ADVANCED APPLICATIONS FOR ARTIFICIAL NEURAL NETWORKS

Edited by **Adel El-Shahat**

Advanced Applications for Artificial Neural Networks
http://dx.doi.org/10.5772/intechopen.68505
Edited by Adel El-Shahat

Contributors
Latifa Guesmi, Mourad Menif, Zhengyong Zhao, Fanrui Meng, Qi Yang, Hangyong Zhu, Ali Babikir, Mustafa Mohammed, Henry Mwambi, Ken Saito, Minami Kaneko, Fumio Uchikoba, Masaya Ohara, Mizuki Abe, Li-Jeng Huang, Adela Bara, Simona Vasilica Oprea, Nasser Mohamed Ramli, Jose Manuel Ortiz-Rodriguez, Carlos Guerrero-Mendez, Maria Del Rosario Martinez-Blanco, Salvador Castro-Tapia, Mireya Moreno-Lucio, Ramon Jaramillo-Martinez, Luis Octavio Solis-Sanchez, Margarita de la Luz Martinez-Fierro, Idalia Garza-Veloz, Jorge Alberto Barrios-Garcia, Alex Oliveira Barradas Filho, Isabelle Moraes Amorim Viegas, Livia Maria Serio, Giovanni Mummolo, Luigi Alberto Ciro De Filippis, Francesco Facchini, Vassili Karanassios, Ines Sansa, Najiba Mrabet Bellaaj, Rosangela Cintra, Haroldo Campos Velho, Adel El-Shahat

Published by InTech
Janeza Trdine 9, 51000 Rijeka, Croatia

Publishing Process Manager Slobodan Momcilovic
Technical Editor SPi Global
Cover InTech Design team

First published February, 2018
Printed in Croatia
Legal deposit, Croatia: National and University Library in Zagreb

Additional hard copies can be obtained from orders@intechopen.com

Advanced Applications for Artificial Neural Networks, Edited by Adel El-Shahat
p. cm.
Print ISBN 978-953-51-3780-1
Online ISBN 978-953-51-3781-8

For EU product safety concerns:
IN TECH d.o.o., Prolaz Marije Krucifikse Kozulić 3, 51000 Rijeka, Croatia,
info@intechopen.com or visit our website at intechopen.com.

Meet the editor

Dr. Adel El-Shahat is an assistant professor in the Department of Electrical and Computer Engineering at Georgia Southern University, USA. He is the founder and director of the Innovative Power Electronics and Nano-Grids Research Lab (IPENG). His research focuses on neural networks, electric machines, renewable energy systems, smart grid systems, power electronics, power systems, energy storage, and optimization. He received some awards, recognitions, and honors for his work. He is a senior member of IEEE and IRED and a member of professional organizations (22 up to now). He is an editor in chief of International Journal of Convergence Computing and a reviewer of 53 journals and conferences. He has published 55 journals, 50 refereed conference papers, 7 books, and 3 book chapters with 77 other publications.

Contents

Preface

This book addresses recent advances and multidisciplinary advanced applications of artificial neural networks (ANNs) in various fields. Artificial neural network technique is one of the most important techniques to help researchers for solving a wide area of problems. This book supplies the reader with an integrative view of latest research based on ANN. It will help graduates, senior-level undergraduate students, professionals, and researchers to learn foundational and advanced topics of ANN technique. It presents both theoretical knowledge and hands-on work from multidisciplinary experts. ANN is a computational structure inspired by a biological nervous system. ANN consists of very simple and highly interconnected processors called neurons. The neurons are connected to each other by weighted links over which signals can pass. Each neuron receives multiple inputs from other neurons in proportion to its connection weights and generates a single output that may propagate to several other neurons. The process consists of data collection, analysis and processing, network structure design, number of hidden layers, number of hidden units, initializing, training the network, network simulation, weights/bias adjustments, and testing the network.

In this book, highly qualified scientists in this field grasp the most recent researches motivated by the importance of artificial neural networks. The chapters selected for this book are to reflect current technologies, new concepts, advanced applications, and methods related to the book's topic from different perspectives. This book introduces innovative case studies for the next-generation optical networks based on modulation recognition using artificial neural networks, hardware ANN for gait generation of multilegged robots, production of high-resolution soil property ANN maps, ANN and dynamic factor models to combine forecasts, ANN parameter recognition of engineering constants in Civil Engineering, ANN electricity consumption and generation forecasting, ANN for advanced process control, ANN breast cancer detection, ANN applications in biofuels, ANN modeling for manufacturing process optimization, spectral interference correction using a large-size spectrometer and ANN-based deep learning, solar radiation ANN prediction using NARX model, and ANN data assimilation for an atmospheric general circulation model. These advanced ANN applications are well prepared and presented in the form of 14 chapters as follows:

Chapter (1): Introductory Chapter: Artificial Neural Networks

Chapter (2): Modulation Format Recognition Using Artificial Neural Networks for the Next-Generation Optical Networks

Chapter (3): Gait Generation of Multilegged Robots by Using Hardware Artificial Neural Networks

Chapter (4): Using Artificial Neural Networks to Produce High-Resolution Soil Property Maps

Chapter (5): Dynamic Factor Model and Artificial Neural Network Models: To Combine Forecasts or Combine Models?

Chapter (6): Parameter Recognition of Engineering Constants of CLSMs in Civil Engineering Using Artificial Neural Networks

Chapter (7): Electricity Consumption and Generation Forecasting with Artificial Neural Networks

Chapter (8): Advanced Process Control

Chapter (9): Breast Cancer Detection by Means of Artificial Neural Networks

Chapter (10): Applications of Artificial Neural Networks in Biofuels

Chapter (11): ANN Modeling to Optimize Manufacturing Process

Chapter (12): Artificial Neural Networks (ANNs) for Spectral Interference Correction Using a Large-Size Spectrometer and ANN-Based Deep Learning for a Miniature One

Chapter (13): Solar Radiation Prediction Using NARX Model

Chapter (14): Data Assimilation by Artificial Neural Networks for an Atmospheric General Circulation Model

This book is dedicated to the victims of the last terrorism accidents in Egypt (my home country). Surely, this cancer will disappear from the world sooner than later.

هذا الكتاب مهدي لضحايا حوادث الارهاب الاخيره بمصر (بلدي الأم). بالتأكيد سوف يختفي هذا السرطان من العالم قريبا.

Best Regards, Adel

Dr. Adel El-Shahat, Senior IEEE Member
Assistant Professor, Department of Electrical Engineering,
Founder & Director of Innovative Power Electronics & Nano-Grids Research Lab. (IPENG),
Georgia Southern University,
Statesboro, Georgia, USA

Chapter 1

Introductory Chapter: Artificial Neural Networks

Adel El-Shahat

Additional information is available at the end of the chapter

http://dx.doi.org/10.5772/intechopen.73530

1. Introduction

Artificial neural network (ANN) is a computational structure inspired by a biological nervous system. An ANN consists of very simple and highly interconnected processors called neurons. The neurons are connected to each other by weighted links over which signals can pass. The process consists of data collection, analysis and processing, network structure design, number of hidden layers, number of hidden units, initializing, training the network, network simulation, weights/bias adjustments, and testing the network. Artificial neural networks are used in many different fields to process large sets of data, often providing useful analyses that allow for prediction and identification of new data. Artificial neural networks are computational structure programs consisting of interconnected processors called neurons connected by weights. They compute structural data through a process of learning and training. Data normally used by these structures have nonlinear relationships between inputs and outputs. They are used in applications such as speech recognition, imaging, control, estimation, optimization, and host of other things. They are also applied in real-world applications in the areas of finance, medical, business, mining, etc. [1].

2. ANN basic fundamentals and architectures

The process of artificial neural network works similarly to the neurons in the brain. First, before an artificial neural network can be tested or used, it must be trained. The process starts with the neuron, the basic element ANNs (see **Figure 1**). The neuron inputs are the outputs of several other neurons. Once a neuron has combined the inputs and produces a single output, it is compared to what is known as a training set, group of known inputs and outputs. The user sets a threshold of maximum that is allowed by the system. If the output value from the neuron does not match the known value in the data set, then the system will adjust the weights. This process is repeated until the error is within the threshold range and at that time the system will hold the weights at their current position to be tested against data that was not used in the training set. At this point in time, the system will be able to back decision and process patterns from the nonlinear data.

An important issue in designing an ANN is knowing how many values are assigned to each layer of an ANN. Assigning too many variables to a layer will lead to overfitting due to the system not being able to process so much information and also will lead to longer computational times during training. Sometimes, proper training may not be possible in a reasonable time given the overload of data. Assigning to few variables in a layer of a complicated set will lead to the system to underfitting the data due to the signals not being fully recognized. Many factors such as the inputs and outputs, noise, complexity of the error function, network architecture, and training algorithm influence what is the best number of hidden units. The neural network is implemented in MATLAB and Simulink toolbox. The performance of the system will be the mean squared error for measuring the average of the squared error. Training of the network will stop when the max number of repetitions is reached, the max time is reached, the performance is minimized to the goal, the performance gradient falls below the minimum value, or mu exceeds the max value [1].

Biological neurons as shown **Figure 2** have a cell nucleus to receive input from other neurons through a web of dendrites. Its learning is accomplished via little changes to a current

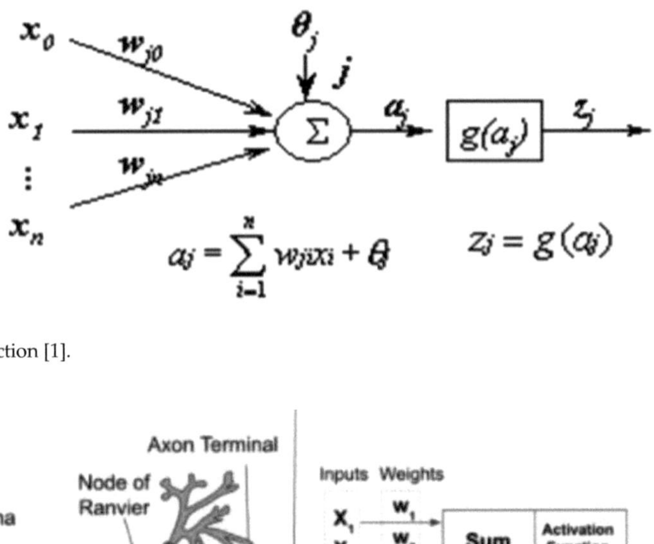

Figure 1. Neuron function [1].

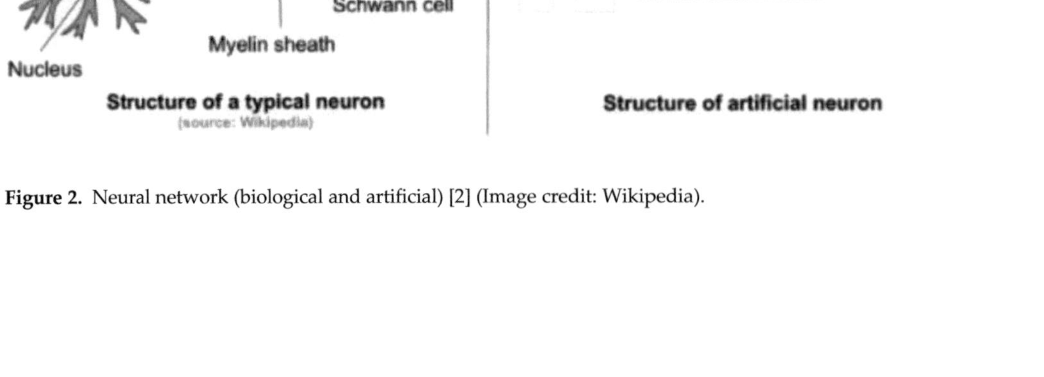

Figure 2. Neural network (biological and artificial) [2] (Image credit: Wikipedia).

portrayal—its setup contains critical data previously, and learning is directed. The qualities of associations between neurons, or weights, don't begin as arbitrary, nor does the structure of the associations. Unlike biological neural networks, artificial neural networks (ANNs) are ordinarily prepared starting with no outside help, utilizing a settled topology decided for the current issue. Be that as it may, ANNs can likewise learn in light of a prior portrayal. Sooner rather than later, ANNs will start to play out extra classes of errands at close human and even superhuman levels, maybe ending up scientifically and fundamentally more like organic neural systems [2].

One of the primary issues with neural systems is that, generally, they have a constrained capacity to recognize causal connections expressly. Engineers of neural systems bolster these systems' huge swathes of information and take into consideration the neural systems to decide autonomously which input factors are generally vital. Another issue with neural systems is the inclination to overfit in light of the fact that the model records for abnormalities and anomalies in the preparation information that may not be available crosswise over real informational indexes. Overfitting of information happens when an information examination model, for example, a neural system, produces great expectations for the preparation information yet more regrettable ones for testing information. Designers can moderate overfitting in neural systems by punishing huge weights and constraining the quantity of neurons in shrouded layers. Decreasing the quantity of neurons in concealed layers lessens overfitting yet in addition restrains the capacity of the neural system to display more intricate, nonlinear connections [3].

Artificial neural network contains various layers as shown in **Figure 3**. These layers are the following: input layer to receive inputs for network's learning and recognition, output layer to react to the data about how it's found out any assignment, and in-between hidden layer to change the contribution to something that yield unit can use somehow.

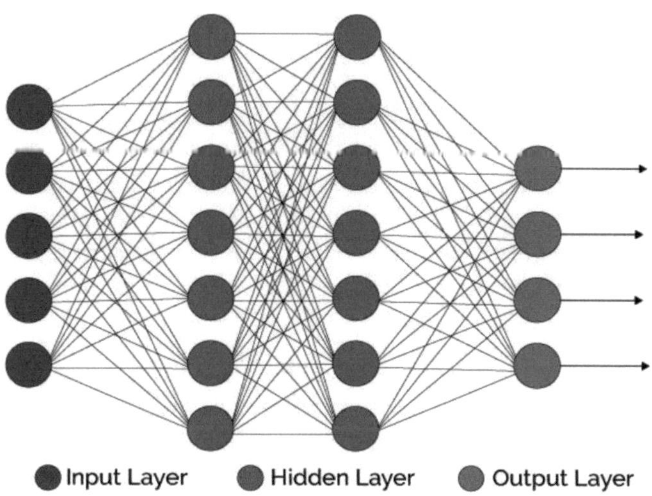

Figure 3. Multilayer neural network [4].

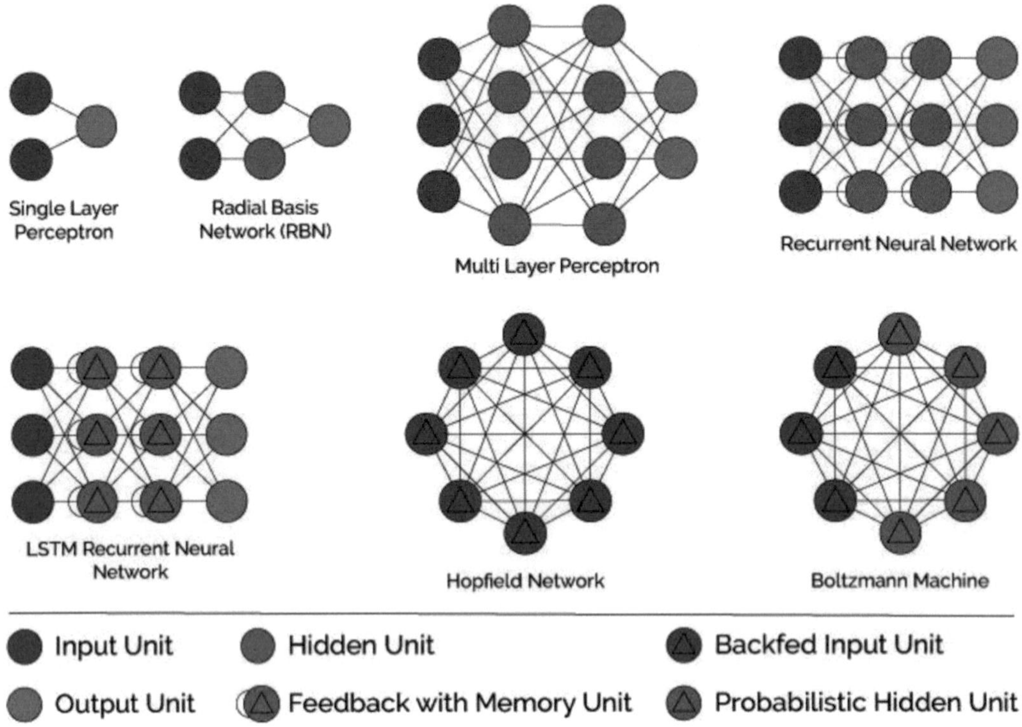

Figure 4. Neural network' different architectures [4].

Moreover, neural network has different architectures such as perceptron model, radial basis function, multilayer perceptron, recurrent neural network, long short-term memory, Hopfield network, Boltzmann machine neural network, convolutional neural network, modular neural network, and physical neural network [4]. These different types are well depicted in **Figure 4**.

Also, neural networks could be used in classification, prediction, clustering (competitive networks, adaptive resonance theory networks, and Kohonen self-organizing maps), association, pattern recognition (supervised classification and unsupervised classification), and in addition machine learning [4].

3. In-brief recent applications

The editor himself has used ANN in different applications such as smart distributed generation systems [5], photovoltaic module and horizontal axis wind turbine modeling [6], wind energy estimation functions for future homes [7], small-scale hydropower generator electrical system modelling [8], robot energy modeling [9], small-scale wind power dispatchable energy source modeling [10], optimum ANN empirical model of capacitive deionization desalination unit [11], lead acid battery modeling for PV applications [12], solar panel modeling-based design technique for distributed generation applications [13], wind turbine (horizontal and vertical) design and simulation aspects for renewable energy applications [14], neural network storage unit parameter modeling [15], empirical capacitive deionization ANN nonparametric modeling for desalination purpose [16], PV module optimum operation modeling [17], ANN interior PM synchronous machine performance improvement unit [18], DC-DC converter duty cycle ANN estimation for DG applications [19], stand-alone PV system simulation for DG applications—Part I: PV module modeling and inverters [20], stand-alone PV system simulation for DG applications—Part II: DC-DC converter feeding maximum power to resistive load [21], maximum power point genetic identification function for photovoltaic system [22], PV cell module modeling and ANN simulation for smart grid applications [23], a neuro-modelling for new biological technique of water pollution control [24], high fundamental frequency PM synchronous motor design neural regression function [25], PM synchronous motor control strategies with their neural network regression functions [26], DC micro-grid pricing and market models [27], battery degradation model based on ANN regression function for EV applications [28], sizing residential photovoltaic systems in the state of georgia [29], an artificial neural network model for wind energy estimation [30], site wind energy appraisal function for future egyptian homes [31], horizontal axis wind turbines modeling [32], wind energy simulation and estimation in egypt [33], petroleum archie parameter estimation [34], storage device unit modeling [35], capacitive deionization (CDI) operational condition nonparametric modeling [36], solar photovoltaic module modeling-based design technique [37], high-speed synchronous motor basic sizing neural function for renewable energy applications [38], generating basic sizing design regression neural function for HSPMSM in aircraft [39], neural unit for PM synchronous machine performance improvement used for renewable energy [40], neural unit for PM synchronous machine performance improvement used for renewable energy [41], a neural model for flat-plate collector [42], a neuro-modeling for new biological technique of water pollution control [43], a neural model for new biological technique of water pollution control: experimental project [44], speed sensorless neural controller for induction motor efficiency optimization [45], and neural model of three-phase induction motor [46].

These book chapters reflect advanced ANN applications for next generation optical networks modulation recognition using artificial neural networks, hardware ANN for gait generation of multi-legged robots, high-resolution soil property ANN map production, ANN dynamic factor models for combined forecasts, ANN parameter recognition of engineering constants in civil engineering, ANN electricity consumption and generation forecasting, ANN for advanced process control, ANN breast cancer detection, ANN applications in biofuels, ANN modeling for manufacturing process optimization, spectral interference correction using a large-sized spectrometer and ANN-based deep learning, solar radiation ANN prediction using NARX model, and ANN data assimilation an atmospheric general circulation model.

Author details

Adel El-Shahat

Address all correspondence to: aahmed@georgiasouthern.edu

Department of Electrical and Computer Engineering, Georgia Southern University, Georgia, USA

References

[1] El-Shahat A. Artificial Neural Network (ANN): Smart & Energy Systems Applications. Germany: Scholar Press Publishing; 2014. ISBN: 978-3-639-71114-1

[2] Schiappa M, Rudd E. Man vs machine: Comparing artificial and biological neural networks, Sophos News. 21 September 2017, https://news.sophos.com/en-us/2017/09/21/man-vs-machine-comparing-artificial-and-biological-neural-networks/

[3] Mahesh S. Machine minds: An exploration of artificial neural networks. Catalyst. May 1, 2017;**10**. Posted in M and tagged with Volume 10, Connections, M, Physical Sciences, Mathematics and Models, http://ricecatalyst.org/volume-10/2017/6/machine-minds-an-exploration-of-artificial-neural-networks

[4] Jagreet KG. Overview of artificial neural networks and its applications. Categories - Artificial Neural Networks, Machine Learning, Deep Learning. May 05, 2017. https://www.xenonstack.com/blog/data-science/overview-of-artificial-neural-networks-and-its-applications

[5] Guha B, Haddad RJ, El-Shahat A, Kalaani Y. Smart distributed generation systems using artificial neural network-based event classification. IEEE Power and Energy Technology Systems Journal. In press;**5**(2):1-8

[6] Eldean MAS, El-Shahat A, Soliman AM. A new modeling technique based on performance data for photovoltaic modules and horizontal axis wind turbines. Wind Engineering Journal. Accepted & In Press; 2017:1-21. http://journals.sagepub.com/doi/abs/10.1177/0309524X17737052, Article first published online: October 30, 2017. https://doi.org/10.1177/0309524X17737052

[7] El-Shahat A, Haddad R, Kalaani Y. Wind energy estimation functions for future homes. Journal of Power Technologies. In Press; 2016:1-10. http://papers.itc.pw.edu.pl/index.php/JPT/article/view/605

[8] Saggus C, Coley R, Floyd Z, El-Shahat A. Small scale hydropower generator electrical system modelling based on real-measurements. European Journal of Advances in Engineering and Technology. 2016;**3**(8):1-12

[9] Rios-Gutierrez F, El-Shahat A, Wahab M. ANN robot energy modeling. IOSR Journal of Electrical and Electronics Engineering (IOSR-JEEE). 2016;**11**(4):66-81. Ver. III (Jul–Aug 2016)

[10] Cannon J, Moore D, Eason S, El Shahat A. Small scale-wind power dispatchable energy source modeling. International Journal of Scientific Engineering and Applied Science (IJSEAS). January 2016;**2**(1):34-39. ISSN: 2395-3470.

[11] El-Shahat A, Haddad R, Kalaani Y. Optimum ANN empirical model of capacitive deionization desalination unit. International Journal of Industrial Electronics and Drives. InderScience. 2015;**2**(2):116-133

[12] Haddad R, El-Shahat A, Kalaani Y. Lead acid battery modeling for PV applications. Journal of Electrical Engineering. June 2015;**15**(2);17-24. ISSN: 1582-4594

[13] Soliman AM, El-Shahat A, Sharaf MA. Solar panels modeling based design technique for distributed generation applications. International Journal of Engineering Research and Management (IJERM). December 2014;**1**(9);213-218. ISSN: 2349-2058

[14] El Shahat A, Soliman AM, Sharaf MA. Wind turbines (horizontal & vertical) design and simulation aspects for renewable energy applications. ARPN Journal of Science and Technology. June 2014;**4**(7):388-396

[15] El Shahat A. Neural network storage unit parameters modeling. International Journal of Industrial Electronics and Drives. 2014:**1**(4);249-274

[16] El Shahat A. Empirical capacitive deionization ANN nonparametric modeling for desalination purpose. Journal of Engineering Research and Technology. June 2014;**1**(2):58-65

[17] El Shahat A. PV module optimum operation modeling. Journal of Power Technologies. 2014;**94**(1):50-66. ISSN: 2083-4187, E-ISSN: 2083-4195

[18] El Shahat A, Kader FA, El Shewy H. ANN interior PM synchronous machine performance improvement unit. Journal of Automation & Systems Engineering (JASE). December 2013;**7**(4, P3):164-175. ISSN: 1112-8542

[19] El Shahat A. DC-DC converter duty cycle ANN estimation for DG applications. Journal of Electrical Systems (JES). March 2013;**9**(1):13-38. ISSN: 1112-5209

[20] El Shahat A. Stand-alone PV system simulation for DG applications, Part I: PV module modeling and inverters. Journal of Automation & Systems Engineering (JASE). 2012;**6**(1): 36-54. ISSN: 1112-8542

[21] El Shahat A. Stand-alone PV system simulation for DG applications, Part II: DC-DC converter feeding maximum power to resistive load. Journal of Automation & Systems Engineering (JASE). 2012;**6**(1):55-72. ISSN: 1112-8542

[22] El Shahat A. Maximum power point genetic identification function for photovoltaic system. International Journal of Research and Reviews in Applied Sciences. June 2010; **3**(3):264-273. ISSN: 2076-734X, EISSN: 2076-7366

[23] El Shahat A. PV cell module modeling & ANN simulation for smart grid applications. Journal of Theoretical and Applied Information Technology. June 2010;**16**(1):9-20. ISSN: 1992-8645, EISSN: 1817-3195

[24] El Shahat A, Tawfik ATY. A neuro-modelling for new biological technique of water pollution control. Journal of Arab Research Institute for Science & Engineering. 2010;**2**(2): 6-17. ISSN: 1994-3253; Second Quarter (April–June)

[25] El Shahat A, El Shewy H. High fundamental frequency PM synchronous motor design neural regression function. Journal of Electrical Engineering. 2010;**10**:1-10. ISSN: 1582-4594; Article 10.1.14, Edition 1, March

[26] El Shahat A, El Shewy H. PM synchronous motor control strategies with their neural network regression functions. Journal of Electrical Systems (JES). December 2009;**5**(4):1-16. ISSN: 1112-5209

[27] Minshew Z, El Shahat A. DC micro-grid pricing and market models. In: Jose HS, editor. IEEE Global Humanitarian Technology Conference. California, USA: DoubleTree; October 19–22, 2017

[28] May G, El Shahat A. Battery-degradation model based on ANN-regression function for EV applications. In: Jose HS, editor. IEEE Global Humanitarian Technology Conference. California, USA: DoubleTree; October 19–22, 2017

[29] El Shahat A, Haddad RJ, Guha B, Kalaani Y. 'Sizing residential photovoltaic systems in the state of Georgia. In: 2015 IEEE International Conference on Smart Grid Communications (SmartGridComm 2015), Miami Florida, USA: IEEE Communications Society; November 2–5, 2015

[30] El Shahat A, Haddad R, Kalaani Y. An artificial neural network model for wind energy estimation. IEEE SoutheastCon 2015 Conference. Fort Lauderdale, Florida: IEEE South East Region; April 9–12, 2015. pp. 1-3

[31] El Shahat A. Site wind energy appraisal function for future egyptian homes. In: 2014 Grid of the Future Symposium. Houston, Texas, USA: The Third Grid of the Future Symposium Sponsored by the CIGRE US National Committee (USNC) and the 10 Electric Power Research Institute (EPRI); October 19–21, 2014. pp. 1-13. http://cigre-usnc.tamu.edu/wp-content/uploads/2015/06/Site-Wind-Energy-Appraisal-Function-for-Future-Egyptian-Homes.pdf

[32] El Shahat A. Horizontal axis wind turbines modeling. In: 16th International Middle East Power Systems Conference. Cairo, Egypt: IEEE; December 23–25, 2014 (MEPCON'14)

[33] Shahien RA, El Shahat A, Sharaf MA, Abbas AMS. Wind energy simulation & estimation in Egypt. In: 12th International Conference on Mining, Petroleum and Metallurgical Engineering MPM12. Suez, Egypt: Suez University; October 20–22, 2014. pp. 13-22

[34] Attia AM, Al Aziz MMA, El Shahat A. Archie parameters estimation (comparative study). In: 12th International Conference on Mining, Petroleum and Metallurgical Engineering MPM12. Suez, Egypt: Suez University; October 20–22, 2014. pp. 43-51

[35] El Shahat A. Storage device unit modeling. In: The 2nd International Conference on Engineering and Technology (ICET 2014), German University in Cairo (GUC). Cairo, Egypt: IEEE Xplore included; April 19–20, 2014

[36] El Shahat A. Capacitive deionization (CDI) operational conditions nonparametric modeling. In: International Conference on Industry Academia Collaboration, IAC 2014, Fairmont Heliopolis, Cairo, Egypt: IEEE; March 3–5, 2014

[37] El Shahat A, Soliman AM, Sharaf MA. Solar photovoltaic modules modeling based design technique. In: The International Conference on Industry Academia Collaboration, IAC 2014, Fairmont Heliopolis, Cairo, Egypt: IEEE; March 3–5, 2014

[38] El Shahat A, El Shewy H. High speed synchronous motor basic sizing neural function for renewable energy applications. In: MDGEN05, The International Conference on Millennium Development Goals (MDG): Role of ICT and Other Technologies. Chennai, India: RMK Engineering College; December 27–29, 2009

[39] El Shahat A. Generating basic sizing design regression neural function for HSPMSM in Aircraft EP-127. In: 13th International Conference on Aerospace Science & Aviation Technology. Cairo, Egypt: ASAT 2009 – Military Technical College; May 26–28, 2009

[40] El Shahat A, El Shewy H. Neural unit for PM synchronous machine performance improvement used for renewable energy. In: Ref: 93, The Third Ain Shams University International Conference on Environmental Engineering (Ascee – 3), Cairo, Egypt: College of Engineering, Ain Shams University; April 14–16, 2009

[41] El Shahat A, El Shewy H. Neural unit for PM synchronous machine performance improvement used for renewable energy. In: Paper Ref.: 910, Global Conference on Renewable and Energy Efficiency for Desert Regions (GCREEDER2009), Amman, Jordan: The University of Jordan

[42] Nafey A, El Shahat A, Sharaf MA. A neural model for flat plate collector. In: EGY – 38, 6th International Conference on Role of Engineering towards a Better Environment, RETBE'06 Conference in Alexandria: College of Engineering, Alexandria University; December 16–18, 2006

[43] Tawfik ATY, El Shahat A. A neuro modeling for new biological technique of water pollution control. In: EGY – 37, 6th International Conference on Role of Engineering towards a Better Environment, RETBE'06 Conference in Alexandria: College of Engineering, Alexandria University; December 16–18, 2006

[44] Tawfik ATY, El Shahat A. A neural model for new biological technique of water pollution control: Experimental project. In: The 6th Syrian – Egyptian Conference of Chemical & Petroleum Engineering, Syria: Baath University; November 8–10, 2005

[45] Tawfik AY, El Shahat A. Speed sensorless neural controller for induction motor efficiency optimization. In: 1st International Conference on Advanced Control Circuits and Systems (ACCS'05), Cairo, Egypt: Electronics Research Institute; March 6–10, 2005. ACCS Catalog No: 080610 M 05, ISBN: 0-146-6310-7933-2

[46] El Shewy H, Tawfik AY, El Shahat A. Neural model of 3 phase induction motor. In: 1st International Conference on Advanced Control Circuits and Systems (ACCS'05), Cairo, Egypt. March 6–10, 2005. ACCS Catalog No: 080610 M 05, ISBN: 0-145-6310-7933-2

Chapter 2

Modulation Format Recognition Using Artificial Neural Networks for the Next Generation Optical Networks

Latifa Guesmi, Habib Fathallah and Mourad Menif

Additional information is available at the end of the chapter

http://dx.doi.org/10.5772/intechopen.70954

Abstract

Transmission systems that use advanced complex modulation schemes have been driving the growth of optical communication networks for nearly a decade. In fact, the adoption of advanced modulation schemes and digital coherent systems has led researchers and industry communities to develop new strategies for network diagnosis and management. A prior knowledge of modulation formats and symbol rates of all received optical signals is needed. Our approach of modulation formats identification is based on artificial neural networks (ANNs) in conjunction with different features extraction approaches. Unlike the existing techniques, our ANN-based pattern recognition algorithm facilitates the modulation format classification with higher accuracies.

Keywords: advanced optical modulation, modulation format recognition, ANN, optical networks

1. Introduction

The challenge of this chapter is to develop precise algorithms for modulation format recognition (MFR) with the highest identification accuracies in the presence of optical channel impairments. For that, we propose and demonstrate the use of ANN-based pattern recognition technique, trained by different feature-based approaches.

In the first method, we implement a new approach using ANN in conjunction with linear optical sampling (LOS) for direct and coherent systems at high data rates. Here, and in accordance to the IEEE 802.3 standards, we have considered the classification of 10 Gbps Non-Return-to-Zero On-Off Keying (NRZ OOK), 40 Gbps NRZ-Differential Quadrature Phase Shift Keying (DQPSK), 100 Gbps NRZ Dual-Polarized (DP)-QPSK, 160 Gbps DP-16 Quadrature Amplitude Modulation (16QAM) and 1 Tbps WDM-Nyquist NRZ-DP-QPSK digital modulation formats for high-speed communication systems. Numerical simulations demonstrate high identification precision in the presence of different impairments, such as chromatic dispersion (CD), differential group delay (DGD) and amplified spontaneous emission (ASE) noise.

In the second method, we propose a novel technique of MFR algorithms using the time-frequency analysis, which is wavelet transform. In conjunction with ANN pattern recognition algorithm, this method is efficient for features extraction when it approximate both the signal envelop and frequency content. Continuous wavelet transform (CWT) is used to extract the classification features of 40 Gbps NRZ-OOK, and used three multi-carriers modulation formats namely 160 Gbps OFDM DP-16QAM, 400 Gbps Dual-Carrier (DC)-Polarization Division Multiplexed (PDM)-QPSK and 1 Tbps WDM-Nyquist NRZ-DP-QPSK. Through simulations, the proposed technique is able to classify these modulation schemes under different transmission impairments with high accuracy.

2. MFR based on ANN trained by LOS

2.1. Principle of the proposed method

An implementation of automatic MFR method of the detected signals, at high data rates is proposed. We consider the recognition of 10 Gbps NRZ-OOK, 40 Gbps NRZ-DQPSK, 100 Gbps NRZ-DP-QPSK, 160 Gbps DP-16QAM and 1 Tbps WDM-Nyquist NRZ-DP-QPSK. The basis of this technique is the use of ANN-based pattern recognition trained by the features of linear optical sampling. The method is validated in the presence of various link impairments including CD, DGD and ASE noise. Thereby, the ANN concept with the principle of asynchronous sampling is described in the following sections.

2.1.1. ANN architecture

The ANN is a computational tool trained by the use of input-output data to generate a desired mapping from an input stimulus to the targeted output. The architecture of an ANN consists of three layers: input, hidden and output layers, also called as multilayer perceptron 3 (MLP3), as shown in **Figure 1**. The role of the input layer is to pass the input vector to the network, without computational role. In addition, the ANN architecture has one or more hidden layers and finally an output layer [1]. Layer of processing elements gives independent computations of received data. Then, it passes the result to another layer. In turn, the next layer also passes on the result to another layer after making it independent computations. At the end, the output of the network is determined by a subgroup of one or more processing elements. Each processing element makes its computation based upon a weighted sum of its inputs.

As shown in **Figure 1**, it is used for MFR by assigning output nodes to represent each format type. In our case, to recognize these modulation formats, five output nodes such as 10 Gbps NRZ-OOK, 40 Gbps NRZ-DQPSK, 100 Gbps NRZ-DP-QPSK, 160 Gbps DP-16QAM and 1 Tbps WDM-Nyquist NRZ-DP-QPSK are required. In the training data, the target output vectors $\mathbf{t}_i$, ($i = 1, \ldots, m$) can be considered as binary vectors with elements with values of "1" indicating the correct modulation formats and elements with values of "0" indicating the incorrect formats. m is the number of modulation formats to be recognized ($m = 5$). In this way, the target vectors of

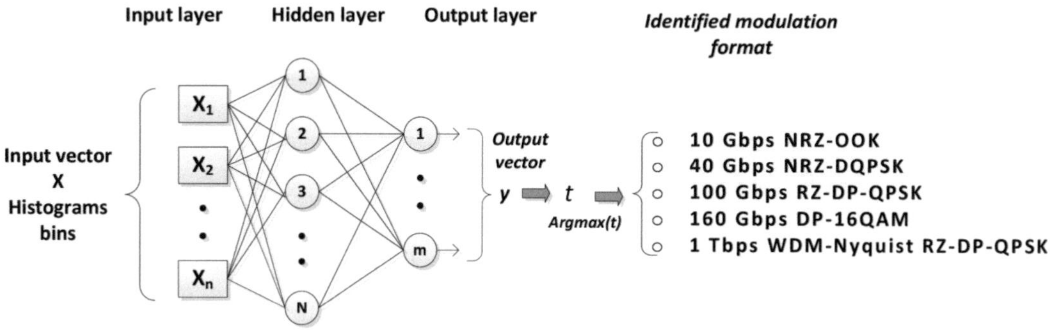

Figure 1. MLP3-ANN structure with amplitude histograms bins vector as input and identified modulation format as output.

these five used modulation formats would be represented by [1, 0, 0, 0, 0], [0, 1, 0, 0, 0], [0, 0, 1, 0, 0], [0, 0, 0, 1, 0] and [0, 0, 0, 0, 1], respectively. The posterior probability is considered at the output of the multilayer perceptron. Hence, the final recognition goes to the node with the highest value *argmax*($\mathbf{y}_i$). Taken an example of output vector with elements [0.05, 0.01, 0.03, 0.9, 0.01], the most probable identification would be 160 Gbps DP-16QAM format.

Amplitude histograms are represented at the input of the ANN with back propagation (BP) learning method. The basic processing elements of the ANN, called neurons, of neighboring layers are interconnected by varying the coefficients that represent the strengths or weights of the respective connections. Each neuron is computed as the weighted sum of the input signals $\mathbf{X}_i$, (i = 1, …, m) transformed by the transfer function, as shown in **Figure 2**. The learning capability of an artificial neuron is achieved by adjusting the weights $\mathbf{W}_{ki}$, (i = 1, …, m) in accordance with the chosen learning algorithm. Weights of the perceptron can amplify or reduce the original input signal. Adding the weighted signals before passing into the activation function is essential to convert the input into a more useful output ($\mathbf{Y}_k$). Different types of activation function exist but one of the simplest would be step function.

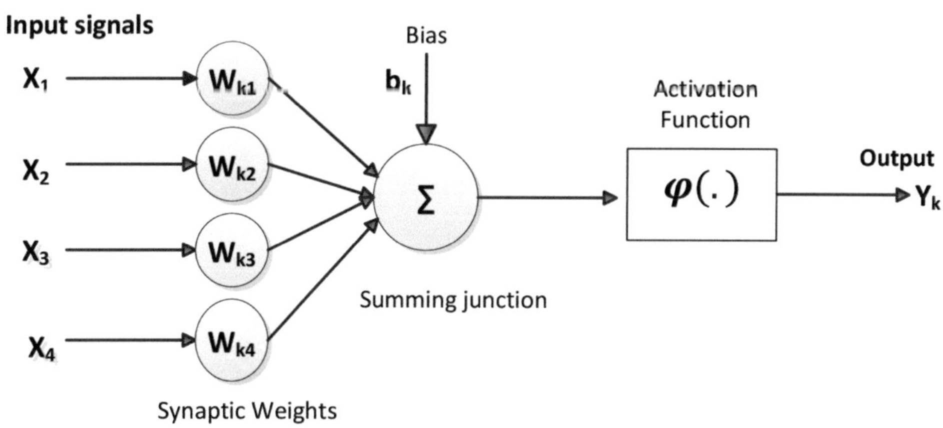

Figure 2. McCulloch-Pitts computational model of a neuron.

The architecture of ANN for recognition problems requires some guidelines. More neurons need more computation and they have a tendency to overfit the data when the number is set too high, which justifies the choice of MLP3 architecture.

2.1.2. *Linear optical sampling for amplitude histograms*

In the literature, optical sampling proved necessary for a variety of experiments. Optical signals are sampled by means of optical or even opto-electrical gates. This technique covers LOS systems that enable the measurement of amplitude histograms and eye diagrams.

Some publications in this field date back to the mid-1990s, when the first optically sampled eye diagrams of 10 Gbps optical data signals were published [2, 3]. The LOS technique allows us the processing of signals at high speeds, like in our case when using WDM-Nyquist system. Received signals are asynchronously oversampled to generate amplitude histograms. These histograms define the own signature or traces of the five used modulation formats. **Figure 3** shows an example of cleaned histogram on back-to-back (a) and an impaired one after a fiber transmission (b,c). Correspondent eye diagram is also showed in the figure (2nd column).

It is clear from the histograms that the location of each peak correspond to a particular intensity level of the formats constellations. By definition, amplitude histograms are the empirical distribution of the received signal power. Therefore, they are sensitive to changes in optical signal-to-noise ratio (OSNR), CD and polarization mode dispersion (PMD) of the transmission

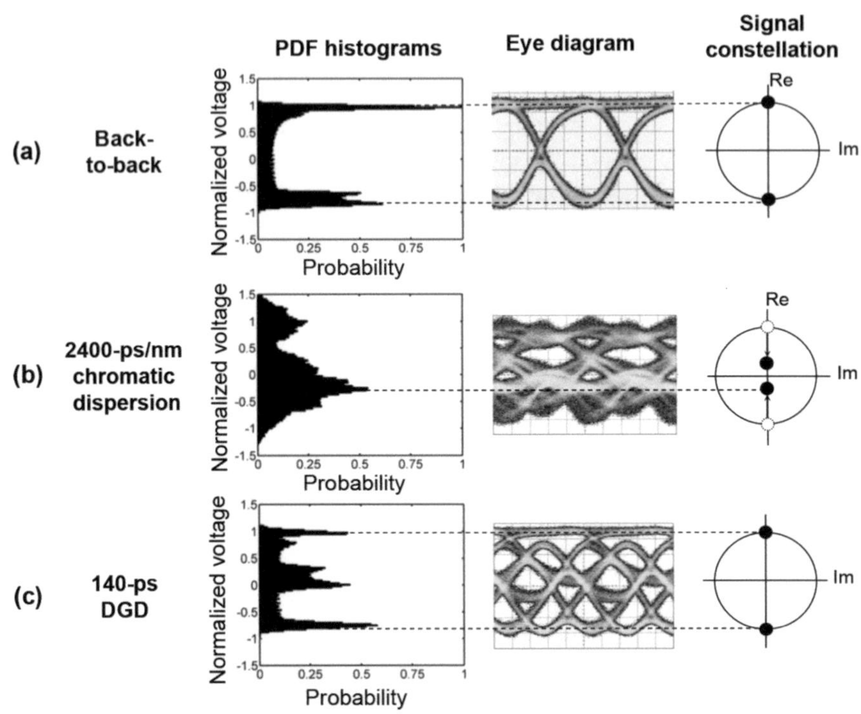

Figure 3. Generated amplitude histograms on back-to-back (b), after fiber transmission (c), and in the presence of DGD (c) [4].

link. As given in **Figure 3(c)**, histogram characteristics changes significantly regarding the optical link impairments and distances.

2.2. Simulation design

In **Figure 4**, the simulation design of the proposed method for automatic MFR is shown. Five different transmitters generates NRZ-OOK at 10 Gbps, NRZ-DQPSK at 40 Gbps, NRZ-DP-QPSK at 100 Gbps, DP-16QAM at 160 Gbps and WDM-Nyquist NRZ-DP-QPSK at 1 Tbps. The pseudorandom binary sequence (PRBS) is of length $2^{14} - 1$. Then, using a variable optical attenuator (VOA), generated output signals are decreased, which affects the gain of the optical amplifier (OA). The latter is used to emulate the effect of optical signal-to-noise ratio (OSNR) by tuning the noise figure and add a variable amount of ASE noise into the signals. As a result, the OSNR values are adjusted in the range between 10 and 30 dB with steps of 2 dB and are then transmitted over a single mode fiber (SMF). By using the CD/PMD (polarization mode dispersion) emulator, the accumulated CD of the link varied in the range of 0–510 ps/nm (steps of 17 ps/nm) to reach 30 km fiber transmission, while the DGD is introduced in the range of 0–14 ps with steps of 2 ps. An optical filter optical band pass filter (OBPF) is used to select the carrier whose modulation format need to be recognized.

Using an optical switch (SW) in the detection stage, the NRZ-OOK signal is directly detected with single photodetector, while coherent receivers detect other formats. Using polarization beam splitter (PBS), the detected signal is split into two orthogonal polarization states. Each output is coupled with the signal derived from the local oscillator (LO). A single-polarization is detected in the case of NRZ-DQPSK signal. In the MFR block, signals are asynchronously oversampled with a rate of 16 samples/bit to have 262,144 amplitude samples. The amplitude histograms of the five used modulation formats are shown in **Figure 5** (2nd and 3rd columns). Besides, when considering the OSNR equal to 16 dB, DGD at 10 ps for 10 km fiber length (3rd column), these histograms stay again different from each other. Typical eye diagrams are also showed in the 1st column of the figure. Later, these histograms are used in the ANN module for formats classification, as described in the previous section. The number of neurons in hidden layer is optimized to be 30 neurons using the incremental-constructive approach [1].

With **n** input and **m** output neurons, the training set is given as $\{(\mathbf{X}_1; \mathbf{t}_1), \ldots, (\mathbf{X}_p; \mathbf{t}_p)\}$, where P = 27,280 is the size of the entire data corresponding to different OSNR (11 values), CD (31 values), DGD (8 values) and modulation types at two polarization states, **n** = 100 is the number of histograms bins. More precisely, we want to minimize the error function of the network, the MSE, defined as $||\mathbf{y} - \mathbf{t}||^2$. When training multilayer networks, the overall data set is randomly divided, with 60% used for training, 15% for validation and 25% for testing. On the other side, the results of the simulations indicate that the Levenberg-Marquardt (LM) training algorithm provides high correct recognition ratios [5].

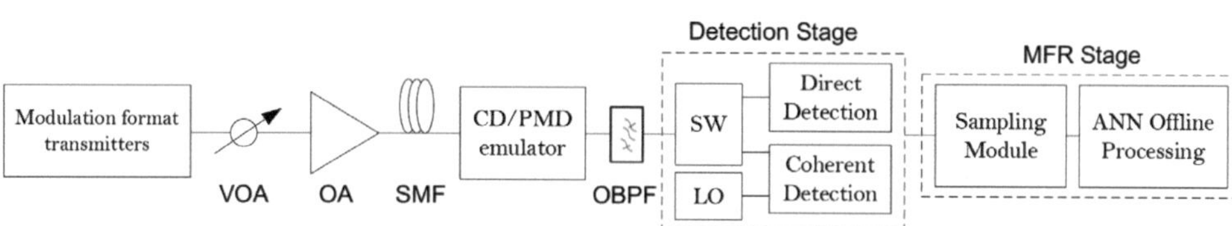

Figure 4. Outline of simulation setup.

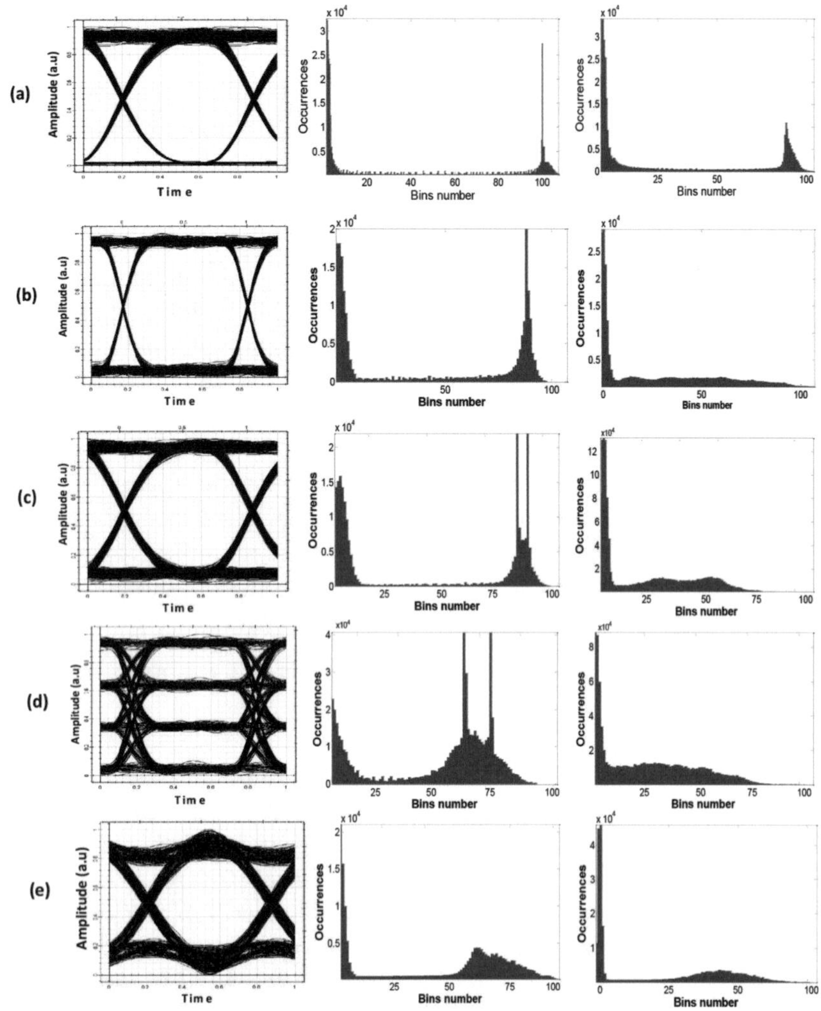

Figure 5. Link impairments variation effect to amplitude histograms and eye diagrams, for the five used modulation formats: (a) 10 Gbps NRZ-OOK, (b) 40 Gbps NRZ-DQPSK, (c) 100 Gbps NRZ-DP-QPSK, (d) 160 Gbps DP-16QAM and (e) 1 Tbps WDM-Nyquist NRZ-DP-QPSK with OSNR = 16 dB (2nd column) and OSNR = 16 dB, DGD = 10 ps, CD = 170 ps/nm (3rd column).

Using our previous settings, we reach the minimum of MSE on 3.67×10^{-7} for 27 epochs leading to abort the training process, as illustrated in **Figure 6**. This amelioration reduces the required time for ANN training process, which depends on ANN size, type of learning algorithm, size of the training data set and the desired degree of accuracy.

2.3. Modulation formats recognition

The previously described system of MFR has validated with test cases comprising five modulation formats. Training data sets are arranged into 16,368 input vectors $\mathbf{x}_i$ (60%), and then numerous simulations using different combinations of OSNR, CD and DGD are performed.

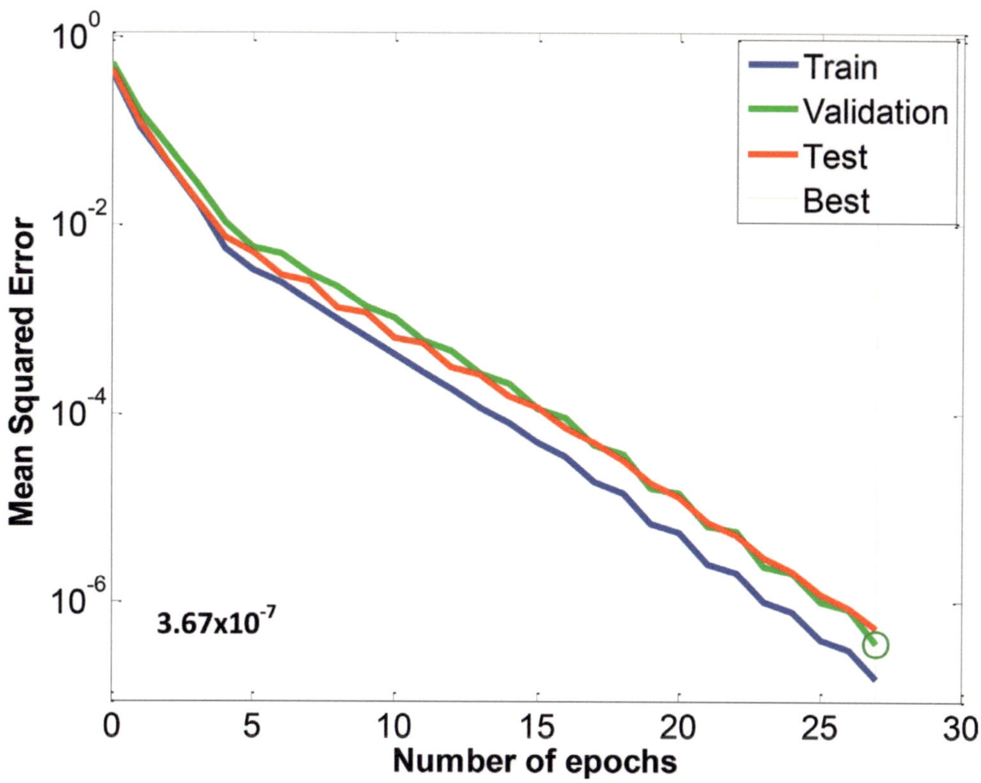

Figure 6. Effect of epoch's number on MSE variation for training (black), validation (grey) and testing (silver) data sets.

The results of the testing data sets (6820 input vectors x_i) are depicted in **Figure 7** and five elements of ANN output vectors $\mathbf{y}_i$ are shown. Each output represents a particular modulation type among 10 Gbps NRZ-OOK, 40 Gbps NRZ-DQPSK, 100 Gbps NRZ-DP-QPSK, 160 Gbps DP-16QAM and 1 Tbps WDM-Nyquist NRZ-DP-QPSK.

Indeed, one output $\mathbf{y}_i$ reaches a maximum value than the others, as clearly shown in the figure, which represents the modulation format. For that, there is no ambiguity in the classification process because of this large separation. The five-used modulation formats are well recognized with good accuracies, as given in the all cases represented in **Figure 7**.

After ANN training, the recognition accuracy is validated with different set of testing data. **Table 1** shows the obtained results, and it is apparent that 100% accuracy is obtained for 10 Gbps NRZ-OOK, 40 Gbps NRZ-DQPSK and 160 Gbps DP-16QAM with small differences in recognition probabilities (i.e., 99.99% and 99.98%) for the other formats.

An unannounced precision ambiguity between 100 Gbps NRZ-DP-QPRK and 1 Tbps WDM-Nyquist NRZ-DP-QPSK modulation formats has observed. This is due to the use of the same coding scheme, which is the QPSK. As previously stated at the outset, our simulations are performed under various impairments of ASE noise, CD and PMD but the recognition accuracy remains high up to 99.99%. This result is an improvement compared to other works presented in the literature (99.6%, 99.95%) [6, 7].

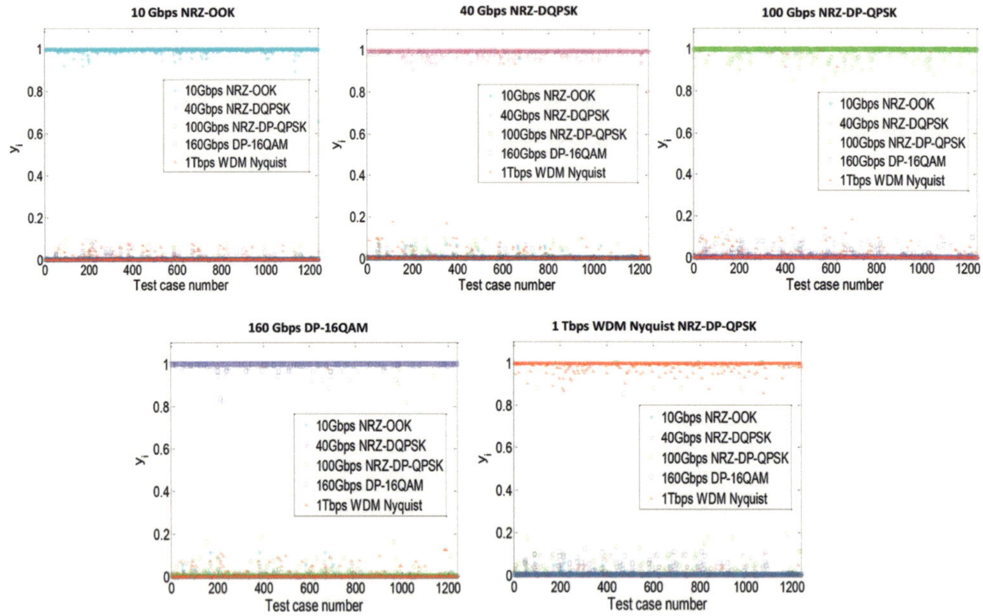

Figure 7. The ANN outputs y_i for 5 used modulation formats in response to the 6200 test cases representing input vectors x_i.

	Recognized modulation format				
Current modulation format	**10 Gbps NRZ-OOK**	**40 Gbps NRZ-DQPSK**	**100 Gbps NRZ-DP-QPSK**	**160 Gbps DP-16QAM**	**1 Tbps WDM-Nyquist NRZ-DP-QPSK**
10 Gbps NRZ-OOK	100%	–	–	–	–
40 Gbps NRZ-DQPSK	–	100%	–	–	–
100 Gbps NRZ-DP-QPSK	–	–	99.99%	–	0.01%
160 Gbps DP-16QAM	–	–	–	100%	–
1 Tbps WDM-Nyquist NRZ-DP-QPSK	–	–	0.02%	–	99.98%

Table 1. Recognition accuracies of the five used modulation formats using the proposed automatic MFR technique.

3. MFR based on ANN trained by wavelet transform

3.1. Theoretical background

Different mathematical guidelines are used in the defined MFR block of this technique. Before moving to the ANN classifier, it allows the features extraction of all received signals. In our study, we chose the wavelet transform for the multiresolution analysis (MRA). In addition, to accomplish the classification mission, the singular value decomposition (SVD), as a factorization tool of matrix, is used. The different blocs of our MFR module are shown in **Figure 8**.

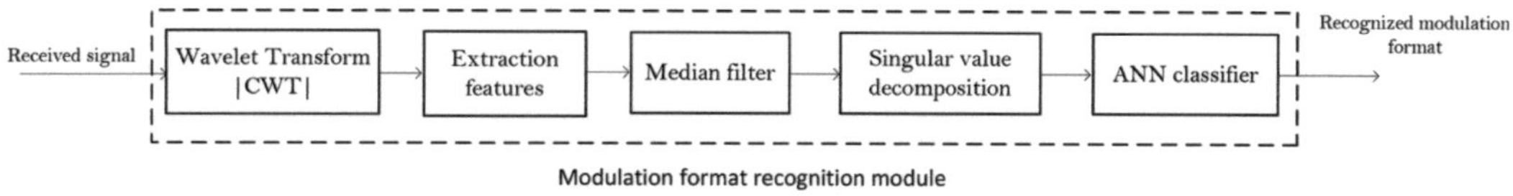

Figure 8. Different blocs of the optical MFR module.

3.1.1. *Wavelet transform and features extraction*

Wavelet transform analysis is one of the most popular non-stationary signals processing tool. In this method, continuous wavelet transform (CWT) is used for its ability to construct in time and frequency domain a good representation of treated signals. It is also used to extract the necessary features of each received modulation format [8].

In the following integral, the CWT of the signal $\mathbf{f(t)} \in \mathbf{Z}$ is expressed at a scale $\mathbf{a} > 0$ and translational value $\mathbf{b} \in \mathrm{R}$:

$$\mathrm{CWT}\ (\mathrm{a,b}) = \int_{-\infty}^{+\infty} f(t)\Psi^*_{\mathrm{a,b}}(\mathrm{t})\mathrm{dt} \tag{1}$$

where CWT(a, b) define the wavelet transform coefficients, * denotes complex conjugate and $\Psi_{\mathrm{a,\ b}}(\mathrm{t})$ is the baby wavelet comes from time-scaling and translation of mother wavelet $\Psi(\mathrm{t})$ as described in Eq. (3).

$$\Psi_{\mathrm{a,b}}(\mathrm{t}) = \frac{1}{\sqrt{\mathrm{a}}}\ \Psi\left(\frac{\mathrm{t-b}}{\mathrm{a}}\right) \tag{2}$$

Recently, the selection of the mother wavelet function as well as the decomposition level of signal is the most indispensable challenge in wavelet analysis. It includes Haar, Meyer, Morlet, Symlet, Daubechies and coiflet wavelets [8]. In our case, the Haar wavelet is chosen due to its simple form and also its computation is still easy. It is given in the following equation as a continuous function in both; the time and frequency domain:

$$\Psi(\mathrm{t}) = \begin{cases} 1 & \text{if } 0 < t < \frac{T}{2}, \\ -1 & \text{if } \frac{T}{2} \le t \le T \\ 0 & \text{otherwise.} \end{cases}, \tag{3}$$

Give s(t), with $0 < \mathrm{t} < \mathrm{T_s}$, the received optical waveform in a complex form described as:

$$\mathrm{s(t)} = \mathrm{f(t)} + \mathrm{n(t)} = \tilde{f}(t)e^{j\left(2\pi f_c t + \theta_c\right)} + n(t), \tag{4}$$

where $\mathrm{T_s}$ is the symbol duration, $\theta_\mathbf{c}$ is the carrier initial phase, $\mathbf{f_c}$ is the carrier frequency, **n(t)** is the complex ASE noise and $\tilde{f}(t)$ is the complex envelope of the signal f(t) defined indifferently for each modulation format:

- For PSK signals:

$$\tilde{f}_{\text{PSK}}(t) = \sqrt{S}\sum_{i=1}^{N} e^{j\phi_i} h_{T_s}(t - iT_s), \tag{5}$$

with N the number of observed symbols, $h_{T_s}(t)$ is the pulse shaping function of duration T_s, S is the average signal power and $\phi_i \in \{(2\pi/N)(m-1), m=1,2, \ldots, N\}$,

- For QAM signals:

$$\tilde{f}_{\text{QAM}}(t) = \sum_{i=1}^{N} (A_i + jB_i) h_{T_s}(t - iT_s), \tag{6}$$

where (A_i, B_i) are the assigned QAM symbols.

- For NRZ-OOK signal:

$$\tilde{f}_{\text{NRZ-OOK}}(t) = \sum_{i=1}^{N} d_i h_{T_s}(t - iT_s), \tag{7}$$

with $d_i = \{0, 1\}$ symbols.

An example of CWT for the four used modulation formats (40 Gbps NRZ-OOK, 160 Gbps OFDM DP- 16QAM, 400 Gbps DC PDM-QPSK and 1 Tbps WDM-Nyquist NRZ-DP-QPSK) is shown in **Figure 9**, where we choose a scale a = 100. From the figure, it is clear that each modulation format has its own features in terms of CWT amplitude and number of peaks.

3.1.2. Singular value decomposition

SVD is the most important applicable matrix factorization used for signal processing and statistics. This tool is used to solve the least squares problems, and provides the best way to approximate a matrix with one of lower rank.

Given a real or complex matrix **A** having **m** rows and **n** columns, the matrix product $U\Sigma V^*$ is the singular value decomposition for the given matrix **A** if:

- U and V, respectively, have orthonormal columns;
- **Σ** has non-negative elements on its principal diagonal and zeros elsewhere and
- **A** = UΣV*.

In addition, if σ is a non-negative scalar, and $\boldsymbol{u}$ and $\boldsymbol{v}$ are nonzero $\boldsymbol{m}$- and $\boldsymbol{n}$-vectors, respectively,

$$\text{A}v = \sigma \boldsymbol{u} \text{ and } \text{Au} = \sigma v \tag{8}$$

where σ is a singular value of A and **u** and **v** are corresponding left and right singular vectors, respectively.

http://dx.doi.org/10.5772/intechopen.70954

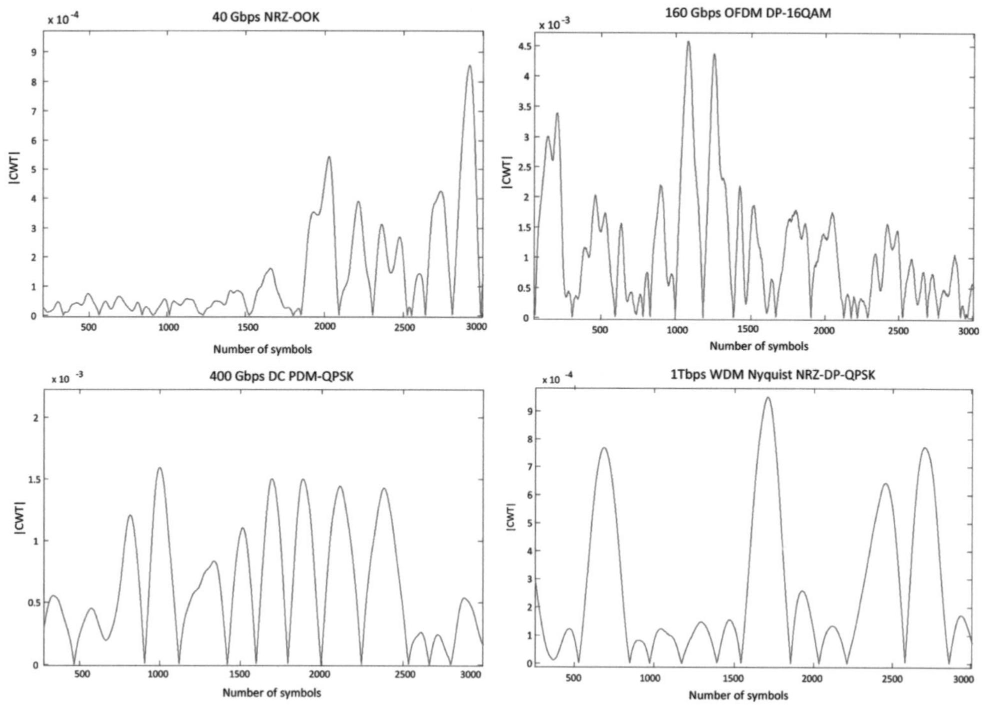

Figure 9. The continuous wavelet transform of four used modulation formats for only 3000 input symbols at OSNR = 20 dB, residual dispersion = 170 ps/nm and DGD = 10 ps where the scale a = 100.

In fact, the diagonal elements $\{\sigma_i\}$ of Σ are the singular values of **A**. The columns $\{u_i\}_{i=1}^{p}$ of U and $\{v_i\}_{i=1}^{q}$ of V are left and right singular vectors of **A**, respectively.

3.1.3. ANN classifier

Features extraction of received signals is accomplished using CWT and SVD. In the last step, the pattern recognition method based on ANN is used for our statistical learning model. Its architecture is described in **Figure 10**. It is structured as an interconnected group of artificial neurons, which use a computational model or mathematical model for information processing. As given in the figure, the ANN is an adaptive system that changes its structure based on external or internal information that flows through the network. Precisely, the architecture of the ANN varies, but generally, it consists of several layers of neurons.

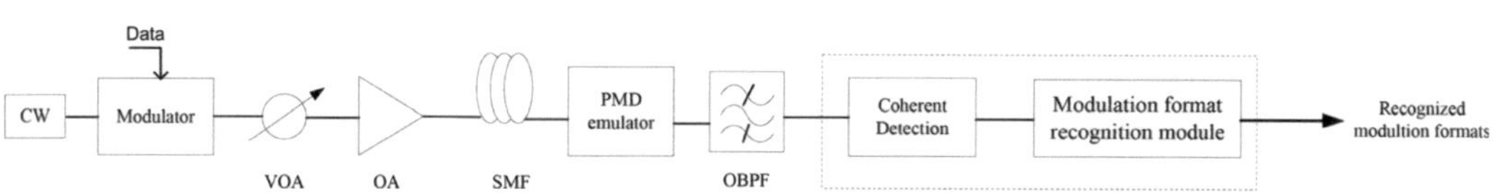

Figure 10. Three-layered feed-forward artificial neural network configuration.

In this technique, we also used the MLP3 for the modulation format identification by assigning output nodes to represent each format. Four output neurons in the output layer represent the 40 Gbps NRZ-OOK, 160 Gbps OFDM DP-16QAM, 400 Gbps DC PDM-QPSK and 1 Tbps WDM-Nyquist NRZ-DP-QPSK modulation formats. As designed previously, before training the network, the multilayer perceptron output can be considered as the highest probability, which represent one from the four modulation types. Eigenvalues after the SVD for each modulation format are represented at the input of the ANN. The multilayer perceptron used in this architecture requires four output neurons representing the number of format types.

3.2. Design of the proposed method

The setup of the proposed MFR technique is shown in **Figure 11**.

The four used modulation formats are generated with carrier frequency equal to 193.1 THz. Using a variable optical attenuator (VOA), the injected power is tuned and passed through an optical amplifier (OA) that undergo the ASE noise effect at higher gain amplifier. As a result, the OSNR of the signals is adjusted in the range of 10–35 dB (steps of 5 dB). Then, using a CD/PMD emulator, chromatic dispersion is varied from 85 to 510 ps/nm (steps of 85 ps/nm) to reach 30 km on SMF, and the DGD between 0 and 20 ps (steps of 5 ps). The appropriate carrier to be classified is selected by an OBPF. As described in **Figure 8**, in MFR block, using the CWT, each received signal is processed by scaling factor up to 128 without amplitude normalization. Moreover, with length equal to 3, the median filter was applied to extract the features set and remove the peaks. In addition, we make the SVD to the time-scale parameters of the wavelet coefficients matrix and obtain the eigenvectors as the final characteristic vectors for each received signal. Finally, we reach the ANN classifier as described in the previous section, where for each modulation format we generate 150 realizations with 65,536 symbols corresponding to different combinations of CD, DGD and OSNR.

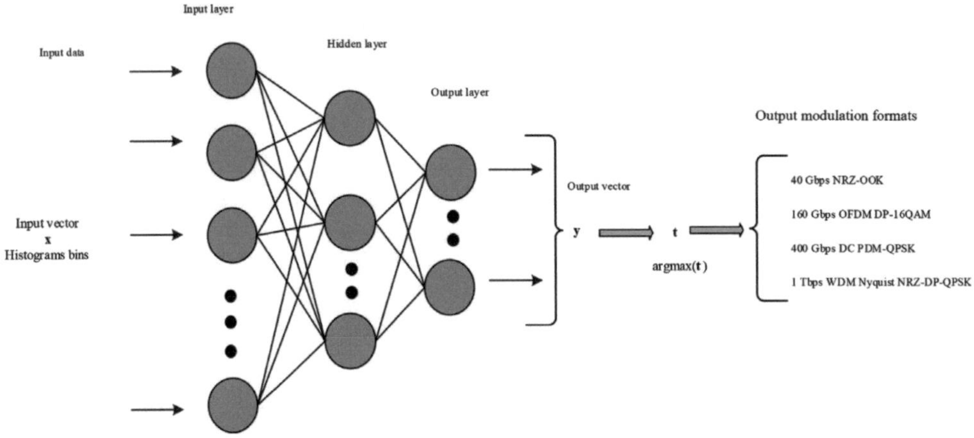

Figure 11. Proposed modulation recognition system.

The number of neurons in hidden layer is optimized to be 25 neurons. In addition, 128 input neurons representing the eigenvalues after SVD for each input modulated signal are used, in addition to 4 output neurons to design the modulation formats to be recognized.

In the training process, the input vectors are randomly divided, with 65% used for training, 20% for validation and 15% for testing. On the other side, using LM training algorithm and reducing the MSE (3.71×10^{-5} for 10 epochs) optimize the identification rates and minimize the computation time.

3.3. Modulation formats classification

The proposed classification method is demonstrated at high bit rates for the four used optical modulation formats including 40 Gbps NRZ-OOK, 160 Gbps OFDM DP-16QAM, 400 Gbps DC PDM-QPSK and 1 Tbps WDM-Nyquist NRZ-DP-QPSK. For each modulation type, to verify the robustness of our method, 150 realizations with 65,536 symbols have been used. All signals are transmitted through ideal (B-to-B) and impaired channels. The simulation results are given **Figures 12–14**.

The plot of the probabilities of recognition against OSNR is given in **Figure 12**. The OSNR is in the range of 10–35 dB. 100% correct identification was observed for 160 Gbps OFDM DP-16QAM and 1 Tbps WDM-Nyquist NRZ-DP-QPSK at higher OSNR values. In contrast, for

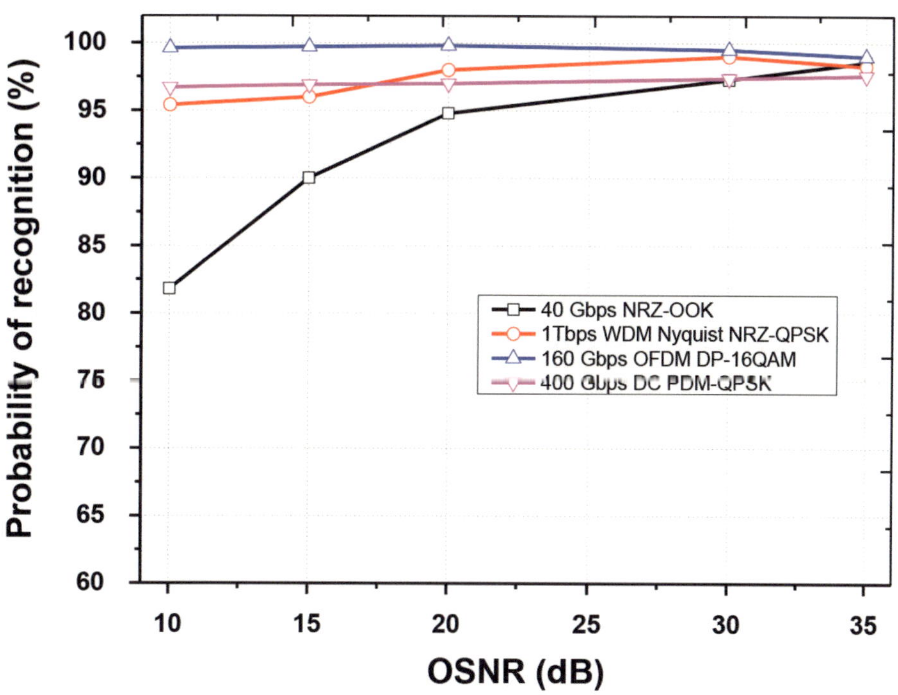

Figure 12. Percentage recognition versus OSNR values for NRZ-OOK, OFDM DP-16QAM, DC PDM-QPSK and WDM-Nyquist NRZ-DP-QPSK modulation types.

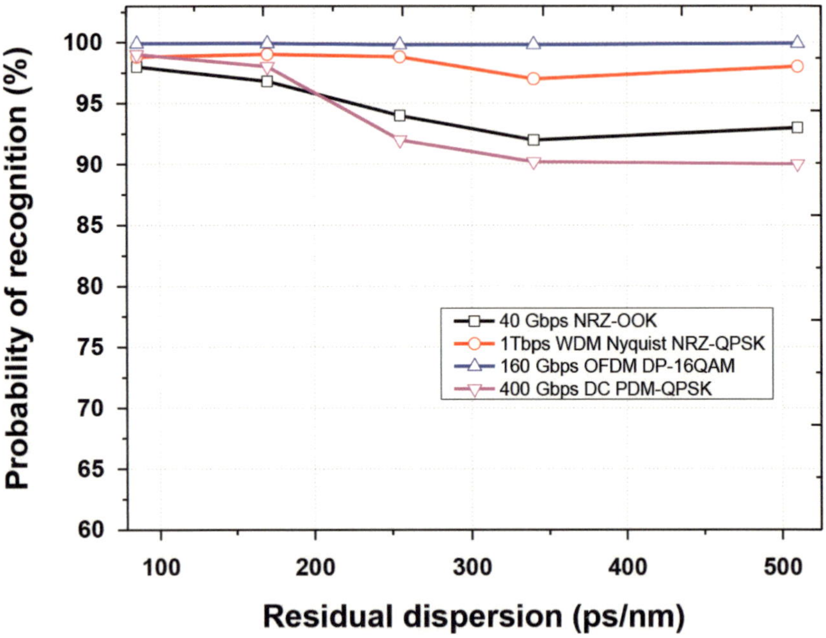

Figure 13. Percentage of correct identification for four used modulation formats depending upon residual dispersion for OSNR = 20 dB.

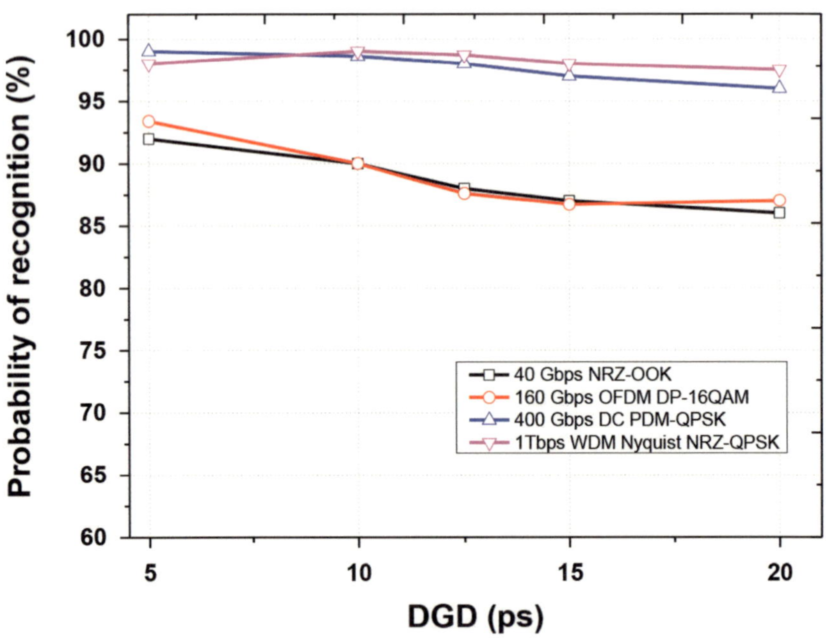

Figure 14. Percentage of correct identification for four used modulation formats depending upon DGD where OSNR = 20 dB.

lower OSNR values (lower than 15 dB), a challenging problem remains for NRZ-OOK identification, which reached values between 80 and 90%. This misclassification is because of its coding properties, where to extract its features, the wavelet transform located ambiguities.

The modulation format can also be recognized correctly when varying the CD, as described earlier in **Figure 13**. From the simulation, the residual dispersion varies between 85 and 510 ps/nm with OSNR = 20 dB. The 160 Gbps OFDM DP-16QAM and 1 Tbps WDM-Nyquist NRZ-DP-QPSK still having the highest recognition probabilities (~100%). Furthermore, 40 Gbps NRZ-OOK and 400 Gbps DC PDM-QPSK reached the minimum values of identification accuracies, that is, 90% for residual dispersion more than 350 ps/nm. In the main, when increasing the residual dispersion values, all probabilities of recognition decreases. This is interpreted by the fact that signal characteristic are widely modified in terms of phase and amplitude with the chromatic dispersion. For that, the wavelet transform will lose its principal features.

In optical transmissions, in the presence of several impairments that broadly modified the signals features and makes the formats recognition issue more difficult. We can cite in this case the impairment caused by the DGD. In **Figure 14**, we show the probabilities of identification versus this parameter.

The DGD is between 0 and 20 ps with steps of 5 ps. The misclassification percentage for 40 Gbps NRZ-OOK signal remains with a small difference for 160 Gbps OFDM DP-16QAM and rises when the DGD is greater than 15 ps. 400 Gbps DC PDM-QPSK and 1 Tbps WDM-Nyquist NRZ-DP-QPSK modulation formats still having the highest accuracies when the DGD is less than 10 ps and begin to decrease for DGD values more than 15 ps. It is suspected that this error is due to the effect of SOP induced by the PMD. It is based on the DGD and the frequency, and it varies differently for each modulation format with the optical carrier, after fiber transmission.

Table 2 shows the recognition results of the neural network when OSNR is equal to 30 dB. For 160 Gbps OFDM DP-16QAM and 1 Tbps WDM-Nyquist NRZ-DP-QPSK formats, we obtain 100% correct classification, while 40 Gbps NRZ-OOK and 400 Gbps DC PDM-QPSK were identified at 96.6% and 98%, respectively. An ambiguity of identification for these formats is increased to 3% at higher DGD and CD. This misclassification is due to the fact that the signal features (phase, amplitude, etc.) are infected in the presence of signal impairments. Thereby, CWT proves a difficulty to sign these formats and extract their eigenvalues.

	Classified modulation format			
Received modulation format	**40 Gbps NRZ-OOK**	**160 Gbps OFDM DP-16QAM**	**400 Gbps CD PDM-QPSK**	**1 Tbps WDM-Nyquist NRZ-DP-QPSK**
40 Gbps NRZ-OOK	96.6%	–	3%	0.4%
160 Gbps OFDM DP-16QAM	–	100%	–	–
400 Gbps CD PDM-QPSK	1.4%	–	98.2%	0.4%
1 Tbps WDM-Nyquist NRZ-DP-QPSK	–	–	–	100%

Table 2. Recognition rates at OSNR = 30 dB.

The robustness of this technique is evaluated and the simulated results show that the correct modulation identification scheme is possible even at all channel parameters ranges: OSNR between 10 and 35 dB, CD from 85 to 510 ps/nm and DGD in the range of 0–20 ps for all modulation formats mentioned previously. We reached higher identification accuracies at high bit rates which facilitates the performance monitoring process (OPM) for the network management.

From the results obtained, it is found that the method employing the amplitude histograms is simple and more robust to impairments link, than the other one using CWT, for features extraction. Moreover, the asynchronous amplitude histograms (AAH) generation followed by ANN is rapid on time response compared to the method using CWT for features extraction. Besides the modulation formats, identification ambiguities is more apparent for the second method.

4. Summary

In this chapter, two cost-effective techniques for intensity and phase-modulated systems have been proposed and demonstrated. Both methods employ ANN for pattern recognition in conjunction with features extraction approaches and digital signal processing.

In the first method, asynchronous amplitude sampling is the features extraction method. For high-speed optical communications, new approach using ANN trained by the features of linear optical sampling is implemented. For the demonstration of the proposed method, 10 Gbps NRZ-OOK, 40 Gbps NRZ-DQPSK, 100 Gbps NRZ DP-QPSK, 160 Gbps DP-16QAM and 1 Tbps WDM-Nyquist NRZ-DP-QPSK modulation formats are considered. The efficiency of this technique is demonstrated in the presence of different transmission link parameters, such as CD, DGD and OSNR. Simulation results demonstrate successful recognition from a known bit rates with higher estimation accuracy, which exceeds 99.8%. For this method, asynchronous sampling with a rate greater than symbol rates is successfully utilized to have the maximum features for each received signal. Thereby, due to the simplicity of ANN implementation and the use of only amplitude samples, the proposed techniques enable the identification of various modulation formats at different bit rates with high accuracies.

The second technique presents a new achievement using the continuous wavelet transform (CWT) for features extraction. It offers the best time and frequency localization. In that case, Haar wavelet and SVD followed by ANN pattern-recognition are used to achieve the classification process. This method is advantageous because its cost effectiveness and its flexibility. To demonstrate the validity of this technique, we consider the classification of 40 Gbps NRZ-OOK, and three multi-carriers modulation schemes such as 160 Gbps OFDM DP-16QAM, 400 Gbps DC-PDM-QPSK and 1 Tbps WDM-Nyquist NRZ-DP-QPSK. The effect of each channel parameter to the probability of recognition has been also observed. In particular, it has been found that the correct identification was observed at higher OSNR values. While, an increase of CD and DGD affects the accuracy of recognition and limits the measurement ranges. Despite the presence of link impairments, and because the CWT is resistant to the noise in the signal, the classification of these formats remains possible with good precision.

Author details

Latifa Guesmi[1]*, Habib Fathallah[2,3] and Mourad Menif[1]

*Address all correspondence to: latifa.guesmi@supcom.tn

1 GresCom Laboratory, University of Carthage, High School of Communication of Tunis (Sup'Com), Ghazala Technopark, Ariana, Tunisia

2 Computer Department, College of Science of Bizerte, University of Carthage, Tunis, Tunisia

3 KACST-TIC in Radio Frequency and Photonics for e-Society, King Saud University, Riyadh, Saudi Arabia

References

[1] Kaastra I, Boyd M. Designing a neural network for forecasting financial and economic time series. Neurocomputing. 1996;**10**(3):215-236. DOI: 10.1016/0925-2312(95)00039-9

[2] Dorrer C. Direct measurement of nonlinear coefficient of optical fibre using linear optical sampling. Electronics Letters. 2005;**41**(1):1. DOI: 10.1049/el:20056688

[3] Dorrer C. Monitoring of optical signals from constellation diagrams measured with linear optical sampling. Journal of Lightwave Technology, IEEE. 2006;**24**(1):313. DOI: 10.1109/JLT.2005.859831

[4] Van Den Borne, Dirk . Robust optical transmission systems: Modulation and equalization [thesis]. 2008

[5] Lera G, Pinzolas M. Neighborhood based Levenberg-Marquardt algorithm for neural network training. IEEE Transactions on Neural Networks. 2002;**13**(5):1200-1203. DOI: 10.1109/TNN.2002.1031951

[6] Khan FN, Zhou Y, Sui Q, Lau APT. Non-data-aided joint bit-rate and modulation format identification for next-generation heterogeneous optical networks. Optical Fiber Technology. 2014;**20**(12):68 71

[7] Khan FN, Zhou Y, Lau APT, Lu C. Modulation format identification in heterogeneous fiber-optic networks using artificial neural networks. Optics Express. 2012;**20**(11):12422-12431. DOI: 10.1364/OE.20.012422

[8] CHUN-LIN, Liu. A tutorial of the wavelet transform. NTUEE, Taiwan, 2010

Chapter 3

Gait Generation of Multilegged Robots by using Hardware Artificial Neural Networks

Ken Saito, Masaya Ohara, Mizuki Abe,
Minami Kaneko and Fumio Uchikoba

Additional information is available at the end of the chapter

http://dx.doi.org/10.5772/intechopen.70693

Abstract

Living organisms can act autonomously because biological neural networks process the environmental information in continuous time. Therefore, living organisms have inspired many applications of autonomous control to small-sized robots. In this chapter, a small-sized robot is controlled by a hardware artificial neural network (ANN) without software programs. Previously, the authors constructed a multilegged walking robot. The link mechanism of the limbs was designed to reduce the number of actuators. The current paper describes the basic characteristics of hardware ANNs that generate the gait for multilegged robots. The pulses emitted by the hardware ANN generate oscillating patterns of electrical activity. The pulse-type hardware ANN model has the basic features of a class II neuron model, which behaves like a resonator. Thus, gait generation by the hardware ANNs mimics the synchronization phenomena in biological neural networks. Consequently, our constructed hardware ANNs can generate multilegged robot gaits without requiring software programs.

Keywords: hardware artificial neural networks, pulse-type hardware neuron model, gait, multilegged robot, MEMS, link mechanism, class II neuron model, synchronization phenomena

1. Introduction

Many types of multilegged robots have been developed for various applications [1–3]. Most of these robots were bioinspired by the structures, features, and excellent functionalities of living organisms [4, 5]. Living organisms autonomously operate under the control of small-sized neural networks. Therefore, researchers have begun studying artificial neural networks (ANNs) for robot control [6–10]. Biological neural networks are universally characterized by oscillatory patterns of electrical activity. These patterns govern several functions of living organisms, such as heart rhythms, movements, and swallowing [11, 12]. The oscillatory patterns of living organisms can be clarified through coupled neuron models, which have two categories: class I and class II [13]. Given that the class II model is more easily synchronized than the class I model, the class II model is applied in studies of synchronization phenomena. Famous class II neuron models include the Hodgkin-Huxley model [14] and Bonhoeffer-van der Pol model [15], mathematical neuron models that form the basis of bioinspired oscillatory pattern generation [16–18]. Most of the central pattern generators (CPGs) designed for the synchronized locomotion control of multilegged robots [6–8] are also constructed by mathematical neuron models. A CPG model using mathematical neuron models can be implemented on a field programmable gate array (FPGA). However, an FPGA board cannot be mounted on a millimeter-sized robot system because of its size. Instead, oscillatory patterns for very small robots can be generated by hardware neuron models. Hardware rings of coupled oscillators, which can generate various oscillatory patterns by using the synchronization phenomena [19, 20], have been employed as the structural elements of ANNs. However, given that most of the hardware neuron models contain inductors in their circuit architectures [19–22], they are difficult to implement in an integrated circuit (IC); thus, the use of such models is disadvantageous on the circuit scale [23]. In particular, ICs can be combined with mechanical parts of the robot by using microelectromechanical system (MEMS) technology, which can reduce the robot size to the millimeter scale.

The authors are studying hardware ANNs based on a pulse-type hardware neuron model [24–27] with the same basic features as biological neurons. Specifically, this model possesses spatiotemporal summation characteristics, a threshold period, and a refractory period and generates oscillating patterns of electrical activity. Furthermore, the pulse-type hardware neuron model requires no inductors; therefore, the system is easily implemented in an IC.

Previously, the authors proposed two types of prototype multilegged robots: a quadruped robot approximately 10 cm in size [26] and a hexapod robot approximately 5 mm in size [27]. Both multilegged robots move their limbs by stepping motions. A multilegged robot usually needs actuators for each joint. In our multilegged robots, the number of actuators is reduced by a link mechanism, and the gait is controlled by a hardware ANN. The hardware ANN consists of 4 excitatory synaptic models, 16 inhibitory synaptic models, and 8 cell body models for the quadruped robot [26], and 12 inhibitory synaptic models and 4 cell body models for the hexapod robot [27–29].

This chapter describes the basic characteristics of the hardware ANNs that generate the gait of multilegged robots. After briefly introducing both types of multilegged robots, it discusses the hardware ANNs and mathematically describes the characteristics of the pulse-type hardware neuron model. The oscillation characteristic of the model requires a negative resistance and is described in a phase plane. The synchronization characteristics of connected hardware ANNs are also discussed. Finally, the hardware ANNs are validated in locomotion tests of the multilegged robot.

2. Multilegged robots

The quadruped and hexapod robots have been described in previous works [26, 27]. This section briefly introduces the mechanical components of the fabricated multilegged robots.

2.1. Quadruped robot

The width, length, and height dimensions of the quadruped robot are 130, 140, and 90 mm, respectively (see **Figure 1**). The quadruped robot is constructed from mechanical and electrical components. The mechanical components comprise the body frame, four servo motors, link mechanisms, and four legs. The electrical components consist of the control board, hardware ANNs, and battery. The limbs and body frame are made from aluminum base alloy 2017 and aluminum base alloy 5052, respectively. The mechanical parts are fabricated by a computerized numerical control machining system. The four legs of the quadruped robot system are actuated by four servo motors, and the stepping motion of each leg is generated by the link mechanisms. The servo motor is an HSR-8498HB (Hitec Multiplex Japan) model, which generates sufficient maximum torque to actuate the robot. The mechanical components of the quadruped robot are detailed in [26].

Figure 2 shows the relative phase difference of the quadruped gait pattern under a given driving rhythm of the actuators. The relative phase difference is referenced to the left forelimb (0°). Under various actuation rhythms, the quadruped robot generates different gait patterns. **Figure 2** displays five typical gait patterns: walk, trot, pace, bound, and gallop. The directional changes and turning of the quadruped robot are not realized at present. The robot gait is easily controlled by software programs implemented on a control board. However, in the proposed robot control, the software program for generating the locomotion rhythms is replaced by a hardware ANN.

2.2. Hexapod robot

The fabricated hexapod robot is displayed in **Figure 3**. The robot is 4.0 mm wide, 2.7 mm long, and 2.5 mm high. Two ground (GND) wires and eight signal wires (all made of copper) extend above the robot. The hexapod robot walks when the signal wires are connected to the hardware ANNs. The structure and stepping motion of the robot mimic those of an ant. The ant-like stepping motion is a series of tripod configurations in which two groups of three legs alternate between swing and stance phases (see **Figure 5** in [29]). The hexapod robot comprises

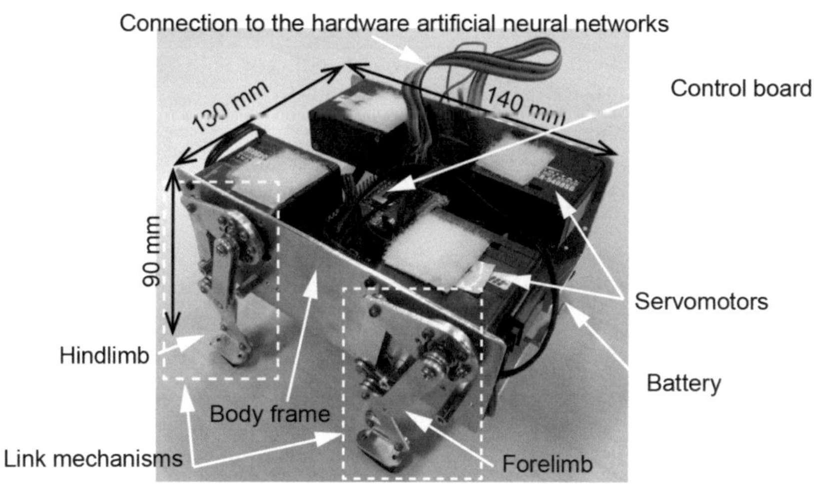

Figure 1. Image of the constructed quadruped robot.

Gait pattern	Leg	Phase difference 0°	90°	180°	270°	Driving rhythm
Walk	LF	D				
	RF			D		
	LH				D	
	RH		D			
Trot	LF	D				
	RF			D		
	LH			D		
	RH	D				
Pace	LF	D				
	RF			D		
	LH	D				
	RH			D		
Bound	LF	D				
	RF	D				
	LH			D		
	RH			D		
Gallop	LF	D				
	RF		D			
	LH				D	
	RH			D		

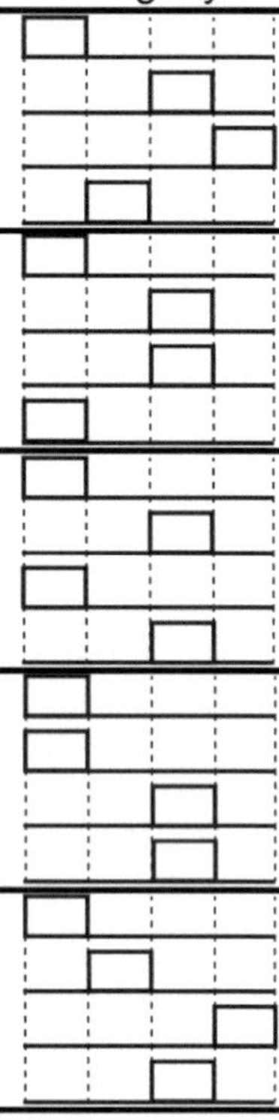

Figure 2. Relative phase difference of quadruped gait patterns for different driving rhythms of the actuators. LF, RF, LH, and RH refer to left forelimb, right forelimb, left hindlimb, and right hindlimb, respectively.

the frame parts, small-sized actuators, and link mechanisms. The small-sized actuators are constructed from artificial muscle wire. All mechanical parts are made from silicon wafers of various thicknesses (100, 200, 385, and 500 μm). The parts were shaped by dry etching by photolithography-based inductively coupled plasma [30]. The small-sized actuator consists of four pieces of artificial muscle wire, as well as the shaft, rotor, and GND wire. The frame components and rotors are connected by the artificial muscle wire, which functions as a shape memory alloy [31]. The artificial muscle wire is BMX50 (BioMetal® Helix, available online at http://www.toki.co.jp [32]). The mechanical components of the hexapod robot are detailed in previous works [27, 29].

Figure 4 shows the leg motions of the hexapod robot. The artificial muscle wire shrinks at high temperatures and extends at low temperatures. Therefore, when an electric current is applied through the wire, the resulting heat displaces the four pieces of artificial muscle wire, and the rotor rotates. The wire is cooled by stopping the current flow. Thus, the actuator is rotated by changing the sequence of the input current. The link mechanism transmits the rotational movements of the rotor to the three legs on one side. This design requires only two small-sized actuators (one on each side of the robot) to actuate the six legs.

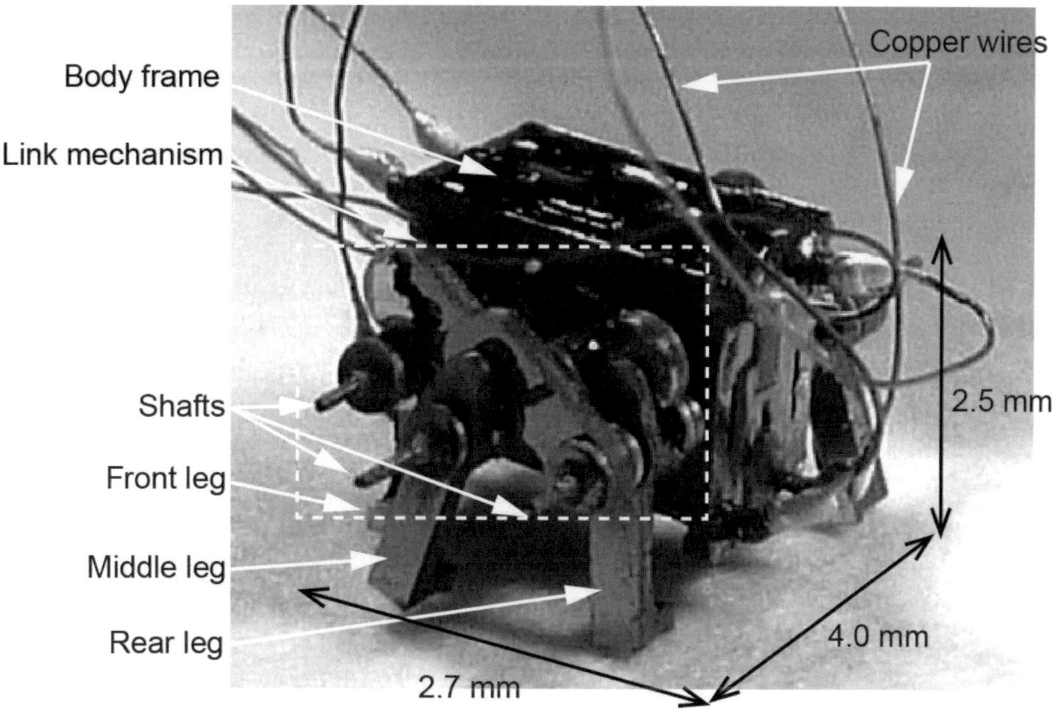

Figure 3. Image of the constructed hexapod robot.

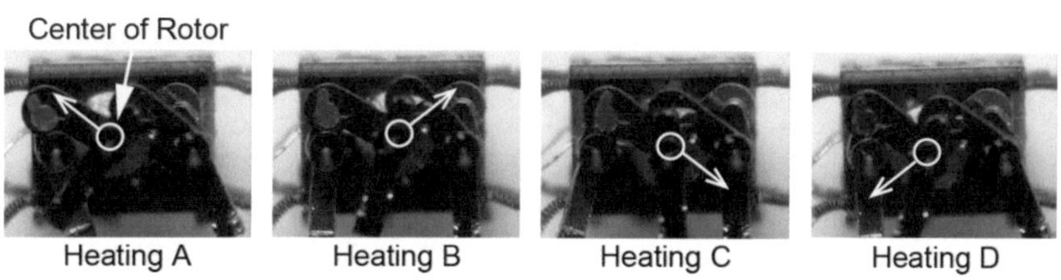

Figure 4. Leg motions of the hexapod robot.

		Phase difference				
Gait pattern	Wire	0°	90°	180°	270°	Driving rhythm
Forward walk	A	D				
	B		D			
	C			D		
	D				D	
Backward walk	A				D	
	B			D		
	C		D			
	D	D				

Figure 5. Relative phase difference of hexapod gait patterns for different driving rhythms of the actuator.

Figure 5 shows the relative phase differences of the hexapod gait patterns for different driving rhythms of the actuator. To heat the artificial muscle wires, an input pulse of amplitude 50–100 mA, period 2 s, and width 0.5 s is required. Therefore, the hexapod robot requires 2 s to complete one locomotion cycle. As mentioned above, the length of the artificial muscle wire depends on the temperature. Specifically, the wire shrinks when heated and extends when cooled. Heating the artificial muscle wires from A to D and from D to A in **Figure 4** drives the hexapod robot forward and backward, respectively. The locomotion pattern is a 180° phase shift at each side, which mimics the locomotion of an ant. If the input pulse is narrower than 0.5 s, the thermal heating by the driving current is insufficient to shrink the wire. By contrast, if the input pulse is wider than 2 s, the thermal heating by the driving current is excessive, and the cooling is insufficient to extend the wire.

3. Hardware artificial neural networks

The hardware ANNs are based on a pulse-type hardware neuron model of class II, specifically, a Hodgkin-Huxley model and a Bonhoeffer-van der Pol model [28]. This section describes the circuit diagrams and the basic characteristics of the pulse-type hardware neuron model. The synchronization phenomena of the hardware ANNs are also discussed.

3.1. Pulse-type hardware neuron model

Figure 6 shows the circuit diagrams of the pulse-type hardware neuron model, which comprises a cell body model and two synaptic models. The cell body model (**Figure 6a**) includes a voltage control-type negative resistance, an equivalent inductance, resistors R_1 and R_2, and a membrane capacitor C_M. The voltage control-type negative resistance circuit with equivalent inductance consists of an n-channel MOSFET M_1, a p-channel MOSFET M_2, a voltage source V_A, a leak resistor R_L, another resistor R_G, and a capacitor C_G. The cell body model generates oscillating patterns of electrical activity v_M (t). v_G (t) is the voltage between both ends of

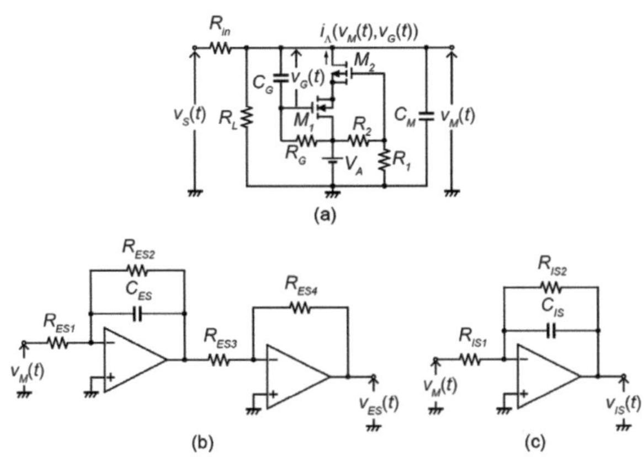

Figure 6. Circuit diagram of the pulse-type hardware neuron model. (a) Cell body model, (b) excitatory synaptic model, and (c) inhibitory synaptic model.

capacitor C_G. v_M (t) and v_G (t) are, respectively, governed by the following simultaneous differential equations.

$$C_M\frac{dv_M(t)}{dt}=\frac{v_s(t)}{R_{in}}-\frac{v_M(t)}{R_L}-\frac{v_M(t)-v_G(t)-V_A}{R_G}+i_\Lambda(v_M(t),v_G(t)), \tag{1}$$

$$C_G\frac{dv_G(t)}{dt}=\frac{v_M(t)-v_G(t)-V_A}{R_G}. \tag{2}$$

A time-dependent nonlinear current $i_\Lambda(v_M(t),v_G(t))$ flows through the negative resistance circuit. The governing equations of $i_\Lambda(v_M(t),v_G(t))$ under the three possible conditions are given by the following:

$$\text{Condition 1}: v_G(t)+V_A+V_{Tn}+V_{Tp}<v_M(t)\le V_{Gp}+V_{Tp},$$

$$i_\Lambda(v_M(t),v_G(t))=\frac{\beta}{8}\left(A+B+V_{Gp}\right)^2 \tag{3}$$

$$\text{Condition 2}: V_{Gp}+V_{Tp}<v_M(t)\le v_G(t)+V_A+V_{Tn},$$

$$i_\Lambda(v_M(t),v_G(t))=\frac{\beta{\cdot}A^2\left(A-2\left(B+V_{Gp}\right)\right)^2}{8\left(A+B+V_{Gp}\right)^2} \tag{4}$$

$$\text{Condition 3}: v_G(t)+V_A+V_{Tn}<v_M(t)\le V_A,$$

$$i_\Lambda(v_M(t),v_G(t))=\frac{\beta\{(V_A-v_M(t))(V_A-v_M(t)+2A)\left(V_A+v_M(t)-2\left(V_{Tp}+V_{Gp}\right)\right)\left(V_A-3v_M(t)+2\left(V_{Tp}+A+V_{Gp}\right)\right)\}}{8\left(A+B+V_{Gp}\right)^2} \tag{5}$$

where $A=v_G(t)+V_{Tn}, B=V_{Tp}-v_M(t), V_{Gp}=\frac{V_A\cdot R_2}{R_1+R_2}, \frac{\beta}{2}=\frac{\mu\varepsilon}{2t}\frac{W}{L}$, and V_{Tn} and V_{Tp} are the threshold voltages of the n and p-channel MOSFETs, respectively. V_{Gp} is the gate voltage of MOSFET M_2. β is the conductance constant of the MOSFETs (with carrier mobility μ, dielectric constant ε of the gate insulator, oxide channel thickness t, channel width $W$and channel length L). Although the value of β differs in the n-type and p-type MOSFETs, Eqs. (3–5) become intractable unless the βs are approximated by the same value. The complex case with different βs is considered in the following numerical analysis.

The circuit parameters of the cell body model are as follows: C_G = 4.7 μF, C_M = 470 nF, R_G = 680 kΩ, R_L = 10 kΩ, R_1 = 15 kΩ, R_2 = 20 kΩ, and R_{in} = 50 kΩ. The voltage source V_A = 3.5 V. The authors have used the BSS83 and BSH205 for M_1 and M_2, respectively. These circuit parameters are set to allow the cell body model to generate oscillation with amplitude 3.5 V, period 8 s, and width of 2 s.

Figure 6b and **c** displays the circuits of the excitatory and inhibitory synaptic models, respectively. The spatiotemporal summation characteristics of the synaptic model resemble those of biological systems. The output $v_S(t)$ of the synaptic model is the spatiotemporal summation of the output voltages of the cell body model $v_M(t)$. v_{ES} (t) and v_{IS} (t) are described by the following equations.

$$v_{ES}\left(t\right)=\frac{R_{ES2}}{R_{ES1}}\cdot\frac{R_{ES4}}{R_{ES3}}\left(1-e^{-\frac{t}{R_{ES2}\cdot C_{ES}}}\right)\cdot v_M(t), \tag{6}$$

$$v_{IS}\left(t\right)=-\frac{R_{IS2}}{R_{IS1}}\left(1-e^{-\frac{t}{R_{IS2}\cdot C_{IS}}}\right)\cdot v_M(t). \tag{7}$$

The spatial summation is performed by the inverting amplifier, whose amplification factor imitates the synaptic weight. Suffixes E and I denote excitatory and inhibitory, respectively. The temporal summation is realized by the operational amplifier RC integrator. The resistors and capacitors in the synaptic model are valued at 1 MΩ and 1 pF, respectively. The operational amplifier is an RC4558D.

3.2. Basic characteristics of the cell body model

Figure 7 shows the negative resistance characteristics of the cell body model. The N-shape characteristic indicates that the negative resistance is voltage control type negative resistance. When $2.3 < v_M(t) < 3.5$ ($v_G(t) = 2.5$ V), the negative resistance is provided by the negative resistance circuit. The amplitude of the negative resistance characteristic can be changed by varying the $v_G(t)$.

Figure 8 shows the phase plane of the cell body model. The attractor (solid line in **Figure 8**) is the limit cycle. The shapes of the $v_M(t)$- and $v_G(t)$-nullclines confirm the class II neuron characteristics of the cell body model. The same characteristics are observed in the Hodgkin-Huxley and Bonhoeffer-van der Pol models. The $v_M(t)$- and $v_G(t)$-nullclines intersect at the equilibrium point. When the equilibrium point $dv_M/dv_G > 0$, the cell body model becomes unstable and self-oscillates. By contrast, when $dv_M/dv_G < 0$, the cell body model becomes stable. In this chapter, the equilibrium point is set to the unstable condition $dv_M/dv_G > 0$. The unstable and stable conditions can be switched by varying V_A.

3.3. Excitatory-inhibitory neuron pair model

The excitatory-inhibitory neuron pair model comprises two cell body models and two synaptic models and generates several oscillatory patterns by using the synchronization phenomena.

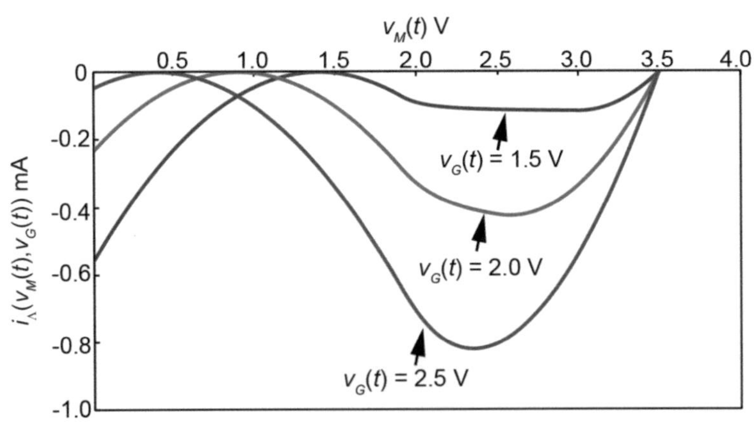

Figure 7. Negative resistance characteristic of the cell body model. The abscissa is $v_M(t)$ and the ordinate is $i_A(v_M(t), v_G(t))$.

http://dx.doi.org/10.5772/intechopen.70693

Figure 9 shows the circuit diagram of the excitatory-inhibitory neuron pair model. The cell body models are mutually coupled by the synaptic models. The excitatory synaptic model sums the excitatory inputs (output voltage of the cell body model v_{ME} and the external input voltage v_{extinE}). Meanwhile, the inhibitory synaptic model sums the inhibitory inputs (output voltage of the cell body model v_{MI} and the external input voltage v_{extinI}). Both cell body models are assigned the same circuit parameters (The synchronization phenomena and oscillatory patterns of the mutually coupled excitatory-inhibitory neuron pair model are provided in [28]).

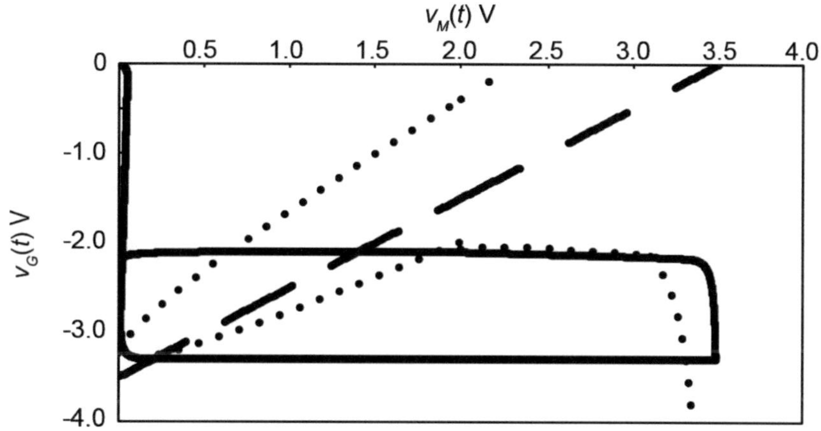

Figure 8. Phase plane of the cell body model. The abscissa is $vM(t)$ and the ordinate is $vG(t)$. The dotted, broken, and solid lines display the $vM(t)$-nullcline, $vG(t)$-nullcline, and attractor, respectively.

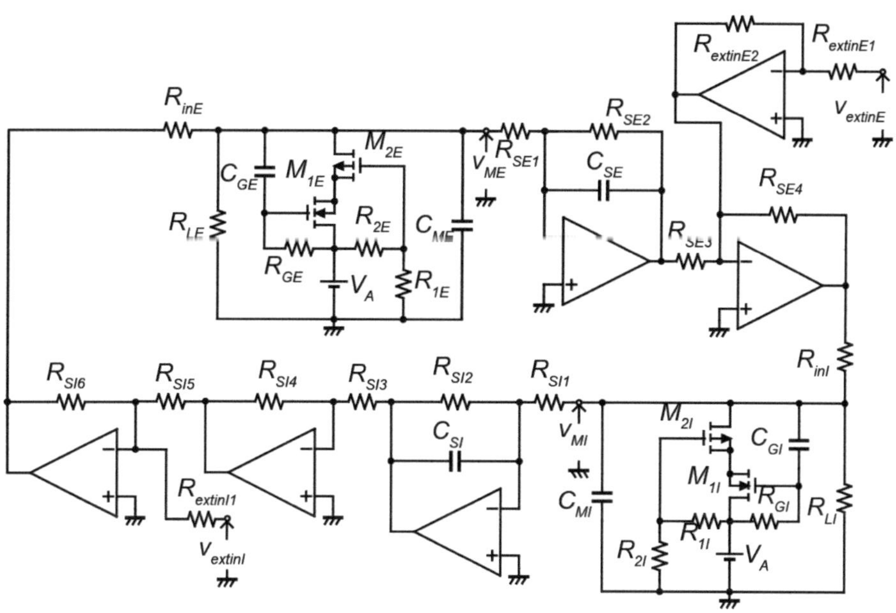

Figure 9. Circuit diagram of the excitatory-inhibitory neuron pair model.

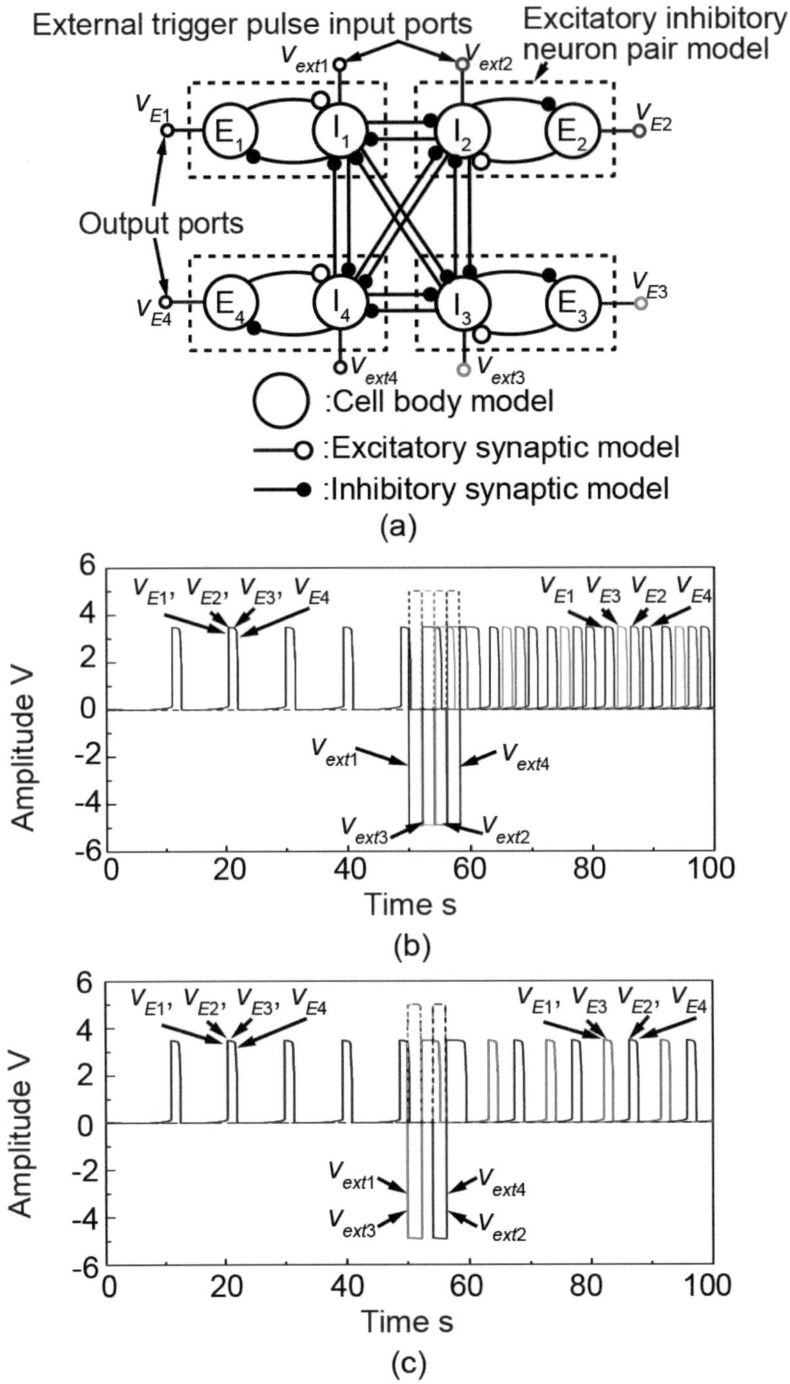

Figure 10. Four sets of excitatory-inhibitory neuron pair models connected by an inhibitory synaptic model. (a) Connection diagram, (b) output waveform when the external trigger pulse generates a walk sequence, (c) output waveform when the external trigger pulse generates a trot sequence (The waveforms in panels (b) and (c) are the simulation results).

The synchronization phenomena of the excitatory-inhibitory neuron pair circuit depend on the connection type of the synaptic model. When the synaptic model connection is excitatory or inhibitory, the synchronization is in-phase and anti-phase, respectively. The excitatory-inhibitory neuron pair circuit was incorporated into the hardware ANN for the quadruped robot.

3.4. Hardware neural networks for quadruped robot

Figure 10 shows the four sets of the excitatory-inhibitory neuron pair model connected by an inhibitory synaptic model. **Figure 10a** shows the connection diagram, and **Figure 10b** and **c** shows the output waveforms during the walking and trotting sequences in **Figure 2**, respectively. The motion sequences are initiated by an external trigger pulse. These results show that to generate a locomotion rhythm of the quadruped robot, the four sets of the excitatory-inhibitory neuron pair model must be connected to the inhibitory synaptic model. The sequences of the gait pattern differ between walk and gallop and between pace/bound and trot. The sequences are easily changed by changing the external trigger pulse.

3.5. Hardware neural networks for hexapod robot

Figure 11 shows the circuit diagrams of the pulse-type hardware neuron model with CMOS circuit. Given that circuit of **Figure 6** is difficult to construct in an IC with a limited layout area, it

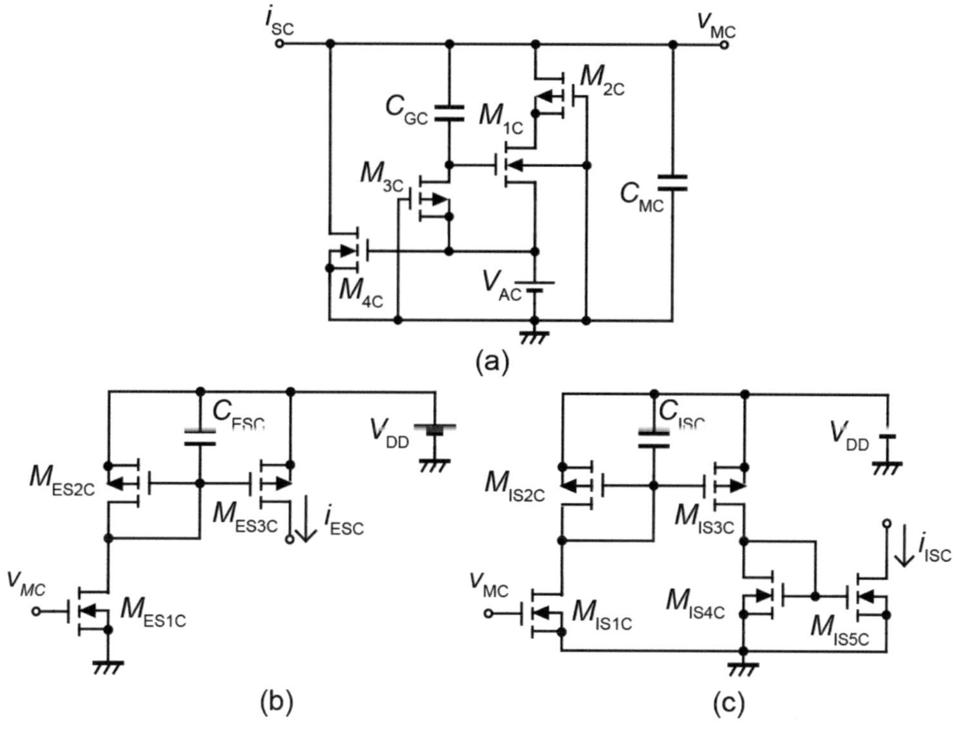

Figure 11. Circuit diagram of the pulse-type hardware neuron model (equivalent CMOS circuit). (a) Cell body model, (b) excitatory synaptic model, and (c) inhibitory synaptic model.

is replaced by a CMOS with an equivalent circuit. In the CMOS circuit, R_L and R_G in **Figure 6a** become the MOS resistors M_{4C} and M_{3C}, respectively. Furthermore, the operational amplifier is replaced by a simple current mirror circuit. However, the basic characteristics of **Figure 11** are unaffected by changing the circuit elements. The circuit parameters are $C_{GC} = 10$ μF, $C_{MC} = 2.2$ μF, M_{1C}, M_{2C}: $W/L = 10$, M_{3C}: $W/L = 0.1$, and M_{4C}: $W/L = 0.3$ for the cell body model and $C_{ESC} = C_{ISC} = 1$ pF, $M_{ES1C\text{-}3C}$, and $M_{IS1C\text{-}5C}$: $W/L = 1$ for the synaptic model. The voltage sources of the cell body and synaptic models are $V_{AC} = 3.0$ V and $V_{DD} = 3.0$ V, respectively.

Figure 12a shows the connection diagram of the inhibitory mutual coupling in the pulse-type hardware neuron model. Four sets of the model are coupled by 12 inhibitory synaptic models. **Figure 12b** shows a typical output waveform of the equivalent CMOS circuit. The inhibitory mutual coupling generates anti-phase synchronization, thus confirming that this coupling will achieve four anti-phase synchronizations. However, the random sequence of the output waveforms must be corrected to the repetitive sequence as shown in **Figure 5**. The correction is made by applying a single external trigger pulse.

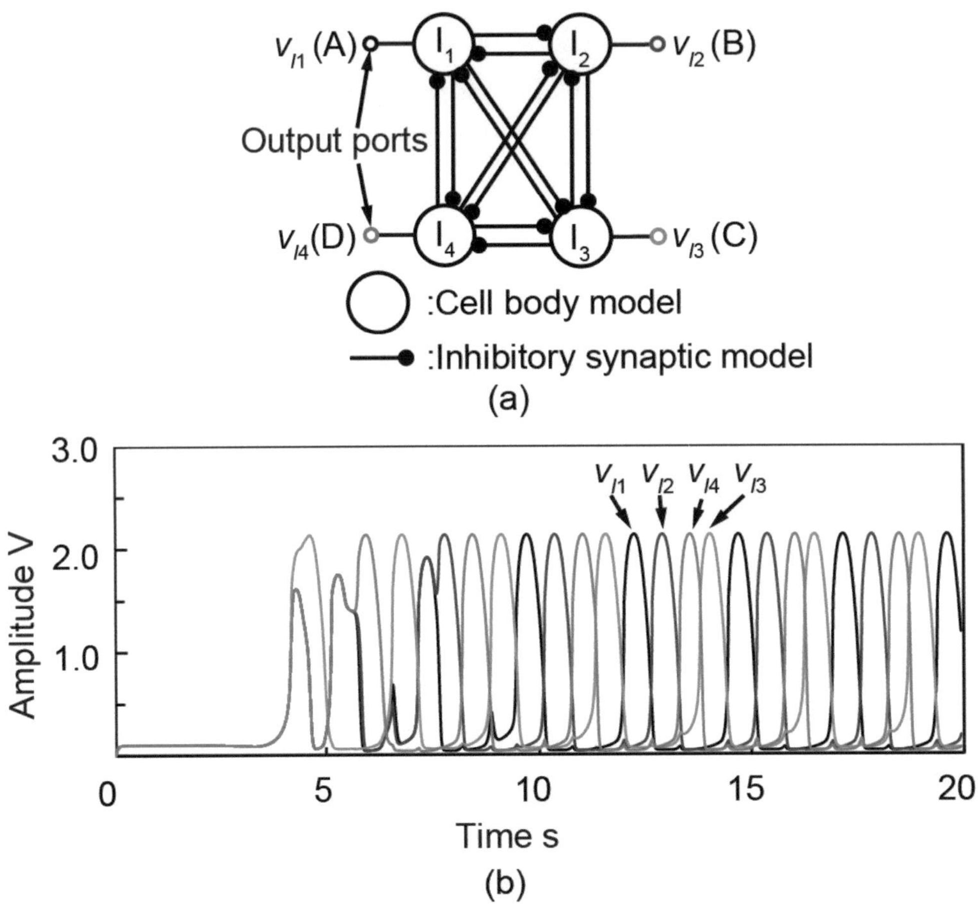

Figure 12. Inhibitory mutual coupling of four pulse-type hardware neuron models. (a) Connection diagram of inhibitory mutual coupling and (b) simulated output waveform of the CMOS equivalent circuit (anti-phase synchronization).

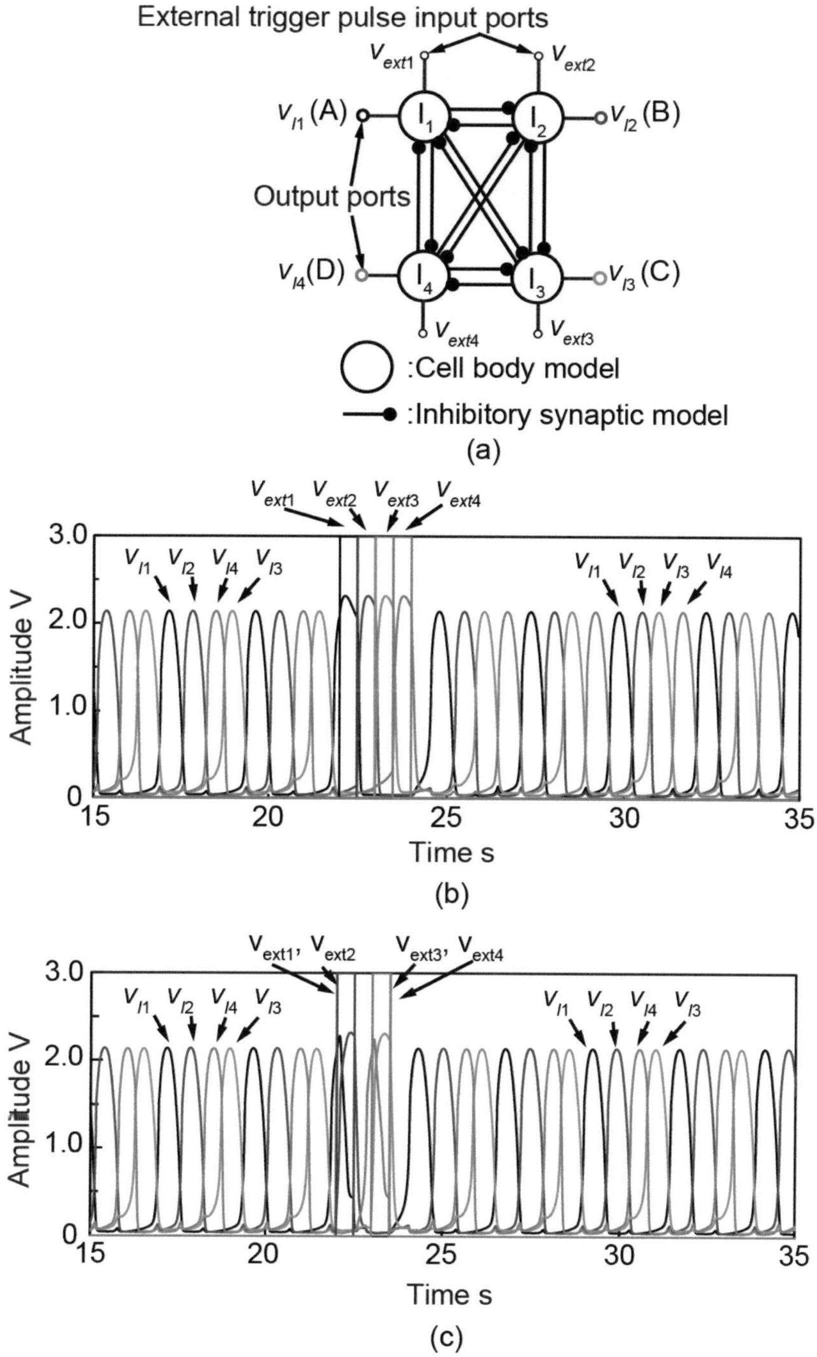

Figure 13. Applying the external trigger pulse to inhibitory mutual coupling of pulse-type hardware neuron models corrected by an external trigger pulse. (a) Connection diagram of inhibitory mutual coupling, (b) output waveform under an external trigger pulse (forward walk sequence in **Figure 5**), and (c) output waveform under an external trigger pulse (bound sequence in **Figure 2**). The waveforms in panels (b) and (c) are simulation results.

Figure 13 shows the inhibitory mutual coupling of the pulse-type hardware neuron models subjected to a single external trigger pulse. (a) The connection diagram of this system, and (b) a typical output waveform under the sequence v_{ext1}, v_{ext2}, v_{ext3}, and v_{ext4} of the trigger pulse (the forward walk sequence in **Figure 5**). Before applying the external trigger pulse, the output sequence was v_{I1}, v_{I2}, v_{I4}, and v_{I3}. After applying the pulse, it was corrected to v_{I1}, v_{I2}, v_{I3}, and v_{I4}. Therefore, the single-pulse correction realizes the forward and backward locomotion patterns in **Figure 5**. Note that walking and galloping in **Figure 2** and forward and backward locomotion patterns in **Figure 5** are all realized by the four-phase alternating oscillation and differ only in the order of their output sequences. **Figure 13c** shows a typical output waveform when the sequence of the external trigger pulse is v_{ext1}, v_{ext2} and (simultaneously) V_{ext3}, V_{ext4} (the bound sequence in **Figure 2**). The bound sequence is not realized by the external trigger pulse. The inhibitory mutual coupling of the pulse-type hardware neuron model cannot by itself generate the locomotion patterns of trot, pace, and bound because these motions are two-phase alternating oscillations.

4. Results and discussion

In this section, the gait rhythms generated by the hardware ANNs are tested in a multilegged robot.

4.1. Locomotion of the quadruped robot

Figure 14 shows the discrete circuits of the hardware ANNs. The electrical components were mounted on a frame-retardant type 4 (FR4) circuit board (The circuit diagram is shown in **Figures 6** and **9**.) The hardware ANN consisted of four sets of an excitatory-inhibitory neuron

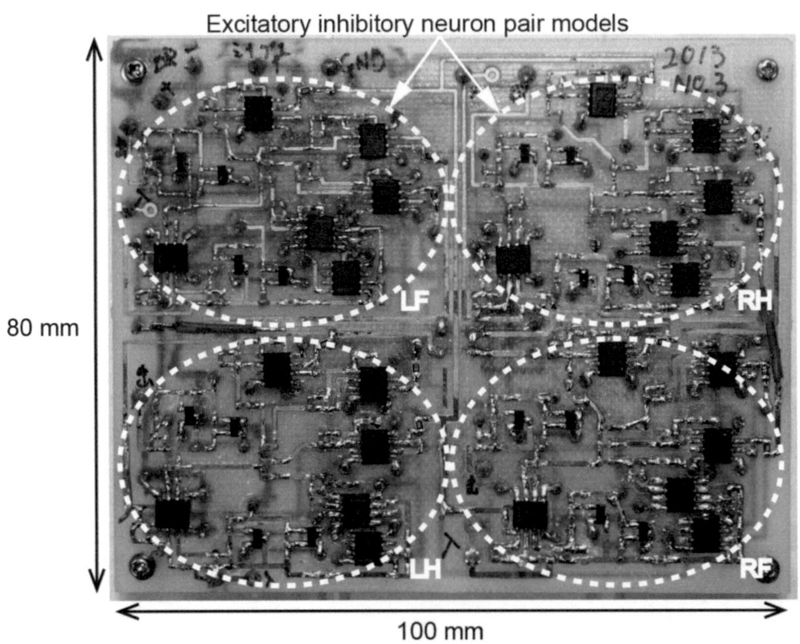

Figure 14. The hardware ANNs are constructed as discrete circuits.

pair model connected as shown in **Figure 10a**. The width and length of the mounted hardware ANNs are 100 and 80 mm, respectively; therefore, the hardware ANNs are sufficiently small to install on the quadruped robot.

Figure 15 shows the quadruped robot mounted with the hardware ANN circuit board. The quadruped robot system is 130 mm wide, 140 mm long, 100 mm high, and 530 g in weight. The power consumption of the hardware ANNs was approximately 360 mWh.

Walk sequence is the basic motion of the quadruped robot. **Figure 16** shows the generated gait pattern and leg motion of a quadruped robot. Panels (a) and (b) show the driving rhythm of the (measured) walking gait pattern and the leg motion of the robot, respectively. Under the

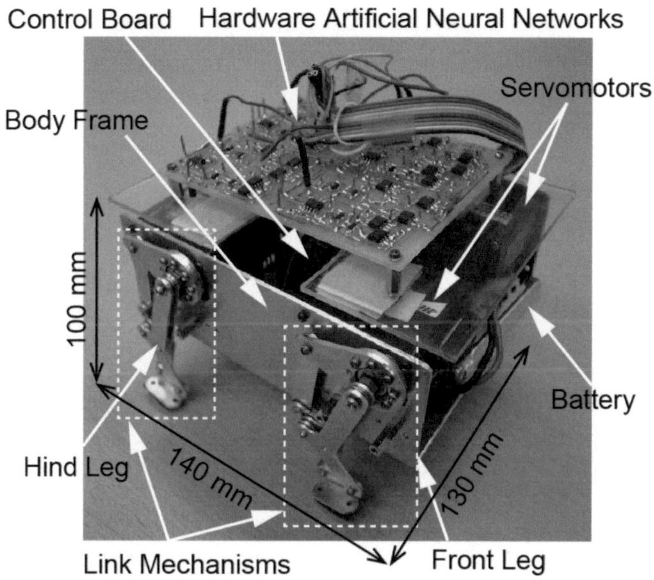

Figure 15. Quadruped robot system mounted with the hardware ANNs as shown in **Figure 14**.

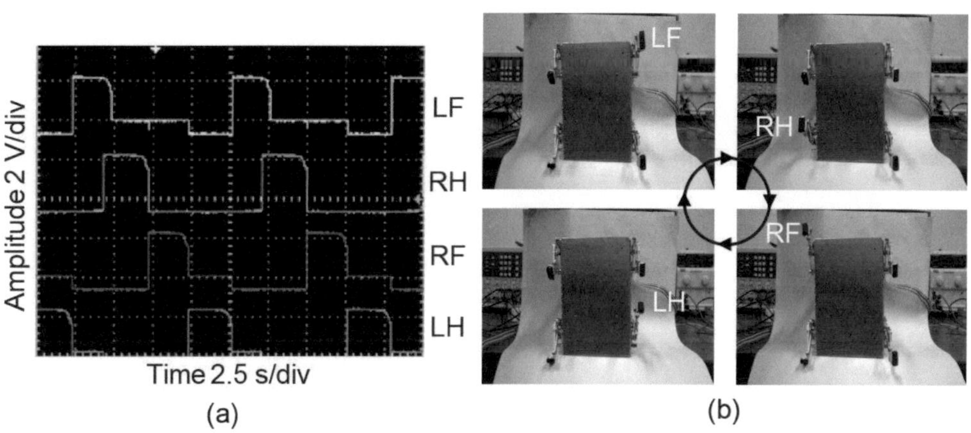

Figure 16. Generated gait pattern and leg motion of a quadruped robot (walk sequence). (a) Waveform and (b) leg motion.

waveform shown in **Figure 16a**, the legs move as shown in **Figure 16b**. In other words, the generated driving rhythm is a four-phase alternating oscillation with the sequence left foreleg (LF), right hindleg (RH), right foreleg (RF), and left hindleg (LH).

The locomotion of a walking quadruped robot driven by the hardware ANNs is captured in **Figure 17**. The motion patterns resemble those of a quadruped animal, thus confirming that the driving rhythms generated by the hardware ANNs can realize proper walking behavior. Moreover, the hardware ANNs can generate various oscillatory patterns without requiring computer programs.

Under an external trigger pulse, the constructed hardware ANNs can change the gait pattern of the quadruped robot. A walk-to-trot gait change is illustrated in **Figure 18**. The external trigger pulse is generated by a waveform generator applied to the input port (see **Figure 10**). Considering that the hardware ANNs can memorize the applied gait rhythm, the quadruped robot can switch its locomotion pattern by applying an external input to its hardware ANNs.

4.2. Locomotion of the hexapod robot

Figure 19 shows the IC of the hardware ANNs. Panel (a) shows the layout pattern of the bare IC chip of the hardware ANNs. The design rule of the bare IC chip is four-metal two-poly CMOS (0.35 μm). The chip is sized (2.45 × 2.45) mm^2. The hardware ANNs are connected as

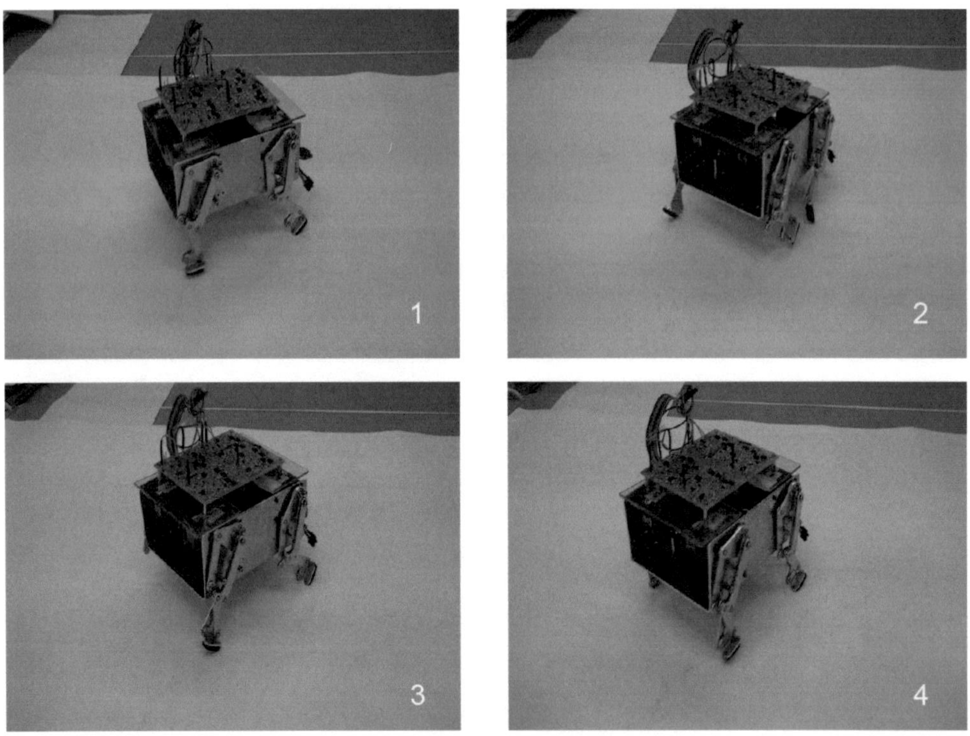

Figure 17. Locomotion (walk) of the quadruped robot driven by hardware ANNs.

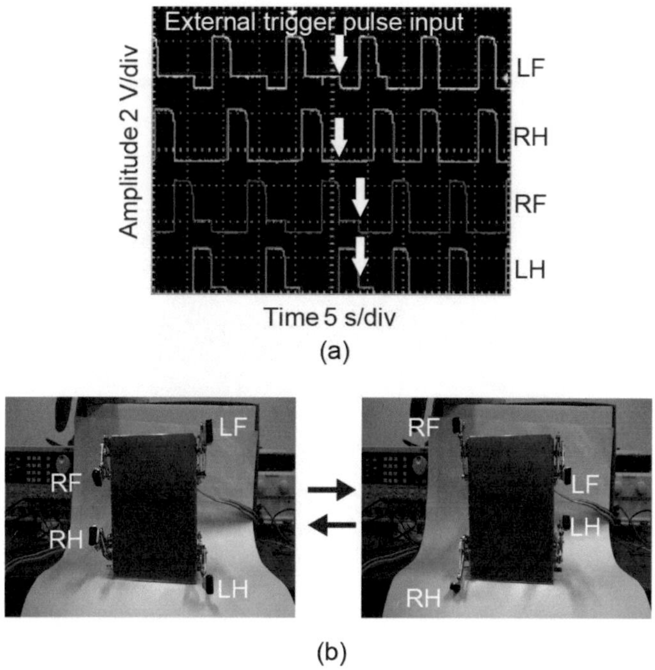

Figure 18. Example of changing the gait pattern from walk to trot. (a) Waveform and (b) leg motion.

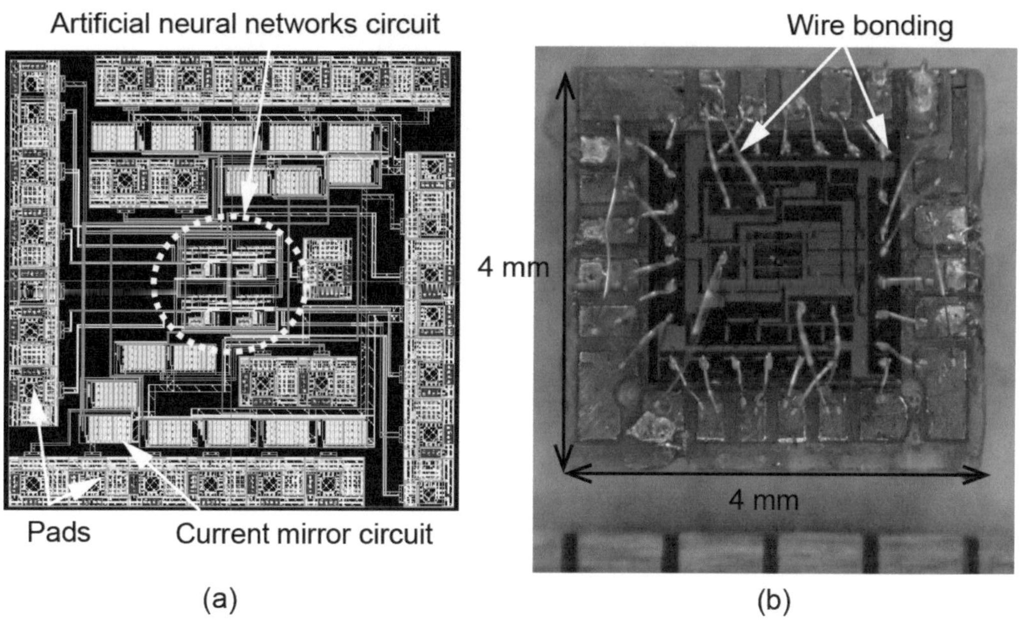

Figure 19. The hardware ANNs are constructed as IC. (a) Layout design and (b) bare IC chip with FR4 circuit board.

shown in **Figure 13**. Four cell body models are mutually coupled by 12 inhibitory synaptic models. The driving waveform of the hexapod robot is generated by the outputs extracted from the hardware ANNs and the current mirror circuit. Four trigger pulse input ports are also extracted from the hardware ANNs. The sequence of the locomotion rhythm depends on the

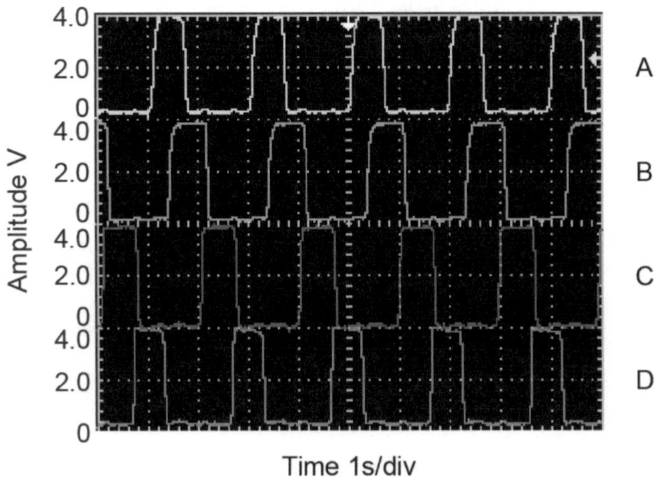

Figure 20. Measured output waveforms of the designed IC.

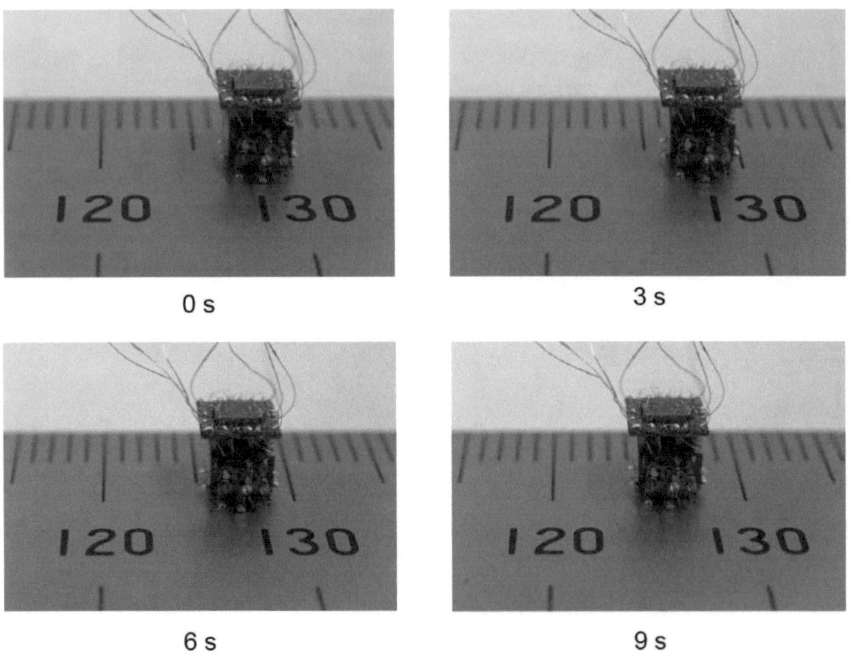

Figure 21. Locomotion (walking) of the hexapod robot mounted with the hardware ANNs.

timing of the single external trigger pulse. **Figure 19b** shows the constructed bare IC chip, which is fixed to the cavity of an FR4 circuit board by wire bonding.

Figure 20 shows the measured output waveform of the designed IC. The hardware ANNs can generate the locomotion rhythms observed in living organisms. To sufficiently heat and cool the artificial muscle wires, the pulse width, period, and amplitude were set to 0.5 s, 2 s, and 75 mA, respectively. The connected helical artificial muscle wires are approximately 50 Ω. As shown in **Figure 20**, the output waveform effectively actuates the actuator of the hexapod robot. The approximate power consumptions of the hardware ANNs and the current mirror circuit were 0.708 and 488 mWh, respectively. The former almost matches the power consumption of biological neural networks, but the power consumption of the artificial muscle wire was excessive.

The circuit in **Figure 19b** was mounted on the hexapod robot. **Figure 21** shows snapshots of the walking hexapod robot system. The driving waveforms generated by the hardware ANNs actuate the hexapod robot, thus enabling successful locomotion.

5. Conclusions

This chapter describes the basic characteristics of the hardware ANNs as gait generators of multilegged robots.

The main findings are summarized below.

1. The basic component of the hardware ANN (namely, the cell body model) has the basic features of a class II neuron model.

2. Gait generation by the hardware ANNs uses synchronization phenomena, as observed in biological neural networks.

3. The hardware ANNs successfully guided the locomotion of two types of multilegged robots without requiring software programs or analog digital converters.

Currently, the authors consider replacing the artificial muscle wire by an electrostatic actuator to reduce the actuating power. The electrostatic actuator will be powered by high-voltage silicon photovoltaic cells installed in the microrobot system. In future works, the ANNs, actuator, power source system, and sensory system will be directly integrated into the silicon frame parts of the microrobot.

Acknowledgements

The authors like to thank Prof. Liwei Lin and the members of Lin laboratory. The VLSI chip in this study was fabricated by Digian Technology Inc. This work was supported by VLSI Design and Education Center (VDEC), the University of Tokyo in collaboration with Synopsys Inc.,

Cadence Design Systems Inc., and Mentor Graphics Inc. The fabrication of the hexapod robot was supported by the Research Center for Micro Functional Devices, Nihon University. The authors appreciate to all above supports.

Author details

Ken Saito[1,2]*, Masaya Ohara[1], Mizuki Abe[3], Minami Kaneko[1] and Fumio Uchikoba[1]

*Address all correspondence to: kensaito@eme.cst.nihon-u.ac.jp

1 Department of Precision Machinery Engineering, College of Science and Technology, Nihon University, Chiba, Japan

2 Department of Mechanical Engineering, University of California, Berkeley, USA

3 Precision Machinery Engineering, Graduate School of Science and Technology, Nihon University, Tokyo, Japan

References

[1] Fujita M, Kitano H. Development of an autonomous quadruped robot for robot entertainment. Autonomous Robots. 1998;**5**:7-18. DOI: 10.1007/978-1-4615-5735-7

[2] Mcghh RB, Iswandhi GI. Adaptive locomotion of a multilegged robot over rough terrain. IEEE Transactions on Systems, Man, and Cybernetics. 1979;**9**(4):176-182. DOI: 10.1109/TSMC.1979.4310180

[3] Raibert M, Blankespoor K, Nelson G, Playter R, The BigDog Team. BigDog, the Rough-Terrain Quadruped Robot. In: Proceedings of the 17th World Congress The International Federation of Automatic Control; July 6–11. Seoul, Korea: Elsevier Ltd; 2008. p. 10822-10825. DOI: 10.3182/20080706–5-KR-1001.01833

[4] Habib MK, Watanabe K, Izumi K. Biomimetics robots: From bio-inspiration to implementation. In: Proceedings of the 33rd Annual Conference of the IEEE Industrial Electronics Society, Nov. 5–8. Taipei, Taiwan: IEEE; 2007. p. 143-148. DOI: 10.1109/IECON.2007.4460382

[5] Habib MK. Biomimetcs: Innovations and Robotics. International Journal of Mechatronics and Manufacturing Systems. 2011;**4**(2):113-134. DOI: 10.1504/IJMMS.2011.039263

[6] Kimura H, Fukuoka Y, Konaga K. Adaptive dynamic walking of a quadruped robot using a neural system model. Advanced Robotics. 2001;**15**(8):859-878. DOI: 10.1163/156855301317198179

[7] Fukuoka Y, Kimura H, Cohen AH. Adaptive dynamic walking of a quadruped robot on irregular terrain based on biological concepts. The International Journal of Robotics Research. 2003;**22**(3–4):187-202. DOI: 10.1177/0278364903022003004

[8] Ijspeert AJ. Central pattern generators for locomotion control in animals and robots: A review. Neural Networks. 2008;**21**(4):642-653. DOI: 10.1016/j.neunet.1 March 2008.4

[9] Schilling M, Hoinville T, Schmitz J, Cruse H. Walknet, a bio-inspired controller for hexapod walking. Biological Cybernetics. 2013;**107**(4):397-419. DOI: 10.1007/s00422-013-0563-5

[10] Schilling M, Paskarbeit J, Huffmeier A, Schneider A, Schmitz J, Cruse H. A hexapod walker using a heterarchical architecture for action selection. Frontiers in Computational Neuroscience. 2013;**7**:1-17/126. DOI: 10.3389/fncom.2013.00126

[11] Delcomyn F. Neural basis of rhythmic behavior in animals. Science. 1980;**210**(4469):492-498. DOI: 10.1126/science.7423199

[12] Arbib MA. The Handbook of Brain Theory and Neural Networks. 2nd ed. Cambridge, MA: The MIT Press; 2002 1308 p

[13] Rinzel J, Ermentrout GB. Analysis of neural excitability and oscillations. In: Koch C, Segev I, editors. Methods in Neuronal Modeling. 2nd ed. Cambridge, MA, The MIT Press; 1998. p. 135-169

[14] Hodgkin AL, Huxley AF. A quantitative description of membrane current and its application to conduction and excitation in nerve. The Journal of Physiology. 1952;**117**(4):500-544

[15] van der Pol B. On "relaxation-oscillations". The London, Edinburgh, and Dublin Philosophical Magazine and Journal of Science. 1926;**2**(11):978–992. DOI: 10.1080/14786442608564127

[16] Tsumoto K, Yoshinaga T, Aihara K, Kawakami H. Bifurcations in synaptically coupled Hodgkin-Huxley neurons with a periodic input. International Journal of Bifurcation and Chaos. 2003;**13**(3):653-666. DOI: 10.1142/S0218127403006832

[17] Tsumoto K, Yoshinaga T, Iida H, Kawakami H, Aihara K. Bifurcations in a mathematical model for circadian oscillations of clock genes. Journal of Theoretical Biology. 2006;**239**(1):101-122. DOI: 10.1016/j.jtbi.2005.07.017

[18] Tsuji S, Ueta T, Kawakami H, Aihara K. Bifurcation analysis of current coupled BVP oscillators. International Journal of Bifurcation and Chaos. 2007;**17**(3):837-850. DOI: 10.1142/S0218127407017586

[19] Endo T, Mori S. Mode analysis of a ring of a large number of mutually coupled van der Pol oscillators. IEEE Transactions on Circuits and Systems. 1978;**25**(1):7-18. DOI: 10.1109/TCS.1978.1084380

[20] Kitajima H, Yoshinaga T, Aihara K, Kawakami H. Chaotic bursts and bifurcation in chaotic neural networks with ring structure. International Journal of Bifurcation and Chaos. 2001;**11**(6):1631-1643. DOI: 10.1142/S0218127401002894

[21] Yamauchi M, Wada M, Nishino Y, Ushida A. Wave propagation phenomena of phase states in oscillators coupled by inductors as a ladder. IEICE Transactions on Fundamentals of Electronics, Communications and Computer Sciences. 1999;**E82-A**(11):2592-2598

[22] Yamauchi M, Okuda M, Nishino Y, Ushida A. Analysis of phase-inversion waves in coupled oscillators synchronizing at in-and-anti-phase. IEICE Transactions on Fundamentals of Electronics, Communications and Computer Sciences. 2003;**86-A**(7):1799-1806

[23] Merolla PA, Arthur JV, Alvarez-Icaza R, Cassidy AS, Sawada J, Akopyan F, et al. A million spiking-neuron integrated circuit with a scalable communication network and interface. Science. 2014;**345**(6197):668-673. DOI: 10.1126/science.1254642

[24] Matsuoka J, Sekine Y, Saeki K, Aihara K. Analog hardware implementation of a mathematical model of an asynchronous chaotic neuron. IEICE Transactions on Fundamentals of Electronics, Communications and Computer Sciences. 2002;**E85-A**(2):389-394

[25] Nakabora Y, Saeki K, Sekine Y. Synchronization of coupled oscillators using pulse-type hardware neuron models with mutual coupling. In: Proceedings of the 2004 International Technical Conference on Circuits/Systems; July 6–8. Miyagi, Japan: Computers and Communications; 2004. p. 8D2L-3-1-8D2L-3-4

[26] Saito K, Ikeda Y, Takato M, Uchikoba F. Locomotion rhythm generation using pulse-type hardware neural networks for quadruped robot. In: Ngo TD, editor. Biomimetic Technologies Principles and Applications. 1st ed. Sawston, Cambridge, UK: Woodhead Publishing; 2015. p. 321-334

[27] Saito K, Takato M, Sekine Y, Uchikoba F. MEMS microrobot with pulse-type hardware neural networks integrated circuit. In: Habib MK, editor. Handbook of Research on Advancements in Robotics and Mechatronics. Hershey, PA, USA: IGI Global; 2014. p. 18-35. DOI: 10.4018/978-1-4666-7387-8.ch002

[28] Saito K, Matsuda A, Saeki K, Uchikoba F, Sekine Y. Synchronization of coupled pulse-type hardware neuron models for CPG model. In: Rao AR, Cecchi GA, editors. The Relevance of the Time Domain to Neural Network Models. Boston, MA: Springer; 2012. p. 117-133. DOI: 10.1007/978-1-4614-0724-9_7

[29] Saito K, Takato M, Sekine Y, Uchikoba F. Biomimetics micro robot with active hardware neural networks locomotion control and insect-like switching behaviour. International Journal of Advanced Robotic Systems. 2012;**9**(226):1-6. DOI: 10.5772/54129

[30] Bhardwaj JK, Ashraf H. Advanced silicon etching using high-density plasmas. In: Proceedings SPIE 2639, Micromachining and Microfabrication Process Technology September 19. Austin, TX, USA: SPIE Press; 1995. p. 224-233. DOI: 10.1117/12.221279

[31] Homma D. Metal artificial muscle "BioMetal Fiber". Journal of the Robotics Society of Japan. 2003;**21**(1):22-24. DOI: 10.7210/jrsj.21.22

[32] Toki Corporation. Welcome to Toki Corporation [Internet]. Available from: http://www.toki.co.jp/. [Accessed: July 27, 2017]

Chapter 4

Using Artificial Neural Networks to Produce High-Resolution Soil Property Maps

Zhengyong Zhao, Fan-Rui Meng, Qi Yang and Hangyong Zhu

Additional information is available at the end of the chapter

http://dx.doi.org/10.5772/intechopen.70705

Abstract

High-resolution maps of soil property are considered as the most important inputs for decision support and policy-making in agriculture, forestry, flood control, and environmental protection. Commonly, soil properties are mainly obtained from field surveys. Field soil surveys are generally time-consuming and expensive, with a limitation of application throughout a large area. As such, high-resolution soil property maps are only available for small areas, very often, being obtained for research purposes. In the chapter, artificial neural network (ANN) models were introduced to produce high-resolution maps of soil property. It was found that ANNs can be used to predict high-resolution soil texture, soil drainage classes, and soil organic content across landscape with reasonable accuracy and low cost. Expanding applications of the ANNs were also presented.

Keywords: ANN, soil drainage, soil texture, soil organic carbon, DEM, topography, hydrological index, vertical slope position

1. Introduction

1.1. Soil properties

Difference of soils in physical and chemical determined what type of plants grows in a soil or what particular crops grow in a region. Jack pine (*Pinus banksiana*), for example, occurs on coarse sands, poor drainage, and shallow soils, and sugar maple (*Acer saccharum*) grows best on deep, fertile, moist, well-drained soils in Ref. [1]. The most important soil properties included soil texture, soil drainage, and soil organic carbon (SOC).

Soil texture is defined as relative proportions (percentages) of clay, sand, and silt contents. These percentages are used to confirm soil textural classes in a soil texture triangle (**Figure 1**).

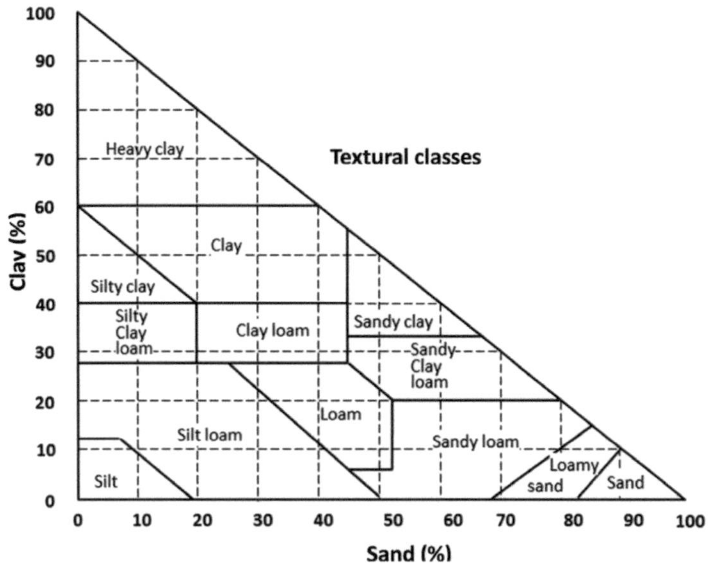

Figure 1. Canadian soil texture triangle in Ref. [2].

Soil texture not only directly affects the porosity of soil, but also determines water-holding and nutrient-holding capacity, flow characteristics, and long-term soil nutrient regime. For example, soils with heavy clay in general have higher percentage of smaller pores, higher water-holding capacity at lower water potentials and are often associated with poorly drained conditions with limited aeration for plant growth. As a contrast, soils with heavy sand normally have relatively higher percentage of larger pores with lower water-holding capacity under relatively dry conditions. Soil texture also affects the risk of soil erosion and soil erodibility.

Soil drainage was defined as the frequency and duration of periods of water saturation or partial saturation, and soil drainage classes reflect average soil moisture conditions in Ref. [3]. Soil drainage is associated with water-holding and nutrient-holding capacities, flow characteristics, and solute transport. Soil drainage is also directly related to plant growth. For example, plants grown on soil with poor drainage often suffer from reduced growth, leaf dieback as a result of root suffocation, and root disease in Ref. [4]. Plants experiencing root decline from excess water are also more susceptible to attack by secondary diseases and insects in Ref. [5]. Under natural conditions, soil drainage characteristic is one important factor that determines which types of plants grow on a particular landscape site. For precision forestry and precision agriculture, high-resolution soil maps are especially important in Ref. [6]. Soil drainage classes are closely related soil texture and slope position (**Figure 2**).

Soil organic carbon refers to the carbon (C) occurring in soil organic matter of the soil. SOC can help to improve soil physical properties by increasing water-holding capacity, stabilizing soil structure in Ref. [8], soil chemical properties, and nutrients holding capacity in Ref. [9]. From a land management perspective, SOC plays important roles in reducing soil erosion and improving crop productivity. For this reason, SOC content has been used as a required input variable

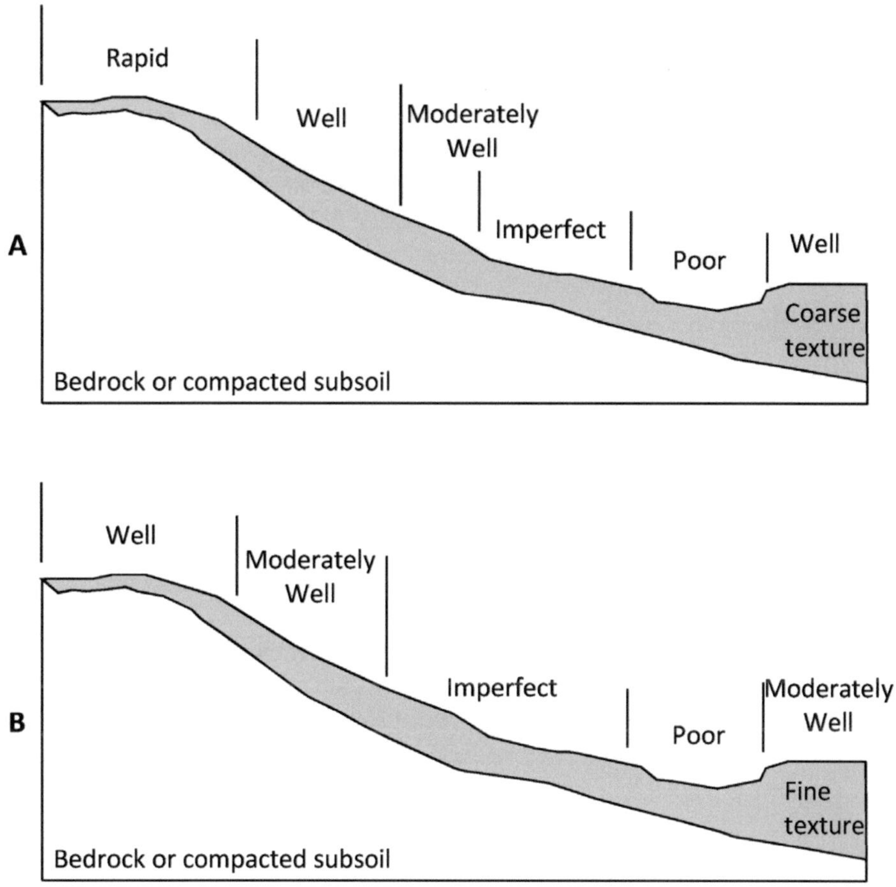

Figure 2. Generalized soil drainage patterns and drainage classes for soils with coarse texture soil (A) and fine texture soil (B) as influenced by slope position in Ref. [7].

for a number of hydrological simulation models in Ref. [10] and many landscape level models for estimating soil water retention, cation exchange capacity, and soil bulk density in Ref. [11]

1.2. Mapping soil properties

Field soil surveys have been the primary method for determination of soil properties, including soil texture, soil drainage, and SOC. For mapping purposes, soil surveys are normally conducted with point samples, either systematically or randomly over a given area, and then the point data are usually interpolated to produce soil maps. Various interpolation methods have been used to produce soil maps, especially the kriging method in Ref. [12]. There is a major limitation about interpolation method, i.e., the assumption that the spatial distributions and changes of the interpolated properties are continuous. Therefore, large amount of data are often required to produce accurate high-resolution soil maps. With the purpose of improving the interpolation accuracy with sparsely distributed sample points, various improved kriging methods have been developed in Ref. [13]. However, the methods still require substantial amounts of field samples to define the spatial autocorrelation and the precision of the resultant maps will still depend upon the density and distribution of original data points in Ref. [14]. Due to high spatial variability of soil characteristics, large numbers of sampling points are required to generate an accurate high-resolution soil map. Although the accuracy of a soil map may be increased with increasing data points, intensive field surveys are expensive and time-consuming. Furthermore, the accuracy is affected by the quality of the data, which, to a great extent, depends on the field experience of the soil surveyors in Ref. [15]. As an alternative, various models have been developed to produce soil property maps.

Statistical models with predictive powers could potentially overcome the problem of interpolation methods in Ref. [16]. Bell et al., for example, related soil drainage class to parent material, terrain, and surface drainage with the help of discriminant function analysis in Pennsylvania, USA in Ref. [17]. According to this method, soil drainage probability maps were predicted well when compared with published soil drainage maps. Campling et al. applied a logistic model to successfully predict the probability of drainage classes in a tropical area using terrain properties (elevation, slope, distance-to-the-river channel) and vegetation indices from a Landsat TM image in Ref. [18]. By applying discriminant function analysis and a co-kriging method, Kravchenko et al. created soil drainage maps using topographical data, i.e., slope, curvature, and flow accumulation, and soil electrical conductivity data in central Illinois, USA in Ref. [19]. But empirical models derived with traditional statistical methods may hinder the real relationships between soil properties and independent data because the relationships are rarely linear in nature.

1.3. Artificial neural networks

In recent years, artificial neural network (ANNs) have been increasingly used to overcome non-linear problems. The ANN is a form of artificial intelligence that was inspired by the studies of the human neuron and has been used to analyze biophysical data in Ref. [20]. ANNs have the ability to auto-analyze the relationships between multi-source inputs (including combinations of qualitative and quantitative data) by self-learning, and produce results without hypothesis. Some ANNs have been successfully used to map soil properties in Ref. [21]. For example, in Licznar and Nearing's study, soil loss was predicted quantitatively from natural runoff plots with the ANN method in Ref. [22]. The results showed that correlation coefficients (predicted soil loss versus measured values) were in the range of 0.7–0.9. Ramadan et al. applied two different multivariate calibration methods (PCA and back-propagation ANN) to predict soil properties (sand, silt, clay, etc.) with the help of DNA data from microbial community in Ref. [23].

1.4. Objectives

In the chapter, we focused on describing a general approach for using ANNs to produce high-resolution soil properties, from preparing data, building ANN structure, training ANNs, optimizing networks, to simulating ANNs.

http://dx.doi.org/10.5772/intechopen.70705

2. Data preparation for modeling soil properties

Preparing data, including input data and target data, is an important and indeed a critical step before building ANN for soil properties.

2.1. Input data

Input data were composed of potential variables that describe or determine the predicting soil properties, including DEM-generated topo-hydrological variables, such as slope steepness, soil terrain factor (STF), sediment delivery ratio (SDR), vertical slope position (VSP), topographic witness index (TWI), and potential solar radiation (PSR) (**Figure 3**), and existing coarse resolution soil map, such as soil property map, geology map, surficial parent material map, and hydrologic map, because (1) at local levels, soil properties are assumed to have been modified by hydrological processes that are associated with topography and they can be modeled with a

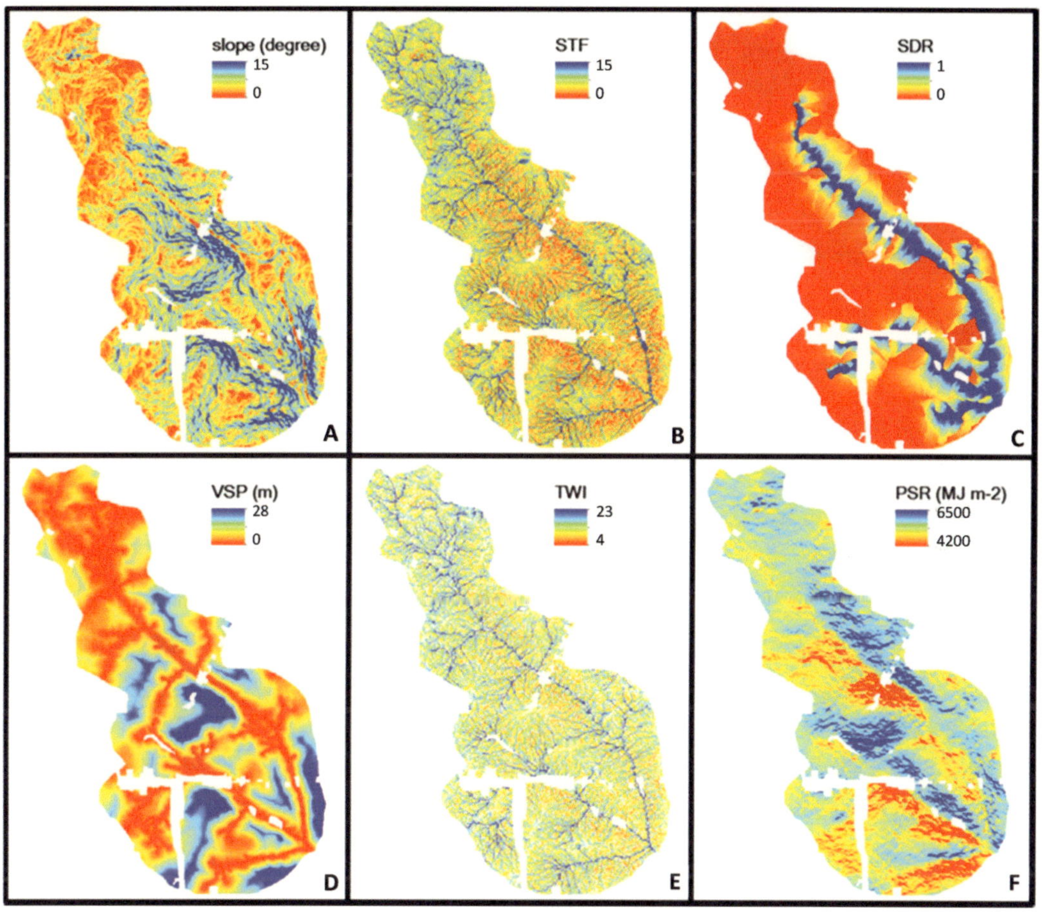

Figure 3. The images of slope (A), soil terrain factor (B), sediment delivery ratio (C), vertical slope position (D), topographic witness index (E), and potential solar radiation (F) in the black brook watershed, New Brunswick, Canada.

DEM in Ref. [24]; (2) at landscape levels, average soil properties were related to geological formations and soil parent materials. These landscape features are assumed to have been captured by existing coarse resolution soil maps.

Soil terrain factor is a modified version of the hydrological similarity index in Ref. [25]. It considers total drainage area and slope as well as the clay content in rooting zone. The STF was calculated using Eq. (1):

$$STF = \ln \frac{(A+1)P_{clay}}{(s+k)^2} \tag{1}$$

where A is the flow accumulation (m^2); P_{clay} is the clay content (wt. %) from the coarse resolution soil data; k is a parameter (=1); and s is the slope steepness ($m\ m^{-1}$).

Sediment delivery ratio is the percent of sediment delivered to surface waters from the total amount of soil eroded in a watershed. The ratio, calculated by Eq. (2), indicates the efficiency of sediment transport in the watershed and is largely influenced by topography and the flow distance to streams in Ref. [26].

$$SDR_i = \exp\left(-\beta t_i\right) \tag{2}$$

where t_i is the travel time from cell i to the nearest channel (s); and β is a watershed-specific constant.

Traveling time, t_i, is defined by Eq. (3):

$$t_i = \sum_{j=1}^{N_p} \frac{l_j}{v_j} \tag{3}$$

where N_p is the total number of cells from cell j to the nearest channel, along the flow path (m); l_j is the length segment cell j along the flow path (m); and v is flow velocity ($m\ s^{-1}$).

Flow velocity, v, is got based on Eq. (4) in Ref. [27].

$$v = ds^{1/2} \tag{4}$$

where s is slope steepness ($m\ m^{-1}$) and d is a coefficient dependent on surface roughness characteristics ($m\ s^{-1}$) for cell i.

By using HYDRO-tools extension in ArcView, the flow length, t_i, was calculated in order to acquire travel time, with an inverse velocity grid used as a weighting factor in Ref. [28].

The watershed parameter, β was estimated by numerically solving Eq. (5):

$$SDR_w = \frac{\sum_{i=1}^{N} \exp\left(-\beta t_i\right) l_i^{0.5} s_i^2 a_i}{\sum_{i=1}^{N} l_i^{0.5} s_i^2 a_i} \tag{5}$$

where SDR_w is the watershed average SDR, which was calculated with an empirical formula similar to $SDR_w = pA_T^c$ in Ref. [29]. Parameters p and c were confirmed as 0.42 and −0.125 because they represent a good general approximation between SDR_w and SDR in Ref. [30].

N is total number of cells over the watershed, a_i is area of the cell (m^2), l_i is the length of cell i along the flow path (m), A_T is the area of the watershed (km^2).

Vertical slope position (m) is defined as the elevation differences between the land and the nearest water surface and calculated by integrating the elevation difference for each cell alone the path to the nearest water body using the following Eq. (6) (**Figure 4**):

$$VSP = \min \sum (ds) \tag{6}$$

where d is the distance between two adjacent cells (m); s is slope steepness ($m\ m^{-1}$).

Topographic wetness index is a steady-state wetness index that reflects soil moisture and drainage conditions, defined as a function of the natural logarithm of the ratio of local upslope contribution area and slope angle in Ref. [32].

$$TWI = \ln \left(\frac{A}{s} \right) \tag{7}$$

where A is the flow accumulation (m^2) ands is the slope steepness ($m\ m^{-1}$).

Potential solar radiation ($MJ\ m^{-2}$) is the total of annual potential solar radiation. PSR reflected the potential light distribution along with the change of topography. The higher the value, the stronger the light radiation. Potential solar radiation takes into account the central Latitude, days of 1 year from 1 to 365 and hours of 1 day from 1 to 24 by an ArcView Extension in Ref. [33].

Coarse resolution soil maps are widely available. These maps usually reflected average soil properties over a large area (**Figure 5**). Researches indicated that coarse resolution soil data had a significant influence on the distribution of high-resolution soil property maps, especially around the boundary in Ref. [34].

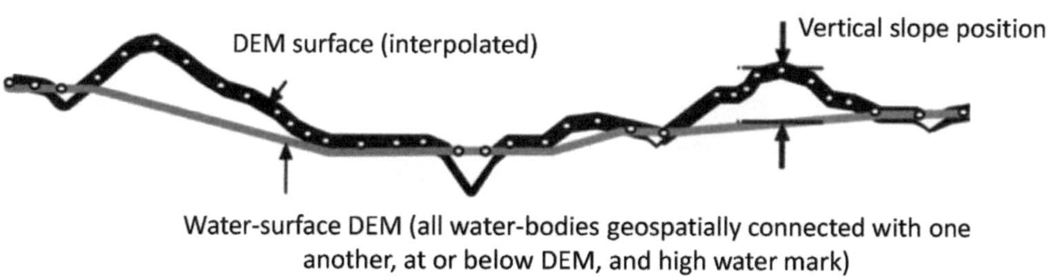

Figure 4. Vertical slope position of a slope profile in ref. [31].

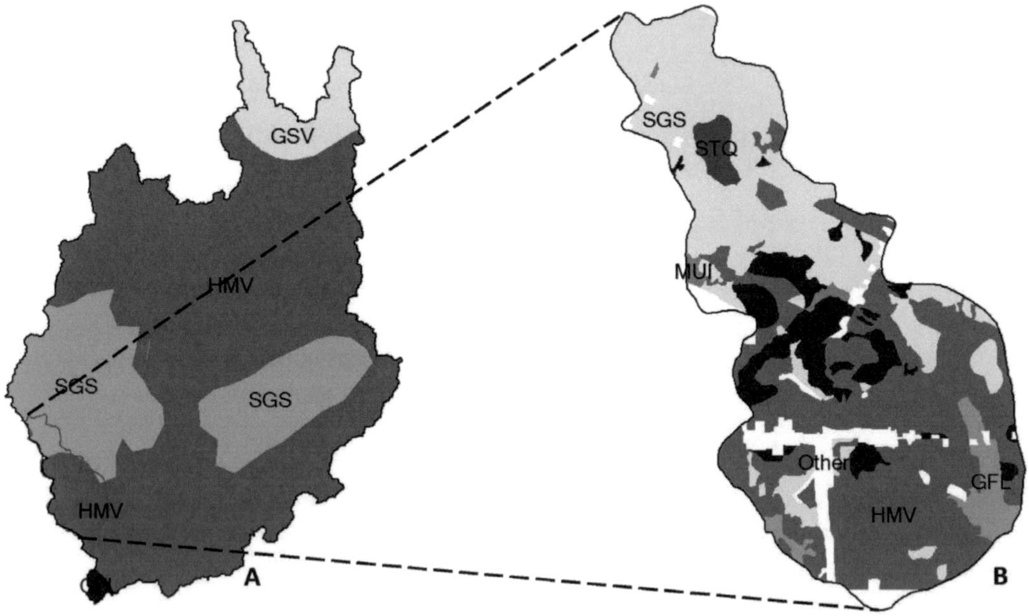

Figure 5. Comparison of coarse resolution soil map (A) and high-resolution soil map (B).

2.2. Target data

Target data, used as reference data in training ANNs, were composed of collecting field soil samples with soil property data (**Figure 6**). Representativeness and density of target data will directly affect the performance of ANNs.

3. Building ANNs for soil properties

A full process of modeling soil properties with ANNs was composed of building ANN structure, training ANNs, and network optimization.

3.1. Building ANN structure

The most popular ANN in modeling soil properties is back-propagation (BP) ANN because this kind of ANNs can map non-linearity when limited discontinuous points exist between input and output data in Ref. [35]. Common BP ANN has three layers: the input layer contains the independent variables used to make model predictions; the output layer contents variables to be predicted; hidden layer connects the input layer and output layer. Each node in one layer is linked with all nodes of the adjacent layer. The number of nodes in the hidden layer determined the complexity of the model. The input weight matrix consisted of all links between the input layer and the hidden layer and the output weight matrix consisted of all links between the hidden layer and the output layer. Weight (w), which affects the propagation value (x) and the output value (o) from each node, was fine-tuned using the value from the preceding layer based on Eq. (8).

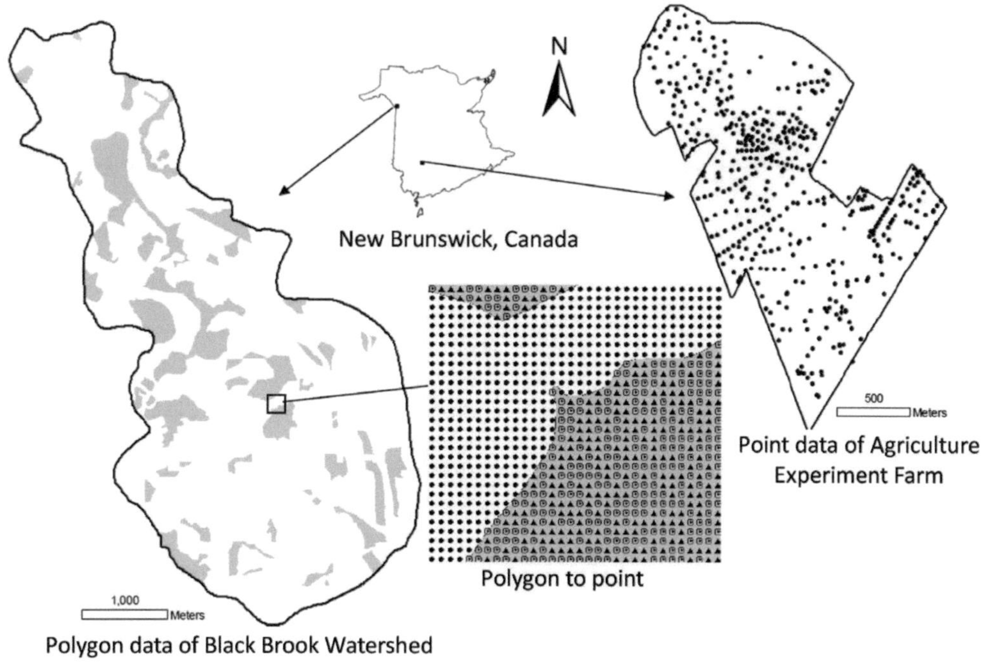

Figure 6. A sample of target data referring to polygons and points.

$$o = f\left(-T + \sum w_i x_i\right) \tag{8}$$

where T was a specific threshold (bias) value for each node; f was a non-linear sigmoid function, which increased monotonically.

When building ANNs for soil properties, the combinations of coarse resolution soil data (i.e., average soil drainage, sand, clay, silt contents) and DEM-derived topo-hydrological data (i.e., slope, STF, SDR, VSP) composed the input layer nodes. Predicted soil properties were the nodes in output layer.

3.2. Training ANNs

The aim of training ANN is confirming coefficients according to different rules or algorithms. BP ANN is trained by self-adjusting weight and bias values of each neuron along a negative gradient descent to minimize the mean squared error (MSE) in Ref. [36]. The MSE between the network outputs (o) and targeted values (t) was calculated through each training cycle (i) by Eq. (9). Training was stopped when the MSE could not be reduced by a set threshold. Frequently-used algorithm included the Levenberg-Marquardt (LM) algorithm and the resilient (RP) algorithm. The LM algorithm was based on Levenberg-Marquardt optimization theory in Ref. [37]. The RP was a kind of rebound back-propagation algorithm in Ref. [38].

$$MSE = \frac{1}{n}\sum_{i=1}^{n}(t_i - o_i)^2 \quad (9)$$

An early stopping method was used to avoid "over-fitting", which has the effect of decreasing prediction accuracy outside of the training data, and improving ANN generalization in Ref. [39, 40]. Through this method, in order to compute the gradient, update the network weights and estimate biases, a training set was used. Another data set, that is, the validation set, was applied to monitor the training process with the purpose of preventing "over-fitting". If training MSE decreased but the validating MSE increased, the training of the ANN model was stopped.

3.3. ANN optimization

The purpose of ANN optimization is adjusting networks structure and improving prediction accuracy of ANNs. It included two parts: (1) selecting the best combination of inputs. The schemes of combining inputs should follow one-variable, two-variable, three-variable, etc. (2) selecting the fittest number of hidden layer's nodes. When the number of hidden layer nodes was too small, prediction accuracy of the ANN was low. When the number of hidden layer nodes was too large, there was a potential over-fitting.

4. Built ANNs for soil properties

4.1. ANNs for soil texture

A BP ANN was developed to estimate soil texture with three-layer structure in **Figure 7** in Ref. [41]. The input layer had six nodes, including average clay and sand contents from coarse

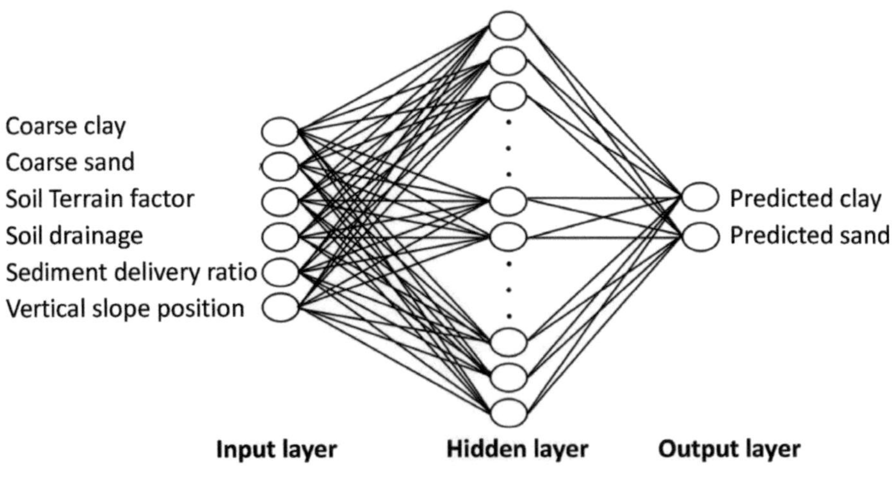

Figure 7. ANN structure for predicting high-resolution clay content and sand content.

resolution soil data, and four DEM-generated topo-hydrologic variables. The output layer contained two nodes: predicted high-resolution clay and sand contents.

The predictive capability of the ANN trained with LM and RP methods was assessed when the hidden layer nodes changed from 5 to 40, and training cycles changed from 25 to 250.

Accuracy of ANN models with the LM and RP training methods when 100 training cycles to various net structures is reported in **Table 1**. Results showed that the ANN models trained with the LM methods had much higher ROA ±5% and lower MSE than the models trained with the RP methods when holding the same number of hidden layer nodes. The LM trained ANN models had better prediction capability. With increasing the number of hidden layer nodes, the MSE of ANNs trained by the LM method was decreasing, but the ROA ±5% got the highest value with 25 hidden layer nodes. According to the results, the best ANN model of predicting clay and sand was a 6-25-2 ANN. Results also directed that when the number of hidden layer nodes was less than 25, the hidden layer scale was too small and the accuracy of model prediction was low. However, over-fitting happened when the number of hidden layer nodes exceeding 25. When the ANN model has been over-fitted, the training accuracy (MSE)

Training algorithm	**Net structure**	**MSE (%)**	**ROA ±5% (%)***	
			Clay	**Sand**
Levenberg-Marquardt back-propagation (LM)	6-5-2	29	81	76
	6-10-2	26	86	76
	6-15-2	25	85	80
	6-20-2	24	86	80
	6-25-2	24	88	81
	6-30-2	24	85	80
	6-35-2	24	86	81
	6-40-2	23	84	74
Resilient back-propagation (RP)	6-5-2	61	34	33
	6-10-2	39	75	70
	6-15-2	38	79	70
	6-20-2	38	74	68
	6-25-2	35	76	71
	6-30-2	33	80	76
	6-35-2	31	75	72
	6-40-2	28	74	72

*Relative overall accuracy (ROA) ±5%, a parameter of assessing the relative accuracy of model predictions, was calculated by counting all predictions within a 5% range of the referenced clay and sand content.

Table 1. Prediction accuracy of ANNs trained with LM and RP algorithms with 100 epochs and nodes of hidden layer changing from 5 to 40 in ref. [41].

increased but the prediction accuracy decreased. In another word, over-fitted ANN models would have poor "generalization" and could lead to inaccurate prediction when using to other input data than the original training set. The same results were presented for the nets trained by the RP method, but the RP method had the highest value of prediction accuracy with 30 hidden layer nodes and the best net structure was 6-30-2.

Prediction accuracies of the 6-25-2 network using the LM training method with training cycles of 25–250 are showed in **Table 2**. As presented, the values of ROA ±5% had the maximum value after 100 epochs. The results indicated that when the epochs of training was more than 100, the ANNs could be over-trained, which is another form of over-fitting.

It can be concluded that net structure, training algorithms, and training cycles would have significant impacts on performance of an ANN.

4.2. ANNs for soil organic carbon

A set of ANNs were developed to predict SOC distribution across the landscape in Ref. [42]. The ANNs used widely available coarse resolution soil map data, high-resolution DEM-generated topo-hydrologic variables, and detailed land use data as inputs. In order to select the best combination of inputs, the various schemes of combining inputs were designed and showed in **Table 3**.

Results from the two-input-node ANN (Level 1) are shown in **Figure 8**. The STF was the poorest predictor of SOC with a MSE of 84 and ROA ±1% (a parameter of assessing model predictions, calculated by counting all predictions within a 1% range of the referenced SOC value) of 66%. The VSP stood out as the best predictor of SOC, with MSE of 29 and ROA ±1% of 70.6%. These results indicated that VSP was the best predictor of SOC distribution across the landscapes.

For Level 2, VSP combined with SDR was the best three-input-node ANN SOC prediction model with MSE of 22. The model of VSP combined with PSR also exhibited a slightly higher

Training cycles	MSE (%)	ROA ± 5% (%)*	
		Clay	Sand
25	27	86	76
50	25	83	72
100	24	88	81
150	24	87	80
200	23	83	80
250	23	84	81

*Relative overall accuracy (ROA) ±5%, a parameter of assessing the relative accuracy of model predictions, was calculated by counting all predictions within a 5% range of the referenced clay and sand content.

Table 2. Predicted soil clay and sand content based on 6-25-2 ANN model using the LM method when the epoch was 25, 50, 100, 150, 200 and 250 times in ref. [41].

Scheme	Level 1	Level 2	Level 3	Level 4	Level 5*
1	CSOC, STF	CSOC, VSP, STF	CSOC, VSP, SDR, slope	CSOC, VSP, slope, PSR, sand	CSOC, VSP, slope, PSR, land use
2	CSOC, slope	CSOC, VSP, slope	CSOC, VSP, SDR, PSR	CSOC, VSP, slope, PSR, silt	CSOC, VSP, slope, PSR, land use, drainage
3	CSOC, PSR	CSOC, VSP, PSR	CSOC, VSP, slope, PSR	CSOC, VSP, slope, PSR, clay	—
4	CSOC, SDR	CSOC, VSP, SDR	CSOC, VSP, SDR, slope, PSR	CSOC, VSP, slope, PSR, drainage	—
5	CSOC, VSP	—	—	—	—

*CSOC: coarse resolution SOC data; sand, silt, clay, drainage: high-resolution sand, silt, clay, and drainage data; land use: detailed land use map with 13 classes.

Table 3. Schemes of combining inputs with different levels.

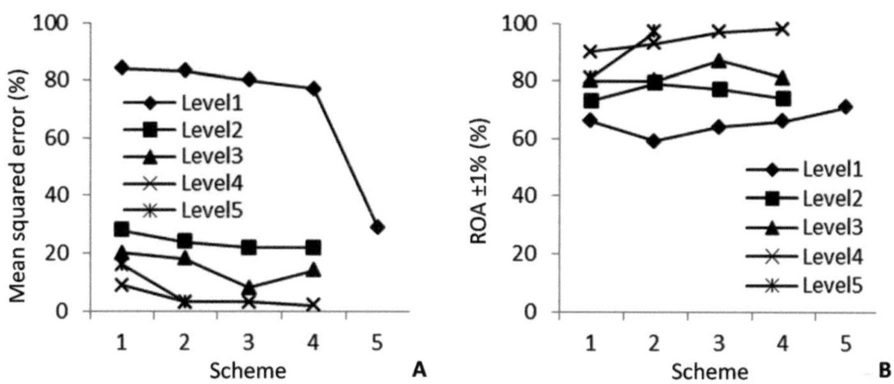

Figure 8. Mean squared error of ANNs (A) and prediction accuracy referring to relative overall accuracy ±1% (B) under different schemes of combining inputs.

MSE (23). However, in terms of MSE, the difference between the two models was considered to be insignificant. Furthermore, the CSOC-VSP-PSR ANN had better performance when measured with ROA ±1% (77 vs. 71%) than the CSOC-VSP-SDR ANN. The model of VSP combined with slope showed the highest values of ROA ±1% (79%).

Within the four input node ANN models (Level 3), the CSOC-VSP-slope-PSR ANN had the best performance, while the CSOC-VSP-SDR-slope ANN had the poorest accuracy of prediction. A further increase of input nodes by adding other DEM-generated topo-hydrological variables could not improve the accuracy of model prediction. As shown in **Figure 8**, the method of adding SDR as a new input node into the CSOC-VSP-slope-PSR ANN could cause a decrease in the accuracy of model prediction.

Input data extracted from high-resolution soil maps significantly improved model prediction accuracy (Level 4). For example, the addition of one soil parameter reduced MSE from a range of 8–20 (level II) to 2–9. Based on the results, soil parameters that were extracted from high-resolution soil maps could significantly improve the accuracy of model prediction. Both of the content of silt and clay and soil drainage classes were better predictors than the sand content. With MSE decreased to 2 and ROA ±1% increased to 98%, soil drainage was the best additional parameter for modeling SOC.

When land use was introduced as an input layer node in addition to the best four-input-node ANN, CSOC-VSP-slope-PSR, the MSE increased from 2 to 3 but the ROA ±1% decreased from 98 to 97% (Level 5).

4.3. ANNs for soil drainage

An ANN was developed and trained to predict high-resolution soil drainage class maps following the flowchart in **Figure 9**. The research indicated that the best ANN for mapping soil drainage had five input nodes (two from coarse resolution soil maps: average soil drainage class, sand content; three from DEM-generated topo-hydrological variables: slope, SDR, and VSP) and 20 hidden nodes in Ref. [34]. After training, the calibration correlation coefficient of the ANN was 0.69, which was slightly higher than the prediction correlation coefficient (0.65), with MSE of 0.758.

The trained ANN was used to produce a high-resolution soil drainage map for a little watershed (**Figure 10**). An error matrix was constructed using soil drainage records (measured soil

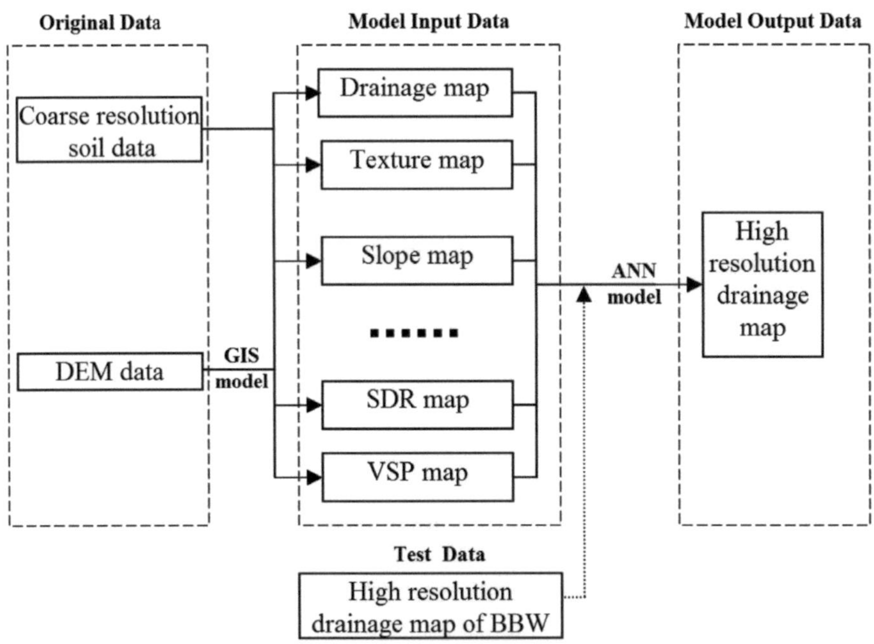

Figure 9. Schematic diagram showing structure and flow of the artificial neural network for predicting soil drainage in ref. [34].

http://dx.doi.org/10.5772/intechopen.70705

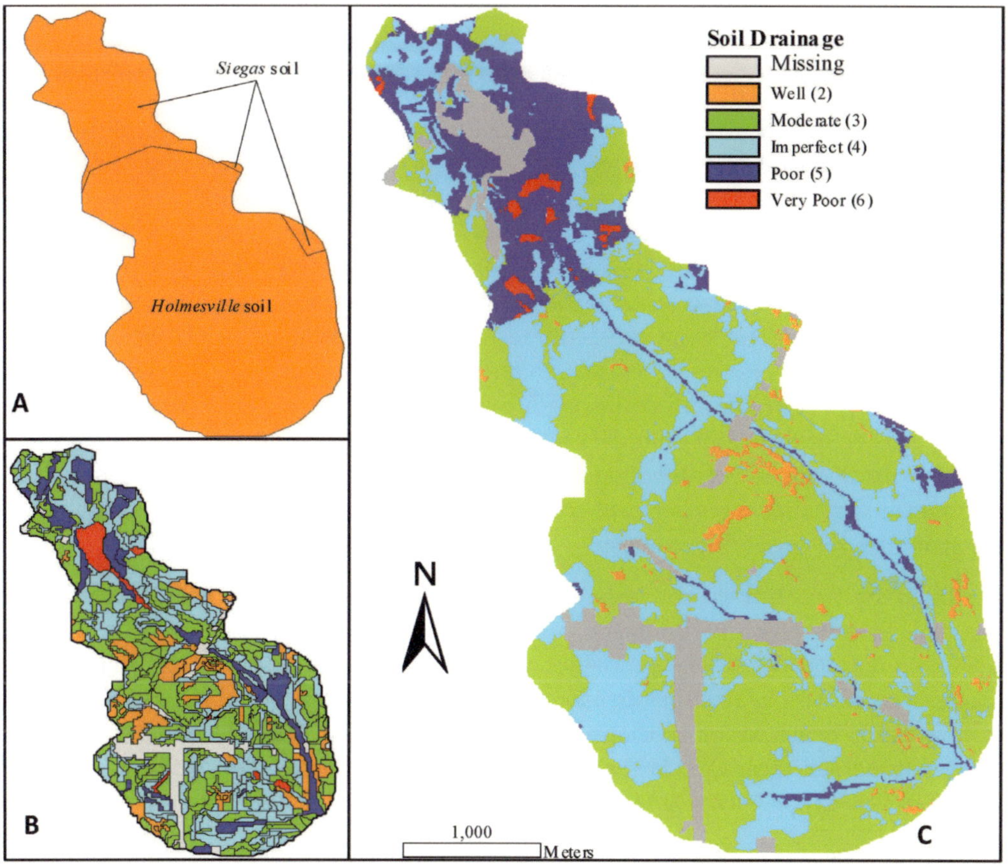

Figure 10. Low-resolution soil drainage map (A), high-resolution soil drainage map (B) and predicted soil drainage map based on artificial neuron network model (C) in ref. [34].

drainage classes) from 1:10,000 soil maps as reference data (**Figure 10B**) and predicted soil drainage classes using the ANN (**Figure 10C**). Results indicated that 52% of model-predicted drainage classes were exactly the same as the field assessment. About 94% of model-predicted drainage classes were within ±1 class compared to the field assessment.

The comparing of coarse resolution soil drainage map (**Figure 10A**) and predicted soil drainage map using ANN model (**Figure 10C**) showed that the predicted soil drainage maps have more detailed soil drainage condition information than the coarse resolution soil drainage map. As shown in **Figure 10C**, the original soil polygon boundaries of coarse resolution soil map are still visible in the high-resolution soil map, which indicated that coarse resolution soil data had a significant influence on the distribution of soil drainage in high-resolution soil drainage map produced. This implied that the accuracy of the coarse resolution soil sand content data, especially around the boundary, will affect the accuracy of predicted high-resolution soil drainage maps.

5. Expanding applications of ANNs

5.1. Deducing general rules from an ANN-analysis approach

It is well documented that soil properties, especially those associated with soil drainage, can be describe in terms of DEM-generated topo-hydrologic variables. However, relationships between soil drainage and these variables are usually difficult to define with conventional statistical methods because of their intense non-linearity. ANNs provide a useful tool to address the non-linear mapping. However, ANNs are "black boxes" with little or no possibility to understand their internal behaviors in Ref. [43] and as a result, relationships between soil drainage class and independent variables are not transparent to users. Furthermore, ANN-prediction accuracy is heavily dependent on the data used to calibrate the model. ANNs also potentially can over-fit the calibration data, which has the effect of decreasing prediction accuracy outside of the calibration data in Ref. [34]. These problems inherently limit the use of ANNs outside areas where the model was originally developed. ANNs could, however, be used to analyze relationships between soil drainage class and topo-hydrologic variables that were quantified by network-parameter.

Once the ANNs were trained and tested, they were used to generate the relationships (curves) between ANN-predicted soil drainage classes and topo-hydrologic variables (**Table 4**). Within ANNs with one topo-hydrologic variables, ANN-predicted soil drainage classes (dependent variable) were plotted against independent single variables, with coarse resolution soil drainage data (CSD) being set as constants. Within ANNs with two topo-hydrologic variables, ANN-predicted soil drainage classes were plotted as three dimension surfaces against the two variables, with CSD being set as constants.

The ANN-generated soil drainage-variable relationships (curves) were subsequently formulated as simple mathematical equations using non-linear regression method. Parameters of soil drainage equations were estimated with the Curve Fitting Tool of MATLAB. The used weighted least-squares regression that minimizes the error estimate was used to avoid biases in Ref. [39], included an additional scale factor (the weight factor; the cell count (%) of topo-hydrologic variables) based on Eq. (10):

$$S = \sum_{i=1}^{n} w_i \left(y_i - \widehat{y}_i\right)^2 \tag{10}$$

where w_i are the weights, n is the number of data points included in the fit, S is summed square of residuals, y_i is the observed response value, $\widehat{y}_i$ is the fitted response.

Soil drainage equations with single topo-hydrologic variables are summarized in **Table 4**. Most of the soil drainage equation curves (fitting curves) compared well to the corresponding ANN-generated curves, it indicated that prediction performance of soil drainage equations agreed with ANNs in most cases. The maps predicted by the best soil drainage-single variable equation (soil drainage-VSP equation) had accuracies of 44%. Compared to the corresponding ANNs, reductions of accuracy were 2% for the equations.

http://dx.doi.org/10.5772/intechopen.70705

Inputs of ANNs*	Soil drainage curves	Soil drainage equation**
Coarse resolution soil drainage (CSD) VSP	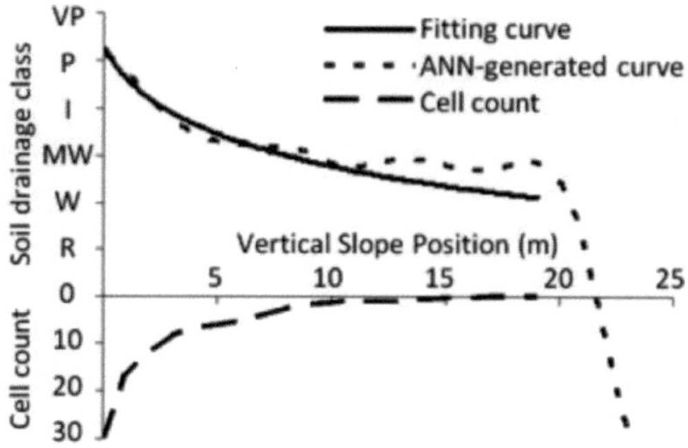	$SD = \frac{319.6}{5.921 + VSP^{0.7543}}$
CSD, slope	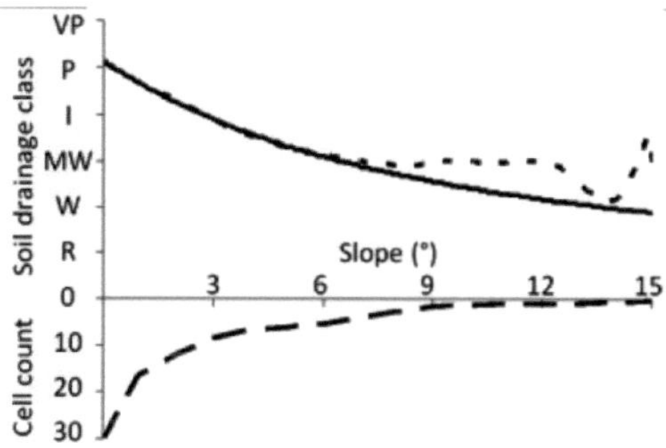	$SD = \frac{504.2}{9.845 + slope^{1.044}}$
CSD, SDR		$SD = a + bSDR^3 + cSDR^2 + dSDR$ a = 43.77 b = 0.00005794 c = −0.004975 d = −0.01193
CSD, TWI	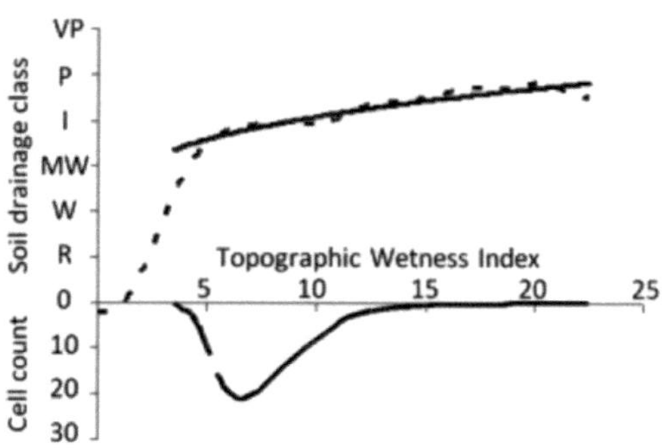	$SD = 12.84 + 14.42TWI^{0.2878}$

Inputs of ANNs[*]	Soil drainage curves	Soil drainage equation[**]
CSD = well, VSP, slope	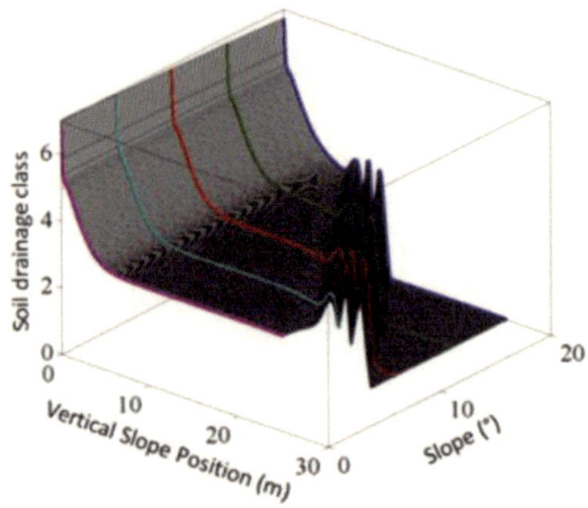	–
CSD = well, VSP, SDR	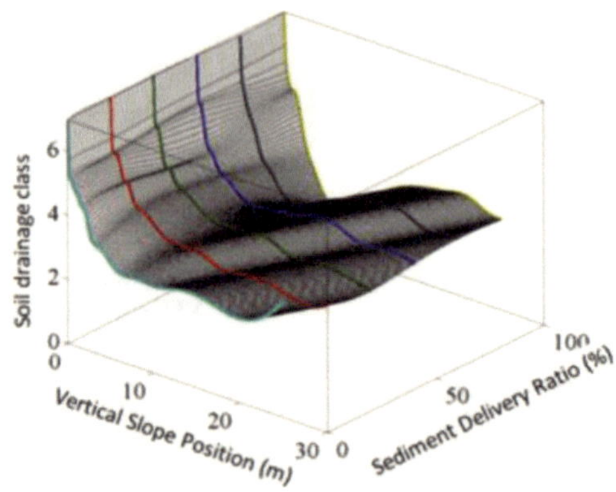	–

[*]ANN structure: input layer's nodes: (inputs) hidden layer's nodes (20) output layer's nodes (1).
[**]Digital soil drainage classes: rapidly drained (VR)-0, rapidly drained (R)-1, well drained (W)-2, moderately well drained (MW)-3, imperfectly drained (I)-4, poorly drained (P)-5, very poorly drained (VP)-6.

Table 4. ANNs, ANN-generated curves with fitting curves, and equations for soil drainage.

Some disagreements also were observed between soil drainage equation curves (fitting curves) and ANN-generated curves. It implied an advantage of soil drainage equations. These disagreed sections are most likely to occur when there are no or few data points in calibration or validation data sets. In these cases, ANN model predictions appeared unrealistic. For example, when VSP was >18.5 m, CSD-VSP ANN predictions demonstrated a sudden change, which could not be explained and was highly unrealistic. In contrast, the corresponding soil drainage equations curve (fitting curve) logically extended its curvilinear trend, which could avoid the unrealistic predictions made by ANNs in value range where there are insufficient calibration data. Thus, the obtained soil drainage equations could overcome the poor generalization problem of ANN models.

In addition, no requirement for special software support when performing predictions was another advantage of soil drainage equation, compared to ANNs using MATLAB software in Ref. [34] or soil landscape models using ARC/INFO software in Ref. [17].

For ANNs with two topo-hydrologic variables, we intended to produce three-dimensional surfaces (**Table 4**). However, the results were not able to produce meaningful mathematical equations because of the complexity of the data and the uneven distributions of data points across the range of independent variables. For example, the soil drainage surface (CSD = well) from the CSD-VSP-slope ANN model has a contour surface that was too difficult to formulize because of lack of general patterns.

5.2. Mapping soil property maps over a very large area

Various models, including ANNs, have been developed to predict soil properties. However, it is difficult to use these existing models to produce high-resolution soil property maps over a very large area (>1000 km^2). This is because these models are either interpolation models or statistics models that were built based on the relationships between local environment variables and observed soil property conditions in the field. When applied over a large area, these models may perform well in areas with similar landforms where field samples were collected, but have trouble in areas with significantly different landforms. It is also difficult to build a new model that can produce soil property maps over a large area because it is very difficult to collect sufficient field samples for either interpolation or model calibration. In order to produce soil drainage map over a very large area with limited number of field samples, a two-stage approach was used to produce soil drainage map over a large area (e.g. the province of Nova Scotia) in Ref. [44]. In the first stage, soil drainage-VSP equation, generated from a soil drainage ANN in BBW, was used as the base model because it can capture the general trend of soil drainage distribution rules along topographic gradient. The base equation was directly used to predict soil drainage maps in the province of Nova Scotia. In the second stage, after dividing the entire provincial area into sub-area (landform) based on different division methods, corresponding linear transformation models were subsequently developed to adapt soil drainage classes produced by the base model to fit field samples. Each linear transformation model is composed of a set of linear equations and each linear equation responded to a special landform. Each linear equation was designed as Eq. (11).

$$SD^i_{linear} = a^i + b^i SD_{base} \tag{11}$$

where SD_{base} is the initial drainage classes produced by base model.

a^i, b^i and SD^i_{linear} responded to a special landform (i) of Nova Scotia. a^i is the shifting parameter, which described average difference of soil drainage conditions between the BBW and a special landform of Nova Scotia. b^i is the stretching parameter, which described the change rate of soil drainage conditions between two the BBW and a special landform of Nova Scotia. SD^i_{linear} is the adapted soil drainage classes. Attributes of coarse soil maps were used as the criteria to divide the entire area of Nova Scotia into sub-area (landforms), including slope, topographic pattern, drainage, and texture. Each dividing criteria responded to a set of landforms (**Table 5**).

For each landform of each linear transformation model, using all of field samples within the landform (sub-area) as calibration data, parameters a^i and b^i of the landform (i) were estimated with the regression analysis tool. Only linear equations that passed $P < 0.05$ based on F and t test for the significance of the correlation coefficient were kept. In order to reduce the number

Attributes of dividing sub-area (landform set)	Deduced soil drainage curves from base equation	Parameters of linear equation $\left(SD^i_{linear} = a^i + b^i SD_{base}\right)$
Slope: level (L)-1 undulating (U)-2 rolling (R)-2	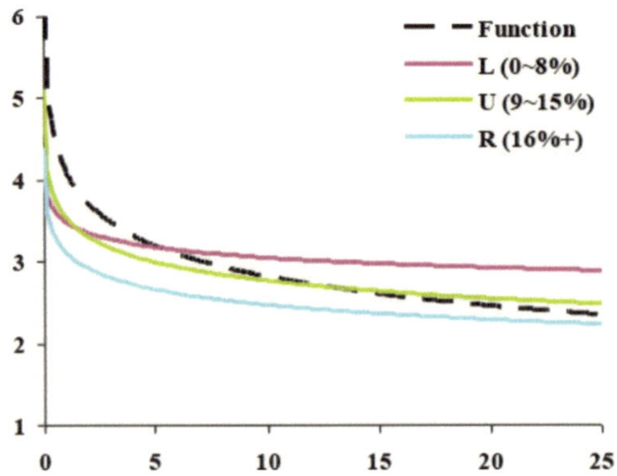	a1 = 2.083; b1 = 0.341 a2 = 1.065; b2 = 0.604 a3 = 1.060; b3 = 0.500
Topographic pattern: drunlinoid-1 hummocky-2 knob&knoll-3 ridged-4 smooth-5	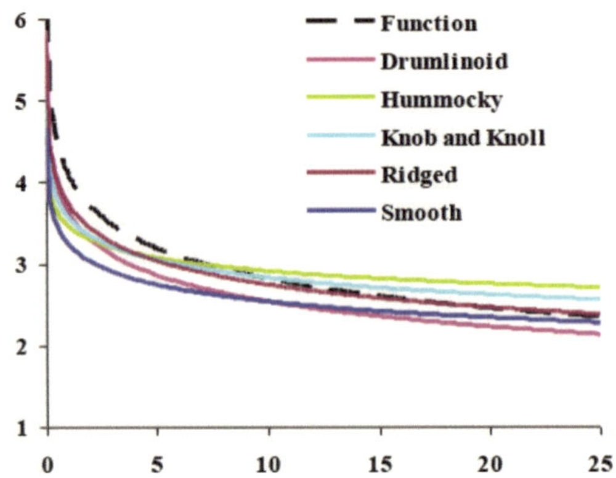	a1 = 0.132; b1 = 0.856 a2 = 1.694; b2 = 0.432 a3 = 1.209; b3 = 0.576 a4 = 0.566; b4 = 0.775 a5 = 0.990; b5 = 0.550
Drainage: well-1 Imperfect-2	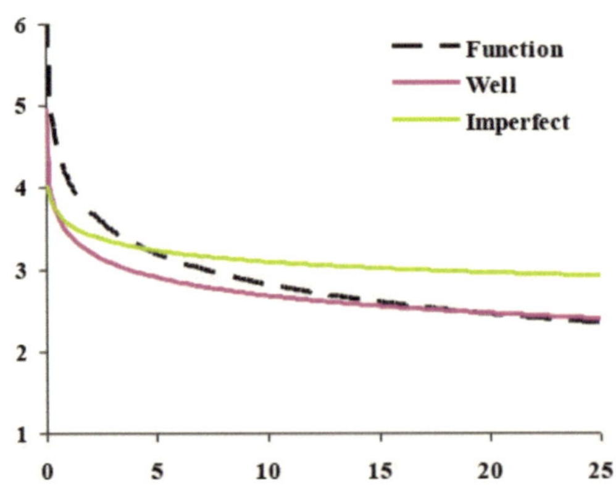	a1 = 1.011; b1 = 0.593 a2 = 1.567; b2 = 0.364

Attributes of dividing sub-area (landform set)	Deduced soil drainage curves from base equation	Parameters of linear equation $\left(SD^i_{linear} = a^i + b^i SD_{base}\right)$
Texture: coarse-1 medium-2 fine-3	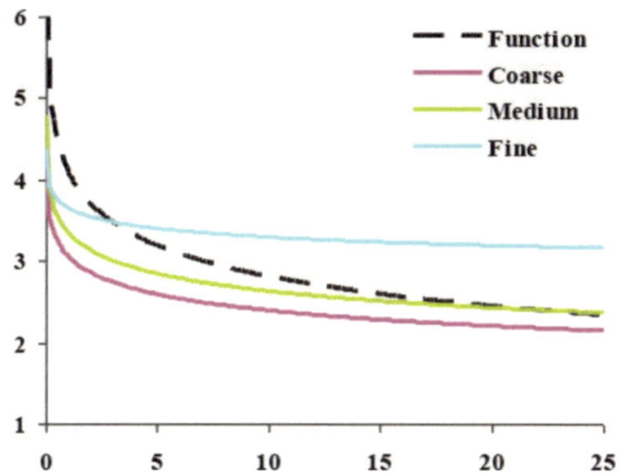	a1 = 0.939; b1 = 0.518 a2 = 1.064; b2 = 0.558 a3 = 2.497; b3 = 0.283

Table 5. Linear transformation models with different landform sets.

of linear equations, field samples that come from different landforms were combined when no significant differences were detected ($P > 0.05$).

As showed in **Figure 11**, prediction accuracies of linear transformation models under different landform sets (**Table 5**) were always better than prediction accuracy of base equation. It indicated that the two-stage methods provide a viable way to extend base equation to generate soil drainage maps over a large area with limited number of field samples.

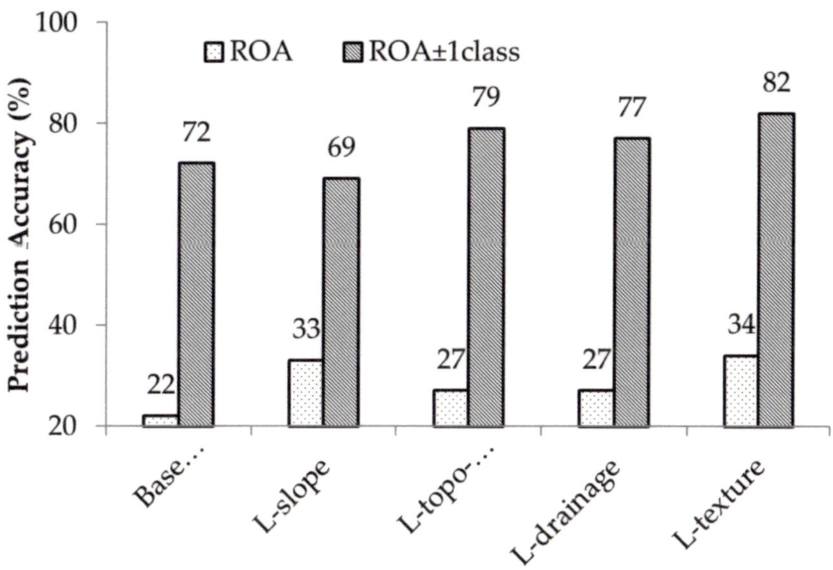

Figure 11. Accuracy comparison of base equation and linear transformation models with different landform sets.

6. Summary

This chapter presented a general approach in using ANNs to produce high-resolution soil properties. It started from preparing input and target data, following by building ANN structure, training ANNs, and optimizing networks. Three successful ANNs for soil texture, SOC, and soil drainage described how to select the fittest hidden layer's nodes, how to select the best combination of inputs, and how to produce high-resolution maps. Two extending applications of the ANNs gave advices in using the obtained ANNs outside the area of ANN calibration.

Acknowledgements

This work was supported by funding from Agriculture and Agri-Food Canada and Ducks Unlimited Canada under a project of the Watershed Evaluation of Beneficial Management Practices and by a Natural Sciences and Engineering Research Council Collaborative Research and Development grant entitled "Development of an advanced growth and yield model for multipurpose sustainable forest management". Zhengyong Zhao was supported by an NSERC Alexander Graham Bell Canada Graduate Scholarship.

Author details

Zhengyong Zhao[1]*, Fan-Rui Meng[2], Qi Yang[1] and Hangyong Zhu[3]

*Address all correspondence to: z.zhao@unb.ca

1 Guangxi Key Laboratory of Forest Ecology and Conservation, Forestry College, Guangxi University, Nanning, China

2 Faculty of Forestry and Environmental Management, University of New Brunswick, Fredericton, New Brunswick, Canada

3 Harbin City Forestry Academy, Harbin, China

References

[1] Farrar JL. Trees in Canada. Ottawa, Canadian Forest Service: Markham: Fitzhenry & Whiteside Limited; 2010

[2] Shields JA, Tarnocai C, Valentine KWG, MacDonald KB. Soil Landscapes of Canada: Procedures Manual and User's Handbook. LRRC Contribution Number 88–29. Land resource Research Centre: Ottawa; 1991

[3] Brady NC, Weil RR. The Nature and Properties of Soils. 14th ed. Upper Saddle River: Pearson Education, Inc.; 2008

[4] Allmaras RR, Fritz VA, Pfleger FL, Copeland SM. Impaired internal drainage and Aphanomyces euteiches root rot of pea caused by soil compaction in a fine-textured soil. Soil & Tillage Research. 2003;**70**:41-52

[5] Colombo SJ, Cherry ML, Graham C, Greifenhagen S, McAlpine RS, Papadopol CS, Parker WC, Scarr T, Ter-Mikaelian MT, Flannigan MD. The impacts of climate change on Ontario's forests. In: Colombo SJ, Buse LJ, editors. Forest Research Information Paper No. 143. Forest Research Institute, Marie, ON, Canada. 1998

[6] Oberthür T, Dobermann A, Neue H. How good is a reconnaissance soil map for agronomic purposes? Soil Use and Management. 1996;**12**:33-43

[7] Arp PA. Soils for Plant Growth: Field and Laboratory Manual. Fredericton: University of New Brunswick; 2005

[8] Leeper GW, Uren NC. Soil Science: An Introduction. 5th ed. Melbourne: Melbourne University Press; 1993

[9] Chivenge PP, Murwira HK, Giller KE, Mapfumo P, Six J. Long-term impact of reduced tillage and residue management on soil carbon stabilization: Implications for conservation agriculture on contrasting soils. Soil & Tillage Research. 2007;**94**:328-337

[10] Somaratne S, Seneviratn G, Coomaraswamy U. Prediction of soil organic carbon across different land-use patterns: A neural network approach. Soil Science Society of America Journal. 2005;**69**:1580-1589

[11] Tranter G, Minasny B, Mcbratney AB, Murphy B, Mckenzie NJ, Grundy M, Brough D. Building and testing conceptual and empirical models for predicting soil bulk density. Soil Use and Management. 2007;**23**:437-443

[12] Voltz M, Webster R. A comparison of kriging, cubic splines and classification for predicting soil properties from sample information. Journal of Soil Science. 1990;**41**:473-490

[13] McBratney AB, Odeh IOA, Bishop TFA, Dunbar MS, Shatar TM. An overview of pedometric techniques for use in soil survey. Geoderma. 2000;**97**:293-327

[14] Thattai D, Islam S. Spatial analysis of remotely sensed soil moisture data. Journal of Hydrologic Engineering. 2000;**5**:386-392

[15] Webster R. Fundamental objections to the 7th approximation. Journal of Soil Science. 1968;**19**:354-365

[16] McBratney AB, Santos MLM, Minasny B. On digital soil mapping. Geoderma. 2003;**117**:3-52

[17] Bell JC, Cunningham RL, Havens MW. Soil drainage class probability mapping using a soil-landscape model. Soil Science Society of America Journal. 1994;**58**:464-470

[18] Campling P, Gobin A, Feyen J. Logistic modeling to spatially predict the probability of soil drainage classes. Soil Science Society of America Journal. 2002;**66**:1390-1401

[19] Kravchenko AN, Bollero GA, Omonode RA, Bullock DG. Quantitative mapping of soil drainage classes using topographical data and soil electrical conductivity. Soil Science Society of America Journal. 2002;**66**:235-243

[20] Wasserman PD. Neural Computing: Theory and Practice. New York: Van Norstrand Reinhold Co.; 1989

[21] Levine ER, Kimes DS, Sigillito VG. Classifying soil structure using neural networks. Ecological Modelling. 1996;**92**:101-108

[22] Licznar P, Nearing MA. Artificial neural networks of soil erosion and runoff prediction at the plot scale. Catena. 2003;**51**:89-114

[23] Ramadan Z, Hopke PK, Johnson MJ, Scow KM. Application of PLS and back-propagation neural networks for the estimation of soil properties. Chemometrics and Intelligent Laboratory Systems. 2005;**75**:23-30

[24] Ren LL, Liu XR. Hydrological processes modeling based on digital elevation model. Geographical Research. 2000;**19**:369-376

[25] Ambroise B, Beven K, Freer J. Toward a generalization of the TOPMODEL concepts: Topographic indices of hydrological similarity. Water Resources Research. 1996;**32**:2135-2146

[26] Fernandez C, JQ W, McCool DK, Stockle CO. Estimating water erosion and sediment yield with GIS, RUSLE, and SEDD. Journal of Soil and Water Conservation. 2003;**58**:128-136

[27] Haan CT, Barfield BJ, Hayes JC. Design Hydrology and Sedimentology for Small Catchments. San Diego: Academic Press; 1994

[28] Schauble EA. Applying stable isotope fractionation theory to new systems. Reviews in Mineralogy and Geochemistry. 2004;**55**:65-111

[29] Vanoni VA. Sedimentation Engineering. ASCE Manuals and Reports on Engineering Practice No. 54. Reston: American Society of Civil Engineers; 2006

[30] Ferro V, Porto P, Tusa G. Testing a distributed approach for modeling sediment delivery. Hydrological Sciences Journal. 1998;**43**:425-442

[31] Murphy PNC, Ogilvie J, Castonguay M, Zhang C-F, Meng F-R, Arp PA. Improving forest operations planning through high-resolution flow-channel and wet-areas mapping. Forestry Chronicle. 2008;**84**:568-574

[32] Beven KJ, Kirkby MJA. Physically based variable contributing area model of basin hydrology. Hydrological Sciences Bulletin. 1979;**24**:43-69

[33] Meng F-R, Castonguay M, Ogilvie J, Murphy PNC, Arp PA. Developing a GIS-based flow-channel and wet areas mapping framework for precision forestry planning. Proceeding for IUFRO precision forestry symposium 2006, 5-10 March, 2006, Stellenbosch, South Africa; 2006.

[34] Zhao Z, Chow TL, Yang Q, Rees HW, Benoy GA, Xing Z, Meng F-R. Model prediction of soil drainage classes based on DEM parameters and soil attributes from coarse resolution soil maps. Canadian Journal of Soil Science. 2008;**88**:787-799

[35] Li ZY. Supervised classification of multispectral remote sensing image using B-P neural network. Journal of Infrared and Millimeter Waves. 1998;**17**:153-156

[36] Sigillito VG, Hutton LV. Case study II: Radar signal processing. In: Eberhart RC, Dobbins RW, editors. Neural Network PC Tools. San Diego: Academic Press Professional, Inc.; 1990

[37] Fun MH. Training modular networks with the Marquardt-Levenberg Algorithm. Master's Thesis. Stillwater, OK: Oklahoma State University; 1996

[38] Riedmiller M, Braun H. A direct adaptive method for faster back propagation learning: The RPROP algorithm. Proceedings of the IEEE international conference on neural networks, 28 March-1 April, 1993, San Francisco, CA; 1993.

[39] The MathWorks Inc. The Help Document. Natick, MA: The MathWorks, Inc.; Copyright 1984–2007

[40] Xu D, Wu Z. System Analysis and Design Based on MATLAB 6.X-Neural Network. Xian: Xidian University Press; 2002

[41] Zhao Z, Chow TL, Rees HW, Yang Q, Xing Z, Meng F-R. Predict soil texture distributions using an artificial neural network model. Computers and Electronics in Agriculture. 2009;**65**:36-48

[42] Zhao Z, Yang Q, Benoy GA, Chow TL, Xing Z, Rees HW, Meng F-R. Using artificial neural network models to produce soil organic carbon content distribution maps across landscapes. Canadian Journal of Soil Science. 2010;**90**:75-87

[43] Lopez C. Looking inside the ANN "black box": classifying individual neurons as outlier detectors. International Joint Conference on Neural Networks, July, 1999, Washington, DC; 1999.

[44] Zhao Z, Ashraf MI, Meng F-R. Model prediction of soil drainage classes over a large area using limited number of field samples: A case study in the province of Nova Scotia. Canada. Canadian Journal of Soil Science. 2013;**93**:73-83

Chapter 5

Dynamic Factor Model and Artificial Neural Network Models: To Combine Forecasts or Combine Models?

Ali Babikir, Mustafa Mohammed and
Henry Mwambi

Additional information is available at the end of the chapter

http://dx.doi.org/10.5772/intechopen.71536

Abstract

In this chapter, we evaluate the forecasting performance of the model combination and forecast combination of the dynamic factor model (DFM) and the artificial neural networks (ANNs). For the model combination, the factors that are extracted from a large dataset are used as additional input to the ANN model that produces the factor-augmented artificial neural network (FAANN). Linear and nonlinear forecasts combining methods are used to combine the DFM and the ANN forecasts. The results of the best combining method are compared to the forecasts result of the FAANN model. The models are applied to forecast three time series variables using large South African monthly data. The out-of-sample root-mean-square error (RMSE) results show that the FAANN model yields substantial improvement over the individual and best combined forecasts from the DFM and ANN forecasting models and the autoregressive AR benchmark model. Further, the Diebold-Mariano test results also confirm the superiority of the FAANN model forecast's performance over the AR benchmark model and the combined forecasts.

Keywords: artificial neural network, dynamic factor model, factor-augmented artificial neural network model, forecasts combination, forecasting

1. Introduction

Prediction of economic or financial variable using related independent variables could be done by either using a super model which contains all the available independent variables or using the forecast combination methodology. Generally, it is admitted in the literature of econometrics that the forecast obtained by all the information integrated in one step is much better than the combination of forecast from individual models. For example, [17] argued that "The best forecast is obtained by combining information sets, not forecasts from information sets. If both models are known, one should combine the information that goes into the models, not the forecasts that come out of the models." Authors of Refs. [13, 23, 25] expressed similar opinions. As it seems the investigators in this field lean more to prefer the combination of information in one model.

The main questions that arise in researchers' minds are "To combine or not to combine" and "how to combine." In this chapter, we are concerned with the question of "combining forecasts from different models or combining information in one model." This is an area that has been discussed by many researchers but not in detail (see [9, 11, 12, 29, 35, 40]).

Huang [29] state that "the common belief that combination of information is better than combination of forecasts might be based on the in-sample analysis." On the contrary, from out-of-sample analysis, they found out that combination of forecasts performs better than combination of information. Many articles typically account for the out-of-sample success of combination of forecasts over combination of information by pointing out various disadvantages that combination of information may possibly possess. For example, (a) in many forecasting situations, particularly in real time, combination of information by pooling all information sets is either impossible or too expensive (see [12, 13, 42]); (b) in a data substantial medium where there are much closed input variables in hand, the super combination of information model may bear from exclusion problem [42]; and (c) in the absence of linearity and, simple dynamics, building an excellent model using combination of information is more likely to be misspecified [26]. We believe that the above-mentioned points can be maintained through the precise selection of the model that is used to estimate the combined information. In our case we used the artificial neural networks to overcome the nonlinearity problem that can be inherent in the series. On the other hand, the factor model is used to tame the problem of the dimensionality, where a large dataset can be summarized in few numbers of factors.

The seminal work of [7] opened the door to examine the prediction combination in different fields of studies in economics and finance. Consequently, a new scope in forecasting study has been to combine the forecasts generated by individual models, using different combinations of techniques. This lets the ultimate forecast result to extract strength from the individual forecasting techniques that cannot be carried out by a single method. Empirically, forecast combinations have been used successfully in diverse areas such as forecasting gross national product, currency market volatility, inflation, money supply, stock prices, interest rates, meteorological data, city populations, and outcomes of football games.

Factor models were introduced in macroeconomics and finance by [22, 36]. The literature on the large factor models starts with [19, 37]. Further theoretical advances were made among others [4, 5, 20]. Upon the successive performance of the DFMs in forecasting, factors augmented to other models are introduced. For example, Bernanke et al. [8] proposed a forecasting model which they called the factor-augmented vector autoregressive (FAVAR) model, a model which merges a factor model with a vector autoregressive component. A factor-augmented vector autoregressive moving average (VARMA) model is suggested by Dufour and Pelletier [16]. Factor-augmented error correction model (FECM) was introduced by Banerjee and Marcellino [6]; Ng and Stevanovic [38] proposed a factor-augmented autoregressive distributed lag (FADL) framework for analyzing the dynamic effects of common and idiosyncratic shocks. Babikir and Mwambi [2] introduced a factor-augmented artificial neural network (FAANN) that showed improved forecasts compared to DFM and AR models.

On the contrary, artificial neural networks (ANNs) have become one of the most scientific projection methods and have been extensively used in different fields of projection goal. Artificial neural networks have several aspects that make them interesting and authentic for projection work. First, ANNs are common functional approximators. Second, ANNs are data-induced self-flexible approach in that there are less a priori presumptions to be stated about the models for the problem under examination; thus, ANN modeling is not similar to classical model-based approaches. Third, an ANN model is a nonlinear model which is in contrast to the conventional time series forecasting models, which postulate linearity of the series under consideration. [45] demonstrated that systems of the real world are often nonlinear. These advantages of ANNs have attracted attention in time series forecasting and have become a competitive method to traditional time series forecasting methods, and the literature is very vast in this area. The hybrid approach or combining models represent the most important developments in ANNs over the last decade. More hybrid models of ANNs with different forecasting models have been introduced in the recent time, which successfully improve the forecasting performance. [44] proposed the integration of the generalized linear autoregression (GLAR) model with artificial neural networks in order to obtain accurate forecasts for foreign exchange market. [43] proposed a hybrid model called SARIMABP that combines the seasonal autoregressive integrated moving average (SARIMA) model and the back-propagation neural network model to predict seasonal time series data. [34] introduced a hybrid model of ANNs and ARIMA models for forecasting purpose. [1] introduced a hybrid model where the factors were used as input to the ANN model. The model produced more accurate forecasts compared to ANN and DFM.

In this chapter, through the artificial neural networks framework and factor model, for in-sample and out-of-sample forecasting, we show analytically that combination of forecasts—of dynamic factor model and artificial neural networks—can be outclassed by combination of models (information)—of the factors to be used as additional input variables to the artificial neural networks.

To the best of our knowledge, the evaluation of the forecasting performance of the combination of information or models of factors and ANN—the FAANN—and combination of forecasts of ANN and DFM using different linear and nonlinear combinations is new, and this is the first attempt in general and in South Africa in particular. The empirical results show sizable gains in terms of the forecasting ability of the FAANN compared to both the standard ANN and the DFM and their forecasts combination; in other words it seems that combination of models outperforms combination of forecasts meaning that combination of information could be better than the combination of forecasts.

The remaining of the chapter is formulated as follow: Section 2 in brief expresses the DFM, the ANN, and the FAANN projection models and the combination techniques; Section 3 introduces the data; the results obtained from forecasting models and their combinations are presented in Section 4; finally, Section 5 gives a concise conclusion of the study and some suggestions for future researches.

2. Individual forecasting models and combination methods

In this section, we introduce briefly the symbols, formation, and estimation methods in forecasting models; also, we introduce and discuss the various combining methods.

2.1. Individual forecasting models

2.1.1. The dynamic factor model and the estimation of factors

This subsection handles DFM to get common elements from a large group of variables; then, these common components are used to predict the variables of interest.

Suppose that we have a group of observations, X_t be the N stationary time series variables having observations at times t = 1,…, T, where it is considered that the series have zero mean. Factor model assumes that most of the variation in the dataset can be explained by a small number $q \ll N$ of factors involved in the vector f_t. We can express the dynamic factor model representation as follows:

$$X_t = \chi_t + \xi_t = \lambda(L)' f_t + \xi_t \tag{1}$$

where χ_t is the common components driven by factor f_t and ξ_t is the idiosyncratic components for each of the variables. ξ_t is the portion of X_t that cannot be explained by the common components. χ_t is a function of the $q \times 1$ vectors of $\lambda(L)' f_t$; the operator $\lambda(L) = 1 + \lambda_1 L + \ldots + \lambda_s L^s$ is a lag polynomial with positive powers on the lag operator L with $Lf_t = f_{t-1}$. The static representation of the model can be rewritten in as

$$X_t = \Lambda' F_t + \xi_t \tag{2}$$

where F_t is a vector of $r \geq q$ static factors that compose of the dynamic factors f_t and all lags of the factors. From a set of data, there are three different methods of estimating the factors in F_t. These methods were developed by Stock and Watson [39] hereafter SW [30] and Forni, Hallin, Lippi, and Reichlin [20] hereafter FHLR[1]. In the current chapter, we employ the estimation method developed by FHLR. For more details of the dynamic factor model estimation, see Babikir and Mwambi [2]. Thus, the estimated factors will be used to forecast the variables of interest. The forecasting model is specified and estimated as a linear projection of an *h*-step ahead transformed variable y_{t+h} into *t*-dated dynamic factors. The forecasting model follows the setup in [3, 21, 41] with the form

$$y_{t+h} = \beta(L)\hat{f}_t + \gamma(L) y_t + u_{t+h} \tag{3}$$

where $\hat{f}_t$ represents the dynamic factors that estimated using the method by FHLR, while $\beta(L)$ *and* $\gamma(L)$ are the lag polynomials, which are determined by the Schwarz information criterion (SIC). The u^h_{t+h} is an error term. The coefficient matrix for factors and autoregressive terms are estimated by ordinary least squares (OLS) for each forecasting horizon *h*. To find

[1]For further technical details on this type of factor models, see [35].

the estimate and forecast of the AR benchmark, we enforce a condition to Eq. (3), where we set$\beta(L) = 0$.

2.1.2. The artificial neural network model

The ANN is one of the most popular and successful biological-inspired forecasting methods, which emulate the framework of the human brain; thus, ANNs have gradually achieved immense importance in forecasting among other fields. The ANN model is one of the generalized nonlinear nonparametric models (GNLNPMs). Compared to the traditional econometric models, the advantage of ANNs is that they can handle complex, nonlinear relationships without any prior assumptions about the underlying data-generating process (see [28]; **Figure 1**).

The properties of the ANN model made the method an attractive alternative to traditional forecasting models. Most importantly, ANN models deal with the limitations of traditional forecasting methods, including misspecification, biased outliers, and assumption of linearity [27]. One of the most recognized ANN structures in time series forecasting problems is the multilayer perceptron (MLP). An MLP is basically a feedforward architecture of an input, one or more hidden, and an output layer. The network structure illustrated in this chapter gives forward network connected with linear neuron activation function. Basically, the input nodes are connected forward to all nodes in the hidden layer, and these latent nodes are joined to the single node in the output layer, as shown in **Figure 1**. The inputs in this model serve as the independent variables in the multiple regression model and are joined to the output node—which is similar to the dependent variable—through the latent layer. We follow [33], in describing the network model. Thus, the model can be specified as follows:

$$n_{k,t} = w_0 + \sum_{i=1}^{p} w_i y_{t-i} + \sum_{j=1}^{J} \varnothing_j N_{t-1,j} \tag{4}$$

$$N_{k,t} = f(n_{k,t}) \tag{5}$$

$$y_t = \alpha_{i,0} + \sum_{k=1}^{K} \alpha_{i,k} N_{k,t} + \sum_{i=1}^{p} \beta_i y_{t-i} \tag{6}$$

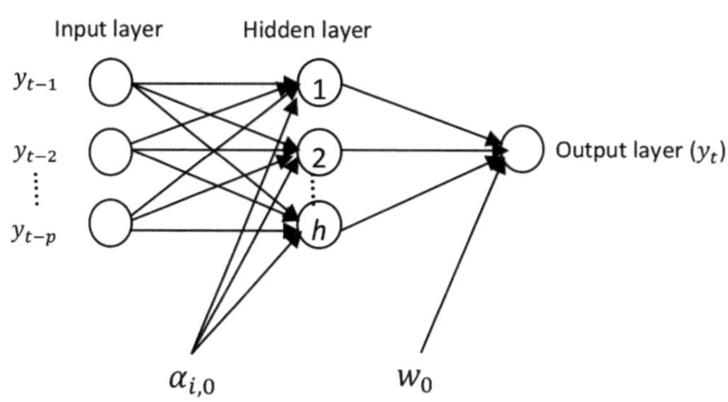

Figure 1. A $p \times h \times 1$ structure of a feed forward neutral network.

where inputs y_{t-i} represent the lagged values of the variable of interest and the output y_t is their forecasts. The w_0 and $\alpha_{i,0}$ are the bias, and w_i and $\alpha_{i,k}$ denote the weights that link the inputs to the latent layer and the latent layer to output, respectively. The $\varnothing_j$ and β_i connect the input to the output via the latent layer. The p-independent variables are connected linearly to form K neurons which then are combined linearly to produce the prediction or output. Eqs. (4)–(6) link inputs y_{t-i} to outputs y through the hidden layer. The function f is a logistic function meaning that $N_{k,t} = f(n_{k,t}) = \frac{1}{1+e^{-n_{k,t}}}$. The second summation in Eq. (6) shows that we also have a jump connection or skip-layer network that directly links the inputs y_{t-i} to the output y_t. The beauty of this ANN structure is that the model combines the true linear model and nonlinear supply-forward neural network. So, if the association between inputs and output is true linear, in this case, the coefficient set β, which is skip layer should be significant, in contrast if the association is a nonlinear in nature the jump connections coefficient β to be insignificant, while the coefficients set w and α be highly significant. Certainly, if the association between input and output is mixed, then we watch for all coefficient sets to be significant. For the best network selection in this chapter, beside the minimum error, we use Bayesian information criterion (BIC), which is usually preferred more than the other three criteria, because it has the ability to penalize the extra parameters more severely; mathematically, BIC is given by the following as described in [31]

$$BIC = N_{p,h} + N_{p,h}\ln(n) + n\ln\left(\frac{S(W)}{n}\right) \tag{7}$$

where $N_{p,h} = h(p+2)+1$ is total number of parameters in the network, $n = N_{train} - p$ is the number of effective observations, N_{train} is the in-sample observation, S(W) is the network misfit function, and W is the space of all weights and biases in the network. The in-sample sum of squared error (SSE) is usually used to determine the function S(W). Eventually, the optimal model is the model with minimum BIC value.

2.1.3. Factor-augmented artificial neural networks (FAANN)

The FAANN model is a hybrid model of artificial neural network and factor model in order to combine information of factors and lagged values of interested variable to be forecasted for more accurate forecasts in hand. The nonlinear function uses the series, its lag, and factors to formulate the FAANN model that defines as follows:

$$y_t = f\left[\left(y_{t-1}, y_{t-2}, \ldots, y_{t-p}\right), (F_1, F_2, F_3, F_4, F_5)\right] \tag{8}$$

where f is the nonlinear functional form determined via ANN. In the first stage, the factor model is used to extract factors from a large related dataset. In the second stage, a neural network model is used to model the nonlinear and linear relationships existing in factors and original data. Thus, based on the model structure depicted on **Figure 2**,

$$y_{t+h} = \alpha_0 + \sum_{j=1}^{h} \alpha_j g\left(\beta_{0j} + \sum_{i=1}^{p} \beta_{ij} y_{t-i} + \sum_{i=p+1}^{p+5} \beta_{ij} F_{t,i}\right) + \varepsilon_t \tag{9}$$

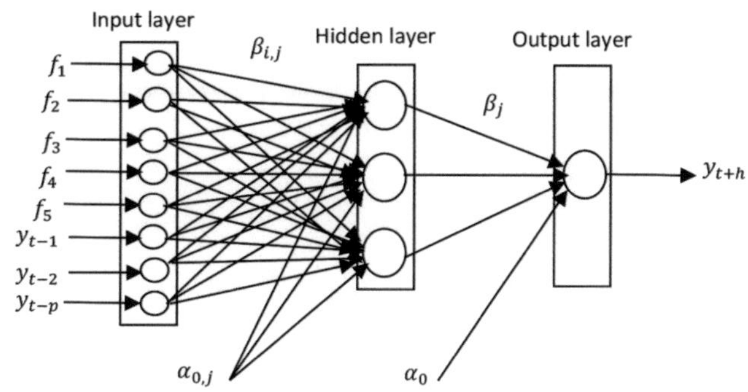

Figure 2. The FAANN model architecture ($N^{(p+5,h,1)}$).

As previously noted, the α_j ($j = 0, 1, \ldots, h$) and $\beta_{ij}(i = 0, 1, \ldots, p; j = 1, 2, \ldots, h)$ are the parameters of the model that called the connection weights. As we have stated earlier, p and h are the numbers of input and hidden nodes, respectively, and ε_t is the error term. **Figure 2** shows the FAANN model structure used.

2.2. Forecast combining methods

To combine individual forecasts composed by the DFM and ANN models, we used four combination methods. The combining methods involve three linear combining methods (the mean, VACO, and discount MSFE-based methods) and one nonlinear combining method (ANN). Just as some of the combining methods need a holdout period to calculate the weights used to combine individual forecasts, we use the first 24 months of the out of sample as holdout observations. For all combining methods, we form combination forecasts over the post holdout out-of-sample period. Brief details about the above combining methods are given below.

2.2.1. Mean combination method

The mean serves as a convenient criterion as has been shown to achieve better results compared to other fancy methods. For instance, see [10, 21, 32]. Compared to single forecasts, the performance of the simple average combination method is found to be superior (see [18]). The simple average combination method can be expressed as

$$\widehat{y}_t^c = \sum_{i=1}^{m} w_i \widehat{y}_t^i \tag{10}$$

where $\widehat{y}_t^c$ is the combined forecast at time t, $\widehat{y}_t^i$ is the forecast from ith individual forecasting model, $w_i = \frac{1}{m}$ is the individual forecast weight for model i, and m is the number of individual models. There are different forms of weights, but generally the weights have to satisfy the condition $\sum_{i=1}^{m} w_i = 1$.

2.2.2. *Variance-covariance (VACO) combination method*

The method uses the historical achievement of the individual forecasts to compute the weights. Thus, according to the VACO method, the weights determined as follows:

$$w_i = \frac{\left[\sum_{j=1}^{T}\left(y_j - \widehat{y}_j^i\right)^2\right]^{-1}}{\sum_{i=1}^{m}\left[\sum_{j=1}^{T}\left(y_j - \widehat{y}_j^i\right)^2\right]^{-1}} \tag{11}$$

Then, the combined forecast is given by $\widehat{y}_t^c = \sum_{i=1}^{m} w_i \widehat{y}_t^i$ where y_j is the jth actual value, $\widehat{y}_j^i$ is the jth forecasting value from ith individual forecasting model, and T is the total number of out-of-sample points. The weight in Eq. (11) is based on the inverse sum of squared deviation for model i as the numerator, and the denominator is the sum of these inverse contributions from all models. This guarantees that $\sum_{i=1}^{m} w_i = 1$.

2.2.3. *Discounted mean square forecast error (DMSFE) combination method*

The DMSFE method weights recent forecasts more heavily than distant ones. [32] suggest that the weights can be calculated as

$$w_i = \frac{\left[\sum_{j=1}^{T}\delta^{T-j+1}\left(y_j - \widehat{y}_j^i\right)^2\right]^{-1}}{\sum_{i=1}^{m}\left[\sum_{j=1}^{T}\delta^{T-j+1}\left(y_j - \widehat{y}_j^i\right)^2\right]^{-1}} \tag{12}$$

where δ is the discount factor with $0 < \delta \leq 1$, if $\delta = 1$ and then the DMSFE and VACO methods become one method, which means that the VACO is a special case of the DMSFE. Note that as mentioned above the sum of all weights is equal to one.

2.2.4. *Artificial neural network (ANN) combination method*

Linearity of combinations of the individual forecasts is the corner stone of linear combination method, but if the individual forecasts are based on nonlinear methods, the combinations are defined to be insufficient or if the true relationship is nonlinear. For the success of the ANN as a combination method over the linear methods, among others, see [15, 25]. Here, we use the same setup used in subsection (2.1.2); the output $\widehat{y}_t^c$ of combined forecasts can be given by

$$\widehat{y}_t^c = \alpha_{i,0} + \sum_{k=1}^{K} \alpha_{i,k} N_{k,t} + \sum_{i=1}^{m} \beta_i \widehat{y}_t^i \tag{13}$$

where $\widehat{y}_t^i$ is the forecast from ith individual forecasting model.

3. Data

For FAANN and DFM models, data are gathered that include 228 monthly time series[2] of which 203 are collected from South Africa, including the financial, real, nominal sectors, and confidence indices, 2 global variables, and 23 series of major trading partners and global financial markets. The AR criterion model will be used for the data which composed only the variable of interest, namely, deposit rate or share prices for gold mining or long-term interest rate. Thus, besides the national variables, the chapter uses a set of global variables such as gold and crude oil prices. Also, the data incorporate series from financial markets of major trading partners, namely, the United Kingdom, the United States, China, and Japan. For estimation data cover the period January 1992 through December 2006, while the period from January 2007 through December 2011 will be used for goodness of fit for the extracted model. For the degree of integration of all series, the augmented Dickey-Fuller (ADF) test will be used. Difference of the series is used for all nonstationary series in this study. The Schwarz information criterion (SIC) is used in selecting the appropriate lag length in such a way that no serial correlation is left in the stochastic error term. Finally, all series are standardized to have a mean of zero and a constant variance.

4. Evaluation of forecast accuracy

To evaluate the forecast accuracy of model combination or information combination, we used three datasets from South Africa, namely, deposit rate, gold mining share prices, and long-term interest rate, in order to demonstrate the in-sample and out-of-sample appropriateness and effectiveness of the combination of models or information of the DFM and ANN models.

4.1. In-sample forecast evaluation

In this subsection, we evaluate the in-sample predictive power of the combined model forecast —the FAANN model—and other fitted models which include AR (benchmark model), DFM, and ANN and best combined forecasts of the DFM and ANN models. To achieve this, a full sample from January 1992 to December 2011, giving a total of 240 observations of the three datasets—deposit rate, gold mining share prices, and long-term interest rate—is used to estimate the forecasting models in order to check the robustness of in-sample results of competed models and compare it to the AR benchmark model. In-sample forecasting is most useful when it comes to investigate the true relationship between the independent variables and the forecast of dependent variable. **Table 1** reports the root-mean-square error (RMSE)[3] of the in-sample forecasting results. The FAANN model outperformed all other models. The maximum reduction in RMSE over the AR benchmark model is around 24%, while the

---

[2]The data sources are the South Africa Reserve Bank, ABSA Bank, Statistics South Africa, National Association of Automobile Manufacturers of South Africa (NAAMSA), South African Revenue Service (SARS), Quantec, and World Bank.

[3]The RMSE statistic can be defined as $\sqrt{\frac{1}{N}\sum\left(Y_{t+n} -_t\widehat{Y}_{t+n}\right)^2}$, where $Yt + n$ denotes the actual value of a specific variable in period $t + n$ $and_t\widehat{Y}_{t+n}$ is the forecast made in period t for $t + n$.

Variable	Model				
	FAANN	**DFM**	**ANN**	**AR**	**Best combined forecasts of DFM and ANN**
Deposit rate	**0.1687**	0.1849	0.1793	0.1954	0.1694
Share prices for gold mining	**1.5922**	1.7782	1.7787	1.8187	1.6215
Long-term interest rate	**0.1253**	0.1537	0.1546	0.1640	0.1438

Table 1. The RMSE of the in-sample forecasts.

minimum reduction is around 14% considering all variables. Regarding the in-sample forecasting, the FAANN model provides lower RMSE with a reduction of between 9 and 19% for all variables compared to the DFM. Despite that the same factors are augmented to AR and ANN to produce the DFM and the FAANN models, the in-sample results provide significant differences between estimation methods which favor the nonlinear method over the linear one. This is potentially due to the flexibility and property of the ANN models as universal approximators that can be used to different time series in order to obtain accurate forecasts. Comparing the forecasting performance of the FAANN and standard ANN model, the FAANN model produced lower RMSE of 6–19% for all variables. These results indicate the importance of the factors—which summarized 228 related series into five factors—that are used as input to the ANN to produce the FAANN model. Regarding the in-sample forecasting performance of the forecasts of combined models or information—the FAANN model—compared to the best forecast combination of the DFM and ANN models, the FAANN model outperforms the best forecast combination with reduction in the RMSE around 0.01–13% for all variables. These results confirm the superiority of the combination of information or models when a precise estimation method is used to estimate the combined information over the combined forecasts of individual models.

4.2. Out-of-sample forecast evaluation of individual models

In this subsection, we estimate the individual forecasts of the AR, DFM, and ANN and the best combined forecasts of the DFM and ANN models and the FAANN model that combine information of the factors and ANN for the three variables of interest, namely, deposit rate, gold mining share prices, and long-term interest rate, over the in-sample period January 1992 to December 2006 using monthly data, and then compute the out of sample for 3-, 6-, and 12-month-ahead forecasts for the period of January 2007 to December 2011. We employ iterative forecast technique to compute the RMSE for the three forecasting horizons used for the three variables across all of the different models in order to compare the forecast accuracy generated by the models. The starting date of the in-sample period depends on data availability of some important financial series. The out-of-sample period includes the occurrence of the financial crisis that affected economies and financial sectors in particular. Thus, we used this period as out of sample in order to show the suitability and efficiency of the combination of information—FAANN model—to produce accurate forecasts for such data that exhibits inherent nonlinearity or the data that faced fluctuations during the financial crisis. The result of each single variable can be summarized as follows:

http://dx.doi.org/10.5772/intechopen.71536

- *Deposit rate forecasting results*: for the FAANN model estimation firstly, MATLAB package is used to estimate the factors. Secondly, R software using Broyden, Fletcher, Goldfarb, and Shanno (BFGS) algorithm is used to find and estimate the optimum network architecture. The network with the lowest in-sample RMSE and the Bayesian information criterion (BIC) is selected as best-fitted network, which is composed of eight inputs, five neurons in the hidden layer, and one output (in abbreviated form $N^{(8-5-1)}$). **Table 2** reports the RMSEs of the 3-, 6-, and 12-month-ahead and the average of the 3-, 6-, and 12-month-ahead RMSEs. The benchmark for all forecast evaluations is the AR model forecast RMSEs. For both long and short horizons, the FAANN model outperforms all other models followed by the DFM for the short horizons and the ANN in long horizon. The RMSE of the FAANN model decreases as the forecast horizon increases which in turn agreed with [24] who found that the ANNs significantly forecast better in long horizon. Results reveal that the FAANN performed better with large reductions in RMSE of around 25–46% of the RMSE compared to the AR benchmark model and the reduction on the average RMSE around 37%.
- *Gold mining share prices*: we used the same steps where software and algorism were implemented to the previous variable to estimate the FAANN model. The optimum network is composed of eight inputs, seven neurons in the hidden layer, and one output (in abbreviated form $N^{(8-7-1)}$). **Table 3** presents the RMSE results of the FAANN, the DFM, the ANN, and the AR benchmark. As expected based on the in-sample results, the FAANN model stands out in forecasting both short and long horizons with a sizable reduction in

Model	3 months	6 months	12 months	Average
FAANN	**0.7465**	**0.6373**	**0.5359**	**0.6399**
DFM	0.9501	0.9153	0.9438	0.9364
ANN	0.9693	0.9160	0.8869	0.9241
AR	0.1862	0.1949	0.2314	0.2041

Note: The last row reports the RMSE for the AR benchmark model; the remaining rows represent the ratio of the RMSE for the forecasting model to the RMSE for the AR. Bold entries indicate the forecasting model with the lowest RMSE.

Table 2. Out-of-sample (January 2007–December 2011) RMSE for deposit rate.

Model	3 months	6 months	12 months	Average
FAANN	**0.9053**	**0.9121**	**0.8227**	**0.8800**
DFM	0.9655	0.9661	0.9532	0.9616
ANN	0.9566	0.9556	0.9215	0.9446
AR	1.7743	1.7924	1.8187	1.7951

Note: See note to **Table 2.**

Table 3. Out-of-sample (January 2007–December 2011) RMSE for gold mining share prices.

Model	3 months	6 months	12 months	Average
FAANN	**0.7281**	**0.6051**	**0.5498**	**0.6277**
DFM	0.9834	0.9042	0.9584	0.9487
ANN	0.9893	0.8981	0.8306	0.9060
AR	0.2052	0.2140	0.2308	0.2167

Note: See note to **Table 2**.

Table 4. Out-of-sample (January 2007–December 2011) RMSE for long-term interest rate.

RMSE relative to the AR benchmark model of 10–18%. The average of the RMSE reduction over the forecast horizons is 12%. On average the FAANN outperforms the ANN and DFM models with reduction in RMSE of 6 and 8%, respectively.

- *Long-term interest rate*: for estimation purpose the same package and algorism that are used with previous variables are implemented. Thus, the optimal network in abbreviated form is $N^{(8-3-1)}$. **Table 4** results show the performance of the FAANN model where the model produces more accurate forecasts compared to all competing model on both the single-level forecast horizons and the average of these horizons. Compared to the AR benchmark, the FAANN provides a reduction in the RMSE range from 45–27%, while the average RMSE reduction is around 38%. The performance of the FAANN model stands out followed by the ANN and the DFM with average reduction in RMSE of 9 and 5%, respectively, relative to the AR benchmark model. Comparing the FAANN performance to the ANN and the DFM, the FAANN model RMSE reduction is around 28 and 32%, respectively.

4.3. Out-of-sample forecast evaluation of the combined forecasts of the DFM and ANN models

Table 5 reports the results of combining forecasts of the DFM and ANN models. We aim of using the DFM and ANN models in particular to merge their advantages where the ANN model with its flexibility to account for potentially complex nonlinear relationships that is not easily captured by traditional linear models, and the DFM model can accommodate a large number of variables. Similar to **Table 2**, **Table 5** shows the ratio of the RMSE for a given combining method to the RMSE for the AR benchmark model. We found that the AR benchmark model poorly performs compared to all combining methods. Generally, the nonlinear ANN combining method outperforms all other combining methods for all variables at all forecasting horizons; hence, it offers a more reliable method for generating forecasts of the variables of interest. Compared to the AR, the nonlinear ANN combining method provides a large reduction in RMSE of around 7–20% relative to the AR model overall forecasting horizons and variables. The nonlinear ANN combining method also beats the best individual forecasting of the DFM and the ANN models for all variables and overall forecasting horizons with sizable reductions in RMSE of around 1–15% of the RMSE of the best individual forecasts. We note in addition that the discount MSFE with $\delta = 0.9$ as a combining method performs

Combination method	h = 3	h = 6	h = 12
	Deposit rate		
AR	0.1862	0.1949	0.2314
Mean	0.915	0.890	0.851
VACO	0.921	0.892	0.846
DMSFE, δ = 0.95	0.923	0.903	0.848
DMSFE, δ = 0.90	0.905	0.884	0.837
ANN	**0.907**	**0.882**	**0.835**
	Gold mining share prices		
AR	1.7743	1.7924	1.8187
Mean	0.946	0.942	0.937
VACO	0.943	0.946	0.951
DMSFE, δ = 0.95	0.945	0.941	0.937
DMSFE, δ = 0.90	0.945	0.942	0.936
ANN	**0.921**	**0.929**	**0.911**
	Long-term interest rate		
AR	0.2052	0.2140	0.2308
Mean	0.951	0.923	0.902
VACO	0.952	0.942	0.922
DMSFE, δ = 0.95	0.956	0.953	0.954
DMSFE, δ = 0.90	0.951	0.952	0.935
ANN	**0.827**	**0.815**	**0.804**

Note: See note to **Table 2.**

Table 5. Forecast combining results of the DFM and ANN-RMSE for variables (January 2007–December 2011).

nearly as well as the best individual model for all variables and forecasting horizons. The combining method of variance–covariance (VACO), on average, performs less accurate compared to other combining methods' overall forecasting horizons and variables. We note that the combined forecasts produce more accurate forecasts for long horizons which we attributed to the contribution of the nonlinear model in the combination as nonlinear models produce more accurate forecast in the long horizon.

4.4. Comparison of forecasting performance of combination of models or information and combination of forecasts

Here, we compare the forecasting performance of the combination of models (information)—the FAANN model—with the best forecast combinations of the ANN and DFM models.

Forecasting model	h = 3	h = 6	h = 12
	Deposit rate		
AR (benchmark model)	0.1862	0.1949	0.2314
FAANN	**0.7465**	**0.6373**	**0.5359**
Combined forecasts of DFM and ANN	0.907	0.882	0.835
	Gold mining share prices		
AR (benchmark model)	1.7743	1.7924	1.8187
FAANN	**0.9053**	**0.9121**	**0.8227**
Best combined forecasts of DFM and ANN	0.921	0.929	0.911
	Long-term interest rate		
AR (benchmark model)	0.2052	0.2140	0.2308
FAANN	**0.7281**	**0.6051**	**0.5498**
Best combined forecasts of DFM and ANN	0.827	0.815	0.804

Note: See note to **Table 2.**

Table 6. Forecast results of the best combination of DFM and ANN model and FAANN-RMSE for variables (January 2007–December 2011).

Table 6 presents the RMSE ratios of the FAANN model and the best forecast combination to the AR benchmark model over the out-of-sample period. Compared to the DFM, the results indicate that the FAANN model generates accurate forecasts for all variables and with all forecast horizons. The improvement of the FAANN model is compared to the DFM between 2 and 10% reduction in RMSE for all variables and horizons. Thus, these results indicate the superiority of augmentation of factors to nonlinear method (FAANN) over the linear one (DFM) across the three different series and three different time horizons.

To confirm the RMSE results, the test of equal forecast accuracy of Diebold and Mariano [14] is used to evaluate forecasts. The test of equal forecast accuracy employed here is given by $S = \frac{\overline{d}}{\sqrt{\widehat{V}(\overline{d})}}$, where $\overline{d} = \frac{1}{T}\sum_{t=1}^{T}\left(e_{1t}^2 - e_{2t}^2\right)$ is the mean difference of the squared prediction error and $\widehat{V}\left(\overline{d}\right)$ is the estimated variance. Here, e_{1t}^2 denotes the forecast errors from the FAANN model, and e_{2t}^2 denotes the forecast errors from the AR benchmark model or the best combined forecasts of DFM and ANN. The *S* statistic follows a standard normal distribution asymptotically. Note, a significant negative value of *S* means that the FAANN model outperforms the other model in out-of-sample forecasting. **Table 7** shows the result of the Diebold and Mariano test between the FAANN and the AR benchmark and between the FAANN and the best combined forecasts of DFM and ANN. The test results confirm that the FAANN models provide the lowest RMSEs. In summary the FAANN models provide significantly better forecasts at the 5% and 10% level compared to the AR and the best combined forecasts of DFM and ANN models.

Model/variable	Forecasting horizons		
	3 months	6 months	12 months
Deposit rate			
FAANN vs. AR	−2.095**	−2.108**	−3.159**
FAANN vs. best combined forecast from DFM and ANN	−1.944*	−1.799*	−2.064**
Share prices for gold mining			
FAANN vs. AR	−2.420**	−2.527**	−2.753**
FAANN vs. best combined forecast from DFM and ANN	−1.812*	−1.673*	−1.961**
Long-term interest rate			
FAANN vs. AR	−2.402**	−2.339**	−2.429**
FAANN vs. best combined forecast from DFM and ANN	−1.741*	−2.138**	−1.861**

Note: ** and * indicate significant value at the 5 and 10% levels, respectively.

Table 7. Diebold-Mariano test (January 2007–December 2011).

5. Conclusion

In this chapter we aim to evaluate the forecasting performance of the model combination and forecast combination for the ANN and DFM models. In the model combination, we merge the factors that were extracted from a large dataset—288 series in our case—with ANN which produces the FAANN model. For the forecast combination, we used different linear and nonlinear combination methods to combine the individual forecasts of the DFM and the ANN models. Using the period of January 1992 to December 2006 as in-sample period and January 2007 to December 2011 as out-of-sample period, we compare the forecast performance of the FAANN with DFM, ANN, and AR benchmark model for 3-, 6-, and 12-month-ahead forecast horizons for three variables, namely, for deposit rate, gold mining share prices, and long-term interest rate. The study has provided evidence using both the RMSE and Diebold and Mariano test as the comparison criteria that FAANN models best fit the three considered variables over the 3-, 6-, and 12-month-ahead forecast horizons.

Tables 2–4 show the ability of the model combination—FAANN model—to produce accurate forecast that outperforms DFM and ANN and their best forecast combination results. The results seem not contradicted with in-sample model forecast performance as in **Table 1**. The FAANN model outperformed the AR benchmark model with large reduction in RMSE of around 25–46% considering all variables and forecast horizons. Compared to the DFM and ANN models, the FAANN model produces more accurate forecasts that yielded a decrease in RMSE of around 6–43% and 5–40%, respectively. We attribute the superiority of the FAANN to the flexibility of ANN to account for potentially complex nonlinear relationships that are not easily captured by linear models and the contribution of the factors to the model. On the other hand, the ANN and the DFM outperformed the AR benchmark with a reduction in the RMSEs of around 1–17% and 2–10%, respectively, for all variables and across all forecast horizons. **Table 6** shows comparison results of the forecasting performance of the combined models—the FAANN—and the best forecast combination of the DFM and the ANN models. The results indicate that the combined models or information produced forecasts that are better than the best combined forecasts of the DFM and the ANN models. In other words, the nonlinear model that uses large dataset of economic and financial variables in addition to the lags of the interested variable improves the forecasting performance over models that are estimated separately—the DFM and the ANN. We also observed that the FAANN residual decreases as the forecast horizon increases.

Author details

Ali Babikir[1]*, Mustafa Mohammed[2] and Henry Mwambi[1]

*Address all correspondence to: ali.basher@gmail.com

1 School of Mathematics, Statistics and Computer Science, University of KwaZulu-Natal, Pietermaritzburg, South Africa

2 Faculty of Science and Arts, University of Jeddah, Saudi Arabia

References

[1] Babikir A, Mwambi H. A Factor—Artificial Neural Network Model for Time Series Forecasting: The Case of South Africa. Proceeding of IEEE International Joint Conference on Neural Networks (IJCNN); Beijing, China. 2014. p. 838–844

[2] Babikir A, Mwambi H. Factor augmented artificial neural network model. Neural Processing Letters. 2016;**45**:507-521. DOI: 10.1007/s11063-016-9538-6

[3] Aruoba S, Diebold F, Scotti C. Real-time measurement of business conditions. Journal of Business & Economic Statistics. 2009;**27**:417-427

[4] Bai J. Inferential theory for factor models of large dimensions. Econometrica. 2003;**71**(1): 135-171

[5] Bai J, Ng S. Determining the number of factors in approximate factor models. Econometrica. 2002;**70**(1):191-221

[6] Banerjee A., Marcellino, M.. Factor augmented error correction models. CEPR Discussion Paper, 6707; 2008

[7] Bates JM, Granger CWJ. The combination of forecasts. Operations Research Quarterly. 1969;**20**:451-468

[8] Bernanke B, Boivin J, Eliasz P. Measuring the effects of monetary policy: A factor-augmented vector autoregressive (FAVAR) approach. Quarterly Journal of Economics. 2005; **120**:387-422

[9] Chong YY, Hendry DF. Econometric evaluation of linear macro-economic models. The Review of Economic Studies. 1986:671-690

[10] Clemen RT, Winkler RL. Combining economic forecasts. Journal of Business & Economic Statistics. 1986;**4**:39-46

[11] Clements MP, Galvao AB. Combining predictors and combining information in Modelling: Forecasting US recession probabilities and output growth. University of Warwick; 2005

[12] Diebold FX. Forecast combination and encompassing: Reconciling two divergent literatures. International Journal of Forecasting. 1989;**5**:589-592

[13] Diebold FX, Pauly P. The use of prior information in forecast combination. International Journal of Forecasting. 1990;**6**:503-508

[14] Diebold FX, Mariano RS. Comparing predictive accuracy. Journal of Business & Economic Statistics. 1995;**13**:253-263

[15] Donaldson RG, Kamstra M. Forecast combining with neural networks. Journal of Forecasting. 1996;**15**:49-61

[16] Dufour J-M, Pelletier D. Practical Methods for Modelling Weak VARMA Processes: Identification, Estimation and Specification with a Macroeconomic Application. Discussion paper; 2013

[17] Engle RF, Granger CWJ, Kraft DF. Combining competing forecasts of in- flation using a bivariate ARCH model. Journal of Economic Dynamics and Control. 1984;**8**:151-165

[18] Fang Y. Forecasting combination and encompassing tests. International Journal of Forecasting. 2003;**19**:87-94

[19] Forni M, Hallin M, Lippi M, Reichlin L. The generalized factor model: Identification and estimation. The Review of Economics and Statistics. 2000;**82**:540-554

[20] Forni M, Hallin M, Lippi M, Reichlin L. The generalized dynamic factor model, one sided estimation and forecasting. Journal of the American Statistical Association. 2005;**100**(471): 830-840

[21] Forni M, Hallin M, Lippi M, Reichlin L. The generalized factor model: Consistency and rates. Journal of Econometrics. 2004;**119**:231-255

[22] Geweke J. The dynamic factor analysis of economic time series. In: Aigner DJ, Goldberger AS, editors. Latent variables in socio-economic models. North Holland: Amsterdam; 1977. pp. 365-383

[23] Granger CWJ. Invited review: Combining forecasts - twenty years later. Journal of Forecasting. 1989;**8**:167-173

[24] Tkacz G, Hu S. Forecasting GDP Growth Using Artificial Neural Networks. Working Paper 3. Bank of Canada; 1999

[25] Harrald PG, Kamstra M. Evolving artificial neural network to combine financial forecasts. IEEE Transactions on Evolutionary Computation. 1997;**1**:40-52

[26] Hendry DF, Clements MP. Pooling of forecasts. The Econometrics Journal. 2004;**7**:1-31

[27] Hill T, O'connor M, Remus W. Neural network models for time series forecasts. Management Science. 1996;**42**:1082-1092

[28] Hornik K, Stinchcombe M, White H. Multi-layer feed forward networks are universal approximators. Neural Networks. 1989;**2**:359-366

[29] Huang H, Lee T-H. To combine forecasts or to combine information? Econometric Reviews. 2010;**29**(5–6):534-570

[30] Kapetanios G, Marcellino M. A parametric estimation method for dynamic factor models of large dimensions. Journal of Time Series Analysis. 2009;**30**:208-238

[31] Kihoro JM, Otieno RO, Wafula C. Seasonal time series forecasting: A comparative study of ARIMA and ANN models. African Journal of Science and Technology. 2004;**5**(2):41-49

[32] Makridakis S, Winkler R. Averages of forecasts: Some empirical results. Management Science. 1983;**29**:987-996

[33] McAdam P, Hughes Hallett AJ. Non linearity, computational complexity and macro economic modeling. Journal of Economic Surveys. 1999;**13**(5):577-618

[34] Khashei M, Bijari M. An artificial neural network (p, d,q) model for time series forecasting. Expert Systems with Applications. 2010;**37**:479-489

[35] Newbold P, Harvey DI. Forecast combination and encompassing. In: Clements MP, Hendry DF, editors. A Companion to Economic Forecasting. Blackwell Publishers; 2001

[36] Sargent TJ, Sims CA. Business cycle modeling without pretending to have too much a priori economic theory. In: Sims C, editor. New Methods in Business Research. Federal Reserve Bank of Minneapolis; 1977

[37] Schumacher C. Forecasting German GDP using alternative factor models based on large datasets. Journal of Forecasting. 2007;**26**:271-302

[38] Serena Ng and Dalibor Stevanovic: Factor Augmented Autoregressive Distributed Lag Models. working paper; 2012

[39] Stock JH, Watson MW. Forecasting using principal components from a large number of predictors. Journal of the American Statistical Association. 2002a;**97**:147-162

[40] Stock JH, Watson M. Combination forecasts of output growth in a seven country data set. Journal of Forecasting. 2004;**23**:405-430

[41] Stock JH, Watson MW. Macroeconomic forecasting using diffusion indexes. Journal of Business & Economic Statistics. 2002b;**20**:147-162

[42] Timmermann A. Forecast combinations. Elliott G, Granger CWJ, Timmermann A, ed. Forthcoming in Handbook of Economic Forecasting. North Holland. 2005

[43] Tseng FM, Yu HC, Tzeng GH. Combining neural network model with seasonal time series ARIMA model. Technological Forecasting and Social Change. 2002;**69**:71-87

[44] Yu L, Wang S, Lai KK. A novel nonlinear ensemble forecasting model incorporating GLAR and ANN for foreign exchange rates. Computers and Operations Research. 2005;**32**:2523-2541

[45] Zhang G, Patuwo BE, Hu MY. Forecasting with artificial neural networks: The state of the art. International Journal of Forecasting. 1998;**14**:35-62

Chapter 6

Parameter Recognition of Engineering Constants of CLSMs in Civil Engineering Using Artificial Neural Networks

Li-Jeng Huang

Additional information is available at the end of the chapter

http://dx.doi.org/10.5772/intechopen.71538

Abstract

Controlled low-strength materials (CLSMs) had been widely applied to excavation and backfill in civil engineering. However, the engineering properties of CLSM in these embankments vary dramatically due to different contents involved. This study is proposed to employ the ANSYS software and two different artificial neural networks (ANNs), that is, back-propagation artificial neural network (BPANN) and radial basis function neural network (RBFNN), to determine the engineering properties of CLSM by considering an inverse problem in which elastic modulus and the Poisson's ratio can be identified from inputting displacements and stress measurements. The PLANE42 element of ANSYS was first used to investigate a 2D problem of a retaining wall with embankment, with $E = 0.02\sim3\ GPa$, $\nu = 0.1\sim0.4$ to obtain totally 270 sampling data for two earth pressures and two top surface settlements of embankment. These data are randomly divided into training and testing set for ANNs. Practical cases of three kinds of backfilled materials, soil, and two kinds of CLSMs (CLSM-B80/30% and CLSM-B130/30%) will be used to check the validity of ANN prediction results. Results showed that maximal errors of CLSM elastic parameters identified by well-trained ANNs can be within 6%.

Keywords: ANNs, ANSYS, CLSM, fem, parameter recognition

1. Introduction

In recent years, sustainable materials have been widely studied and developed especially for construction, highway, and civil engineering. Controlled low-strength material (CLSM) is commonly used as backfilled materials. It would be a friendly environment-cheap material and typically consists of small amount of cement, supplementary, fine aggregates, and a large amount of mixing water. Self-compacting/self-leveling, significantly low strength, as well as almost no measured settlement after hardening are remarkable characteristics of CLSM.

CLSM can be defined as a kind of self-compacting cementitious material that is in a flowable state at the initial period of placement and has specified compressive strength of 1200 *psi* (8.27 *MPa*) (or less at 28 days) or is defined as excavatable if the compressive strength is 300 psi (2.07 *MPa*) (or less at 28 days) [1]. Recent studies have reported that the maximum CLSM strength of approximately up to 1.4 MPa is suitable for most of backfilling applications when re-excavation is required [2, 3] It is also recommended that depending upon the availability and project requirements, any recycle material would be acceptable in the production of CLSM with prior tests its feasibility before uses [4]. The special features of CLSM can be summarized as follows: durable, excavatable, erosion-resistant, self-leveling, rapid curing, flowable around confined spacing, wasting material usage, elimination of compaction labors and equipment, and so on.

There are several studies on the engineering properties of CLSMs by laboratory experiments [5–10], and numerical analyses of applications of CLSM to civil engineering, such as excavation and backfill after retaining walls [11–13], bridge abutments [14–17], pipeline and trench ducts [18], pavement bases [19–24], and so on. All these studies reflect requirement of the identification of mechanical constants of the CLSMs. Though it is known that the Young's modulus of CLSMs lies between soil and commonly used concrete, precise determination of engineering material properties of CLSMs (even for soil and concretes) is a questionable and difficult problem. For example, modulus of elasticity is evaluated by experiments using secant modulus of stress-strain curve or estimated from empirical formula of Young's modulus with 28-day compressive strength or weight of concrete.

Besides, artificial neural networks had been widely applied to various engineering [25], especially to civil and construction engineering [26, 27]. Alternately, several studies were conducted on the application of inverse problems in structural and geotechnical problems [28–32].

2. Problem definition and data preparation

2.1. Parameter recognition considered as inverse problem

In a classical mechanical analysis of civil engineering problems, we determinate displacements and/or stresses of a structure with known engineering constants, such as the Young's modulus, E (with the unit *GPa)*, and the Poisson's ratio, ν, which had been identified from laboratory or in-site experiments. This kind of problems can be termed *forward problems*, that is, we evaluate the unknown dependent variables (physical quantities) from prescribed parameters and dimensions analytically if there exist some closed-form relationships, or numerically using computational schemes (such as the finite element methods, FEMs) if the domain and/or boundary conditions are complicated.

On the other hand, an *inverse problem* in this case is to identify the engineering constants of a structure through evaluated or measured displacements and/or stresses. For a simple problem which can be analyzed and the results can be expressed in closed-form mathematical relationship, the inverse problem can be easily obtained from mathematical operation. However, for a practical huge structure of complicated shape, closed-form relationship cannot be obtained. Recently, a lot of schemes had been developed for parameter recognition (classification and regression) in the

Problem	Process	Problem with closed-form expression	Problem without closed-form expression
Forward	model parameters → model→ prediction of data	$y=f(p_1)$ (e.g., $\Delta = \frac{PL^3}{3EI}$)	parameters→ numerical models (FEM) → displacements, stresses
Inverse	data → model → estimation of model parameters	$p_1 = f^{-1}(y)$ (e.g.,$E = \frac{PL^3}{3I\Delta}$)	displacements, stresses → welled trained ANNs → parameters

Table 1. Comparison of forward problem and inverse problem.

field of machine learning and artificial intelligence, among which neural networks such as back-propagation artificial neural network (BPANN) and radial basis function neural network (RBFNN) are proven to be powerful and efficient if well designed, trained, and tested.

The two problems are compared and illustrated in **Table 1**, where problems with and without closed-form relationship between parameters and physical quantities are shown, respectively. In **Table 1**, a well-known example in civil engineering, displacement at the end of a cantilevered beam subjected to a concentrated load is shown, in which Δ, P, L, E, I denotes the end displacement, loading, length, Young's modulus, and moment of inertia, respectively.

This research study aims to consider the identification of engineering constant of a typical CLSM-backfilled region as an inverse problem. The processes employed are as follows: (1) preparation of training data, and testing data through numerical analysis (using ANSYS); (2) preparation of verification data (from experiments on CLSMs); (3) normalization of training data, testing data, and verification data; (4) conducting prediction using neural networks of BPANN and RBFNN along with comparison study of parameters involved in the networks; and (5) selection of a useful network topology for parameter recognition.

In the following sections, the procedures are explained with numerical results.

2.2. Typical problem employed for the recognition of engineering constants

A typical problem of backfilled region after a retaining wall is considered (**Figure 1**). The length and height of backfilled region is $L=20\ m$, $H=5\ m$, respectively. For simplicity, the

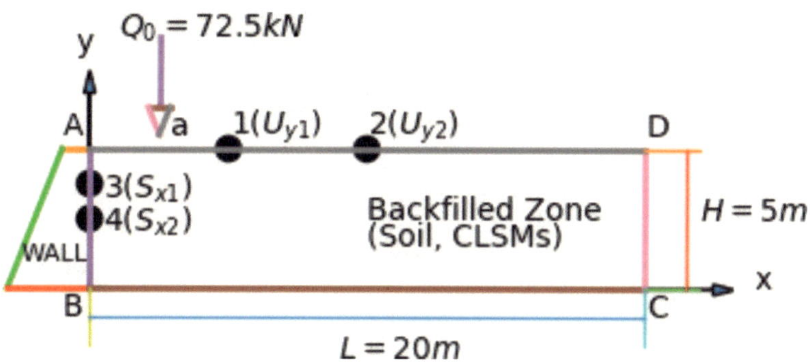

Figure 1. Schematic of a typical CLSM-backfilled region for the analysis of parameter recognition.

backfilled materials are considered to be linearly elastic and are within small deformation under external loadings; therefore, linear elastic analysis can be performed using only two engineering constants, that is, the Young's modulus, E (with the unit GPa), and the Poisson's ratio, ν. Furthermore, considering the width of backfilled zone is infinitely long, and a two-dimensional analysis can be used. In order to evaluate the engineering constants through displacements and stresses, the backfilled region is assumed to be subjected to a concentrated vertical loading (surcharge) $Q_0 = 72.5\ kN$ acting at the point behind the retaining wall$a = 0.5\ H$.

In order to provide training data and testing data in parameter recognition using neural networks, the following four quantities are defined:

$x_1 = U_{y1}$: vertical displacement (settlement) at upper surface ($x = L/4$), (positive downward, m).

$x_2 = U_{y2}$: vertical displacement (settlement) at upper surface ($x = L/2$), (positive downward, m).

$x_3 = S_{x1}$: horizontal normal stress (lateral earth pressure) on wall ($y = 3H/4$), (tensile positive, Pa).

$x_4 = S_{x2}$: horizontal normal stress (lateral earth pressure) on wall ($y = H/2$), (tensile positive, Pa).

These sampling points are illustrated in **Figure 1**.

2.3. FEM analysis using ANSYS

Finite element equation for elastic analysis of displacement and stress of a plane deformation problem can be expressed in matrix form [33]:

$$[K]\{X\} = \{F\} \tag{1}$$

where $[K]$, $\{X\}$, $\{F\}$ denotes global stiffness matrix, global degrees of freedom vector and global load vector respectively, defined as follows:

$$\begin{aligned} [K] &= \sum_{e=1}^{NE} [k]^e = \sum_{e=1}^{NE} t \iint_{A^e} [B]^T [D][B]\ dx\,dy \\ \{F\} &= \sum_{e=1}^{NE} \{f\}^e = \sum_{e=1}^{NE} t \oint_{S^e} [N\}^T\ \{q\}\ dS \end{aligned} \tag{2}$$

If a plane 4-node isoparametric element is used, the shape functions in Eq. (2) can be expressed as

$$\begin{aligned} N_1(\xi,\eta) &= (1-\xi)(1-\eta)/4 \\ N_2(\xi,\eta) &= (1+\xi)(1-\eta)/4 \\ N_3(\xi,\eta) &= (1+\xi)(1+\eta)/4 \\ N_4(\xi,\eta) &= (1-\xi)(1+\eta)/4 \end{aligned} \tag{3}$$

where ξ, η are local coordinates. A typical PLANE42 element in ANSYS is shown in **Figure 2**.

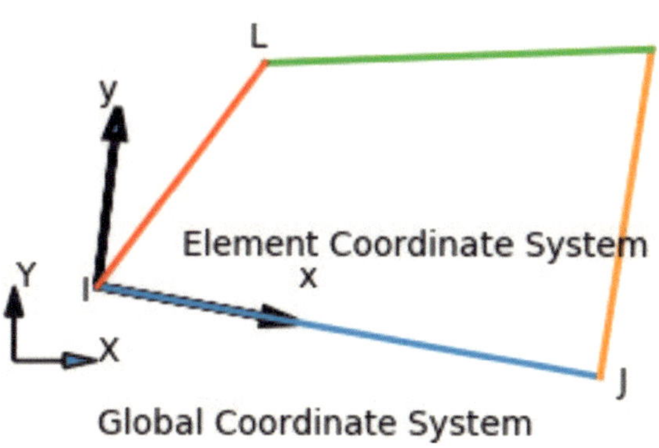

Figure 2. Definition of PLANE42 element of ANSYS [34].

2.4. Numerical experiments for different combination of engineering constants

A finite element mesh with $40 \times 10 = 400$ elements, $41 \times 11 = 451$ nodes, $451 \times 2 = 902$ degrees of freedom (displacements) is employed for a numerical analysis of backfilled zone (**Figure 3**). The left-hand side and right-hand side can only move freely in vertical direction, while the bottom of backfilled zone is considered fixed in both directions. In order to provide enough sampling data for later training and testing process using supervised neural networks, the Young's modulus (E) ranges from 0.02 to 3 GPa (covering the general values of soil and

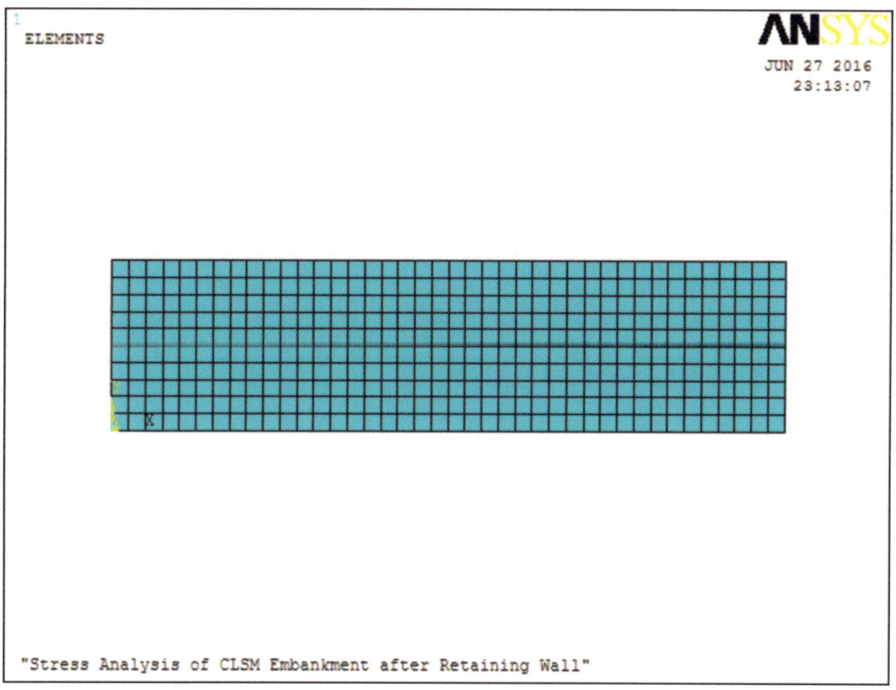

Figure 3. FEM mesh of the typical example of CLSM-backfilled region using ANSYS of PLANE42 elements.

CLSMs), while the Poisson's ratio (ν) is selected to be 0.1, 0.2, 0.25, 0.3, and 0.4. A total of 270 data samples with different combinations of E and ν are used.

2.5. Data preparation

2.5.1. Data collection from FEM analysis using ANSYS

Table 2 shows part of the 270 numerical results of computed displacements and stresses for different Young's moduli and Poisson's ratio using the ANSYS PLANE42 model.

2.5.2. Normalization of data

Since the output range of the sigmoid function is within [0, 1], and in order to have a better performance of training of neural network, the input data should be normalized to have a uniformly ranged data.

The relationship between normalized and original data can be expressed as follows:

$$\begin{aligned} \tilde{x} &= a_x x + b_x \\ \tilde{y} &= a_y y + b_y \end{aligned} \tag{4}$$

where a_x, b_x are selected such that $\tilde{x} \in [-1,\ 1]$, a_y, b_y are chosen to let $\tilde{y} \in [0\ \ 1]$. In this case, the relations are

$$\begin{aligned} \tilde{x}_1 &= x_1/0.001 \\ \tilde{x}_2 &= x_2/0.001 \\ \tilde{x}_3 &= x_3/9000 \\ \tilde{x}_4 &= x_4/9000 \\ \tilde{y}_1 &= 3^* y_1/10^{10} \\ \tilde{y}_2 &= y_2 \end{aligned} \tag{5}$$

Data	x_1,U_{y1} (m)	x_2,U_{y2} (m)	x_3, S_{x1} (Pa)	x_4, S_{x2} (Pa)	y_1,E(GPa)	y_2,ν
1	−0.00098	1.9447E-05	−4452.6	−4029.1	0.02	0.1
2	−4.91E-04	9.72E-06	−4452.6	−4029.1	0.04	0.1
55	−0.0008607	2.6951E-05	−5434.05	−5196	0.02	0.2
56	−0.0004303	1.3476E-05	−5434.05	−5196	0.04	0.2
109	−7.61E-04	4.36E-05	−5979.35	−5862.9	0.02	0.25
110	−3.80E-04	2.18E-05	−5979.35	−5862.9	0.04	0.25
163	−0.62826E-03	0.72850E-04	−6567.6	−6599	0.02	0.3
164	−3.14E-04	3.64E-05	−6567.6	−6599	0.04	0.3
269	−1.88E-06	1.50E-06	−7896.55	−8337.1	2.5	0.4
270	−1.56E-06	1.25E-06	−7896.55	−8337.1	3	0.4

Table 2. Computed displacements and stresses for different Young's moduli and Poisson's ratio using the ANSYS PLANE42 model.

Data	x_1, U_{y1} (m)	x_2, U_{y2} (m)	x_3, S_{x1} (Pa)	x_4, S_{x2} (Pa)	y_1, E(GPa)	y_2, ν
1	0.980000	0.019447	−0.494733	−0.447678	0.006000	0.100000
2	0.491200	0.009721	−0.494733	−0.447678	0.012000	0.100000
55	0.860680	0.026951	−0.603783	−0.577333	0.006000	0.200000
56	0.430340	0.013476	−0.603783	−0.577333	0.012000	0.200000
109	0.760910	0.043562	−0.664372	−0.651433	0.006000	0.250000
110	0.380450	0.021781	−0.664372	−0.651433	0.012000	0.250000
163	0.628260	0.072850	−0.729733	−0.733222	0.006000	0.300000
164	0.314130	0.036425	−0.729733	−0.733222	0.012000	0.300000
269	0.001876	0.001505	−0.877394	−0.926344	0.750000	0.400000
270	0.001564	0.001254	−0.877394	−0.926344	0.900000	0.400000

Table 3. Typical normalized FEM computed displacements and stress at sampling points.

Part of typical normalized FEM computed displacements and stress at sampling points are shown in **Table 3**. Among these normalized data, 216 set (216/270 ≒ 80%) are selected randomly for training and 54 set (54/270 ≒ 20%) for testing in the later neural work analyses.

2.5.3. Data for verification

In order to verify the trained and tested neural networks, three data set of backfilled materials are used: (1) the first is commonly used soil (E = 0.1 *GPa*, ν = 0.30); (2) CLSM-B80/30% (E = 0.27 *GPa*, ν = 0.25); and (3) CLSM-B130/30% (E = 0.87 *GPa*, ν = 0.25). The CLSM-B80/30% and CLSM-B130/30% denote unit weight of binder of the CLSM is 80 and 130 kg/m^3 with 30% of replacement of cement by fly ash. Selection of materials for the CLSM mixture in this study consisted of fine aggregate, type I Portland cement, stainless steel reducing slag (SSRS), and water. Fine aggregate for CLSM was formed by well blending between river sand and residual soil with a given proportion (e.g., 6:4, by volume) for grading improvement. The soil was obtained from a construction site. The experimental work was conducted on two binder content levels in mixtures (i.e., 80- and 130 kg/m^3). The water-to-binder ratio was selected via few trial mixes until the acceptable flowability for CLSM of 150−300 *mm* was achieved. The detailed information can be seen in [8].

In **Table 4**, computed displacements and stresses for verified soil and two CLSMs using the ANSYS PLANE42 model are summarized, while the normalized data for verification are tabulated in **Table 5**.

Data	$x_1, Uy1$ (m)	x_2, U_{y2} (m)	x_3, S_{x1} (Pa)	x_4, S_{x2} (Pa)	y_1, E(GPa)	y_2, ν
Soil	−1.26E-04	1.46E-05	−6567.6	−6599	0.1	0.3
CLSM-B80/30%	−5.64E-05	3.23E-06	−5979.35	−5862.9	0.27	0.25
CLSM-B130/30%	−1.75E-05	1.00E-06	−5979.35	−5862.9	0.87	0.25

Table 4. Computed displacements and stresses for verified soil and two CLSMs using the ANSYS PLANE42 model.

Data	x_1, U_{y1} (m)	x_2, U_{y2} (m)	x_3, S_{x1} (Pa)	x_4, S_{x2} (Pa)	y_1, E(GPa)	y_2, ν
Soil	−0.126	0.0146	−0.72973	−0.73322	0.003	0.3
CLSM-B80/30%	−0.0564	0.00323	−0.66437	−0.65143	0.0081	0.25
CLSM-B130/30%	−0.0175	0.001	−0.66437	−0.65143	0.0261	0.25

Table 5. Normalized FEM computed displacements and stress for verified soil and two CLSMs using the ANSYS PLANE42model.

3. Parameter recognition using BPANN

3.1. Application of BPANN for parameter recognition

Figure 4 demonstrates a typical BPANN for the identification of engineering constants of CLSM. The BPANN shown in **Figure 4** contains a single output, that is, the Young's modulus ($y1 = E$, $y2 = \nu$), L input neurons (x_i, $i = 1, 2, \cdots, L$), and M hidden neurons (h_j, $j = 1, 2, \cdots, M$). The predicted outputs can be expressed as [35–37]:

a. from input layer (IL) to hidden layer (HL):

$$h_j = f(n_j) = f\left(\sum_{i=1}^{L} w_{ji} x_i - b_j\right) \tag{6a}$$

b. from hidden layer (HL) to output layer (OL):

$$y_k = f(n_k) = f\left(\sum_{j=1}^{M} w_{kj} h_j - b_k\right) \tag{6b}$$

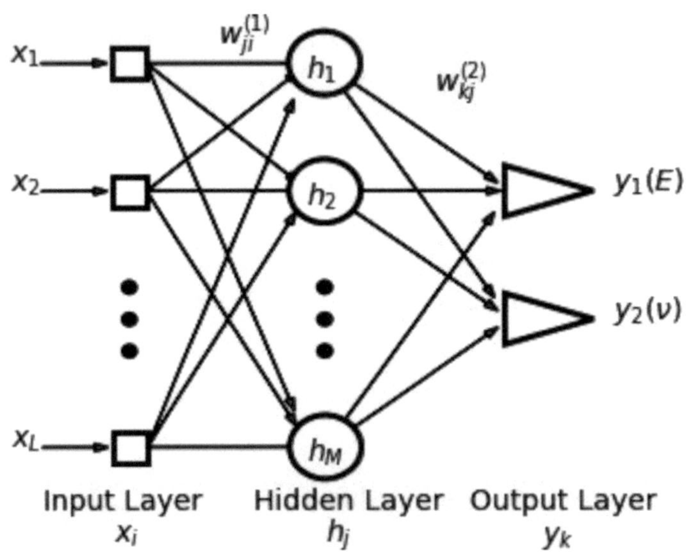

Figure 4. Schematic of a BPANN topology for single parameter recognition.

Where the activating function (the sigmoid function) and its derivative can be expressed as.

$$f(n) = \frac{1}{1+e^{-n}}$$
$$f'(n) = f(n)[1 - f(n)]. \tag{7}$$

3.2. Learning algorithms of BPANN for parameter recognition

There exist many approaches for the determination of the network parameters in BPANN (w_{kj}, b_k, w_{ji}, b_j). The most basic and popular generalized delta rule based on the method of the steepest descent along with two learning parameters (i.e., the learning rate η and the momentum factor μ)is employed, which can be expressed as

$$\begin{aligned}
w_{kj}(p+1) &= w_{kj}(p) - \eta \frac{\partial E}{\partial w_{kj}}(p) + \mu w_{kj}(p) \\
b_k(p+1) &= b_k(p) - \eta \frac{\partial E}{\partial b_k}(p) + \mu b_k(p) \\
w_{ji}(p+1) &= w_{ji}(p) - \eta \frac{\partial E}{\partial w_{ji}}(p) + \mu w_{ji}(p) \\
b_j(p+1) &= b_j(p) - \eta \frac{\partial E}{\partial b_j}(p) + \mu b_j(p)
\end{aligned} \tag{8}$$

where

$$E(p) = \frac{1}{2}\sum_{k=1}^{N} e_k^2(p) = \sum_{k=1}^{N} \frac{1}{2}\left[d_k(p) - y_k(p)\right]^2 \tag{9}$$

denotes the error between targets and trained output results.

$$\begin{aligned}
\frac{\partial E}{\partial w_{kj}}(p) &= -e_k(p) f'(n_k)\ h_j \\
\frac{\partial E}{\partial b_k}(p) &= -e_k(p) f'(n_k)^2 \\
\frac{\partial E}{\partial w_{ji}}(p) &= -\sum_{k=1}^{N}\left[e_k(p) f'(n_k)\ w_{kj}\right] f'(n_j)\ x_i \\
\frac{\partial E}{\partial b_j}(p) &= -\sum_{k=1}^{N}\left[e_k(p) f'(n_k)\ w_{kj}\right] f'(n_j)
\end{aligned} \tag{10}$$

The MATLAB toolbox *nntool* provides a lot of training methods along with BPANN [38], among which four kinds of training algorithms were tested in the current research as follows:

a. Generalized steepest decent (GD):

The learning rule can be written as Eq. (8) with $\eta \neq 0, \ \mu = 0$.

b. Generalized steepest decent including momentum (GDM):

The learning rule can be written as Eq. (8) with $\eta \neq 0, \quad \mu \neq 0$.

c. Generalized steepest decent with adjustable learning rate (GDA):

In this algorithm, the basic learning rule is the same as Eq. (6) but adding a conditional judgment. When stable learning can be kept under a learning rate, then the learning rate is increased, otherwise it is decreased. The learning rate increment and decrement can be denoted as ζ_{inc} and ζ_{dec} [35].

d. Levenberg-Marquardt (LM):

The learning rule can be written as

$$\Delta w_{ij}(t+1) = w_{ij}(t+1) - w_{ij}(t) = -\left[[J]^T[J] + \lambda[I]\right]^{-1} [J]^T \{e\} \tag{11}$$

where λ denotes a constant to assure the inversion of matrix, and the learning rule becomes Gauss-Newton algorithm when $\lambda = 0$, while it approaches GD with small learning rate with large λ [35].

3.3. Numerical results of parameter recognition using BPANN

The first supervised learning employed for parameter recognition of engineering constants is the BPANN, which can be easily implemented for multiple inputs and multiple outputs. Since there are various design parameters in the construction of a BPANN, we study some influence factors (such as different algorithms of training rules, different combination of input variables, and number of neurons of hidden layer), and then we propose and analyze an appropriate topology of BPANN. The MATLAB nntool is used for network simulation.

3.3.1. Comparison of different algorithms of learning rules

The convergence of RSME with iteration of BPANN by using different training algorithms under a BPANN topology with 4–6-2 (NI = 4, NH = 6, NO = 2) for the 216 training set is shown in **Figure 5**. The training functions in MATLAB are as follows: (1) GD (*traingd*); (2) GDM (*traingdm*); (3) GDA (*traingda*); and (4) LM (*trainlm*). Some parameters employed in the four BPANN algorithms are also shown in **Figure 5**. It can be observed that except LM (*trainlm*), all another three algorithms cannot allow the root mean square errors (RMSEs) approach to zero quickly. (The results had been verified by the self-developed BPANN by using GD learning rule programming in Python). This reflects the current problem that contains a special feature that first-order method of the steepest decent cannot help to find the global minimum quickly, while the Levenberg-Marquardt (LM) algorithms based on Hessian matrix containing second-order derivative of cost function work well.

Table 6 summarizes the effect of different training algorithms of BPANN on the predicted accuracy. It can be shown that LM (*trainlm*) gives accurate prediction of both the Young's modulus (error is within 6% for CLSMs) and Poisson's ratio (error is 1% for all) for three kinds of backfilled materials.

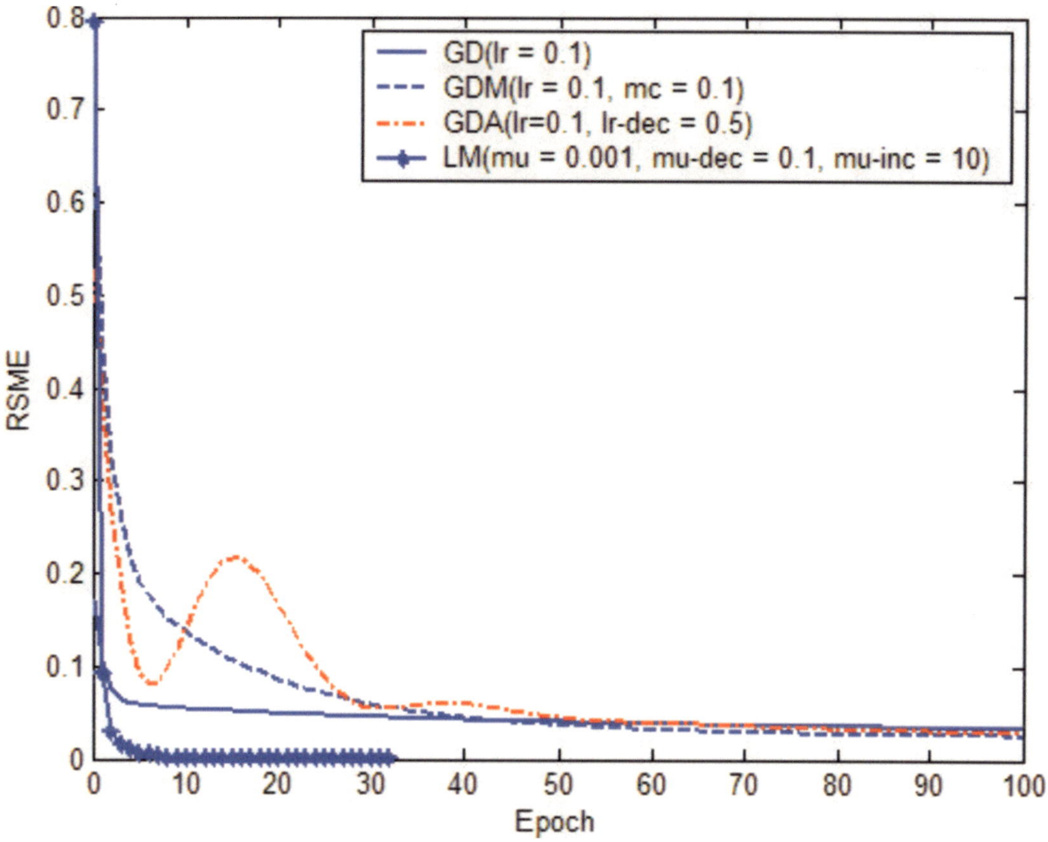

Figure 5. Convergence of RSME with iteration of BPANN using different training algorithms (NI = 4, NH = 6, NO = 2).

Case	Training method	RSME	Soil		CLSM-B80/30%		CLSM-B130/30%	
			E(Error%)	ν(Error%)	E(Error%)	ν(Error%)	E(Error%)	ν(Error%)
1	*traingd*	0.02	0.5855 (485.5%)	0.4109 (36.95%)	0.6875 (154.6%)	0.2769 (10.75%)	0.7356 (−15.45%)	0.2717 (8.69%)
2	*traingdm*	0.02	0.5234 (423.4%)	0.3307 (10.24%)	0.6700 (148.2%)	0.2628 (5.11%)	0.6875 (−20.97%)	0.2581 (3.25%)
3	*traingda*	0.02	0.5148 (414.8%)	0.2181 (−27.30%)	0.5695 (110.92%)	0.1999 (−20.06%)	0.5766 (−33.72%)	0.2049 (−18.06%)
4	*trainlm*	0.00	**0.0729 (−27.11%)**	**0.2991 (−0.31%)**	**0.2862 (5.99%)**	**0.2512 (0.49%)**	**0.8561 (−1.60%)**	**0.2510 (0.40%)**
Experimental value			0.1	0.3	0.27	0.25	0.87	0.25

Table 6. Effect of different training algorithms of BPANN on the predicted accuracy.

3.3.2. Effects of input variable combinations

In a practical engineering situation, we are interested in a question: what physical variables should we measure? To solve this problem, five cases of different combination of input variables are investigated:

Case 1: (U_{y1},U_{y2}, S_{x1}, S_{x2}) (NI =4) (two displacements, two stresses).

Case 2: (U_{y1},U_{y2}, S_{x1}) (NI =3) (two displacements, one stress).

Case 3: (U_{y1},U_{y2}) (NI =2) (two displacements).

Case 4: (U_{y1}, S_{x1},) (NI =2) (one displacement, one stress).

Case 5: (S_{x1}, S_{x2}) (NI =2) (two stresses).

The convergence of RSME with iteration of BPANN using different combinations of input variables using LM training algorithms (NH = 6, NO = 2) for the 216 training set is shown in **Figure 6**. Again, LM works well, but the predicted accuracy shown in **Table 7** depicts that only cases 1, 2, and 3 are appropriate for use. The result of case 5 reflects the fact that only stresses information cannot predict the material constant. Therefore, in the following analysis, we basically consider input variables of case 1; this means we need to measure two displacements and two stresses.

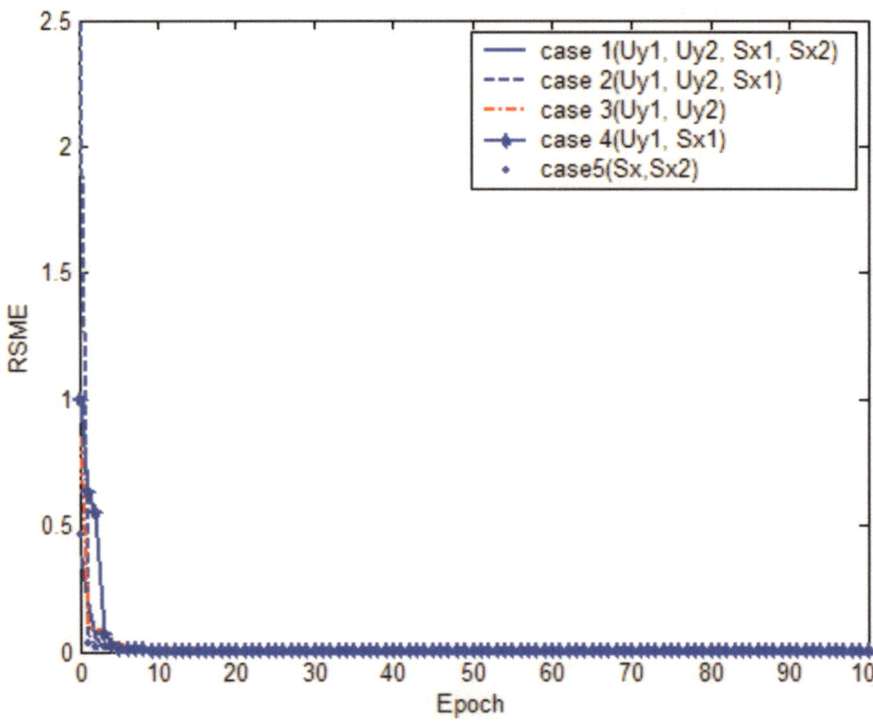

Figure 6. Convergence of RSME with iteration of BPANN using different combinations of input variables (trainlm, NI = 4, NH = 6, NO = 2).

Case	NI	Input variables	Soil		CLSM-B80/30%		CLSM-B130/30%	
			E(Error%)	ν(Error%)	E(Error%)	ν(Error%)	E(Error%)	ν(Error%)
1	4	Uy1, Uy2, Sx1, Sx2	0.1363 (36.28%)	0.3003 (0.11%)	0.2368 (−12.30%)	0.2470 (−0.86%)	0.8636 (−0.73%)	0.2480 (−0.79%)
2	3	Uy1,Uy2, Sx1	0.0895 (−10.50%)	−0.2997 (−0.09%)	0.2795 (3.50%)	0.2518 (0.71%)	0.8618 (−0.95%)	0.2516 (0.65%)
3	2	Uy1, Uy2	0.0747 (−25.31%)	0.2997 (−0.10%)	0.2555 (−5.337%)	0.2501 (0.04%)	0.8485 (−2.48%)	0.2505 (0.21%)
4	2	Uy1, Sx1	7.5206 (7420%)	−0.1752 (−158.4%)	7.5706 (2704%)	−0.1768 (−17.7%)	7.6544 (779.8%)	−0.1724 (−168.9%)
5	2	Sx1, Sx2	1.3530 (1253%)	1.6716 (457.2%)	1.3079 (384.4%)	1.6449 (557.9%)	1.2985 (49.25%)	1.6331 (553.3%)
Experimental values			0.1	0.3	0.27	0.25	0.87	0.25

Table 7. Effect of input variables on the prediction accuracy of engineering constants using BPANN.

3.3.3. *Effect of number of hidden neurons*

The results of BPANN results using different number of neurons of hidden layer (NH) are shown in **Figure 7** and **Table 8**. From the results it is recommended to employ NH > 2 for the accurate prediction of engineering constants if training algorithms LM (*trainlm*) are employed.

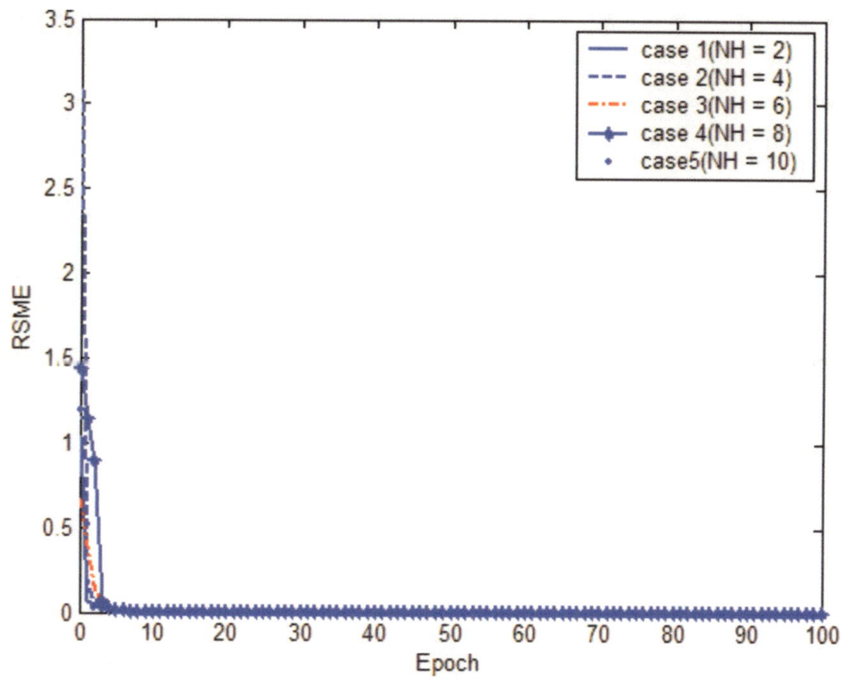

Figure 7. Convergence of RSME with iteration of BPANN using different number of neurons of hidden layer (trainlm, NI = 4, NO = 2).

Case	NH	NI-NH-NO	Soil		CLSM-B80/30%		CLSM-B130/30%	
			E(Error%)	ν(Error%)	E(Error%)	ν(Error%)	E(Error%)	ν(Error%)
1	2	4–2-2-	0.2088 (108.80%)	0.3007 (0.22%)	0.2327 (−13.80%)	0.2498 (−0.08%)	0.9413 (8.20%)	0.2499 (−0.04%)
2	4	4–4-2	0.1562 (56.19%)	0.2878 (−4.06%)	0.3097 (14.69%)	0.2453 (−1.87%)	0.8903 (2.33%)	0.2498 (−0.09%)
3	6	4–6-2	0.1653 (65.35%)	0.2985 (−0.50%)	0.3238 (19.94%)	0.2491 (−0.36%)	0.8859 (1.83%)	0.2492 (−0.31%)
4	8	4–8-2	0.0811 (−11.91%)	0.3015 (0.51%)	0.2392 (−11.43%)	0.2507 (0.29%)	0.8566 (−1.54%)	0.2508 (0.34%
5	10	4–10-2	0.1174 (17.39%)	0.2992 (−0.28%)	0.2777 (2.86%)	0.2531 (1.23%)	0.8833 (1.53%)	0.2542 (1.69%)
Experimental values			0.1	0.3	0.27	0.25	0.87	0.25

Table 8. Effect of number of neurons of hidden layer on the prediction accuracy of engineering constants using BPANN.

3.3.4. Selection of a BPANN topology

After some parametric studies, a BPANN with 4–6-2 topology using LM training algorithm is proposed for current parameter recognition problems. The convergence of RMSE is shown in **Figure 8** to depict very fast decay of RSME. **Figure 9** shows the QQ plot of tested results and predicted results during testing stage after training process. The R^2value for the Young's modulus and Poisson's ratio are 0.99454 and 0.99864, respectively. It reflects that the training

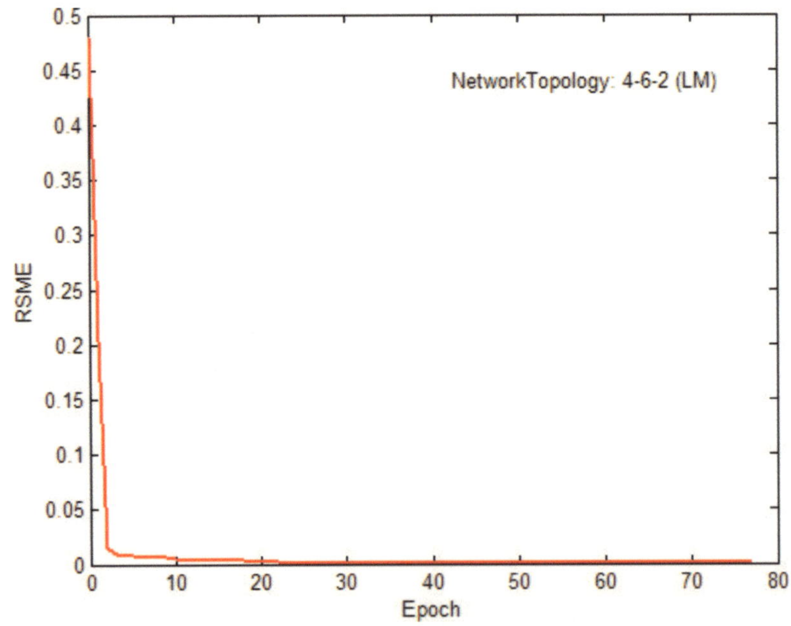

Figure 8. Convergence of RSME with iteration of finally selected of BPANN (trainlm, NI = 4, NH = 6, NO = 2).

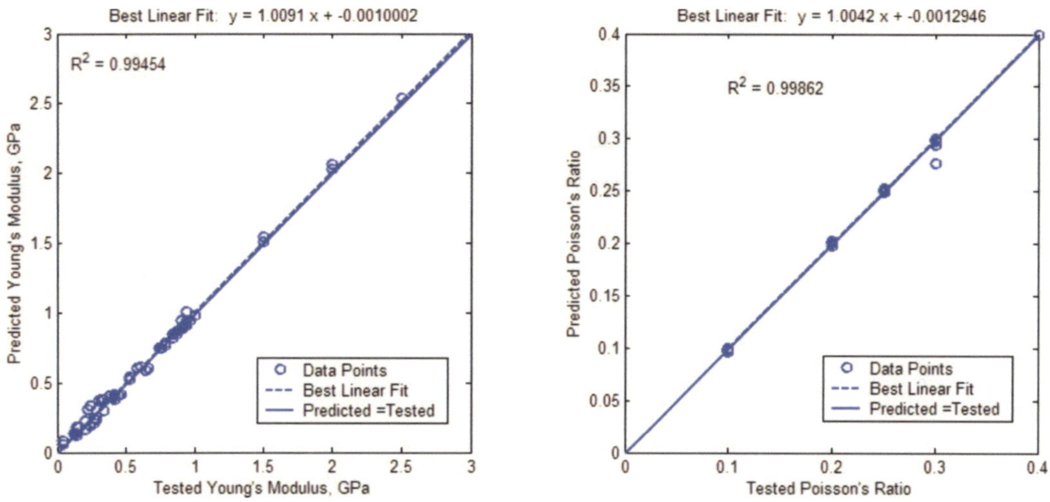

Figure 9. QQ plot of testing data of finally selected of BPANN (trainlm, NI = 4, NH = 6, NO = 2).

Training method	Input variables	NI-NH-NO	Soil		CLSM-B80/30%		CLSM-B130/30%	
			E(Error%)	ν(Error%)	E(Error%)	ν(Error%)	E(Error%)	ν(Error%)
trainlm	Uy1, Uy2, Sx1,Sx2	4-6-2-	0.0729 (−27.11%)	0.2991 (0.31%)	0.2862 (5.99%)	0.2512 (0.49%)	0.8561 (−1.60%)	0.2510 (0.40%)
Experimental values			0.1	0.3	0.27	0.25	0.87	0.25

Table 9. Predicted results using final design of a BPANN for the recognition of engineering constants of CLSM.

BPANN works well for testing data. **Table 9** shows predicted results using final design of a BPANN for the recognition of engineering constants of CLSM.

4. Parameter recognition using RBFNN

4.1. Application of RBFNN for parameter recognition

Figure 10 demonstrates a typical RBFNN for the identification of engineering constants of CLSM. The RBFNN shown in **Figure 10** contains a single output, that is, the Young's modulus ($y_1 = E,\ y_2 = \nu$), L input neurons ($x_i,\ i = 1, 2, \cdots, L$), and M hidden neurons ($h_j,\ j = 1, 2, \cdots, M$). Suppose we have S samples for training, we can select $M \leq S$. The predicted output can be expressed as [35–37]:

$$y_k = F_k(x_i) = \sum_{j=1}^{M} w_j\ K(\|x_i - C_j\|) = \sum_{j=1}^{M} w_j e^{\frac{-1}{2\sigma_j^2}\|x_i - C_j\|^2} \tag{12}$$

where the kernel function $K(\|x_i - C_j\|) = e^{\frac{-1}{2\sigma_j^2}\|x_i - C_j\|^2}$ is the Gaussian basis function.

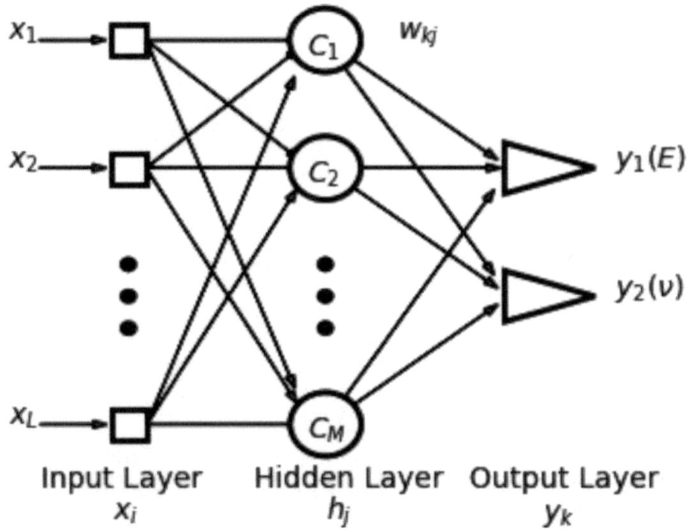

Figure 10. Schematic of a RBFNN topology for single parameter recognition.

4.2. Learning algorithms for RBFNN for parameter recognition

There exist many approaches for the determination of the network parameters in RBFNN (C_j, σ_j, w_{kj}). For parallel comparison, here the supervised learning algorithm, that is, the generalized delta rule based on the method of the steepest descent is used, which can be expressed as [35–37]:

$$\begin{aligned} w_{kj}(p+1) &= w_{kj}(p) - \eta \ \frac{\partial E}{\partial w_{kj}}(p) + \mu w_{kj}(p) \\ C_j(p+1) &= wC_j(p) - \eta \ \frac{\partial E}{\partial C_j}(p) + \mu C_j(p) \\ \sigma_j(p+1) &= \sigma_j(p) - \eta \ \frac{\partial E}{\partial \sigma_j}(p) + \mu \sigma_j(p) \end{aligned} \tag{13}$$

where

$$E(p) = \frac{1}{2}\sum_{k=1}^{N} e_k^2(p) = \frac{1}{2}\sum_{k=1}^{N} \left[d_k(p) - y_k(p)\right]^2 \tag{14}$$

denotes the error between targets and trained output results.

$$\begin{aligned} \frac{\partial E}{\partial w_{kj}}(p) &= -K(\|x_i(p) - C_j(p)\|) \\ \frac{\partial E}{\partial C_j}(p) &= -w_{kj}(p) \ \frac{1}{\sigma_j^2(p)} K(\|x_i(p) - C_j(p)\|) \bullet [x_i(p) - C_j(p)] \\ \frac{\partial E}{\partial \sigma_j}(p) &= -w_{kj}(p) \ \frac{1}{\sigma_j^3(p)} K(\|x_i(p) - C_j(p)\|) \bullet \|x_i(p) - C_j(p)\|^2 \end{aligned} \tag{15}$$

There also exist many algorithms for learning RBFNN; among those, some are unsupervised ones such as using kNN for determination of C_j and using the pseudo-inversion method to evaluate w_{kj} [35–37].

4.3. Numerical results of parameter recognition using RBFNN

Table 10 summarizes the accuracy of predicted results by using RBFNN with different combinations of input variables. MATLAB *nntool* (*newrb*) is used for numerical experiments [38]. Unfortunately, the results are not as good as those obtained using BPANN with the LM training method. **Figure 11** also reflects the same results that Young's modulus cannot be

Case	NI	Input variables	Soil		CLSM-B80/30%		CLSM-B130/30%	
			E(Error%)	ν(Error%)	E(Error%)	ν(Error%)	E(Error%)	ν(Error%)
1	4	Uy1, Uy2, Sx1, Sx2	0.1877 (87.73%)	0.3009 (0.30%)	0.5786 (114.29%)	0.2498 (−0.08%)	0.8085 (−7.07%)	0.2498 (−0.08)
2	3	Uy1,Uy2, Sx1	0.1649 (64.85%)	0.300 (0.00%)	0.5561 (105.95%)	0.2486 (−0.55%)	0.7832 (−9.98%)	0.2487 (−0.53%)
3	2	Uy1, Uy2	0.2124 (112.44%)	0.2151 (−28.31%)	0.5809 (115.15%)	0.2309 (−7.63%)	0.7983 (−8.25%)	0.2549 (1.98%)
4	2	Uy1, Sx1	0.1774 (77.44%)	0.3001 (0.02)	0.5072 (87.85%)	0.2450 (−2.01%)	0.7017 (−19.34%)	0.2425 (−3.00%)
5	2	Sx1, Sx2	0.6023 (502.27%)	0.300 (0.00)	0.6365 (135.74%)	0.2500 (0.01%)	0.6365 (−26.84%)	0.2500 (0.01%)
Experimental values			0.1	0.3	0.27	0.25	0.87	0.25

Table 10. Effect of input variables on the prediction accuracy of engineering constants using RBFNN.

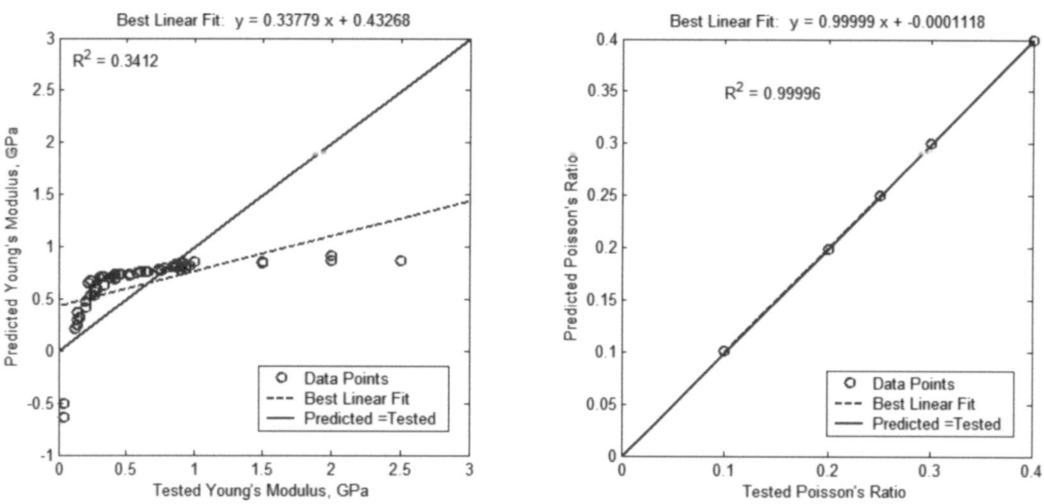

Figure 11. QQ plot of predicted and tested engineering constants of CLSM using RBFNN (NI = 4).

predicted well using RBFNN (even though a lot of trials on selection of spread constants cannot obtain satisfying results).

5. Conclusions

This chapter presents a trial of application of two supervised learning artificial neural networks (BPANN and RBFNN) to predict engineering material constants, Young's modulus and Poisson's ratio, of backfilled materials (soil and CLSMs). The training and testing data are obtained from numerical experiments using ANSYS. Concluding remarks can be summarized as follows:

1. BPANN with training method LM (such as trainlm in MATLAB) works well for parameter recognition of engineering constant. For example, a well-designed BPANN with LM (*trainlm*) can give accurate prediction of both Young's modulus (error is within 6% for CLSMs) and Poisson's ratio (error is with 1% for all) for three kinds of backfilled materials;
2. In the BPANN framework, at least two displacements at different points should be measured, together with optional 0, 1, or 2 stress measurements;
3. In the BPANN structure, for example, small number of neurons of hidden layer is enough for parameter recognition;
4. RBFNN is not appropriate for the parameter recognition of engineering constants, for example, as compared with BPANN.

In future, another neural network which is appropriate for regression, such as probabilistic neural networks (PNN) and supporting vector machines (SVM), maybe used for the study on the parameter recognition of engineering constants of problems in civil engineering.

Author details

Li-Jeng Huang

Address all correspondence to: ljhuang@kuas.edu.tw

Department of Civil Engineering, National Kaohsiung University of Applied Sciences, Taiwan, R. O. C

References

[1] ACI-229R. Controlled-Low Strength Materials (Reproved 2005). Farmington Hills, MI, USA: American Concrete Institute (ACI); 2005.

[2] Lachemi M, Şahmaran M, Hossain KMA, Lotfy A. Properties of controlled low-strength materials incorporating cement kiln dust and slag. Cement and Concrete Composites. 2010;**32**:623-629

[3] Finney AJ, Shorey EF, Anderson, J. Use of native soil in place of aggregate in controlled low strength material (CLSM), International pipelines conference 2008 Atlanta, Georgia, United States, 2008; 1–13

[4] Howard A, Gaughan M, Hattan S, Wilkerson M. Lean, green, and mean: The IPL Project. International Conference on Sustainable Design, Engineering, and Construction 2012 (ICSDEC 2012), November 7-9, 2012. Fort Worth, Texas, United States: ASCE. 2013;**1**:359-366

[5] Huang LJ, Wang HY, Wei CT. Engineering properties of controlled low strength desulfurization slags (CLSDS). Construction and Building Materials. 2016;**115**:6-12

[6] Huang LJ, Wang HY, Wu YY. Properties of the mechanical in controlled low-strength rubber lightweight aggregate concrete (CLSRLC). Construction and Building Materials. 2016;**112**:1054-1058

[7] Huang LJ, Wang HY, Wang SYA. Study of the durability of recycled green building materials in lightweight aggregate concrete. Construction and Building Materials. 2015;**96**:353-359

[8] Sheen YN, Huang LJ, Le DH. Engineering properties of controlled low-strength material made with residual soil and class F fly ash, 3rd International conference for advanced materials design and mechanics and workshop on android robotics, paper no. 54, Singapore, May 23–24, 2014

[9] Huang LJ, Sheen YN, Le DH. On the multiple linear regression and artificial neural networks for strength prediction of soil-based controlled low-strength material, 3rd international conference for advanced materials design and mechanics and workshop on android robotics, paper no. 55, Singapore, May 23–24, 2014

[10] Sheen YN, Hsiao DH, Huang LJ, Le DH. Stress-strain behavior of soil-based controlled low-strength material, The International Conference on Green Technology for Sustainable Development 2014, Ho Chi Minh, Viet Nam, October 30–312014

[11] Alizadeh V, Helwany S, Ghorbanpoor A, Sobolev K. Design and application of controlled kow strength materials as a structural fill. Construction and Building Materials. 2014;**53**: 425-431

[12] Huang LJ, Sheen YN, Hsiao DH, Le DH. Numerical analysis of excavation backfilled with soil-based controlled low-strength materials: Part I- static analysis. IJETAE. 2014;**4**(12):132-139

[13] Huang LJ, Sheen YN, Hsiao DH, Le DH. Numerical analysis of excavation backfilled with soil-based controlled low-strength materials: Part II- steady state elastodynamic analysis. IJETAE. 2014;**4**(12):140-148

[14] Helwany S, Ghorbanpoor A, Alizadeh V, Oliva MA. Novel Abutment Construction Technique for Rapid Bridge Construction: CLSM with Full-Height Concrete Panels. DTRT06-G-0020,

National Center for Freight and Infrasrructure Research and Education (CFIRE). University of Wisonsin-Madison; January, 2012

[15] Schmitz ME, Parsons RL, Ramirez G, Zhao Y. Use of Controlled Low-Strength Material as Abutment Backfill. Technical report K-TRAN: KU-02-6, the Kansas Department of Transportation, Topeka, Kansas, University of Kansas, USA, June 2004

[16] Huang LJ, Sheen YN, Le DH. Numerical analysis of controlled low-strength material bridge abutments: Part-I: Static analysis. The eighth structural engineering and construction conference (ISEC-8), Sydney, Australia, November 23–28, 2015

[17] Huang LJ, Sheen YN, Le DH. Numerical analysis of controlled low-strength material bridge abutments: Part-II: Steady-state elasodynamic analysis. The eighth structural engineering and construction conference (ISEC-8), Sydney, Australia, November 23–28, 2015

[18] Huang LJ, Wang HY, Sheen YN, Le DH. Earth pressure and settlement analysis of trench ducts backfilled with controlled low-strength materials. Procedia Engineering. 2016;**142**: 173-180

[19] Lin DF, Luo HL, Wang HY, Hung MJ. Successful application of clsm on a weak pavement base/subgrade for heavy truck traffic. Journal of Performance of Constructed Facilities. 2007:70-77

[20] Bassani M, Khosravifar S, Goulias DG, Schwartz CW. Long-term resilient and permanent deformation behavior of controlled low-strength materials for pavement applications. Transportation Geotechnics. 2015;**2**:108-118

[21] Huang LJ, Wang HY, Huang WL, Lin MC. Finite element analysis of controlled low strength material pavement bases: Part-I: Static analysis. Resilient structures and sustainable construction. 9th International Conference in Structural Engineering and Construction. (ISEC-9), Valencia, Spain, July 24–29, 2017

[22] Huang LJ, Wang HY, Huang WL, Lin MC. Finite element analysis of controlled low-strength material pavement bases: Part-II: Free vibration analysis. Resilient structures and sustainable construction. 9th International Conference in Structural Engineering and Construction. (ISEC-9), Valencia, Spain, July 24–29, 2017

[23] Huang WL, Wang HY, Huang LJ. Viscoelastic analysis of flexible pavements embedded with controlled low-strength material bases using finite element method. The 2nd International Conference on Mechanics, Materials and Structural Engineering (ICMMSE 2017). Beijing, April 14-16, 2017

[24] Tu TW, Wang HY, Huang LJ. Finite element analysis of cracked flexible pavements embedded with controlled low-strength material bases. The 2nd International Conference on Mechanics, Materials and Structural Engineering (ICMMSE 2017). Beijing, April 14-16, 2017

[25] Oludele A, Olawale J. Neural networks and its application in engineering. Proceedings of Informing Science & IT Education Conference (InSITE). 2009

[26] Kapania RK, Liu Y. Applications of artificial neural networks in structural engineering with emphasis on continuum models. Department of Aerospace and Ocean Engineering, Virginia Polytechnic Institute and State University Blacksburg, VA, USA

[27] Jaina M, Pathak KK. Applications of artificial neural network in construction engineering and management-a review. International Journal of Engineering Technology, Management and Applied Sciences. 2014;**2**(3):134-142

[28] Elshafiey I. Neural Network Approach for Solving Inverse Problems, MS thesis. Department of Electric Engineering and Computer Engineering, Iowa State University; 1991

[29] Raiche A. Pattern recognition approach to geophysical inversion using neural nets. Geophysics Journal International. 1991;**105**(6):692-698

[30] Li S-J, Liu Y-X, Zhang Z-P, Huang W, Shen G-H. Parameter identification of concrete dam with neural networks. Proceedings of Da-Lien University of Science and Engineering. 2000;**40**(5):531-535 (in Chinese)

[31] Li S-J, Liu Y-X, Liu Y-J. Identification of elastic parameters of rock body in slope based on improved BP neural networks. Proceedings of College of Xian-Tan Mineral Engineering. 2002;**17**(1):58-61 (in Chinese)

[32] Chang R-C, Ru E-L, Jien K-L. Mordern Computational Mechanics, Chapter 10. In: Artifical Neural Networks and their Applications to Mechanics. Tsung-Chin University Press; 2004

[33] Movaveni S. Finite Element Analysis: Theory and Application with ANSYS. Prentice Hall, Upper Saddle River, NJ, USA; 1999

[34] ANSYS User's manual: Elements, Vol. III. Canonsburg, PA, USA: Swanson Analysis Systems, Inc; 1999

[35] Hagen MT, Dmuth HB, Deale M. Neural Network Design. Boston, MA, USA: PWS Publishing Co.; 1996

[36] Jang J-SR, Sun CT, Mizutani E. Neuro-Fuzzy and Soft Computing-A Computational Approach to Learning and Machine Intelligence, Chapter 9. Prentice-Hall, Upper Saddle River, NJ, USA; 1997

[37] Haykin S. Neural Networks and Learning Machines. 3rd ed. Upper Saddle River, NJ, USA: Pearson Education, Inc; 2009 Chapter 4, Chapter 5

[38] Neural Networks Toolbox User's Guide, The MathWorks, MA, USA; 2002

Chapter 7

Electricity Consumption and Generation Forecasting with Artificial Neural Networks

Adela Bâra and Simona Vasilica Oprea

Additional information is available at the end of the chapter

http://dx.doi.org/10.5772/intechopen.71239

Abstract

Nowadays, smart meters, sensors and advanced electricity tariff mechanisms such as time-of-use tariff (ToUT), critical peak pricing tariff and real time tariff enable the electricity consumption optimization for residential consumers. Therefore, consumers will play an active role by shifting their peak consumption and change dynamically their behavior by scheduling home appliances, invest in small generation or storage devices (such as small wind turbines, photovoltaic (PV) panels and electrical vehicles). Thus, the current load profile curves for household consumers will become obsolete and electricity suppliers will require dynamical load profiles calculation and new advanced methods for consumption forecast. In this chapter, we aim to present some developments of artificial neural networks for energy demand side management system that determines consumers' profiles and patterns, consumption forecasting and also small generation estimations.

Keywords: forecast, renewable energy, smart metering, demand side management, consumers' profiles

1. Introduction

Recently, many national and international communities and authorities developed energy efficiency strategies and programs in order to reduce energy poverty. In Ref. [1], European Economic and Social Committee (EESC) stated that more than 50 million Europeans are affected by energy poverty in 2009. EESC also recommends to establish a European poverty observatory that will bring together all stakeholders to take correct measures to reduce the gaps between different countries and regions in terms of energy poverty and propose a set of statistics indicators to monitor the evolution of energy efficiency. EESC draw attention that energy prices are constantly increasing with more than 10% annually, while most of the Europeans spending an increasing share of their income on energy.

In 2012, European Commission adopted Energy Efficiency Directive that proposed measures to increase with 20% energy efficiency target by 2020 [2]. On November 30, 2016, the Commission updated the Directive, by targeting 30% energy efficiency for 2030. The proposed measures for energy are oriented toward increasing consumers' awareness regarding their consumption management through electronic bills and information and communications technology (ICT) solutions, encourage them to become prosumers by investing in their own generation sources such as photovoltaic (PV) panels, wind turbines and storage devices.

The main objective of the chapter is to present an implementation of artificial neural networks (ANNs) for the electricity consumption management based on smart metering (SM) data. This objective will be reached by following topics:

- determining consumers' profiles and patterns with clustering and self-organizing maps (SOM);
- forecasting aggregated electricity consumption for short-term period on a typical week day with autoregressive (AR) neural networks;
- forecasting energy generation for small wind turbines and photovoltaic panels installed at consumers side (prosumers) with feed-forward neural networks;
- presenting the main components of an informatics prototype that allows the prosumers to configure and schedule their appliances in an interactive manner to optimize the electricity consumption.

The ANN performance will be compared with stochastic methods (classification, ARMA and ARIMA models) and the best solution is adopted for ICT prototype.

2. Current problems in electricity consumption and generation

Regarding ICT solutions, the most important measures to reduce the energy poverty and to increase consumers' awareness toward energy efficiency concern both electricity suppliers and consumers. For electricity suppliers, market segmentation can be used to determine dynamic consumes' profiles to better understand consumption behavior and also to set up strategies and plans for different consumers groups. Another important measure for electricity suppliers consists in consumption (load) forecasting for short and medium term, used for planning the grid resources and wholesale electricity markets bids. For consumers, with the introduction of smart metering (SM) systems, their awareness increased and new methods must be taken into consideration such as consumption optimization of household appliances through user-friendly interfaces, micro-generation (through photovoltaic panels, small wind turbines and storage devices), mobile applications for real time billing with detailed information regarding appliances' consumption or own generation sources.

2.1. Determine consumers' profiles

Determining dynamic profiles for consumers represents a challenge for energy suppliers due to the widespread implementation of smart metering (SM). Comparing with previous period before SM implementation, the consumers can play an active role, having the opportunity to control and schedule their consumption by programming some devices such as washing machine, electric heating, ventilation systems or car batteries. Another aspect that can be considered is to use micro-generation sources (photovoltaic panels installed on the roofs or buildings' facades or small wind turbines) to unload back into the grid the generated electricity according to the tariff systems. Based on activities that are carried out by consuming electricity, final consumers are categorized into household and non-household consumers. Final non-household consumers are characterized by specific consumption, defined by profiles (consumption curves) defined in Romania by procedure [3] and are split into several categories such as industry, gas stations, civil works, hospitals, public utilities, hotels, retailers, etc. For household consumers in Romania, there is no official procedure or study used by energy suppliers, although SM is targeted for 80% implementation until 2020. Based on international studies such as [4] conducted in UK during 2010–2011 by the Department of Energy and Climate Change (DECC), the Department for the Environment Food and Rural Affairs (DEFRA) and the Energy Saving Trust (EST), demonstrated clearly the influence of time-of-use tariff (ToUT) on domestic demand response. The consumers shifted their evening peak consumption due to the various ToUT prices without significantly affecting their comfort and lifestyle. In Ref. [5], it is considered a multivariate statistical lifestyle analysis of household consumers in US. The study identified five factors reflecting social and behavioral profiles (patterns) determined by air conditioning, washing machines, climate conditions, PC and TV use. A detailed analyses for market segmentation is presented in Ref. [6] based on effect of lifestyles, socio-demographic factors, smart appliances, electricity and heat supply. Authors also identified the most influenced factors that determined the segmentation: socio-demographic factors (household size, net income and employment status), types of electric appliances and the use of new (smart) technologies. They also correlated the link between socio-demographic factors and the use of new technologies and smart appliances. The household profiles are determined in Ref. [7] by applying a time series auto-regression model—Periodic Autoregression with eXogenous variables (PARX) algorithm, taking into consideration temperature and occupants' daily habits. Thus, the consumption is correlated with life style influenced by temperature that leads to air conditioning and heating electricity consumption variations.

In Ref. [8], we analyzed several methods for profile calculation including fuzzy C-means clustering, autoregression with exogenous variables and multi-linear regression. For National Grid UK, the load profiles are determined with multiple regression taking into consideration seven variables such as noon temperature, two variables regarding sunset moments compare to 6 o'clock in the afternoon and four variables related to the week days [9]. Thus eight profiles are obtained that can be used further for electricity consumption forecasts and simulation.

In Ref. [10], authors applied autoregression on hourly consumption data measured for 1000 household consumers in Canada (Ontario). The household consumption represents 30% of the total consumption and its contribution to the peak load is important due to the ventilation or AC devices. For autoregression, the variables also include hourly temperature data measured at local stations and occupation degree of each house.

In Ref. [11], clustering methods are used for determining load profiles for 300 electricity consumers from Malaysia. Authors proposed C-means fuzzy clustering algorithm by using average consumption values, thus obtaining four clusters, each of them being split into sub-clusters for a better and detailed typical consumption profiles.

In Section 3.1, we proposed a new method based on self-organizing maps (SOM) that allows us to determine six profiles clearly delimited for consumers having the following types of consumption: heating, cooling, ventilation, interior lighting, exterior lighting, water heating, usual devices (washing machine, refrigerator) and other smaller devices (TV, audio and computer). These profiles were compared with other profiles obtained by stochastic methods such as clustering and classification.

2.2. Consumption and micro-generation short-term forecasting

Regression is seen as part of the first generation of consumption (load) forecasting methods. It is one of most widely used statistical methods due to its undoubtable advantages such as simplicity and transparency. For electricity load forecasting, regression methods are usually applied to effectively model the relationship of consumption level and other factors such as weather (i.e. temperature, humidity, etc.), day type (workdays and holidays) and consumers profiles.

Several methods based on regression have been used for short-term load forecasting with different levels of success such as ARMAX models [12], multiple regression [13, 14] and regression with neural networks [15–17].

In Ref. [18], authors describe several regression models for the next day peak forecasting. Their models incorporate deterministic influences such as weekend days, stochastic influences such as historical loads, and exogenous factors influences such as temperature. In papers [19–22], authors described other applications of regression models to load forecasting.

According to [23, 24], ARIMA models have proven appropriate for forecasting electricity consumption.

In Section 3.2, we proposed a method based on autoregressive neural networks for short-term forecasting the electricity consumption aggregated at supplier's level for a typical day of the week. The forecasting method is applied on each profile previously determined by SOM. Also, we considered ARIMA method for load forecasting and at the end of Section 3.2, we compared the results for both methods.

Regarding the micro-generation forecasting (small wind turbines and photovoltaic panels installed at consumers' side), the methods depend on the time interval. For example, stochastic methods (persistence and autoregressive patterns) are recommended in Ref. [25] for very short-term prediction (up to 4–6 hours). In addition, other authors [26] proposed Kalman integrated support vector machine (SVM) method to achieve a 10% accuracy improvement by comparing with artificial neural networks or autoregressive (AR) methods. Also a consistent approach is given by the use of ANNs for short-term generation forecast in case of wind turbines and photovoltaic (PV) panels. Various ANN-based algorithms are described in [27, 28], it is proposed Bayesian Regularization algorithms for forecasting. Also in [29, 30], authors proposed back propagation neural networks based on the optimization of Swarm particles.

Stochastic methods can be successfully used in order to determine the PV generation. The authors of the paper [31] analyzed and compared different models for forecasting and concluded that the accuracy of the ARMA model is better than other models.

In Section 4, we analyzed two methods for PV and small wind turbines generation: stochastic method based on ARIMA and feed-forward ANN. The results are compared and conclusions are drawn at the end of the section.

2.3. Consumption optimization

Residential consumers usually have certain types of appliances: washing machine, dryer, dish machine, water heater, refrigerator, electric oven/grill, blender, iron machine, electric centralized heating system, coffee maker, vacuum cleaner, AC/ventilation systems, TV and other multimedia appliances. Out of these appliances only some of them can be automatically controlled and used at certain time intervals when electricity price is lower (e.g. washing machine, dish machine, electric oven, car batteries can be charged at night). Electricity suppliers may use several methods for consumption optimization using different optimization functions. In Ref. [32], it is described as stochastic optimization based on Monte Carlo simulation for minimization of estimated payment for entire day. Authors proposed a mixed integer linear programing (MILP) algorithm for optimization of the electricity residential consumption taking into account real time tariffs. In [33, 34], authors proposed genetic algorithms for consumption optimization. We proposed in Ref. [35] a method based on MILP with two optimization functions: cost-based function that minimizes the electricity costs depending on the time-of-use tariffs (ToUT) and a peak-shaving optimization function that minimizes the peak consumption. Both functions provide savings to electricity bills for consumers, but the second method also brings benefits for electricity suppliers and grid operators. In Section 5, we presented informatics solution that integrates the optimization methods presented in Ref. [35] and allows consumers to schedule their appliances in order to minimize the electricity costs.

2.4. Smart applications for real time billing

Until the expansion of smart meters, consumers were charged based on meters' reads made by an electricity supplier employee on different time intervals (usually 2–3 months) and most of the time the bills are based on estimations determined by the energy supplier on historical data regarding each household's consumption. Therefore, the electricity consumer was unable to customize and adjust his consumption based on ToUT or schedule his appliances to avoid peak consumption because he cannot benefit from real time information and his behavior is not reflected in the demand management system in real time. Since the widespread implementation of smart meters in most European countries, various informatics solutions were developed by software companies or by energy suppliers in order to provide consumers accurate electricity bills, near real time. A review of the top utility billing software products is available in Ref. [36]. These solutions are user-friendly, accessible online through mobile devices, intuitive and ease to use even for ICT novices.

Besides information regarding the total consumption, the billing systems have to provide consumptions data for different type of appliances measured by SM or by other smart measurement devices. Thus, consumers can analyze their consumption for heating, cooling, washing, lighting and other home appliances and they can schedule it based on ToUT. In Section 5, we proposed an informatics solution that provides friendly user interfaces and integrates methods for consumption optimization and micro-generation forecasting for electricity consumers.

3. Forecasting the electricity consumption

3.1. Determining the consumption profiles

In order to dynamically determine consumer profiles, first we considered a series of algorithms based on classification and clustering techniques. In order to implement and test the model, we used a data set with hourly electricity consumption recorded in different US cities between January 1, 2014 and December 31, 2014. Each record contains values for the following types of consumption: heating, cooling, ventilators, indoor lighting, outdoor lighting, water heating, household equipment (washing machine and refrigerator) and other interior devices (TV and computer). Data were imported into Oracle Database 11 g R2 in the *LOAD_PROFILE_T* table with approximately 1,900,000 hourly records for 212 consumers. We analyzed the distribution of electricity consumption at different value ranges, consumption types and time periods as shown in **Figure 1**.

The analyses shows that the consumption curve has the same aspect as the consumption for heating and interior equipment, which makes these types of consumption significant attributes for the total consumption value.

Data being imported into Oracle Database, we consider data mining algorithms developed in Oracle SQL Developer. So, for the first method, we approached support vector machines (SVMs) classification method and we build six profiles (classes) and the profiles with the most cases (over 30,000) have the highest degree of accuracy (about 90%), which can be considered a

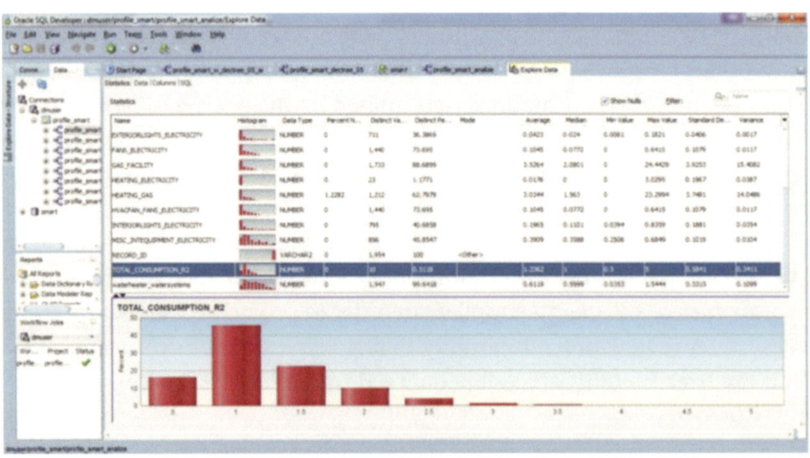

Figure 1. Data set statistics.

good result for classification. Performing classes' analyses, we observed that the profiles are very sensitive to changes in consumer behavior, due to the fact that classes with a small number of items recorded the highest prediction errors.

To eliminate these shortcomings, we considered it useful to apply a second solution for determining profiles dynamically by using clustering methods. For building the profiles, we applied the K-means method and for measuring similarity within a cluster, the variance (the sum of the squares of the differences between the main element and each element) is used, being the best clusters in which the variance is small. We analyzed the confidence level for each cluster and it is noticeable that the confidence is high, in most cases being over 85%. Regarding the clustering rules, from our results we noticed that the grouping rules do not take into account the attributes such as water heating, fans, cooling, household equipment, indoor/outdoor lighting, but only heating and total consumption (the most important attributes). This may be due to the fact that we choose a small number of clusters comparing to the data set population. In conclusion, the lower the number of clusters, the more people in the group and less sensitive to changes in consumer behavior.

In order to divide the obtained profiles into smaller groups, we choose another clustering method in order to establish consumption patterns. So, we refined the K-mean results and we applied O-cluster method (Orthogonal partitioning clustering). This method is owned by Oracle Corporation [37] and uses a recursive data grouping algorithm through orthogonal data partitioning. On top of the previous 6 profiles determined by K-means, we build 10 sub-clusters, representing consumption patterns for each profile on hourly intervals. Analyzing the training rules and the weight of each consumption category in each cluster, we noticed that they have a varied composition, each cluster identifying a primary profile determined by the K-means method and one or more consumption patterns determined by the O-cluster method. For example, we considered the distribution of consumption patterns of a consumer within the P5 profile within 24 h. **Figure 2** shows profile P5 split into 10 patterns (T1, …, T10) for a detailed perspective on electricity consumption.

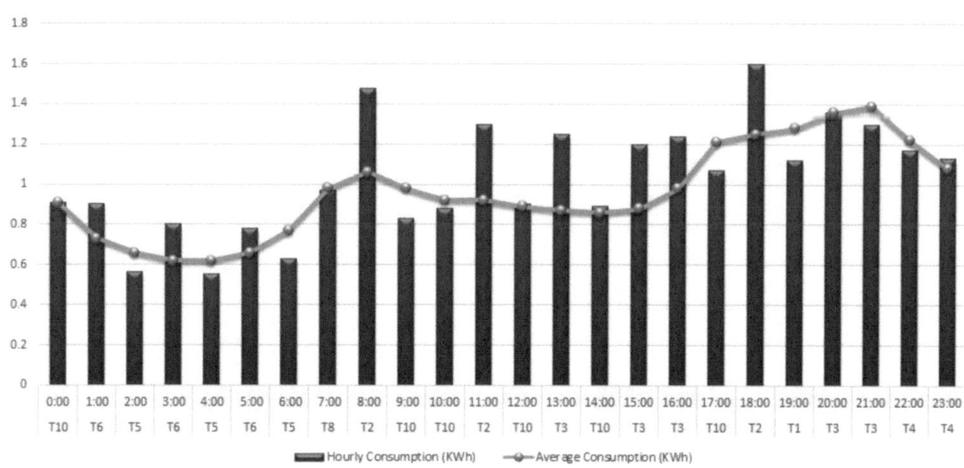

Figure 2. Profile P5 patterns with O-cluster.

The patterns build with O-cluster refine the clusters and gives a better understanding about consumption behavior regarding smaller groups of consumers and thus adjusting the ToUT for these groups. Also, the consumption patterns shape more accurately the consumer's dynamic behavior within 24 h, the profiles being in fact an approximation of the variation of hourly consumption. The deviations of the actual consumption compared to the average consumption of the profile are small, which again validates the clustering model.

As an option to clustering methods, we approached also a third method based on artificial neural networks (ANN). In Matlab R2015a, we imported data from Oracle Database from *LOAD_PROFILE_T* table and we organized input vectors as $x(t) \in R^n$, where n = 13 for each consumption type (heating, ventilation, indoor lighting, etc.) and t represents time interval (hours) between January 1, 2014 and December 31, 2014.

We developed a self-organizing maps (SOM) algorithm, setting the following parameters for the neural network:

- SOM architecture—2D with 2 × 3 neurons/layer (dimensions) = [2 3];
- number of steps for initially processing the input space (coverSteps) = 100;
- initial neighbor (initNeighbor) = 2;
- network topology (topologyFcn) = 'hextop' and
- distance between neurons (distanceFcn) = 'linkdist'.

The network is initialized with random values for each neuron. We used the *trainbu* training function that adjusts weights and bias after each iteration. We plotted the results and observed the distribution of the input set in **Figure 3**:

From the representation of the consumption curves corresponding to six clusters, it can be observed a clear delimitation between profiles P2 and P5. Also, a difference of approx. 30% of the evening consumption peak is observed between P6 and P1, P3, P4 (**Figure 4**).

Following the analysis of the obtained results, we noticed a correct and efficient grouping of the consumer profiles using the self-organizing neural networks.

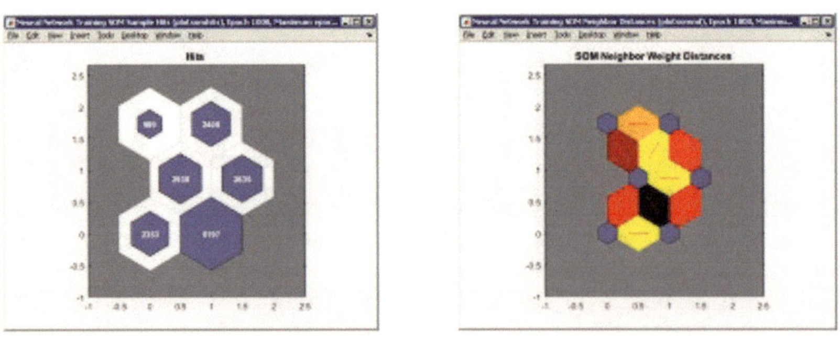

Figure 3. Distances among clusters distribution.

http://dx.doi.org/10.5772/intechopen.71239

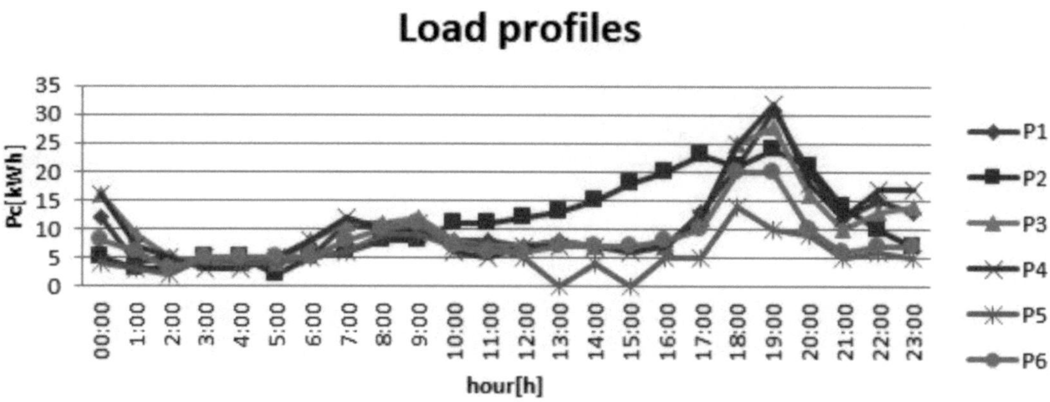

Figure 4. Profiles obtained with SOM.

A short comparison of the results obtained with the three analyzed methods is summarized in **Table 1**.

From the analysis, we can conclude that for the determination of dynamic consumption profiles, which surprising a series of consumption patterns, the optimal method is the clustering method, and for the determination of clearly delimited profiles the most efficient method is the use of self-organizing maps.

3.2. Consumption forecasting solution with ANN

Analyzing the consumption data set for 212 consumers during 4–6 weeks, a regular pattern is observed between working days or weekdays (Monday to Friday) and some differences in weekend or holidays. Therefore, for load forecasting hourly aggregated at grid operator or electricity supplier level for a typical day of the week, we can consider an autoregressive model. In this section, we approach and compare two methods for forecasting electricity consumption: statistics methods based on ARIMA and autoregressive artificial neural networks.

Autoregressive-moving-average (ARMA) models are suitable for stationary series, but most of the series are non-stationary, their mean and variance not being constant over time. The ARMA model was adapted for non-stationary time series that become stationary by differentiation,

Method	SVM	K-means and O-cluster	SOM
Number of profiles	6 profiles	6 profiles with 10 patterns	6 profiles
Sensitivity to consumption variations	High, small classes with lower confidence	Medium, variations are included in patterns	Medium, each group is clearly delimited
Detailed consumption information	High (sub-types of profiles)	High (by patterns of O-cluster)	Low
Overall performance	Medium	High	High

Table 1. Comparison of the profiles obtained by SVM, K-means and O-cluster and SOM.

the resultant models being called autoregressive integrated moving average ARIMA (p, d, q). The ARIMA model (p, d, q) consists of three parts: autoregressive (AR), where p represents the autoregression order, d represents the order of differentiation required for staging the series (I) and the moving average, q being the order of the moving average. Unlike autoregression, the moving average describes phenomena with certain irregularities. Moving average is described by the following equation:

$$Y_t = c + \theta_1 e_{t-1} + \theta_2 e_{t-2} + \ldots + \theta_p e_{t-p} + e_t \quad (1)$$

where Y_t is the consumption, c is a constant coefficient and the θ are the parameters of the moving average and e_t represents the time series error.

To evaluate the results of the analysis, we used the mean squared error (MSE) and also mean absolute percentage error (MAPE) to compare the accuracy of the forecast obtained in various variants of the ARIMA model.

Data from the *LOAD_PROFILE_T* table were imported into the SAS Guide Enterprise 7.1. Starting from the input data set, we applied the autoregressive integrated moving average models. In **Table 2**, we presented MAPE for the AR model first order, ARMA(1,1) and ARIMA(1,1,1).

Table 2 shows that MAPE is the lowest in the autoregressive model, the accuracy of the electricity consumption forecast being the best (about 93%). The accuracy of other forecasts is over 70%. In all analyses, the degree of correlation indicates an average or poor inverse dependence.

In addition to ARIMA models, we approached the autoregressive neural networks in Matlab. We built the *LOAD_PROFILE_HOURLY* virtual table based on the *LOAD_PROFILE_T* table and the *LOAD_PROFILE_SOM_6* table, which includes six consumption profiles previously determined by the self-organizing maps. For simulation we considered a single profile—P6 with the largest number of consumers (6197).

Due to the structure of the input data and the fact that there is an autoregressive component of electricity consumption during a typical week, we have built a nonlinear autoregressive neural network (*narnet*). We configured ANN parameters as follows:

- feedbackDelays—number of delays;
- hiddenSizes—number of neurons in the hidden layer;
- trainFcn—training function.

We considered 50 neurons in the hidden layer and a single input y(t)—the total consumption determined according to the formula:

Model	**MAPE [%]**
AR(1)	7.29
MA(1)	24.45
ARMA(1,1)	29.05
ARIMA(1,1,1)	24.97

Table 2. ARIMA models' results.

$$y(t) = f(y(t-1), \ldots, y(t-d)) \tag{2}$$

where d represents the number of records considered delays. For the first iteration of the model, we considered d = 5 and for the second iteration with better results d = 10. The architecture of the network is shown in **Figure 5**.

For the hidden layer, we used a bipolar sigmoid activation function and a linear activation function for the output layer. As for the training algorithm, Matlab provides the following algorithms: the Levenberg-Marquardt (LM) algorithm (*trainlm*), the Bayesian Regularization (BR) algorithm (*trainbr*) and the Scaled Conjugate Gradient (SCG) algorithm (*trainscg*). We developed the autoregressive neural network and compared the results obtained with the three training algorithms. The performance of the network is very good, the mean square error (MSE) being 0.0046 attained at epoch 936 for the BR training algorithm and the correlation coefficient R between the prediction and the actual value is 0.996 (**Figure 6**).

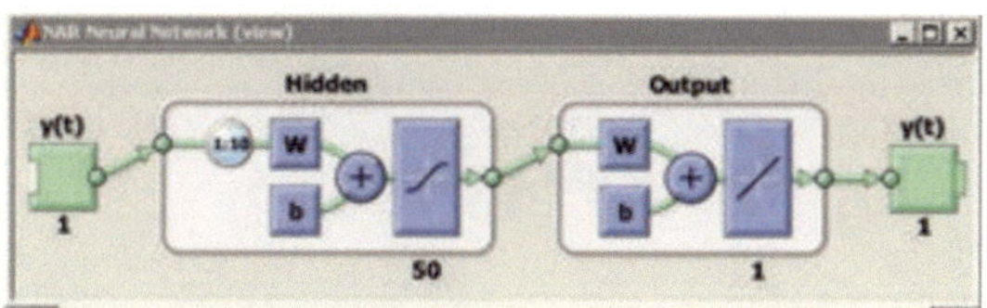

Figure 5. The architecture of the autoregressive neural network.

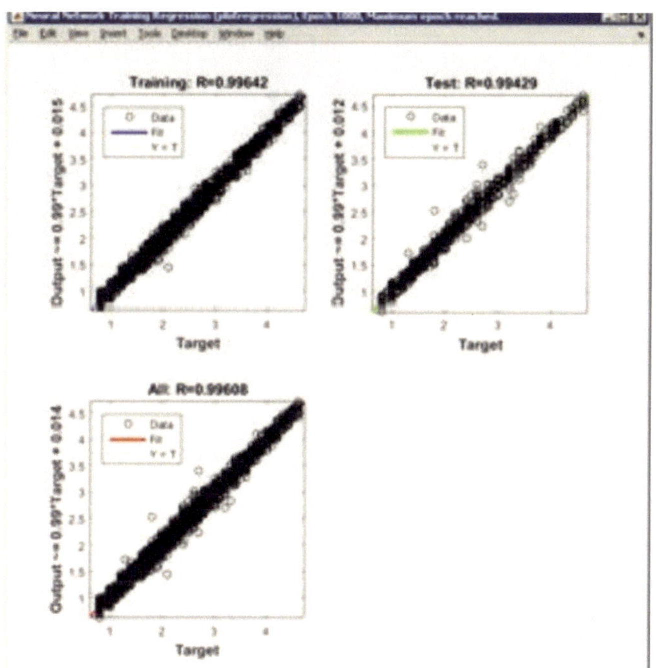

Figure 6. Results for R coefficient for BR algorithm.

From the error histogram (**Figure 7**), it can be observed that the errors are between −0.13 and +0.12, which can be considered an acceptable distribution.

We trained the network using the three algorithms (LM, RB and SCG), the best results being recorded using the Bayesian Regularization algorithm, although the Levenberg-Marquardt algorithm recorded good results with an increased performance in training.

In **Table 3**, the results obtained with autoregressive neural networks are compared with stochastic methods (ARMA, ARIMA and AR).

The accuracy of ANN algorithms is better (about 95%) compared to the accuracy of stochastic models. Also, the Levenberg-Marquardt and Bayesian regularization algorithms are also superior regarding the lowest MSE. The R coefficient and error distribution for neural network algorithms are better than AR, MA, ARMA and ARIMA models.

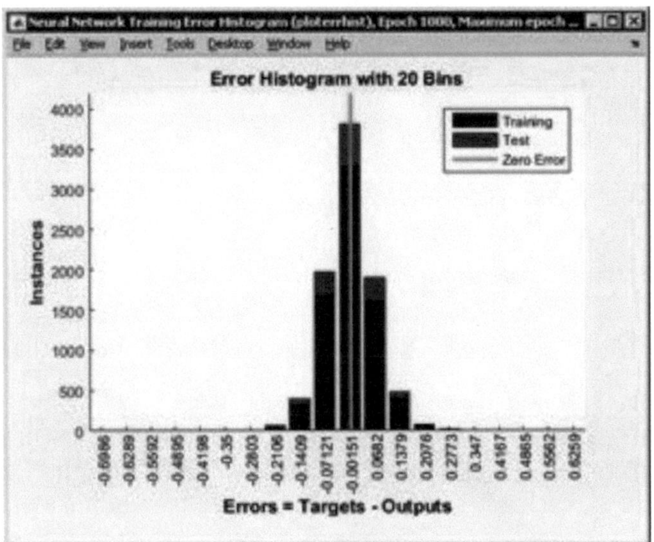

Figure 7. Errors histogram.

Performance/ method	LM	RB	GCS	AR	MA	ARMA	ARIMA
MSE	0.0064	0.0046	0.167	0.0091	0.0275	0.0316	0.0287
MAPE	4.26	4.21	6.21	7.29	24.45	29.05	24.97
Errors distribution	−0.3 to 0.12	−0.13 to 0.12	−0.18 to 0.22	−1.24 to 1.16	−1.36 to 1.44	−1.11 to 0.99	−1.14 to 0.66

Table 3. Autoregressive neural networks versus stochastic methods.

4. Forecasting the electricity generation

In this section we will analyze stochastic methods based on ARMA and ARIMA models compared with feed-forward artificial neural networks for small wind turbines and photovoltaic panels generation in case of short-term forecasting.

4.1. Photovoltaic panels generation forecasting

In order to forecast the electricity produced by photovoltaic panels, we used input data from one PV power plant of 7.6 kW located in Giurgiu City, Romania, installed at a prosumer side on his building facade. PV generates electricity for the consumption of the prosumer, and when the consumption is lower than the PV output, the electricity is sent to the grid. For our experiments, data was recorded at 10 minutes interval, from January to December 2015 and includes the following attributes: ambient temperature, humidity, solar radiation, wind direction, wind speed and PV output (generated power), having more than 50,000 records.

First, we applied the ARIMA models and we calculated the error distribution, MSE, MAPE and R correlation coefficient (**Table 4**).

From our observations, the correlation coefficient indicates a strong relationship between solar radiation and the PV power forecast. This close dependence showed that regression models are appropriate for this time series. The best results were obtained with ARIMA model where the accuracy is 96.5% that indicates that the model can be used in PV panels generation forecast.

We consider a second method based on feed-forward neural networks. Therefore, we trained and validated a set of ANN in Matlab using Levenberg-Marquardt (LM), Bayesian Regularization (BR) and Scaled Conjugate Gradient (SCG).

For ANN architecture, we analyzed various settings regarding the number of neurons per layer, number of hidden layers and training algorithms. After several tests, we chose the following architecture: the input layer with 5 neurons (ambient temperature, humidity, solar irradiation, wind direction and wind speed) 60 neurons on a hidden layer and a single output (the energy produced).

Models	MSE	R	MAPE [%]
AR(1)	0.006505	0.989558	3.716167
AR(2)	0.013464	0.978219	5.008174
MA(1)	0.094253	0.948153	59.89228
MA(2)	0.102734	0.923199	63.59939
ARMA(1,1)	0.006478	0.98958	3.803265
ARMA(2,2)	0.013297	0.978492	5.439663
ARIMA(1,1,1)	0.006372	0.989939	3.633844
ARIMA(2,1,2)	0.006435	0.989787	3.566530

Table 4. Stochastic models results in case of PV generation forecasting.

For training, validating and testing: we have allocated 70% of the records for the training process, 15% for the validation process and 15% for the testing process. For training errors, we used the mean square error (MSE) by applying an error normalization process by configuring the normalization parameter to "standard". Thus, output parameter values were standardized, ranging from [−1, 1].

Taking into account the seasonal variations of the influence factors in Romania, we built artificial neural networks based on the three algorithms for each month and we compared the results in **Table 5**.

Comparing the ARIMA and ANN results, we consider that the most efficient approach is to use ANN on monthly data sets, which leads to excellent accuracy for every analyzed month. We also found that in almost 70% of cases, BR algorithm has a better generalization than LM or SCG algorithms. In 30% of cases, the highest accuracy was obtained with LM algorithm.

4.2. Wind turbines generation forecasting

For forecasting simulations, we used recorded data for one small wind turbines (micro-generators) with a total power of 5 kW and another wind turbine of 10 kW, belonging to two consumers-producers (prosumers) located in two different areas of County of Tulcea, Romania. The two prosumers uses the energy produced by wind turbines for pumping water. For each turbine, the data set contains hourly data recorded from January 2013 to December 2014 with the following attributes: ambient temperature, wind direction, wind speed, atmospheric pressure and humidity. For each wind turbine, the measuring devices provides different values such as average, maximum and minimum wind speeds. Starting from the input data,

Period	MSE			Coefficient R		
	LM	BR	SCG	LM	BR	SCG
January	0.0818	0.0872	0.1132	0.9994	0.9993	0.9992
February	0.0387	0.0317	0.0679	0.9994	0.9993	0.9990
March	0.0617	0.0570	0.1174	0.9985	0.9987	0.9978
April	0.0201	0.0191	0.0319	0.9990	0.9989	0.9984
May	0.0539	0.0505	0.0640	0.9980	0.9981	0.9975
June	0.0705	0.0675	0.0865	0.9991	0.9992	0.9989
July	0.0439	0.0474	0.0577	0.9967	0.9969	0.9962
August	0.0870	0.0658	0.1019	0.9991	0.9993	0.9989
September	0.0348	0.0308	0.0512	0.9997	0.9997	0.9996
October	0.0601	0.0628	0.0877	0.9996	0.9997	0.9996
November	0.0369	0.0295	0.0650	0.9999	0.9999	0.9999
December	0.1002	0.0839	0.1091	0.9997	0.9997	0.9997

Table 5. Performance of ANN for solar generation forecasting in case of the PV panel.

we have developed several forecast scenarios by applying ARIMA models. The data recorded at the turbines' locations were analyzed using ARIMA Modeling and Forecasting time series in SAS Guide Enterprise 7.1. Applying the autoregressive model of the first AR (1), we obtained an extremely high average error (MAPE) of 86.5% for the wind turbine of 10 kW, which means that the accuracy of the model is only 13.5%. We tested also with first-order moving average (ARMA(1,1)) for both turbines and obtained the following results:

- for 5 kW turbine: AR(1) MA(1) model with MSE = 0.047 and MAPE = 93.6 and
- for 10 kW turbine: AR(1) MA(1) model with MSE =0.021 and MAPE = 50.7.

Although the moving average improves the results (especially for the 10 kW wind turbine) as a consequence of the wind's unpredictable nature, because of the very low accuracy, the ARIMA models cannot be used for forecasting wind turbines' generation.

As a consequence, we approached the feed-forward neural networks. We used the three algorithms available in Matlab for feed-forward ANN: Levenberg-Marquardt (LM), Bayesian Regularization (BR) and Scaled Conjugate Gradient (SCG).

Considering seasonal characteristics of wind generation in Romania, where during spring and autumn the weather is windy, we split the data set into four seasons and trained and tested a dedicated ANN for each data set.

The ANN architecture was as follows: 5 neurons for the input layer (wind speed, wind direction, atmospheric pressure, temperature and humidity), 50 neurons for the hidden layer and one output (generated energy). The data set was randomly divided as follows: for training 70% of the records, for testing 15% and the remaining 15% for validation. The results obtained from each network testing and validation are synthesized in **Table 6**, which shows that the LM algorithm obtained the best correlation coefficient R (0.96) for spring and autumn data sets.

The results are good for all algorithms, analyzing the errors distribution we observed that most of them are between −0.1 and +0.1, which can be considered acceptable for the 5 kW turbine.

We experiment the ANN training and validation for the second turbine of 10 kW registering similar results, so we can conclude that the networks are efficient for generation forecasting in case of small wind turbines.

Season	**MSE**			**Coefficient R**		
	LM	**BR**	**SCG**	**LM**	**BR**	**SCG**
Spring	0.0372	0.0387	0.0489	0.96	0.96	0.95
Summer	0.0578	0.0603	0.0610	0.95	0.95	0.94
Autumn	0.0553	0.0610	0.0845	0.96	0.94	0.93
Winter	0.0604	0.0623	0.0636	0.95	0.95	0.94

Table 6. Performance of ANN for wind generation forecasting in case of 5 kW turbine.

5. Informatics solutions for electricity consumption and generation

In order to increase the consumer awareness toward energy efficiency, new informatics solutions must be developed and offered by the electricity supplier. An informatics solution for demand management must fulfill the following requirements:

- describing and modeling consumer's electrical appliances;
- real time consumption monitoring;
- monitor and forecast generation in case of prosumers;
- scheduling electrical appliances;
- optimizing the consumption;
- offering advanced analysis for consumption and micro-generation and
- monitoring the costs of electricity consumption according to advanced tariffs systems.

Our proposed informatics solution is part of a research project and it is addressed mainly to household consumers, but it also contains a management consumption module for electricity supplier. The informatics solution contains the following modules: data acquisition from smart metering and smart appliances, models for consumption management and user-friendly interfaces.

5.1. Data management

Data acquisition module extract data from heterogeneous sources such as smart meters and appliances in *.csv* or *.raw* format, micro-generation equipment (small photovoltaic panels, wind turbines and electrical vehicles), manual reading done by electricity supplier' employees or via web interfaces. Data are loaded first into local databases (concentrators) via Wi-Fi or RF. From local concentrators, data are synchronized periodically and loaded into a central data stage for proper cleansing and validation. We also designed an extract, transform and load (ETL) patterns for different types of SM and also procedures for extracting data from heterogeneous appliances. After ETL process completes, data are loaded into a central relational database running Oracle Database 12c or MySQL for operational management and then into a data warehouse for advanced analytics.

5.2. Models

The models' layer integrates previously described methods for determine the consumers' profiles based on SOM, methods for short-term consumption forecasting based on autoregressive neural networks and in case of prosumers, short-term generation forecasting from small wind turbines and PV panels. Also the layer includes an optimization model based on two optimization functions as described in detailed in Ref. [35].

5.3. Interfaces

Our proposed solutions are integrated into a web-based application using business intelligence components that allow both electricity supplier and prosumers to interact with the proposed models. We set up a business intelligence server installed in a cloud computing using Software as a Service (SaaS) that offers access for prosumers/electricity supplier to services via internet connection for advanced analytics. The application includes the following consumers' facilities (**Figure 8**):

- monitoring their own consumption/generation;
- customize appliances and schedule their consumption;
- optimize consumption/generation based on advanced tariffs systems and
- real time electricity bills.

For electricity suppliers, the application will include an advanced analytics interface (**Figure 9**) that allow them to:

- set up advanced tariffs systems;
- analyze aggregate consumption;
- determine consumers' profiles and
- forecast electricity consumption.

The informatics solution is developed on a scalable platform, using Java with Application Development Framework and Oracle Database 12c that enables Cloud management and services. Thus, the solution can be adopted by the energy suppliers without expensive investments in infrastructure. Also, it offers an user-friendly interfaces that can be easily understand and managed by end-users on personal computers and mobile devices.

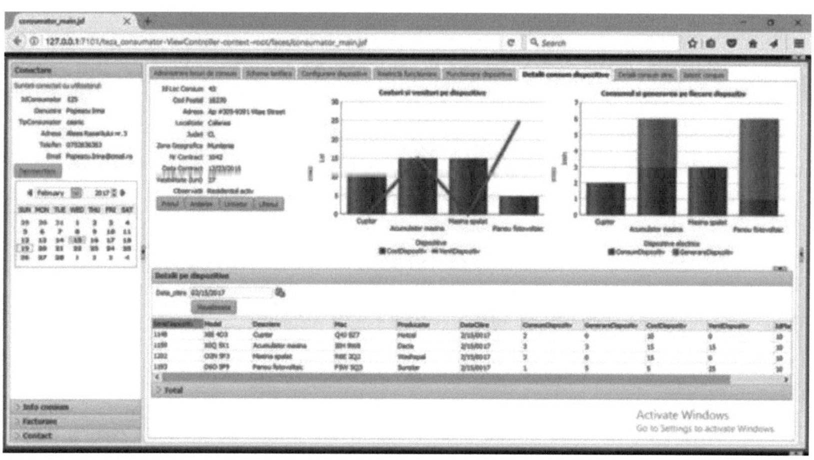

Figure 8. Monitoring consumption and generation in case of prosumers.

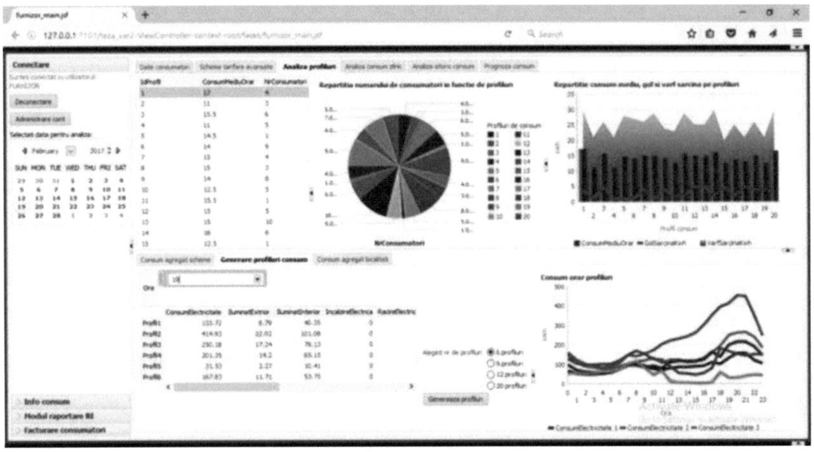

Figure 9. Determine consumers' profiles through web interfaces in case of electricity suppliers.

6. Conclusion and future work

Householders' profiles and patterns will allow electricity suppliers to understand consumers' behavior, set up more flexible and customized electricity prices to avoid peak consumption. One the other hand, prosumers will benefit from the forecasting solutions that will estimate wind and PV generation, therefore they will schedule their appliances according to electricity prices and their generation resources.

From our experiments, we consider artificial neural networks a good solution for determining the consumption profiles, for short-term load forecasting on each profile and also for short-term micro-generation forecasting.

A disadvantage of neural networks is that the most appropriate solution in a particular case is found by successive attempts on the number of hidden layers and the number of neurons on each layer, so in the case of another set of data from another geographic area with different characteristics regarding consumption or meteorological conditions that affect the wind or solar generation, it is necessary to re-configure the ANN parameters.

An advantage of artificial neural networks in case of consumption and generation forecasting is that they perform predictions with very good results in a very short time, which makes ANN particularly useful for real time short-term forecasting.

Acknowledgements

This paper presents some results of the research project: Informatics solutions for optimizing the operation of photovoltaic power plants (OPTIM-PV), project code: PN-III-P2-2.1-PTE-2016-0032, 4PTE/06/10/2016, PNIII - PTE 2016.

Author details

Adela Bâra* and Simona Vasilica Oprea

*Address all correspondence to: bara.adela@ie.ase.ro

The Bucharest University of Economic Studies, Romania

References

[1] European Economic and Social Committee. For coordinated European measures to prevent and combat energy poverty (own-initiative opinion) (2013/C/341/05). Official Journal of the European Union. 2013

[2] Directive 2012/27/EU of the European Parliament and of the Council (2012/27/EU). Official Journal of the European Union. 2012

[3] ANRE Decision 143/23.01.2013. The procedure for elaboration and application of specific consumption profiles in the license area of CEZ Distributie. 2013

[4] Chan A, Moreno JG, Hughes M. Electricity Price Signals and Demand Response [Internet]. 2014. Available from: https://www.gov.uk/government/collections/household-electricity-survey. [Accessed: 24-04-2017]

[5] Sanquista TF, Orrb H, Shuic B, Bittnerd AC. Lifestyle factors in U.S. residential electricity consumption. Energy Policy. 2012;**42**:354-364

[6] Hayn M, Bertsch V, Fichtner W. Electricity load profiles in Europe: The importance of household segmentation. Energy Research & Social Science. 2014;**3**:30-45

[7] Ardakanian O, Koochakzadeh N, Singh RP. Computing electricity consumption profiles from household smart meter data. In: 3rd Workshop on Energy Data Management (EnDM 2014); 28 March 2014; Athens, Greece; 2014

[8] Oprea SV, Bâra A. Electricity load profile calculation using self-organizing maps. In: 20th International Conference on System Theory, Control and Computing (ICSTCC), (Joint conference SINTES 20, SACCS 16, SIMSIS 20); 13-15 October 2016; Sinaia, Romania; 2016

[9] ELEXON. Load Profiles and their use in Electricity Settlement, Guidance [Internet]. 2013. Available from: https://www.elexon.co.uk/wp-content/uploads/2013/11/load_profiles_v2.0_cgi.pdf [Accessed: 2017]

[10] Ardakanian O, Koochakzadeh N, Singh RP, Golab L, Keshav S. Computing electricity consumption profiles from household smart meter data. In: Workshop Proceedings of the EDBT/ICDT 2014 Joint Conference. Greece: Athens. p. 2014

[11] Lo KL, Zakaria Z, Sohod MH. Determination of consumers' load profiles based on two-stage fuzzy C-means. In: Proceedings of the 5th WSEAS Int. Conf. on Power Systems and Electromagnetic Compatibility; 2005; Greece. 2005

[12] Yang HT, Huang CM, Huang CL. Identification of ARMAX model for short term load forecasting: An evolutionary programming approach. IEEE Transactions on Power Apparatus and Systems. 1996;**11**(1):403-408

[13] Haidda T, Muto S. Regression based peak load forecasting using a transformation technique. IEEE Transactions on Power Apparatus and Systems. 1994;**9**(4):1788-1794

[14] Charytoniuk W, Chen MS, Van Olinda P. Nonparametric regression based short-term load forecasting. IEEE Transactions on Power Apparatus and Systems. 1998;**13**(3):725-730

[15] Ko CN, Lee CM. Short-term load forecasting using SVR (support vector regression)-based radial basis function neural network with dual extended Kalman filter. Energy. 2013;**49**:413-422

[16] Sevlian R, Rajagopal R. Short Term Electricity Load Forecasting on Varying Levels of Aggregation [Internet]. 2014. Available from: https://arxiv.org/abs/1404.0058 [Accessed: 2017]

[17] Aung Z, Toukhy M, Williams JR, Sanchez A, Herrero S. Towards accurate electricity load forecasting in smart grids. In: The Fourth International Conference on Advances in Databases, Knowledge and Data Applications; 2012

[18] Engle RF, Mustafa C, Rice J. Modeling peak electricity demand. Journal of Forecasting. 1992;**11**:241-251

[19] Hyde O, Hodnett PF. An adaptable automated procedure for short-term electricity load forecasting. IEEE Transactions on Power Systems. 1997;**12**:84-93

[20] Ruzic S, Vuckovic A, Nikolic N. Weather sensitive method for short-term load forecasting in electric power utility of Serbia. IEEE Transactions on Power Systems. 2003;**18**:1581-1586

[21] Haida T, Muto S. Regression based peak load forecasting using a transformation technique. IEEE Transactions on Power Systems. 1994;**9**:1788-1794

[22] Charytoniuk W, Chen MS, Van Olinda P. Nonparametric regression based short-term load forecasting. IEEE Transactions on Power Systems. 1998;**13**:725-730

[23] Mohamed Z, Bodger PS. Forecasting Electricity Consumption: A Comparison of Models for New Zealand [Internet]. Available from: http://ir.canterbury.ac.nz/bitstream/handle/10092/821/12593635_C47.pdf?sequence=1 [Accessed: 2017]

[24] Chujai P, Kerdprasop N, Kerdprasop K. Time series analysis of household electric consumption with ARIMA and ARMA models. In: Proceedings of the International MultiConference of Engineers and Computer Scientists; 13–15 March 2013; Hong Kong; 2013

[25] Costa A, Crespo A, Navarro J, Lizcano G, Madsen H, Feitosa E. A review on the young history of the wind power short-term prediction. Renewable and Sustainable Energy Reviews. 2008;**12**(6):1725-1744

[26] Yu Chen KJ. Short-term wind speed prediction using an unscented Kalman filter based state-space support vector regression approach. Applied Energy. 2014;**113**:690-705

[27] Chitsaz H, Amjady N, Zareipour H. Wind power forecast using wavelet neural network trained by improved clonal selection algorithm. Energy Conversion and Management. 2015;**89**:588-598

[28] Blonbou R. Very short-term wind power forecasting with neural networks and adaptive Bayesian learning. Renewable Energy. 2011;**36**(3):1118-1124

[29] Yeh WC, Yeh YM, Chang PC, Ke YC, Chung V. Forecasting wind power in the Mai Liao Wind Farm based on the multi-layer perceptron artificial neural network model with improved simplified swarm optimization. International Journal of Electrical Power & Energy Systems. 2014;**55**:741-748

[30] Ren C, An N, Wang J, Li L, Hu B, Shang D. Optimal parameters selection for BP neural network based on particle swarm optimization: A case study of wind speed forecasting. Knowledge-Based Systems. 2014;**56**:226-239

[31] Huang R, Huang T, Gadh R, Li N. Solar generation prediction using the ARMA model in a laboratory-level micro-grid. In: IEEE Third International Conference on Smart Grid Communications (SmartGridComm); 5–9 November 2012. Taiwan: Tainan. p. 2012

[32] Zhi C, Lei W, Yong F. Real-time price-based demand response management for residential appliances via stochastic optimization and robust optimization. IEEE Transaction om Smart Grid. 2012;**3**:1949-3053

[33] Yang X, Guo S, Yang HT.The establishment of energy consumption optimization model based on genetic algorithm. In: IEEE Int. Conf. on Automation and Logistics; 1–3 September 2008; Chindao, China. New York, NY, USA: IEEE. 1426-1431

[34] Omari M, Abdelkarim H, Salem B. Optimization of energy consumption based on genetic algorithms optimization and fuzzy classification. In: 2nd World Symposium on Web Applications and Networking; 21-23 March 2015; Sousse, Tunisia. New York, NY, USA. IEEE. 2015

[35] Oprea S, Bara A, Cebeci ME, Tör OB. Promoting peak shaving while minimizing electricity consumption payment for residential consumers by using storage devices. Turkish Journal of Electrical Engineering & Computer Sciences. 2017;**25**(5):3725-3737. DOI: 10.3906/elk-1606-152

[36] Capterra. Top Utility Billing Software Products [Internet]. Available from: http://www.capterra.com/utility-billing-software [Accessed: 24-04-2017]

[37] Campos MM, Milenova BL. O-cluster: Scalable Clustering of Large High Dimensional Data Sets. Oracle Data Mining Technologies. Oracle Corporation; 2002

Chapter 8

Advanced Process Control

Nasser Mohamed Ramli

Additional information is available at the end of the chapter

http://dx.doi.org/10.5772/intechopen.70704

Abstract

The debutanizer column is an important unit operation in petroleum refining industries. The top product is liquefied petroleum gas and the bottom product is light naphtha. This system is difficult to handle. This is because due to its non-linear behavior, multivariable interaction and existence of numerous constraints on its manipulated variable. Neural network techniques have been increasingly used for a wide variety of applications. In this book, equation-based multi-input multi-output (MIMO) neural network has been proposed for multivariable control strategy to control the top and bottom temperatures of the column. The manipulated variables for column are reflux and reboiler flow rates, respectively. This neural network model are based on multivariable equation, instead of the normal black box structure. It has the advantage of being robust in nature while being easier to interpret in terms of its input-output variables. It has been employed for set point changes and disturbance changes. The results show that the neural network equation-based model for direct inverse and internal model approach performs better than the conventional proportional, integral and derivative (PID) controller.

Keywords: distillation column, artificial neural network, equation-based method, multivariable process control

1. Introduction

Controlling two compositions require more complex instrumentation. The top and bottom composition loops interact and dynamic stability problems can arise. Holding heat input or reflux constant simplifies the control system and avoid interaction problem. Composition of the column are based on online measurement performance variable directly related to composition. The common measurement is temperature. However, temperature-composition relationship is influenced by column pressure control. If temperature is used as a control variable, the sensing element is usually not placed directly in the product stream. Often, product streams are relatively pure so that boiling point is relatively insensitive to small changes in concentration. Instead of investigating the steady state column temperature profile, the sensing element should be located at the tray from the end, at a point where the gradient is large. At this point, a fixed change in product composition causes a larger temperature change. Controlling the temperature gives tight control on product composition despite wide variations in other factors such as internal reflux ratio [1]. The variables that need to be controlled are the top and bottom temperatures and the variables that need to be estimated is top and bottom compositions. Application of composition control to both ends of a debutanizer column has been considered with generally little success. The difficulty results because two individual control loops interact. The top loop controls the heavy key in the overhead stream and the bottom loop controls the light key in the bottom stream. Some disturbances cause the light key concentration in the bottom stream to increase. The lower loop acts to reduce the concentration by adding heat. This action lowers the light key concentration sends more heavy key up the column. If both loops are tuned tightly, the column becomes unstable, and the system can be stable by detuning one loop. Processes with only one output being controlled by a single manipulated variable are classified as single-input single-output (SISO) system. Many processes do not conform to such a simple control configuration. In the process industries, any unit operation cannot do so with only a single loop. In fact each unit operation requires control over at least two variables, product rate and product quality. Systems with more than one control loop are known as multi-input multi-output (MIMO) or multivariable control system. There will therefore be a composition control loop and temperature control loop. Minimization of energy usage is achievable if the compositions of both the top and bottom product streams are controlled to their design values, which are called dual composition control [1]. A common scheme to overcome this problem is to use reflux flow to control top product composition while the heat input is used to control bottom product composition. Loop interaction may also arise as a consequence of process design, typically the use of recycle streams for heat recovery purposes. Changes in the feed temperature will in turn influence bottom product composition. It is clear that interaction exists between the composition and pre heat control loops. The simple approach in dealing with loop interactions is by the design of multivariable control strategies. This is to eliminate interactions between control loops [1]. The outline in the book for this chapter is the multivariable controller used consists of neural network equation based for the forward model and inverse model. The multivariable control system is to control the top and bottom temperature and estimating the top and bottom composition. The use of the neural network-based controller compared to conventional PID controllers is because all the process variables surrounding the debutanizer column are non-linear in nature and PID could not handle non-linearities.

The use of neural network models and controllers from available literature involve the use of black box models. This method is non-versatile and non-robust in nature and difficult to handle due to the relationship between the inputs and outputs of the system, which are important for industry. In this book, the main contribution and novelty, the proposed is to use an equation based inverse neural network models in a multi-input multi-output (MIMO) system to control the top and bottom temperature of the column simultaneously. The control structure is by using the direct inverse control (DIC) and internal model control (IMC) approach. Neural network equation-based models have also been used for the column to estimate the compositions as estimator. The other contribution of this book is that it utilizes a mixture of online close loop and open loop data that are available from industry for training the neural network models.

2. Application of artificial neural network

Artificial neural network (ANN) is a reliable and popular tool when dealing with problems involving prediction of variables in engineering at the present age. Details of the ANN application can be found in literature [2–7]. The main advantage of ANN is in its ability to estimate an arbitrary function mechanism that learns from data that is input to the network. However, it is not an easy step to apply neural network for control purposes. Good understanding of the underlying theory is essential and important. The first important criteria are the model selection which depends on the data representation and its application. A significant number of experiments are required for selecting and tuning an algorithm for training. The other criteria that are involve for training is robustness analysis. For the model, cost function and learning algorithm are important to be selected appropriately, so that the ANN final result can be robust. Neural network has been extensively used for a wide of chemical engineering applications which involve identification, control and prediction. Work has been done of various applications using neural network for control simulation and online implementation for chemical processes can be seen in literature [2].

As for today feed forward neural network (FANN) architecture is the widely used neural network architecture. It has a global approximation model for a multi-input multi-output function for fitting a low-order polynomial through a set of data. Various collection of different learning and network algorithms are available [8, 9] but the network is important to be selected as the basic building block. The formula describing the networks in mathematical form takes the following equation

$$y = F_i\left[\sum_{j=1}^{n_k} W_{i,j}.f_j\left(\sum_{l=1}^{n_\varphi} w_{j,l}\varphi_l + w_{j.0}\right) + W_{i.0}\right] \tag{1}$$

where φ is the external input, n_φ is the number of input in an input layer, n_k is the number of hidden neurons in a hidden layer, W and w are the weights. The activation functions for hidden layer and output layer are f and F, respectively.

In order to model the system dynamically using recurrent neural network (ELMAN) or neural network with ARX, in this book neural network with non-linear autoregressive network with exogenous inputs (NARX) structure which are used to model the dynamic system based on time-series data gives optimum result. The equations describing the NARX structure can be expressed as follows

$$Y = f(Y_1, Y_2, \ldots, Y_n,\ U_1, U_2, \ldots, U_m) \tag{2}$$

where $Y = [y_1(k+1)\ y_2(k+1)]^T$; $Y_1 = [y_1(k), y_1(k-1), \ldots, y_1(k-ny_1)]$, … , $Y_n = [y_n(k), y_n(k-1), \ldots, y_n(k-ny_n)]$; $U_1 = [u_1(k), u_1(k-1), \ldots, u_1(k-nu_1)]$, … , $U_m = [u_m(k), u_m(k-1), \ldots, u_m(k-nu_m)]$ and

m is number of input variables n is number of output variables and n_y and n_u are the history length for output variables and input variables, respectively. The model was trained, validated and test for different number of neurons together with the n_y and n_u values. The time lags in the input and manipulated variables, that is, n_y and n_u are chosen based on trial and error and the values are give to be n_y = 3 and n_u = 2, respectively, on the combination that gives the lowest RMSE values with the least lag time. It is observed that the lowest RMSE for the top and bottom temperature during training, validation and test occurs at same configuration. This is also based on experience from various literatures on dynamic modeling using NN-based models for non-linear chemical processes [10, 11].

However, the applications used previously have neural network utilized as a black box model, which has its own disadvantages. This limitation using black box model is due to robustness. In this book, the proper choice of the activation function and the neural network model can be represented by equation in form of algebraic. The equation used to approximate the output from the neural network model can estimate for a two layer network as follows

$$y = f^2\left(LW^{2,1}f^1\left(IW^{1,1}p + b^1\right) + b^2\right) \tag{3}$$

where $IW^{1,1}$ = weight at layer 1; b^1 = bias value at layer 1; $LW^{2,1}$ = weight at layer 2 (hidden layer); b^2 = bias value at layer 2; p = inputs to the neural network; y = outputs from the neural network; f = activation function at layer i.

By multiplying the matrix input layer and the biases value with the matrix hidden layer, the f^1 and f^2 are simplified. By choosing the activation function to be linear, the equation can be simplified in the form of

$$y = \begin{bmatrix} y_1 \\ y_2 \end{bmatrix} = \left[LW^{2,1}\left[IW^{1,1}p + b^1\right] + b^2\right] \tag{4}$$

where the matrix definition $LW^{2,1}$, $IW^{1,1}$, b^1 and $b^2$are given as

$IW^{1,1}$ = weight at layer 1 (input layer); b^1 = bias value at layer 1; $LW^{2,1}$ = weight at layer 2 (hidden layer); b^2 = layer 2 bias value.

These representations can also be used in this book to estimate the top and bottom compositions. While the multivariable controllers are used to control the top and bottom temperatures simultaneously that will be shown in the next sections.

3. Control strategies neural network

There are two types of control strategies which are direct inverse control (DIC) and internal model control (IMC) methods are to be implemented for neural networks, which is the inverse model-based control schemes. These methods are described briefly in **Figures 1** and **2**.

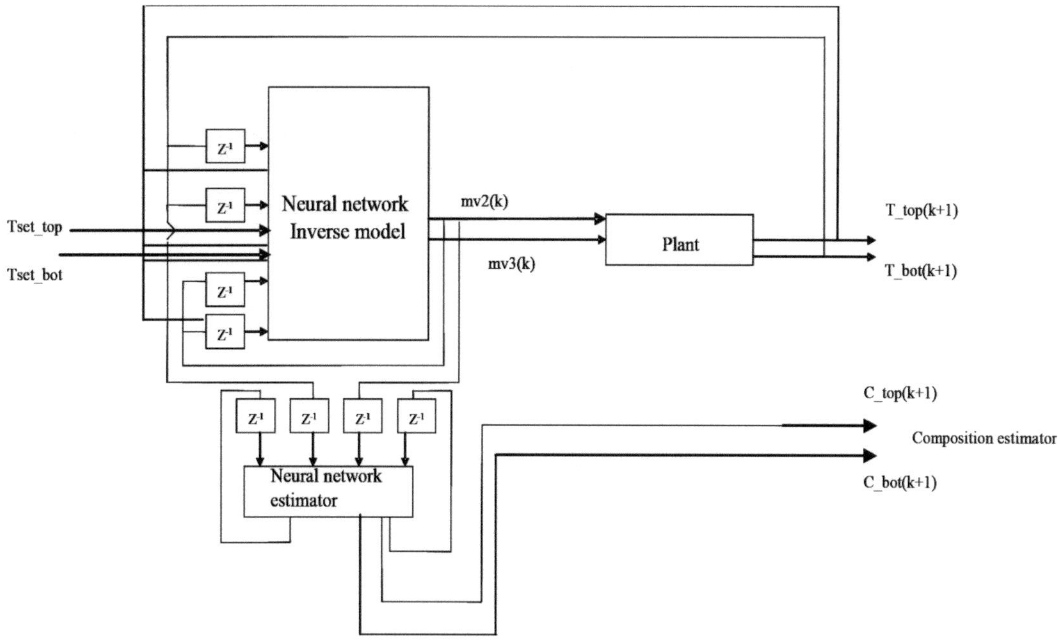

Figure 1. Control loop of neural network-based direct inverse model control (DIC).

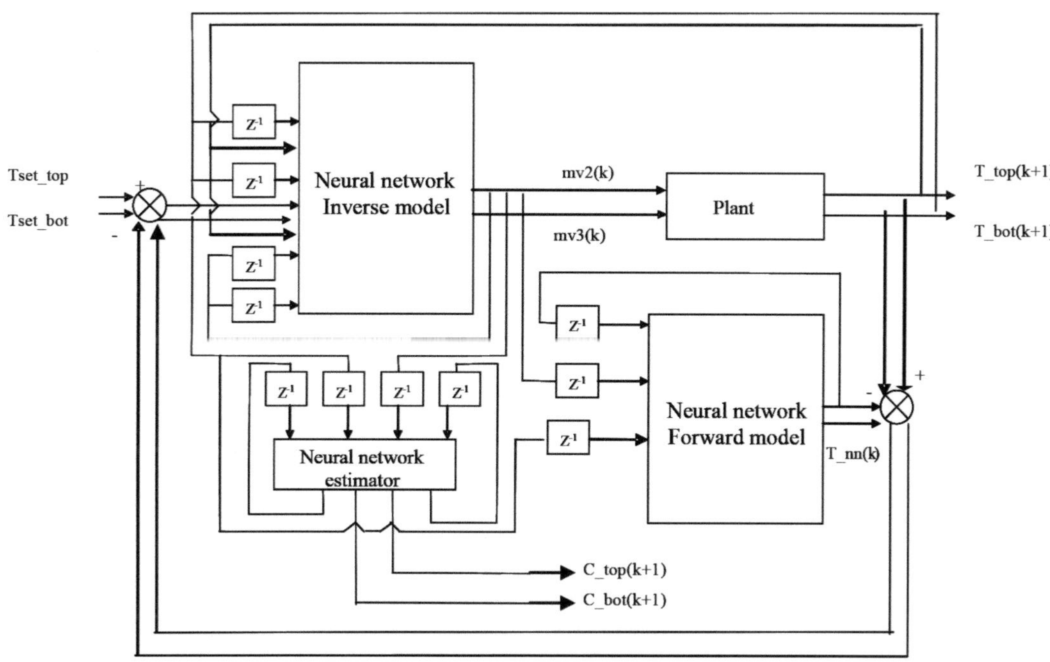

Figure 2. Control loop of neural network-based internal model controller (IMC).

3.1. Method 1: direct inverse control (DIC)

This control strategy which is placed in series with neural network inverse models acts as a controllers. In this scheme, the outputs will predict the system input, while the desired set point acts as the output which is then fed to the network with the past plant inputs. In this case, the appropriate control parameter for the desired target will be predicted based on its input. Neural networks acting as the controller has to learn to supply at its input. As shown in **Figure 1**, the inverse model is then utilized in the control strategy by cascading it with the controlled system or plant. This method depends on the accuracy of the inverse model. The controlled variables used in this method are the top and bottom temperatures. The manipulated variables are the reflux and reboiler flow rate for the DIC method.

3.2. Method 2: internal model control (IMC)

Neural network-based IMC method highlighted in this book are presented in both inverse and forward model control scheme. The dynamic forward model of the process represents it is placed in parallel within the system. This is important to cater for mismatches of the model during implementation [12]. On the other hand, the inverse model could also be used as a controller. In this scheme, the error between the plant output and the neural network forward model is then subtracted from the set point before being fed into the inverse model, as shown in **Figure 2**. With this detection feature, the internal model-based controller can be used to move forward the controlled parameter to the desired set point even when disturbances and noise are present. The optimum performance for controller performance is the IMC method. The error produced by the process model could be minimized and compensated by the error produced by the neural network forward process model [12]. The controlled and manipulated variables used in the IMC method are similar to the DIC method.

3.3. Neural networks models

Before applying the inverse model neural network control strategies for the debutanizer column, it is crucial to discuss the development and configuration of the forward and inverse models. Using neural network architecture and equation-based neural network are important fundamentals to these model-based control strategies as necessary.

3.3.1. Forward models

The procedure of training a neural network to represent the forward dynamics of a column is by predicting the outputs using the required inputs. This method is called forward modeling. The straightforward and good approach is to augment the network inputs data in real forms, from the model and system being identified [13, 14]. Other fundamental variables under state can also be fed into the network and considered as inputs. In this method, the network is fed with the present input, past inputs as well as the past outputs to predict the desired output. The neural network model is placed in parallel with the system. The error between the system output and network output are the prediction error which is used as the training signal for the network. The forward models that have been mentioned previously are used to determine the inverse model. The forward model which is inversed to get the inverse model is then changed to the equation based. The equation-based method has been used to replace the black box

http://dx.doi.org/10.5772/intechopen.70704

model neural network for IMC and DIC method. The inverse models as controllers are used in the IMC and DIC methods. The composition forward models are used as a neural network estimator to predict the top and bottom compositions.

The forward model for temperature is as follows

In this case, p is the input to the neural network temperature given by the vector

$$\begin{array}{l}[mv1(k)\ mv1(k-1)\ mv2(k)\ mv2(k-1)\ mv3(k)\\ mv3(k-1)\ f(k)\ f(k-1)\ T_{top}(k)\ T_{top}(k-1)\ T_{bot}(k)\ T_{bot}(k-1)]^{T}\end{array} \tag{5}$$

After pruning the neural network structure (simplifying the weights and biases values), p is given as matrix vector are defined in Eq. (6)

$$y=\begin{bmatrix}T_1\\T_2\end{bmatrix}=\begin{bmatrix}-0.16 & -0.14 & 0.04 & -0.002 & -0.094 & -0.95 & 1.03 & -0.61 & -0.71 & 0.81 & 0.16 & -0.049\\ 0.42 & 0.07 & 0.04 & 0.20 & -0.30 & -0.19 & 0.12 & -0.28 & 0.35 & -0.29 & -0.48 & 0.168\end{bmatrix}p+\begin{bmatrix}-0.28\\-0.22\end{bmatrix} \tag{6}$$

T_1 and T_2 is the output neural network top and bottom temperature prediction.

3.3.2. Neural network estimator

The forward model for neural network for composition is composition n-butane used for control system IMC method is as follows

In this case, p is the input to the neural network composition given by the vector

$$\left[mv2(k)\ mv2(k-1)\ mv3(k)\ mv3(k-1)\ f(k)\ f(k-1)\ p_{top}(k)\ p_{top}(k-1)\ p_{bot}(k)\ p_{bot}(k-1)\right]^{T} \tag{7}$$

After pruning the neural network structure (simplifying the weights and biases values), Eq. (7) can further be simplified to give the composition Eq. (8)

$$\begin{bmatrix}y1\\y2\end{bmatrix}=\begin{bmatrix}-0.26 & 0.15 & 0.37 & 0.23 & 0.38 & 0.40 & -0.50 & 0.97 & 0.12 & -0.31\\ -0.09 & 0.006 & 0.31 & -0.10 & 0.02 & 0.02 & -0.42 & -0.12 & 0.36 & -0.085\end{bmatrix}p+\begin{bmatrix}-0.28\\-0.21\end{bmatrix} \tag{8}$$

y_1 and y_2 is the output neural network bottom and top composition predictions.

3.3.3. Models for inverse

Inverse models are basically the structure by representing the inverse of the network dynamics after the completion of training. The methods for inverse models are achieved by switching the required outputs and inputs. The important manipulated variable that is used for switching the inputs of the neural net is the manipulated variable reboiler and reflux. The outputs predicted are the future predictions of top and bottom temperatures are switched with the manipulated variables. The sequence of the inputs of the network needs to be maintained. The training procedure outlined in this book is called inversed modeling. $y(k+1)$ is the required set point. The network representation of the inverse is finally given below

$$u(k) = f^{-1}\left[y_p(k+1), y_p(k), y_p(k-1), u(k), u(k-1)\right] \tag{9}$$

where f^{-1} represents the inverse map of the forward model.

In this case the manipulated variable reboiler and reflux flow rate are the output variable which are used in inverse model. The one-step ahead prediction of the control output, $mv2$ (k) and $mv3$ (k) is performed inconformity with that of the forward model. The one-step ahead control action application in the control strategies involving the neural network-based strategies.

The training and validation data set are predicted for inverse model for the networks are similar to that used for forward modeling. Nevertheless, inverse model will have different input and output configuration.

The inverse model for temperature is as follows

In this case, p is the input to the neural network inverse temperature given by the vector

$$\begin{array}{l}\left[mv1(k)\ mv1(k-1)\ mv2(k-1)\ mv3(k-1)\ f(k)\ f(k-1)\ T_{top}(k+1)\ T_{top}(k)T_{top}(k-1)\right. \\ \left. T_{bot}(k+1)\ T_{bot}(k)\ T_{bot}(k-1)\right]^T\end{array} \tag{10}$$

After simplifying the weights and biases values by pruning the neural network structure Eq. (10) can further be simplified in order to give the inverse temperature below in a form of equation

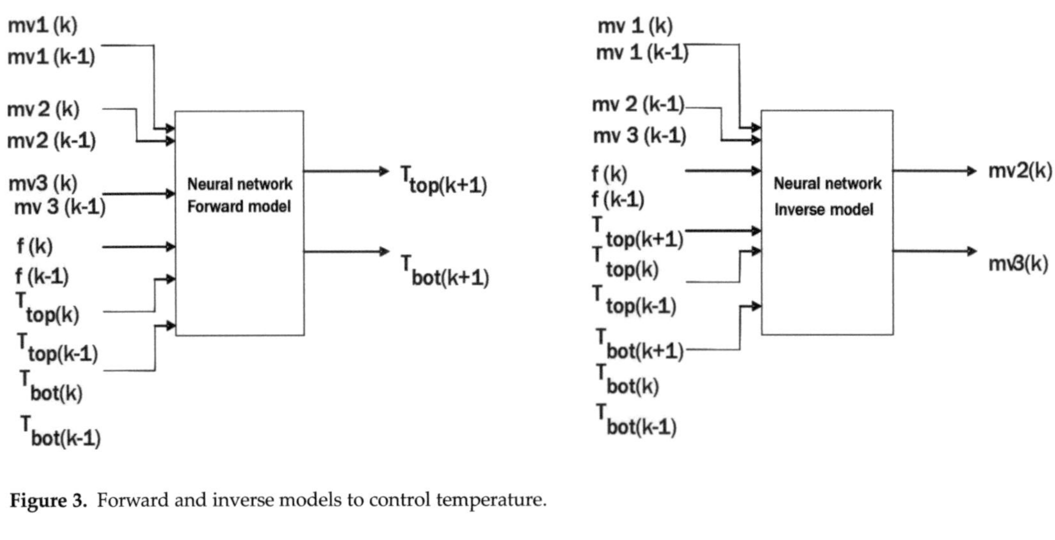

Figure 3. Forward and inverse models to control temperature.

$$\begin{bmatrix} mv2(k) \\ mv3(k) \end{bmatrix} = \begin{bmatrix} -0.16\ 0.14\ 0.039\ -0.004\ -0.09\ -0.95\ 1.03\ -0.61\ -0.72\ 0.81\ 0.17\ -0.05 \\ 0.42\ 0.077\ 0.039\ 0.20\ -0.30\ -0.19\ 0.13\ -0.27\ 0.34\ -0.28\ -0.47\ 0.16 \end{bmatrix} p + \begin{bmatrix} -0.79 \\ -0.008 \end{bmatrix} \quad (11)$$

$mv2(k)$ and $mv3(k)$ is the manipulated variable reflux and reboiler flow rate, respectively. The equation is implemented in SIMULINK in MATLAB by having the system with more than one control loop which are multi-input and multi-output (MIMO) or multivariable control. **Figure 3** shows the forward and inverse model to control temperature.

4. Neural network development

The control strategies used in this work are DIC and IMC method. In order to develop and analyze the controller performance for the debutanizer column, there are two criteria for advanced process control which are the set point changes and disturbances changes applied to the column. The set point changes is the step increases for the temperature and the disturbances changes is by introducing a disturbance of the column feed temperature. The performance of the composition are used based on using a neural network estimator.

4.1. Set point changes

First the top temperature is increased from 30 to 58°C. The bottom temperature is increased from 60 to 137°C. The starting point for the top temperature is 30°C and for bottom temperature is 60°C. This is because the starting point temperature mentioned here is based on the experience of the engineers to maintain and control that particular temperature. **Figures 4** and **5** show the fluctuation of the top and bottom temperature due to set point changes. There are three types of control strategies implemented for the control strategies which are the IMC, DIC and PID controller. It can be seen that IMC and DIC show similar trends with small error, no overshoot and fast settling time and straight goes to the set point. The settling time for top and bottom temperatures fluctuation is at 200 min. The IMC and DIC method gives the least fluctuations for the set point changes. The fluctuations during step point changes for the PID controller does not give good results because it has large overshoot and small decay ratio. The settling time for PID also shows large value compared to the IMC and DIC methods. The PID controller also produces some offset when there are changes made for set point changes. This applies to the top and bottom temperatures, respectively. **Table 1** shows the PID tuning for the column. **Table 2** shows the performance of the controller to control the top and bottom temperature. The results indicate that IMC equation gives the optimum performance as the Integral absolute error (IAE), Integral square error (ISE) and Integral time weighted error (ITAE) values is the smallest compared to the result of the controller. **Figures 6** and **7** show the fluctuation of the manipulated variables to control temperature. The neural network would be able to predict the manipulated variable for reboiler and reflux accurately compared to PID

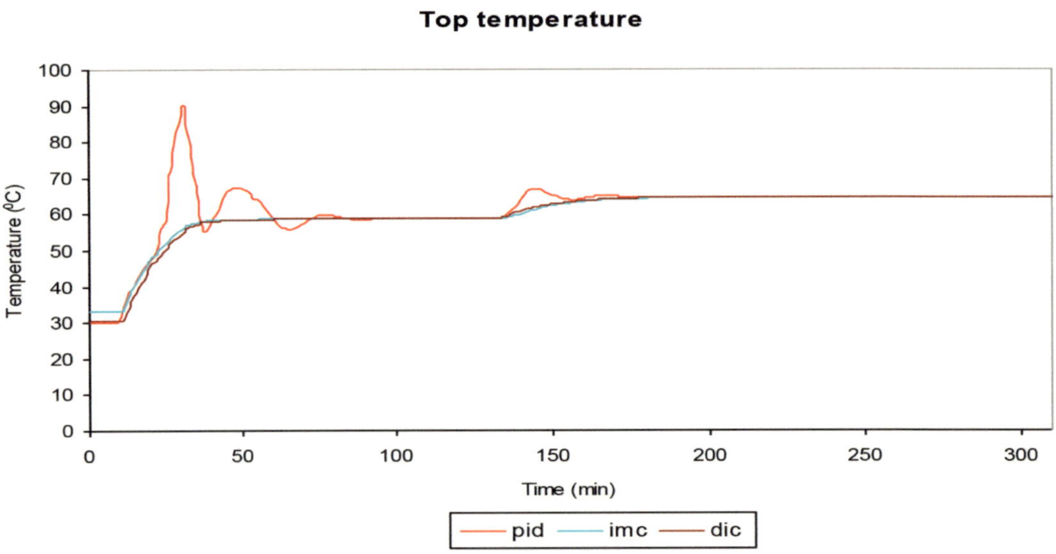

Figure 4. Set point top temperature.

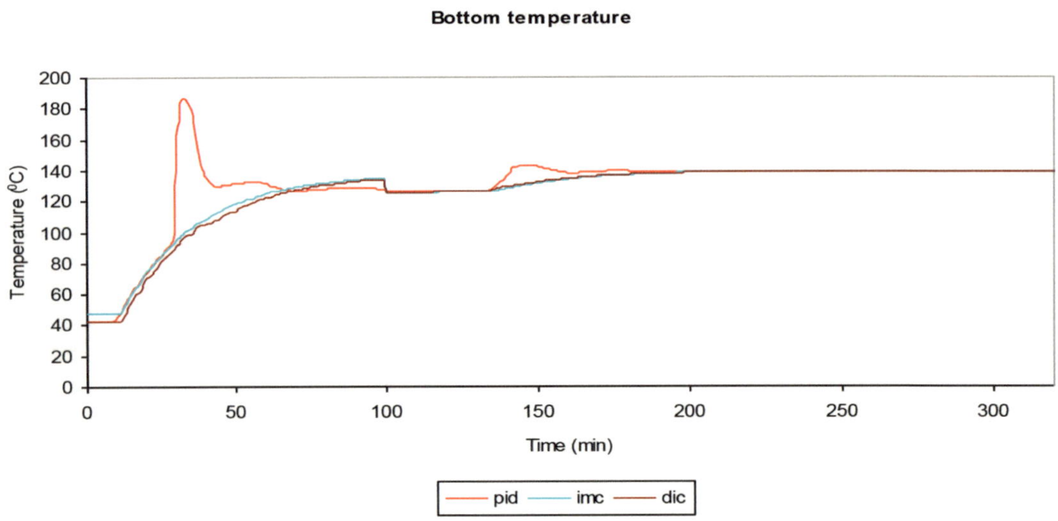

Figure 5. Set point bottom temperature.

Parameter	K_c	T_i	T_d
Top temperature	0.71	1.41	20
Bottom temperature	1.76	3.25	15
Top composition	137.32	3.26	10
Bottom compositon	87.36	3.26	5

Table 1. PID tuning.

http://dx.doi.org/10.5772/intechopen.70704

	IMC eq	DIC eq	PID
IAE top	830.76	912.78	1219.70
IAE bottom	3809	4289	4666
ISE top	2.10E+02	2.23E+02	2.69E+02
ISE bottom	1.21E+02	2.67E+02	3.06E+02
ITAE top	4.25E+02	4.48E+02	1.44E+03
ITAE bottom	1.92E+02	2.16E+02	4.45E+02

Table 2. Controller performance during set point changes.

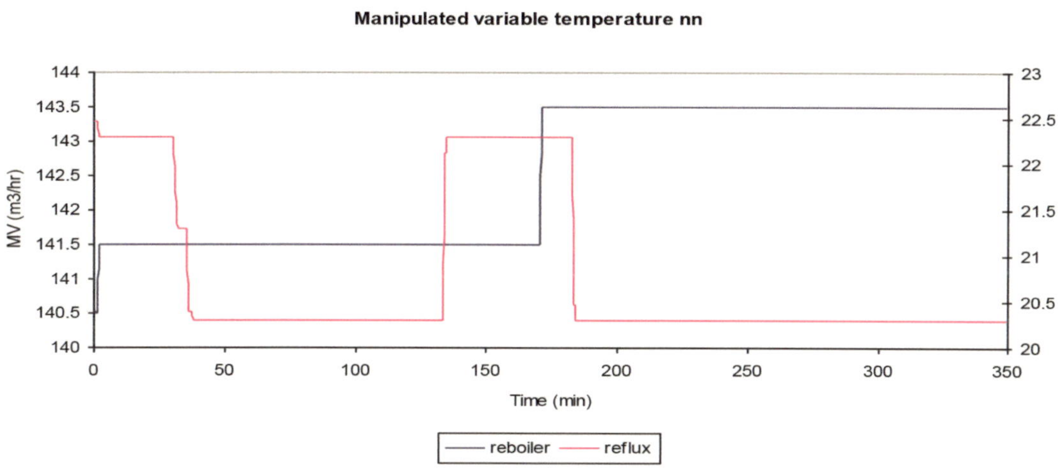

Figure 6. Manipulated variable temperature neural network.

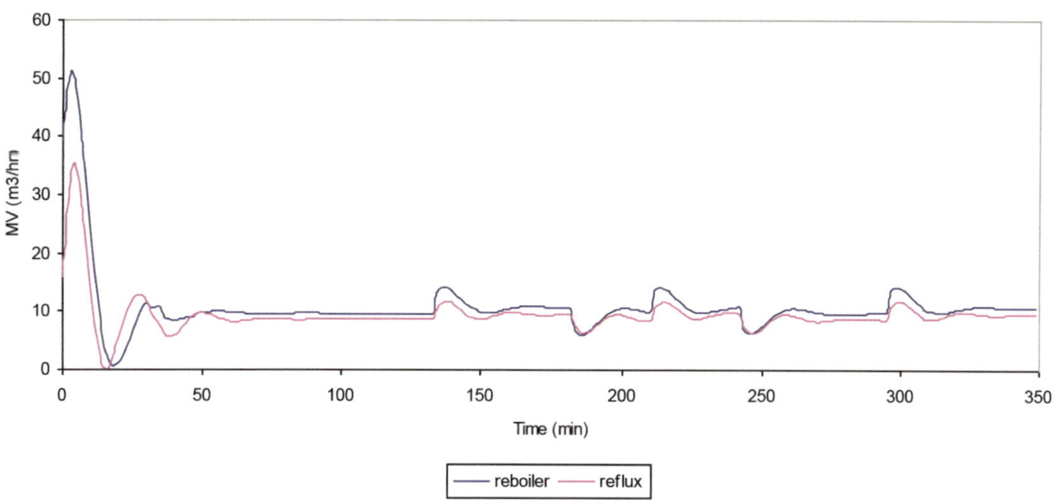

Figure 7. Manipulated variable temperature PID.

controller. Therefore the performance of neural network is better. The fluctuations of the manipulated variable for the reboiler and reflux are very important to see how the controller calculates the error for a control system. The fluctuations for reboiler and reflux flow rate for temperature based on PID show similar trends as time progresses. The units for the calculated IA, ISE and ITAE are dimensionless.

4.2. Disturbances test

Figures 8 and **9** show the fluctuations for the top and bottom temperatures due to disturbances. The disturbances introduced to the debutanizer column are the feed temperature. Similar trends are observed for DIC and IMC methods for the top and bottom temperatures because of disturbances. The neural network control performs well compared to PID controller because there is no overshoot, fast settling time and small error. The PID controller gives unacceptable results as they perform with high overshoot, some offset and large error. This also applies to the top and bottom temperatures. **Table 3** shows the performance of the controller to control the top and bottom temperatures. Results indicate that IMC equation gives the optimum performance as the values of IAE, ISE and ITAE are the smallest compared to other controller. **Figures 10** and **11** show the fluctuation of the manipulated variable to control temperature. The neural network would be able to predict the manipulated variable for reboiler and reflux accurately compared to PID controller. Therefore the performance of neural network is better. The fluctuation of the manipulated variable for the reboiler and reflux flow rate is very important in order to see how the controller calculates the error for a given control system. The fluctuations for reboiler and reflux flow rate for temperature based on PID shows similar trends as time progresses.

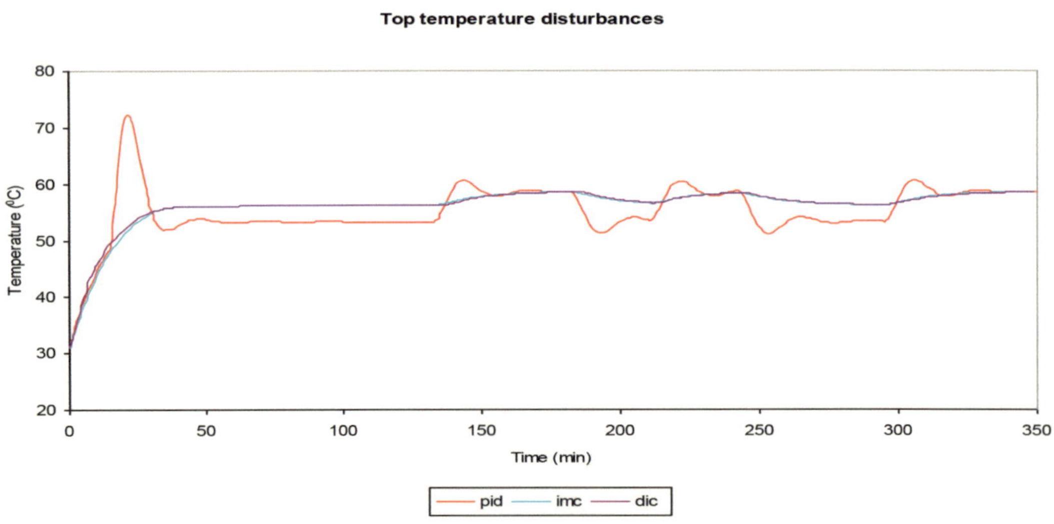

Figure 8. Disturbances top temperature.

http://dx.doi.org/10.5772/intechopen.70704

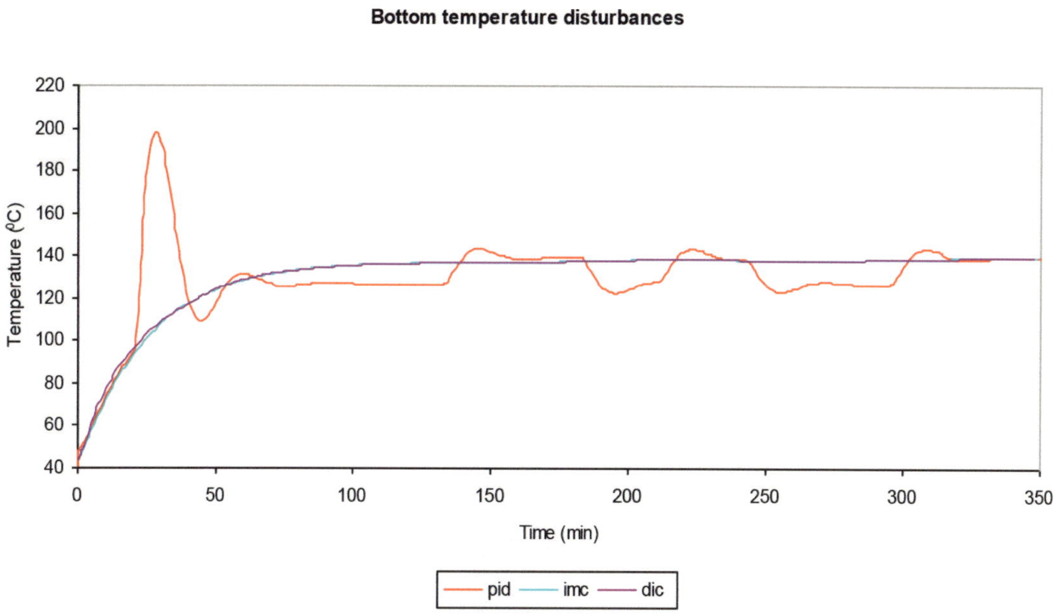

Figure 9. Disturbances bottom temperature.

	IMC eq	DIC eq	PID
IAE top	817.21	836.95	1736.30
IAE bottom	2811.80	2876.00	7891.20
ISE top	6.02E+02	6.63E+02	3.37E+03
ISE bottom	1.14E+02	1.23E+02	1.75E+03
ITAE top	7.78E+02	7.90E+02	1.78E+03
ITAE bottom	1.28E+02	1.30E+02	4.64E+02

Table 3. Controller performance during disturbance changes.

4.3. Estimator neural network

The neural network estimator used in the IMC and DIC method is to estimate and monitor the top and bottom compositions. **Figures 12** and **13** show the fluctuations for the top and bottom compositions which are due to set point changes. For the neural network estimator for IMC for top composition are favorable than DIC method. This is due to the settling time to settle to the required set point for the composition is fastest. This could conclude that both IMC and DIC method perform better compared to the conventional PID controller. This is because the error is small with no overshoot. The results for PID controller are unacceptable because of large overshoot, large error and longer settling time. For the bottom composition fluctuations, the IMC and DIC methods show similar trends. Both methods show better fluctuations compared to PID controller. **Figure 14** shows the fluctuation of the manipulated variable for composition.

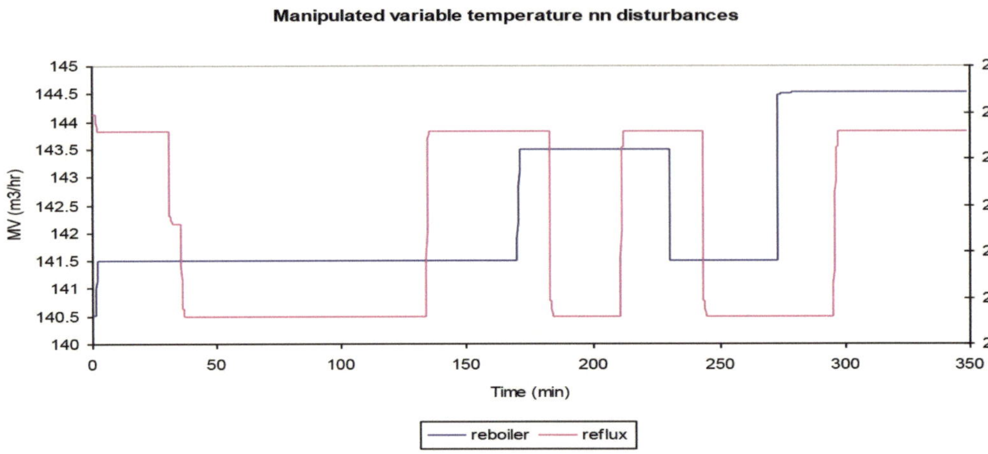

Figure 10. Manipulated variable temperature neural network disturbances.

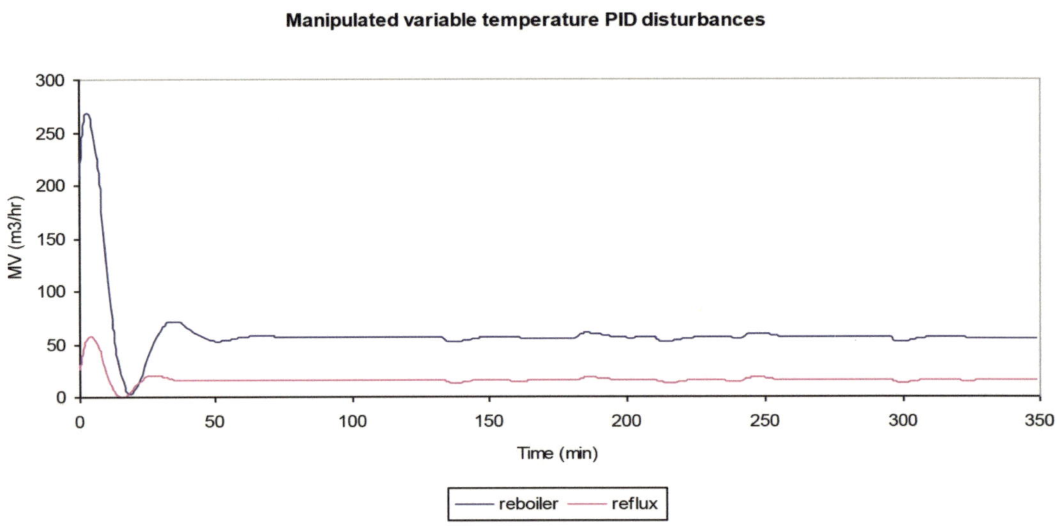

Figure 11. Manipulated variable temperature PID disturbances.

Figures 15 and **16** show the fluctuations for the top and bottom compositions due to disturbances. For the top composition for neural network controller for IMC and DIC methods, it could be concluded that the IMC trend shows similar results to the DIC method. The settling time for the required set point for the composition is similar. Both IMC and DIC methods are superior in comparison to the conventional PID controller. This is because the error is small with no overshoot. The results for PID controller are unacceptable that are due to large overshoot, large error and longer time to settle. For the bottom composition fluctuations, the

http://dx.doi.org/10.5772/intechopen.70704

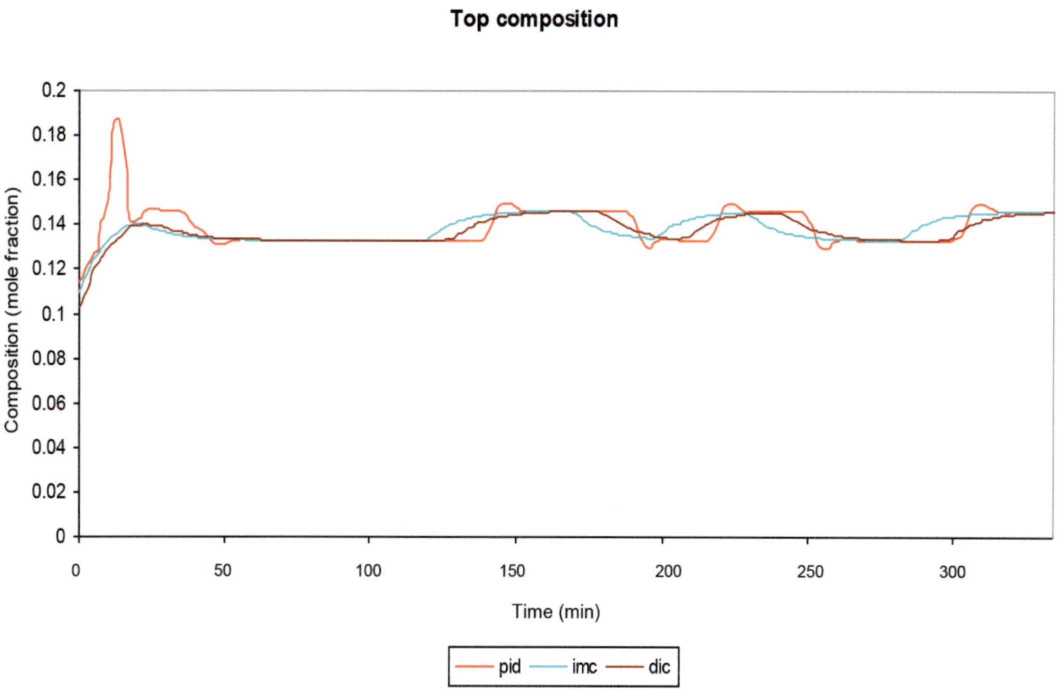

Figure 12. Neural network estimator for the top composition.

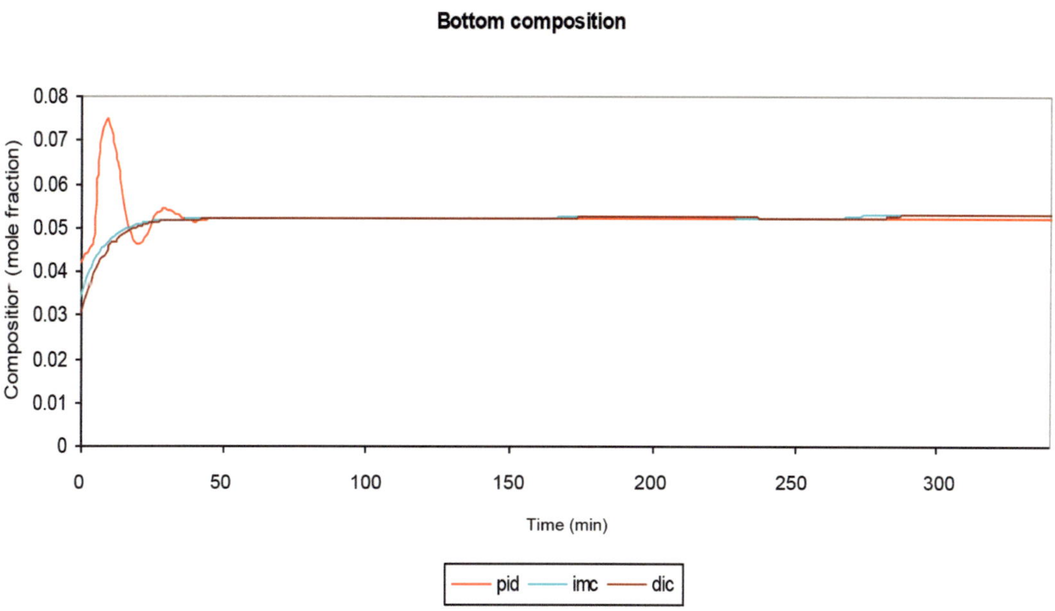

Figure 13. Neural network estimator for the bottom composition.

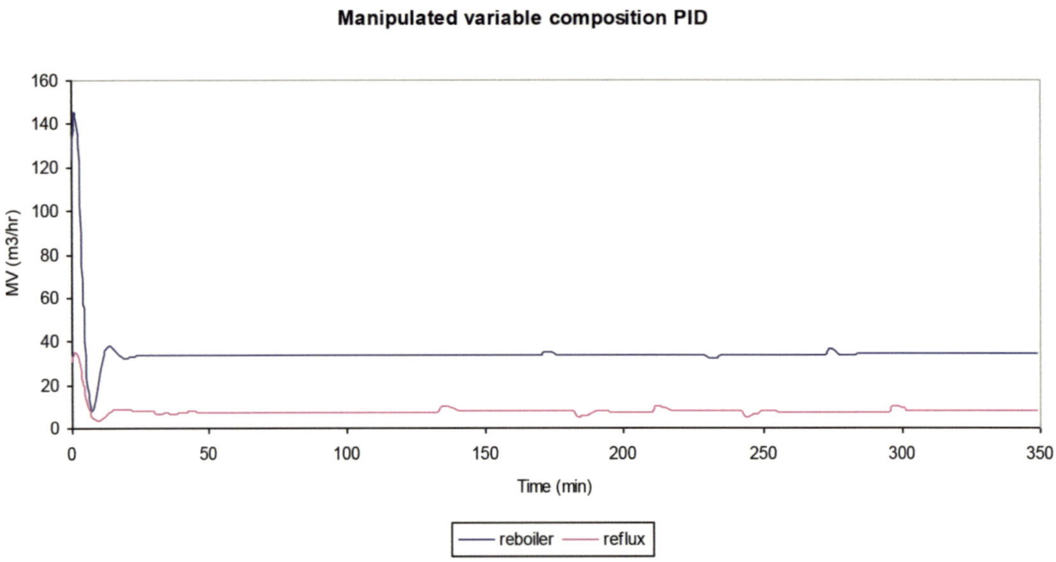

Figure 14. Manipulated variable compositions for PID.

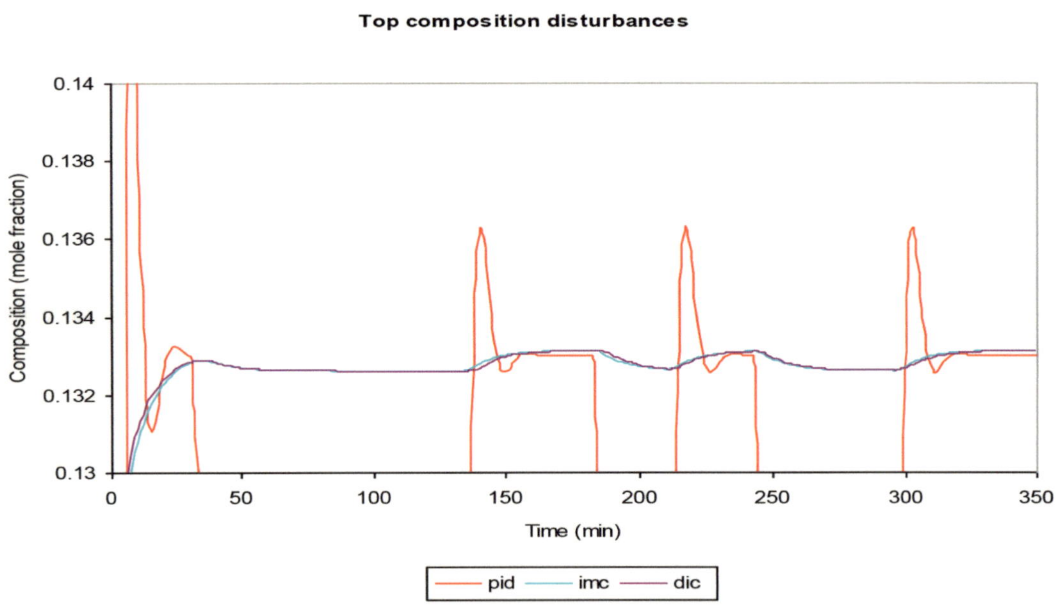

Figure 15. Top composition disturbances.

IMC and DIC methods show similar trends. Both methods show better fluctuations compared to PID controller. **Figure 17** shows the fluctuation of the manipulated variable for composition PID which is due to disturbances.

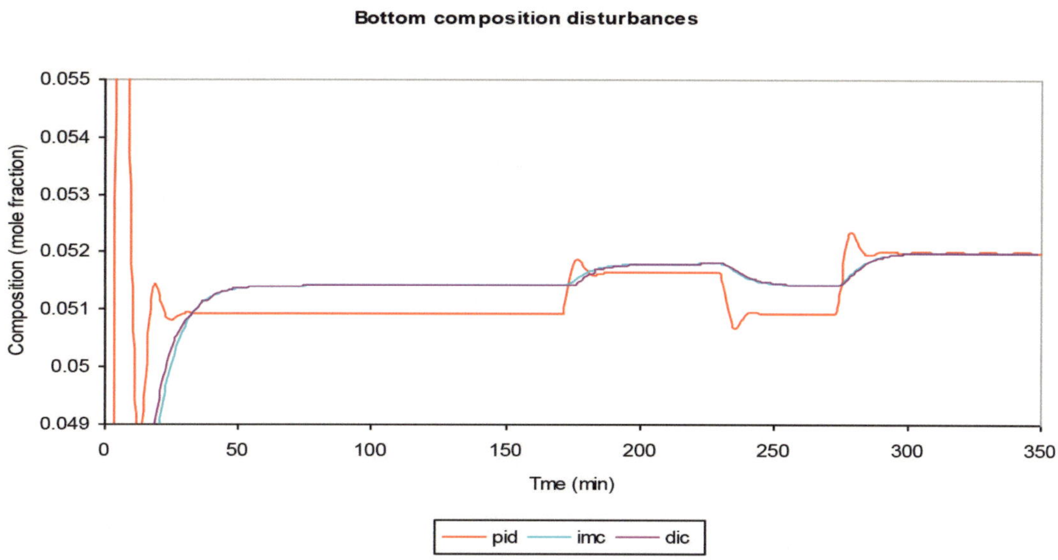

Figure 16. Bottom composition disturbances.

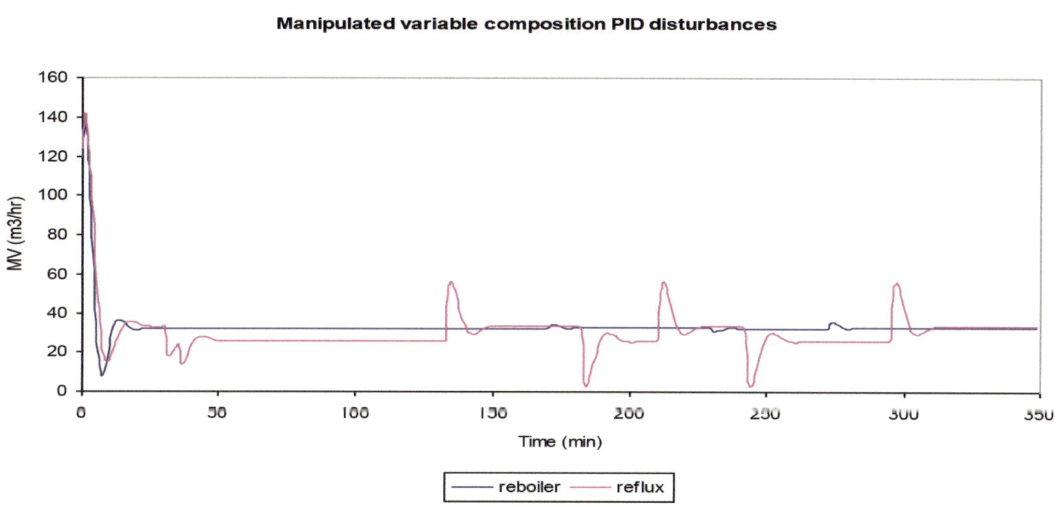

Figure 17. Manipulated variable compositions PID due to disturbances.

Acknowledgements

The authors would like to acknowledge PETRONAS for providing the required data and information for the research. I would like to acknowledge University Malaya for providing the grant for the research (PS107/2010B).

Author details

Nasser Mohamed Ramli

Address all correspondence to: nasser_mramli@utp.edu.my

Chemical Engineering Department, Faculty of Engineering, Universiti Teknologi PETRONAS, Perak, Malaysia

References

[1] Smith Cecil L. Industrial process control. Proceedings AIChe Continuing Education Department, American Institute of Chemical Engineers; 1979

[2] Hussain MA. Review of the application of neural networks in chemical process control—Simulation and online implementation. Artificial Intelligence in Engineering. 1999;**13**:55-68. DOI: S0954-1810(98)00011-9

[3] Greaves MA, Mujtaba IM, Barolo M, Trotta A, Hussain MA. Neural network approach to dynamic optimization of batch distillation application to a middle vessel column. Transactions of the Institution of Chemical Engineers. 2003;**81**:393-401. DOI: 0263-8762/03

[4] Rahman MS, Rashid MM, Hussain MA. Thermal conductivity prediction of foods by neural network and fuzzy (ANFIS) modeling techniques. Food and Bioproducts Processing. 2012;**90**:333-340. DOI: 10.1016/j.fbp.2011.07.001

[5] Hosen MA, Hussain MA, Mjalli F. Control of polystyrene batch reactors using neural network based model predictive control (NNMPC): An experimental investigation. Control Engineering Practice. 2011;**19**:454-467. DOI: 10.1016/j.conengprac.2011.01.007

[6] Arpornwichanop A, Kittisupakorn P, Hussain MA. Model based control strategies for a chemical batch reactor with exothermic reactions. Korean Journal of Chemical Engineering. 2002;**19**:221-226

[7] Ghasem NM, Sata SA, Hussain MA. Temperature control of a bench scale batch polymerization reactor for polystyrene production. Chemical Engineering Technology. 2007;**30**: 1193-1202

[8] Norgaad M, Poulsen N, Hansen L. Neural Networks for Modeling and Control of Dynamic Systems. London: Springer Verlag; 2000. DOI: 10.1002/rnc.585/pdf

[9] Haykin S. Neural Network—A Comprehensive Foundation. New Jersey: Prentice Hall Inc; 1999. DOI: 10.1017/S0269888998004019

[10] Chen G, McAvoy TJ, Pivoso MJ. A multivariable statistical controller for online quality improvement. Journal of Process Control. 1998;**8**:139-149. DOI: 0959-1524/98

[11] Ayala HVH, Coelho LS. Cascaded evolutionary algorithm for non-linear system identification based on correlation functions and radial basis functions neural networks. Mechanical System and Signal Processing. 2016;**11**:378-393. DOI: 10.1016/j.ymssp.2015.05.022 0888-3270

[12] Mujtaba IM, Aziz N, Hussain MA. Neural network based modeling and control in batch reactor. Chemical Engineering Research and Design. 2006;**84**:635-644. DOI: 10.1205/cherd.05096

[13] Ng CW, Hussain MA. Hybrid neural network prior knolwledge model in temperature control of a semi batch polymerization process. Chemical Engineering and Processing. 2004;**43**:559-570. DOI: 10.1016/S0255-2701(03)00109-0

[14] Kittisupakorn P, Thitiyasook P, Hussain MA, Daosud W. Neural network based model predictive for a steel pickling process. Journal of Process Control. 2009;**19**:579-590. DOI: 10.1016/j.jprocont.2008.09.003

Chapter 9

Breast Cancer Detection by Means of Artificial Neural Networks

Jose Manuel Ortiz-Rodriguez,
Carlos Guerrero-Mendez,
Maria del Rosario Martinez-Blanco,
Salvador Castro-Tapia, Mireya Moreno-Lucio,
Ramon Jaramillo-Martinez,
Luis Octavio Solis-Sanchez,
Margarita de la Luz Martinez-Fierro,
Idalia Garza-Veloz, Jose Cruz Moreira Galvan and
Jorge Alberto Barrios Garcia

Additional information is available at the end of the chapter

http://dx.doi.org/10.5772/intechopen.71256

Abstract

Breast cancer is a fatal disease causing high mortality in women. Constant efforts are being made for creating more efficient techniques for early and accurate diagnosis. Classical methods require oncologists to examine the breast lesions for detection and classification of various stages of cancer. Such manual attempts are time consuming and inefficient in many cases. Hence, there is a need for efficient methods that diagnoses the cancerous cells without human involvement with high accuracies. In this research, image processing techniques were used to develop imaging biomarkers through mammography analysis and based on artificial intelligence technology aiming to detect breast cancer in early stages to support diagnosis and prioritization of high-risk patients. For automatic classification of breast cancer on mammograms, a generalized regression artificial neural network was trained and tested to separate malignant and benign tumors reaching an accuracy of 95.83%. With the biomarker and trained neural net, a computer-aided diagnosis system is being designed. The results obtained show that generalized regression artificial neural network is a promising and robust system for breast cancer detection. The Laboratorio de Innovacion y Desarrollo Tecnologico en Inteligencia Artificial is seeking collaboration with research groups interested in validating the technology being developed.

Keywords: breast cancer detection, digital image processing, artificial neural networks, biomarkers, computer-aided diagnosis

1. Introduction

1.1. Breast cancer and early detection

Nowadays, cancer is a massive public health problem around the world. According to the International Agency for Research on Cancer (IARC) [1], part of the World Health Organization (WHO), there were 8.2 million deaths caused by cancer in 2012 and 27 million of new cases of this disease are expected to occur until 2030 [2].

Cancer, medically defined as a malignant neoplasm, is a board group of disease involving unregulated cell growth [2]. In cancer, cell divides and grows uncontrollably forming malignant tumors, invading nearby parts of the body. The cancer can spread to all parts of the body through the lymphatic systems or blood streams [3].

Cancer can be diagnosed by classifying tumors in two different types such as malignant and benign. Benign tumors represent an unnatural outgrowth but rarely lead to a patient's death; yet, some types of benign tumors, too, can increase the possibility of developing cancer [4]. On the other hand, malignant tumors are more serious and their timely diagnosis contributes to a successful treatment. As a result, predication and diagnosis of cancer can boost the chances of treatment, decreasing the usually high costs of medical procedures for such patients [5].

Breast cancer (BC) is the most commonly diagnosed cancer and the most common cause of death in women all over the world. Among the cancer types, BC is the second most common cancer for women, excluding skin cancer [6]. Besides, the mortality of BC is very high when compared to other types of cancer [7]. BC, similar to other cancers, starts with a rapid and uncontrolled outgrowth and multiplication of a part of the breast tissue, which depending on its potential harm, is divided into benign and malignant types.

Generally, there are two types of BC that are in situ and invasive. In situ starts in the milk duct and does not spread to other organs even if it grows [8]. Invasive breast cancer on the contrary, is very aggressive and spreads to other nearby organs, and destroys them as well [9]. It is very important to detect the cancerous cell before it spreads to other organs; thus, the survival rate for patient will increase to more than 97% [10].

A major class of problems in medical science involves the diagnosis of disease, based upon various tests performed upon the patient. The evaluation of data taken from patients and decisions of experts are the most important factors in diagnosis. The correct diagnosis of BC is one of the major problems in the medical field. As BC can be very aggressive, only early detection can prevent mortality. Clinical diagnosis of BC helps in predicting the malignant cases and timely diagnosis can increase the chances of a patient's life expectancy from 56 to 86% [11].

BC has four early signs: microcalcification, mass, architectural distortion, and breast asymmetries [12]. The various common methods used for breast cancer diagnosis (BCD) are positron emission tomography (PET), magnetic resonance imaging (MRI), CT scan, X-ray, ultrasound, photo-acoustic imaging, tomography, diffuse optical tomography, elastography, electrical impedance tomography, opto-acoustic imaging, ophthalmology, mammogram, etc. [13]. The results obtained from these methods are used to recognize the patterns, which are aiming to help the doctors for classifying the malignant and benign cases.

Despite of recent advances in the comprehension of the molecular biology of BC progression and the discovery of new related molecular markers, the histopathological analysis remains the most widely used method for BC diagnosis [14]. Despite significant progress reached by diagnostic imaging technologies, the final BCD, including grading and staging, continues being done by pathologists applying visual inspection of histological samples under the microscope [15].

However, manual classification of images is a challenging and time-consuming task, being highly susceptible to interobserver variability and human errors, resulting in extremely poor critical outcomes, thus markedly increasing the workload of radiologists because of their significant shortage. In addition, medical care costs that are relevant to imaging rapidly increase. Therefore, new methods for diagnosis are required.

Currently, bioimaging quantification is an emerging technique in the field of radiology with a growing implantation in hospital centers. It provides relevant information that is not appreciable by the naked eye in conventional radiological reading. It consists of the generation of quantitative (numerical) data from images, mainly of high resolution, to provide information on which to support a clinical assessment [16]. Biomarkers can be said to be the transition from radiology to personalized medicine.

1.2. Bioimagen markers in breast cancer detection

Bioimagen markers allow to characterize and to study different diseases using some kind of information, such as genetic, histological, clinical imaging, etc. These biomarkers can be used to detect abnormalities in the data as genetic mutations that cause some diseases and can also be used in the clinic for the detection of patients with some types of disease [17].

The application of quantification of bioimaging markers to aid in the diagnosis, treatment, and follow-up of pathologies provides added value throughout the clinical practice process by providing additional information to conventional diagnostic tests [18]. From imaging tests processed in the right way, abnormalities in a tissue are evidenced before they are perceptible in the reading of the radiologist, fundamental objective of this type of biomarkers [19]. In addition, they allow the monitoring of the treatment effect from a quantitative point of view.

As mentioned before, BC is one of the leading causes of death in women around the world, accounting for nearly one-third of cancer-related deaths. Currently, the clinical screening by mammography is the most effective way for the early detection of this disease. Using analysis of mammograms obtained through X-rays allows radiologists to visualize early signs of cancer, such as calcifications, masses, and architectural distortions among other early signs of cancer. However, this analysis is a routine, monotonous, and exhausting task and it is estimated that only 0.3–0.4% of the cases are actually carcinogenic [20].

It has been shown that because of these problems and other factors intrinsic to cancer such as obscuration of abnormalities by fatty tissue, a radiologist can omit up to 30% of cancers. Moreover, because this type of analysis produces many false positives, the number of unnecessary biopsies is increased up to 35%, causing a high level of stress in the patient, and in turn saturating the health systems [21].

Due to all the problems presented by mammography screening, great efforts have been made to support the radiologist in the search for these lesions through computer-aided detection (CAD) or biomarker systems, which try to help the radiologist by taking advantage of the latest advances in computer vision and their manipulation in digital form [22].

At present, computer-aided detection/diagnosis (CAD/CADx) systems are one of the numerous major research topics in diagnostic radiology and medical imaging. CAD systems allow the radiologist to manipulate mammography to highlight certain features that would otherwise be difficult to visualize. One of the most used techniques is the improvement of contrast, which allows to highlight objects in areas of low intensity. To date, CAD is a more suitable method for primary diagnosis of cancer in computed tomography, X-ray, MRI, or mammogram images. CAD system is an effective intermediate between input images and the radiologist. The output from CAD is not considered as an end result; nevertheless, the result is used as reference with regard to additional testing in the related field [23].

The CAD approach helps medical doctors to diagnose diseases with a higher degree of efficiency, while minimizing examination time and cost, as well as avoiding unnecessary biopsy procedures. However, CAD systems not only allow a better visualization of mammograms, but also using different digital image processing (DIP), knowledge discovery from data (KDD), artificial intelligence (AI) techniques such artificial neural networks (ANN) allow to preselect certain regions of interests (ROIs) for later analysis by the radiologist [24].

Classification of histopathology images into distinct histopathology patterns, corresponding to the noncancerous or cancerous condition of the analyzed tissue, is often the primordial goal in image analysis systems for cancer automatic-aided diagnosis applications. Recent advances in DIP, KDD, and AI techniques allow to build CAD/CADx that can assist pathologists to be more productive, objective, and consistent in diagnosis. The main challenge of such systems is dealing with the inherent complexity of histopathological images.

The aim of this research is to use advanced DIP to investigate and develop specific imaging biomarkers for Mexican patients through the quantitative mammography analysis and with this information to develop technology based on advanced KDD and AI techniques, aiming to detect breast cancer in the early stages in order to support the diagnosis and prioritization of high-risk patients.

2. Development of a CADx system to identify breast abnormalities in digital mammograms images using artificial neural networks

In this research, the study of BC disease using advanced techniques of DIP, KDD, and AI was carried out in order to develop imaging biomarkers that allow to carry out diverse studies for BCD. As is showed in **Figure 1**, the research was divided in three main stages.

Currently, there are no public databases of BC in Latin America or Mexico. Therefore, at first stage, different public mammography databases were used for developing and validating digital image processing algorithms capable to select ROIs from mammograms to extract

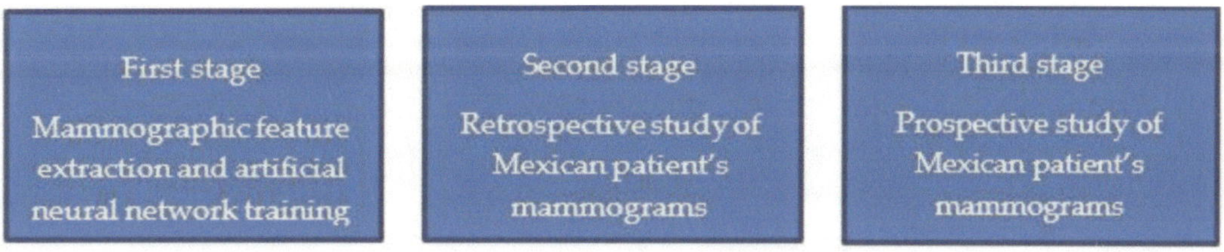

Figure 1. Main stages of research.

image features used to train a generalized regression artificial neural network (GRANN). The aim was to generate a methodology for the characterization of mammograms and their association with risk factors in BC patients as well as to integrate and to develop the technological tools for mammography analysis for BCD using AI technology. In this work, results obtained at first stage are presented.

Because there are no public databases of BC for Mexican patients, it was proposed to establish two protocols for the acquisition of mammograms. The first protocol, second stage, seeks to obtain data retrospectively, which will allow obtaining the mammograms necessary to validate in Mexican patients the methodology and technological tools developed at stage one. The aim of the second stage is the generation of an anonymous database of Mexican patients for free use by the scientific community for the study of BC in Mexican patients and to validate the methodologies developed in collaboration with the General Hospital of Zacatecas (GHZ) and the Molecular Medicine Laboratory (MML) from Autonomous University of Zacatecas, Mexico.

In the second protocol, third stage, it is sought to generate a long-term prospective protocol, which will allow the creation of a database with different risk factors associated with the development of BC. This protocol will allow to collect clinical data of patients with both high and low probabilities of developing cancer. These data will be able to validate the methodologies of cancer detection by the scientific community.

The generation of a prospective protocol will allow the expansion of the database for the study of breast cancer in Mexican patients. Unlike the retrospective protocol, prospective protocol aims to include clinical data, risk factors, and mammograms, among others. This database would present to the scientific community a reference for the development of new breast cancer detection techniques in Mexican patients.

2.1. Methodology: feature extraction and neural network training

Patient prioritization can play a very important role in the reach of health services in developing countries such as Mexico, where not all have access to these specialized oncology services. Therefore, this research seeks the study of BC by generating a methodology that allows the detection of patients with a high probability of BC. In this work, a new technology to generate mammographic biomarkers and a CADx system for breast cancer diagnosis was designed in order to analyze Digital Image Mammograms (DIM). With this knowledge, it is proposed to create a biomarker specifically designed for the Mexican population. As is showed in **Figure 2**, the first stage was divided into six main stages.

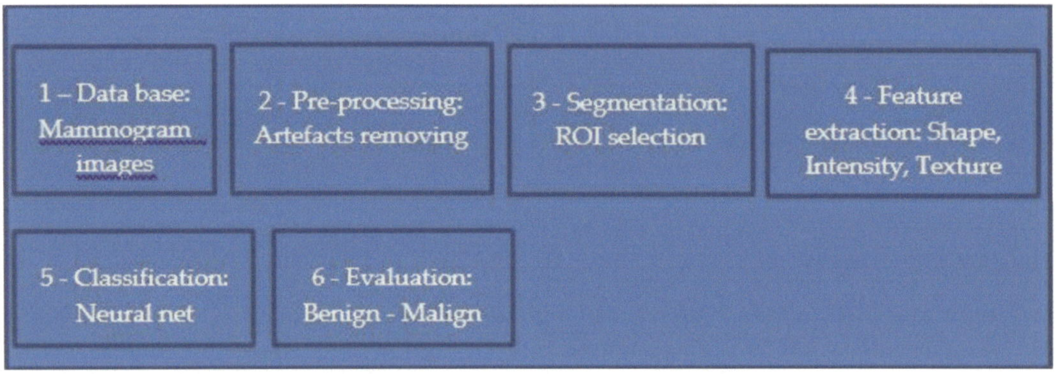

Figure 2. First stage of research. Mammographic feature extraction and artificial neural network training.

2.1.1. Data base: mammogram images

The development of CAD/CADx systems involves their generation and validation by using mammograms obtained from clinical studies, or using public databases. However, at the global level, there are few public databases available to the scientific community to investigate. As mentioned before, currently, there are no public databases of BC in Latin America or Mexico for conducting this kind of studies. Therefore, at first stage, different public mammography databases were used for developing and validating digital image processing algorithms capable to select ROIs from mammograms and to extract image features used to train a GRANN capable to diagnose BC as an aid for radiologists.

Currently, there are only three public databases to conduct this type of research: the first one is the Digital Database for Screening Mammography (DDSM) that has a total of 2620 cases distributed in 625 normal, 1011 benign and 914 malignant and includes the two standardized views CC and MLO. Another available database is the Mammographic Image Analysis Society - Digital Mammogram Data Base (mini-MIAS) that has 322 cases; however, it only has the MLO view. DDSM and mini-MIAS databases are both form North America.

A newly created database is the Breast Cancer Digital Repository (BCDR) from Europe. The creation of BDR is supported by the IMED Project (Development of Algorithms for Medical Image Analysis). The IMED project was created by INEGI, FMUP-CHSJ University of Porto, Portugal and CIEMAT, Spain from 2009 to 2013. This database has 724 patients (723 women and 1 man), aged between 27 and 92 years.

In the first stage of this research, the mini-MIAS, DDSM, and BCDR databases were used to generate and validate the development of a biomarker, an artificial neural network approach with incremental learning and with both, the design of a CADx methodology, carried out in a general scope. However, it is important to highlight that these databases are formed by patients with ethnic characteristics typical of their region, which makes it difficult to transfer knowledge to other countries and their own features.

Moreover, as has been shown by the scientific community, BC varies widely between different etiologies and may prove that systems created for a population may not work for a different population in the way they were thought. This is further aggravated by different types of diets, customs, and lifestyle. Due to this, the development of biomarkers and CAD systems for the Mexican population needs an adaptation to the characteristics of our population. In second and third stages of this research, the designed methodology will be focused and refined for its operation in Mexican patients.

In this work, results obtained with BCDR database are presented. BCDR database contains useful information of each mammogram such as gender: masculine or feminine; segmentations of mammogram, marked in red pixels the ROI that contains the lesion found by the radiologist; patient ID; the age of the patient; breast density, i.e., the percentage of breast density according to Breast Imaging Reporting and Data System (BI-RADS) standard expressed as percentage of glandular and fibrous tissue; breast localization, depending on the location of breast of the RIO with the lesions; mammography, the type of lesion found by the mammographic image expert; biopsy result, anatomical pathology of the biopsy; categorization of the definitive diagnosis; the BI-RADS classification of the lesion; and finally, intensity and shape descriptors of ROI. However, it is important to mention that for this research, these descriptors were not used to train the neural network. Instead, a set of computer algorithms were designed in order to extract image descriptors of ROI of mammograms as described in later section.

2.1.2. Preprocessing: artifact removing and segmentation process

A mammogram image can be considered as a representation of the X-ray radiation density that reflects the tissue of the breast. A risk factor for BC in a patient is recognized when a white region appears on the mammogram image, which means a high tissue density, that may be considered abnormal. A breast abnormality is commonly called ROI. According to DIP techniques, segmentation of breast abnormalities on mammograms is a crucial step in CAD systems. It is a difficult task, since these types of medical images are in low-intensity contrast, making it difficult to identify the edges of a suspicious mass.

In the methodology used in this research, only lateral mammographic images taken from BCDR database were used. In all selected images, a lesion exists, which is considered as benign or malignant; digital mammographic images of BCDR database can be accessed in two forms: the first one from films (photographic films) and the second one from digital images taken from X-ray system (mammography images). Films' images require the design of digital image processing algorithms to eliminate artifacts such as red pixels and prenoise such as labels used by radiologists to identify left or right breast as well as patient identification information. Conversely, digital mammography images only require the design of algorithms for removing red pixels.

The films approach improves digital mammography images increasing the high frequency and eliminating the noise and unwanted artifacts in the ROI. As can be appreciated in **Figure 3**, at preprocessing stage, a computer tool was designed to automate the preprocessing of film digital mammographic images (FDMIs). All FDMIs are treated to eliminate image artifacts such as background, noise, and image labels. In the FDMIs, a common threshold was applied to create a region of the breast and other regions with the labels and artifacts on the mammography.

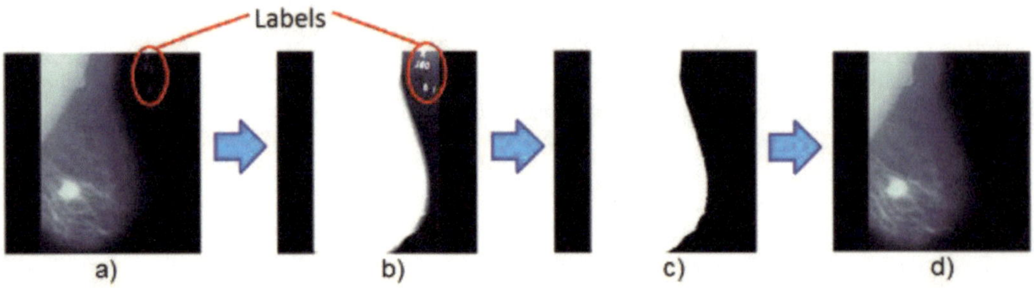

Figure 3. Preprocessing of a mammographic image. (a) Original image, (b) breast region, highlighting labels and background noise, (c) clean breast binary image, and (d) mammography image cleaned.

Using the designed automated computer tool, after creating the logical image, all small regions (less than 10,000 pixels) are eliminated to remove the regions considered as unnecessary in FDMIs. Then, the logical image (mask) is used instead of the original image to obtain an image of the breast without artifacts and labels. **Figure 3** shows the preprocessing method to remove noise and labels in a digital mammography image.

Converting a greyscale to a digital or logical image is a common task of digital image processing. There are many methods for calculating the threshold value for creating logical images. As can be appreciated in **Figure 4**, in this research, the threshold was calculated by converting the nonzero pixel's values to 1. To create a logical image that contains the ROI and the pectoral muscle, the gray tones were converted to white level.

For removing the pectoral region in the logical image, as is showed in **Figure 4**, the white region that is connected to the border of the binary image was eliminated. Therefore, the surplus white region represents the ROI detected in the mammography image. With a cleaned image, the next step is the segmentation process.

On the other hand, the digital mammographic approach works as follows: to calculate the descriptors, the ROI of the lesion is manually segmented by the expert radiologist as can be appreciated in **Figure 5**. At preprocessing stage, the image is fitted for the segmentation. The pixels in red are turned into black. Using the black pixels, the ROI is separated from the rest of the breast image for making a segmentation of the ROI as is showed in **Figure 6**.

For the segmentation of the ROI, a binary or logical image with a very high binarization threshold is created where low gray levels become white. This approach considers most of

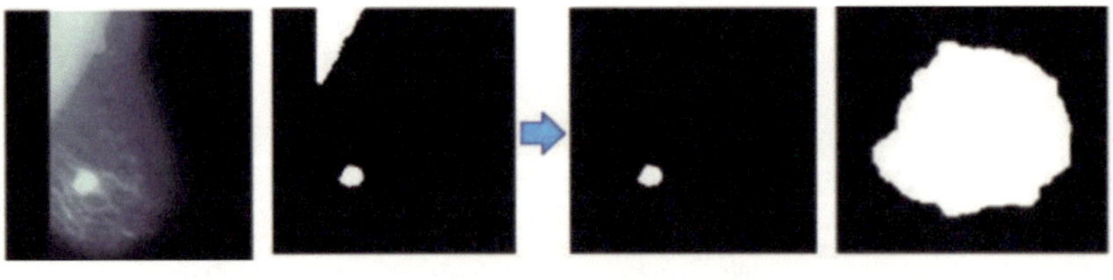

Figure 4. Pectoral region removing process.

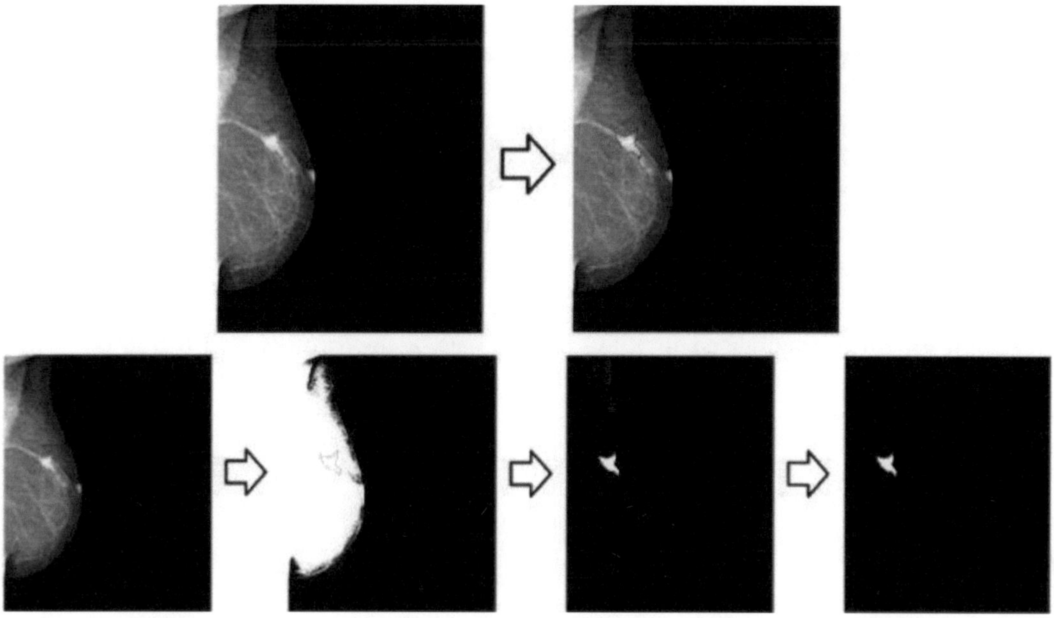

Figure 5. Preprocessing stage of digital mammogram approach.

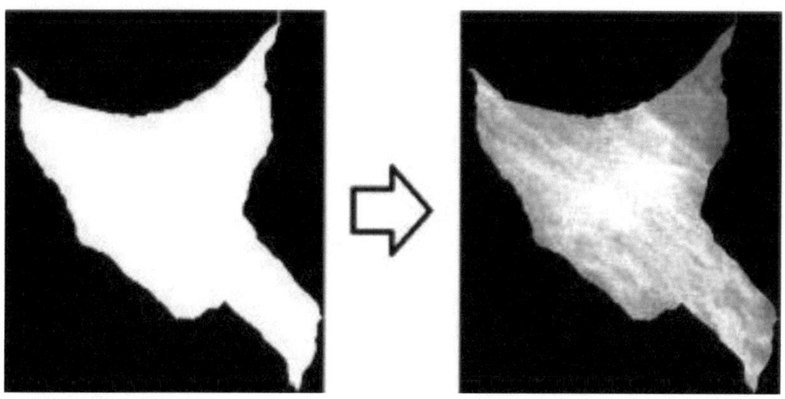

Figure 6. Binary mask and ROI in tones of grays.

gray pixels of the image looking not to lose many pixels from ROI. Afterward, the white logical region that is connected to the edge of the mammographic image is removed. Some white pixels pertaining to the contour of the breast are discarded when the pixels in the image with a small area are removed. Finally, the white region with a greater number of pixels is extracted, which would be considered as the neoplasia.

Next, a binary mask is created using the ROI obtained in the segmentation stage. With the mask and together with the complete image in shades of gray, we will get the ROI in shades of gray as is showed in **Figure 6**.

The next step in the operation of regular CAD systems is the feature extraction of the RIO. The feature extraction can be defined as the process to infer and quantify the parameters that characterize the object being studied. The feature extraction contributes to the analysis of the ROI. It is possible to quantify the shape, texture, size, border, and other tissue parameters that can contribute to the diagnosis and detection of a cancer risk factor. As is showed in **Figure 7**, in this work, shape, intensity, and texture features were extracted in order to create a biomarker for BCD using a CADx system that uses AI technology.

The image features of all Digital Image Mammography (DIM) of BCDR database were extracted and used to build a biomarker to train an ANN. The BCDR digital images are in RGB and gray-level digitalized in JEPG format with a depth of 24 and 8 bits per pixel, respectively, and a resolution of 3328 × 4084. The RGB mammograms are used to show the red remarked section by a radiologist to delimit the found anomaly.

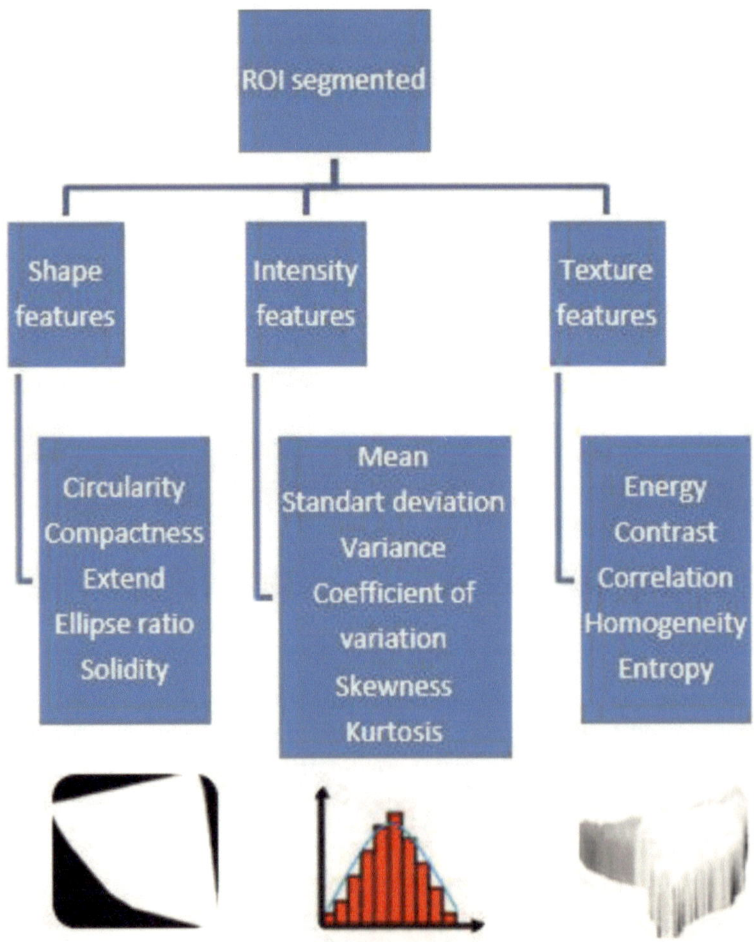

Figure 7. Image features extracted.

http://dx.doi.org/10.5772/intechopen.71256

The segmentation process use the red section remarked in the RGB mediolateral oblique view mammograms to obtain the ROI. In the RGB mammograms, all the red pixels in the image and the pixels outside the original red region were eliminated. Finally, the remained pixels in the gray-level mammogram were used to get the ROI used for the features' calculation.

Using a custom-designed automated computer tool, a total of 361 images (36 malignant and 325 with benign abnormalities) from 239 patients were segmented in order to get the RIOs. This information was used as the entrance data for training and testing a GRANN. This computer tool saves a lot of time in the preprocessing stage of mammography analysis. This tool will be used at second and third stages of research to analyze the mammograms of Mexican patients in order to create a Mexican biomarker and a CADx system for BCD.

Feature extraction of digital images, such as obtained in digital mammograms, as is showed in **Figure 7**, is a manner to represent an element or an ROI in an image like a fingerprint, and these features are used in many research areas such as machine learning, patter recognition, image processing, or diagnosis of disease in medical science. Feature extraction is a crucial task before classifying an ROI or a pattern in an image.

2.1.3. Feature extraction: shape, intensity, and texture

Image processing is the most important area where the feature extraction is applied, in which mathematical algorithms are used to detect and isolate various desired portions or shapes, features, of digitalized images or video streams, it is particularly important in the area of pattern recognition or character recognition.

The feature extraction method is the measure of physical parameters visualized in a segmented region of an image. The aim of feature extraction is to find a mathematical way to represent the image information, which is important, in a compact form, for solving a computational task. In BCD, these features help to determine the kind of tumor detected in a mammogram image. The choice of features has a crucial influence on the accuracy of classification, the time needed for classification, the number of examples needed for learning, and the cost of performing classification. In breast abnormalities, classification of the differences in mass between benign and malignant on a mammography can be distinguished from their shape, textures, and the intensity in the image.

In this research, an automated computer tool was designed to calculate shape, intensity, and texture features from ROI extracted from BCDR mammograms. The shape features of MDI use the pixels inside and the border of the ROI. These descriptors, showed in **Table 1**, only have a valid meaning in binary or logical images, and some simple shape features are used to describe a ratio between some geometrical figures; for example: extend, ellipse_ratio, and solidity. Most common shape features are the area and perimeter of the region, but they are applied when the ROI size is invariant. However, the area and perimeter can be used to create a relation as the circularity and compactness.

The intensity features, showed in **Table 2**, use the shape intensity histogram to get information that describes the image; i.e., the intensity features use the probability and statistics from the values of the pixels in the image. The mean is the average intensity level. The standard is used

Shape features	
Circularity	Extend
$Circularity = \frac{4\pi ROI_{Area}}{ROI_{Perimeter}{}^2}$	$Extend = \frac{ROI_{Area}}{Box_{Area}}$
Compactness	Ellipse_ratio
$Compactness = \frac{ROI_{Perimeter}{}^2}{ROI_{Area}}$	$Ellipse_{ratio} = \frac{ROI_{Area}}{Ellipse_{Area}}$
	Solidity
	$Solidity = \frac{ROI_{Area}}{Convex_{Hull_{Area}}}$

Table 1. Shape features.

Intensity features	**Texture features**
Mean	Energy
$\overline{\mu} = \frac{1}{MN}\sum_{x=1}^{M}\sum_{y=1}^{N} P_{RIO}(x,y)$, where P_{RIO} is the intensity pixel value in the coordinates x and y.	$Energy = \sum_{x=1}^{M}\sum_{y=1}^{N} P_{RIO}(x,y)^2$
Standard deviation	Contrast
$\sigma = \sqrt{\frac{1}{MN-1}\sum_{x=1}^{M}\sum_{y=1}^{N}\left\|P_{RIO}(x,y) - \overline{\mu}\right\|^2}$	$Contrast = \sum_{x=1}^{M}\sum_{y=1}^{N}(x-y)^2 P_{RIO}(x,y)$
Variance	Correlation
$variance = \sqrt{\sigma}$	$Correlation = \sum_{x=1}^{M}\sum_{y=1}^{N}\frac{(x-\overline{\mu_x})(y-\overline{\mu_y})P_{RIO}(x,y)}{\sigma_x\sigma_y}$, where $\overline{\mu_x}$, $\overline{\mu_y}$, σ_x, and σ_y are the mean values and the standard deviation P_{xRIO} and P_{yRIO}, respectively.
Coefficient of variation	Homogeneity
$Coefficient\ of\ variation = \frac{\sigma}{\overline{\mu}}$	$Homogeneity = \sum_{x=1}^{M}\sum_{y=1}^{N}\frac{P_{RIO}(x,y)}{1+\|x-y\|}$
Skewness	Entropy
$Skewness = \frac{1}{MN}\sum_{x=1}^{M}\sum_{y=1}^{N}\left(\frac{P_{RIO}(x,y)-\overline{\mu}}{\sigma}\right)^3$	$Entropy = -\sum_{x=1}^{M}\sum_{y=1}^{N} P_{RIO}(x,y)\ \log\left[P_{RIO}(x,y)\right]$
Kurtosis	
$Kurtosis = \left\{\frac{1}{MN}\sum_{x=1}^{M}\sum_{y=1}^{N}\left[\frac{P_{RIO}(x,y)-\overline{\mu}}{\sigma}\right]^4\right\} - 3$	

Table 2. Intensity and texture features.

to quantify the amount of variation of the set of intensities levels. The variance refers to the variation of the intensities around the mean value. The coefficient of variation is a standardized measure of dispersion in the values. Finally, the skewness and kurtosis measure the histogram symmetric.

The texture features, **Table 2**, describe the *roughness* of an image. Texture features attempt to capture features of the intensity fluctuations between groups of neighboring pixels. The texture is something to which the human eye is very sensitive. In this research, the energy, contrast, correlation, homogeneity, and entropy were used. The energy is a measure of textural uniformity of an image. The contrast refers to the difference in luminance in the ROI. Correlation texture measures the dependence of gray levels on those of neighboring pixels. Homogeneity measures the similarity of values in the ROI. Entropy measures the disorder of value pixels of an image.

As before mentioned, medical diagnosis is an important and complicated task that needs to be executed accurately and efficiently. At present, new techniques based on data mining, KDD, and AI in healthcare are being used mainly for predicting various diseases as well as assisting doctors in diagnosis in their clinical decision. One area where this effort has been most felt is the diagnosis of breast cancer in women. However, the absence of any fully effective, efficient method of BCD has led researchers to develop automated computational systems. In this research, automated CADx technology based on ANN as decision-making tool in the field of BCD is being developed.

2.1.4. *Classification and evaluation*

For automatic classification of BC on DIM, a GRANN was used to separate malignant and benign tumors [25]. GRANN falls into the category of probabilistic neural networks (PNN) [26–30]. GRANN is a neural network architecture of one-step-only learning that can solve any function approximation problem. The learning process is equivalent to finding a surface in a multidimensional space that provides a best fit to the training data. During the training process, it just stores training data and later uses it for predictions. This neural net is very useful to perform predictions and comparisons of system performance in practice. In GRANN architecture, there are no training parameters, just a smoothing factor (σ) that is applied after the network is trained. The choice of this factor is very important [26–30].

In this research, as is showed in **Figure 8**, a GRANN was trained and tested using a data set of 361 mammograms extracted from BCDR public database. For each mammogram, 35 image descriptors were calculated through an automated computer tool specifically designed for this purpose. These image features were used to train the neural net in order to classify benign and malignant BC for decision making in BDC.

As can be appreciated from **Figure 8**, the image features were used as entrance data, and the malignant (cancerous) and benign (noncancerous) instances were used as output data. In order to train the network, the dataset was randomly divided into two subsets, one with about 80% of the instances to training and another with around the remaining 20% of instances to testing.

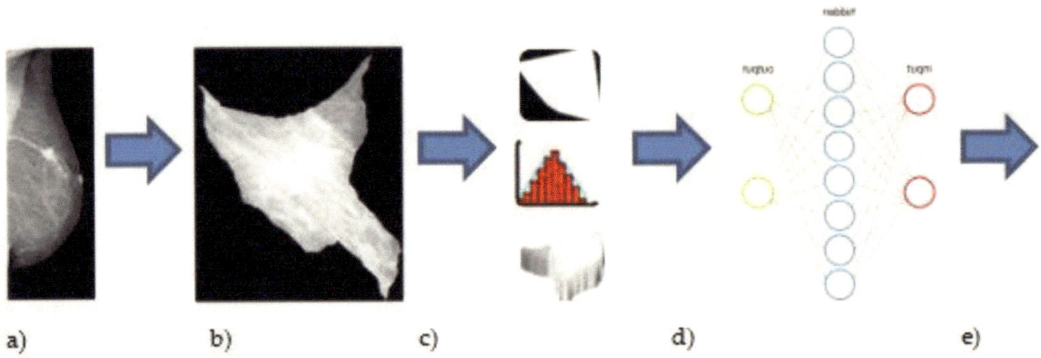

Figure 8. Training of GRANN for BCD. (a) Breast image, (b) segmentation, (c) image descriptors, (d) network training, and (e) BCD.

After 2000 network trainings, a smoothing factor equal to 1e−4 was calculated. This value was used for training the neural net reaching an accuracy of 95.83%. The results obtained in this work show that GRANN is a promising and robust system for BCD. The performance of a trained GRANN was evaluated using four performance measures: accuracy, sensitivity, specificity, and precision. These measures are defined by four decisions: true positive (TP), true negative (TN), false positive (FN), and false negative (FN). TP decision occurs when malignant instances are predicted rightly. TN decision benign instances are predicted rightly. FP decision occurs when benign instances are predicted as malignant. FN decision occurs when malignant instances are predicted as benign.

Accuracy can be calculated as:

$$Accuracy = \frac{TP + TN}{TP + TN + FP + FN} \quad (1)$$

Sensitivity can be calculated as:

$$Sensitivity(recall) = \frac{TP}{TP + FN} \quad (2)$$

Specificity can be calculated as:

$$Specificity = \frac{TN}{TN + FP} \quad (3)$$

Precision can be calculated as:

$$Precision = \frac{TP}{TP + FP} \quad (4)$$

The confusion matrix for the data set, showed in **Table 3**, was computed using these values into above equations to find accuracy, sensitivity, specificity, and precision. **Table 3** shows the

		Obtained		
		0	1	
Goal	0	66	2	
		91.70%	2.80%	
	1	1	3	
		1.40%	**4.20%**	
				95.80%
				4.20%

Table 3. Confusion matrix.

classification results of BC. The confusion matrix is a table that allows to visualize the execution of an algorithm, usually a supervised learning. In this case, it is a classifier of two classes, the current or expected and those obtained by the system (predictions). Each column of the matrix represents the cases that the system, in this case, the neural network, predicted, while the rows represent the expected values.

The diagonal indicates the successes achieved by the system; that is, the trained neural network obtained 91.7% + 4.2% = 95.8% of accuracy, successfully predicting 66 + 3 = 69 lesions of a population of 72, representing an error of 4.2% with three errors from a population of 72 lesions.

With both biomarkers obtained from mammograms and the trained GRANN, a CADx technology system, as showed in **Figure 9**, is being created to be used at second stage in collaboration with GHZ and MML.

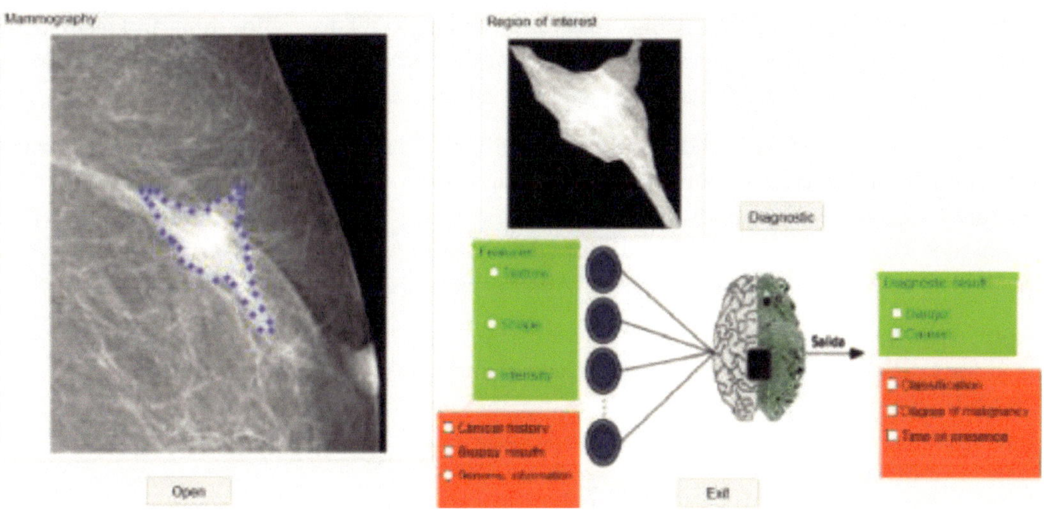

Figure 9. CADx system being developed based on DIP, KDD, and AI methodologies.

The Computer Aided Diagnosis system consists of two main stages: the first one detects the suspicious regions with high sensitivity presenting the results to the radiologist aiming to reduce false positives. This process is given in the first instance by a preprocessing algorithm based on advanced DIP techniques designed to reduce the noise acquired in the image and in an improvement of the same, and then it executed a segmentation process of different ROIs designed to detect high suspicion of some signs of cancer. By using the information obtained in the segmentation process, the classification of positives or negatives prediction of BC is obtained through a GRANN. After concluding the development of this CADx technological computer tool, it is planned to be used at real workplaces such as GHZ, making a validation of the prediction obtained by the neural network compared with predictions made by specialized oncologists aiming that it can be used as an aid in the early breast cancer diagnosis.

The aim of developing this CADx system for Mexican patients is to expand the knowledge of the database of BCD including image mammograms information, clinical data, risk factors, biopsy results, genomic information, etc., as is showed in **Figure 9**, at the bottom of the main window, with the aim to obtain more information on the resulting diagnostics such as degree of malignancy, time of presence, etc.

3. Conclusions

As mentioned before, conventionally, BCD and classification is performed by a clinician or a pathologist by observing stained biopsy images under the microscope. However, this is time consuming and can lead to erroneous results. Therefore, there is a rise in the need for developing intelligent and automated technology. As this problem can be computationally modeled as a problem of retrieving relevant information from a plethora of reports or tests, the development of a computationally efficient and detection-wise effective system for BCD can be seen as an issue from the field of KDD. Being cross-dimensional, KDD uses algorithms and techniques from a vast array of fields like soft computing, pattern recognition, machine learning statistics, artificial intelligence (AI), natural language processing (NLP), etc.

In this research, a method based on advanced DIP, KDD, and AI techniques was used for the extraction of fundamental features in DIM in order to detect breast lesions by using a GRANN. The used methodology was divided in two main stages. The first one used advanced DIP techniques for extracting image features of DMI in order to create a biomarker for BCD. With this information, in the second stage, a GRANN was trained and tested in order to classify BC.

After 2000 network trainings, a smoothing factor equal to 1e−4 was calculated. This value was used for training the neural net reaching an accuracy of 95.83%. The performance of trained GRANN was evaluated using four performance measures: accuracy, sensitivity, specificity, and precision. The results obtained in this work show that GRANN is a promising and robust system for BCD.

In a third stage, a CADx system based on AI technology is being designed in order to be applied in Mexican patients in collaboration with GHZ and MML. The proposed system aims to eliminate the unnecessary waiting time as well as reducing human and technical errors in diagnosing BC. The Laboratorio de Innovacion y Desarrollo Tecnologico en Inteligencia Artificial is seeking collaboration with research groups interested in validating the technology being developed.

Acknowledgements

This work was partially supported by Fondo Sectorial de Investigación para la Eduación under contract no. 241771 and PRODEP under contract no. 511-6/17-7763. The second and sixth authors want to thank the postdoctorate and doctorate scholarships, with scholarship holder numbers 25467 and 25976, respectively, received by Fondo Sectorial de Investigación para la Eduación under contract no. 241771. The fourth and fifth authors want to thank CONACYT PNPC scholarships, with scholarship holder numbers 285593 and 577554, respectively, received through Posgrado en Ingenieria y Tecnologia Aplicada, member of Programa Nacional de Posgrados de Calidad (PNPC) of CONACYT, México.

Authors want to thank the participation of Arturo Serrano Muñoz, an undergraduate student of Information Technology and Communication Bachelor from Universidad Tecnologica del Estado de Zacatecas, México, who is receiving a scholarship from PRODEP under contract no. 511-6/17-7763. This student performed the installation and configuration of the software and several services on the server where calculations were performed for extracting the features of the mammographic images and the neural network trainings.

Authors want to thank the participation of Edgar Viveros Llamas, an undergraduate student of Robotics and Mechatronics Bachelor from Universidad Autonoma de Zacatecas, Mexico. This student is making a social service in Laboratorio de Innovacion y Desarrollo Tecnologico en Inteligencia Artificial, helping with general activities related to this research.

Author details

Jose Manuel Ortiz-Rodriguez[1]*, Carlos Guerrero-Mendez[1], Maria del Rosario Martinez-Blanco[1], Salvador Castro-Tapia[1], Mireya Moreno-Lucio[1], Ramon Jaramillo-Martinez[1], Luis Octavio Solis-Sanchez[1], Margarita de la Luz Martinez-Fierro[2], Idalia Garza-Veloz[2], Jose Cruz Moreira Galvan[3] and Jorge Alberto Barrios Garcia[3]

*Address all correspondence to: morvymm@yahoo.com.mx

1 Laboratorio de Innovación y Desarrollo Tecnológico en Inteligencia Artificial, Unidad Académica de Ingeniería Eléctrica, Universidad Autónoma de Zacatecas, Zacatecas, México

2 Laboratorio de Medicina Molecular, Unidad Académica de Medicina Humana y Ciencias de la Salud, Universidad Autónoma de Zacatecas, Zacatecas, México

3 Tecnologías de Información y Comunicación, Universidad Tecnológica del Estado de Zacatecas, Guadalupe, Zacatecas, México

References

[1] Bernard WS, Christopher PW. World Cancer Report 2014. International Agency for Research on Cancer. WHO Press. World Health Organization; Switzerland. 2014

[2] Bray F, Jemal A, Grey N, Ferlay J, Forman D. Global cancer transitions according to the human development index (2008-2030): A population base study. The Lancet Oncology. 2012;**13**(8):790-801

[3] Weinberg RA, editor. One Renegade Cell: How Cancer Begins. Basic Books; New York, USA. 1999

[4] Kinzler KW, Vogelstein B. Lessons from hereditary colorectal cancer. Cell. 1996;**87**(2):159-170

[5] Steyeberg E. Clinical Prediction Models: A Practical Approach to Development, Validation and Updating. Springer Science & Business Media; New York, USA. 2008

[6] Siegel R, Ward E, Brawley O, Jemal A. Cancer statistics. CA: A Cancer Journal for Clinicians. 2011;**61**(4):212-236

[7] Miller KD, Siegel RL, Lin CC, Mariotto AB, Kramer JL, Rowland JH, JA. Cancer treatment and survivorship statistics. CA: A Cancer Journal for Clinicians. 2016;**66**(4):271-289

[8] Love SM, Barsky SH. Breast-duct endoscopy to study stages of cancerous breast disease. The Lancet. 1996;**348**(9033):997-999

[9] Hortobagyi GN. Treatment of breast cancer. New England Journal of Medicine. 1998;**339**(14): 974-984

[10] Osborne C, Ostir GV, Du X, Peek MK, Goodwin JS. The influence of marital status on the stage at diagnosis, treatment and survival of alder women with breast cancer. Breast Cancer Research and Treatment. 2005;**93**(1):41-47

[11] Frank SA. Genetic predisposition to cancer — Insights from population genetics. Nature Reviews. 2004;**5**(10):764

[12] Sickles EA. Mammographic features of "early" breast cancer. American Journal of Roentgenology. 1984;**143**(3):461-464

[13] Nover AB, Jagtap S, Anjum W, Yegingil H, Shih WY, Shih WH, Brooks AD. Modern breast cancer detection: A technological review. Journal of Biomedical Imaging. 2009;**26**

[14] Kollias J, Elston CW, Ellis IO, Robertson JF, Blamey RW. Early-onset breast cancer — Histopathological and prognostic considerations. British Journal of Cancer. 1997;**75**(9):1318

[15] Krishnamurthy S, Mathews K, McClure S, Murray M, Gilcrease M, Albarracin C, Cohen A. Multi-institutional comparison of whole slide digital imaging and optical microscopy for interpretation of hematoxylin-eosin–stained breast tissue sections. Archives of Pathology and Laboratory Medicine. 2013;**137**(2):1733-1739

[16] Ganesan K, Acharya UR, Chua CK, Min LC, Abraham KT, Ng KH. Computer-aided breast cancer detection using mammograms: A review. IEEE Reviews in Biomedical Engineering. 2013;**6**:77-98

[17] Gelasca ED, Obara B, Fedorov D, Kvilekval K, Manjunath BS. A biosegmentation benchmark for evaluation of bioimage analysis methods. BMC Bioinformatics. 2009;**10**(1): 368

[18] Shamir L, Delaney JD, Orlov N, Eckley DM, Goldberg IG. Pattern recognition software and techniques for biological image analysis. PLoS Computational Biology. 2010;**6**(11)

[19] Kaplan SS. Clinical utility of bilateral whole-breast US in the evaluation of women with dense breast tissue. Radiology. 2001;**221**(3):641-649

[20] Rosenblatt P, Suzuki I, DeRidder A, Patel N. Breast cancer survivorship. Handbook of Breast Cancer and Related Breast Disease; New York, USA. Demos Medical Publishing. 2016

[21] Preventive Services US. Task force. Screening for breast cancer: Recommendations and rationale. Annals of Internal Medicine. 2002;**137**(5):344

[22] Pisano ED, Gatsonis C, Hendrick E, Yaffe M, Baum JK, Acharyya S, Jong R. Diagnostic performance of digital versus film mammography for breast-cancer screening. New England Journal of Medicine. 2005;**353**:1773-1783

[23] Júnior G, de Oliveira Martins L, Silva A, de Paiva A. Computer-Aided Detection and Diagnosis of Breast Cancer Using Machine Learning Texture and Shape Features. IGI Global; Hersey, PA, UZA. 2010

[24] Velayutham C, Thangavel K. Unsupervised feature selection in digital mammogram image using rough set based entropy measure. Information and Communication Technologies (WICT), 2011 World Congress; 2011

[25] Gupta M, Jin L, Homma N. Static and Dynamic Neural Networks: From Fundamentals to Advanced Theory. John Wiley Sons: New Jersey, USA; 2003

[26] Huang DS. Radial basis probabilistic neural networks: Model and applications. International Journal of Pattern Recognition and Artificial Intelligence. 1999;**13**(7):1083 1101

[27] Mao K, Tan K, Ser W. Probabilistic neural network structure determination for pattern classification. IEEE Transactions on Neural Networks. 2000;**11**(4):1009-1016

[28] Spetch DF. Probabilistic neural networks for classification, mapping or associative memory. IEEE International Conference on Neural Networks. 1998;**1**:525-532

[29] Spetch DF. Probabilistic neural networks. Neural Networks. 1990;**3**(1):109-118

[30] Spetch DF, Romsdhal H. Experience with adaptive probabilistic neural networks and adaptive general regression neural networks. IEEE International Conference on Neural networks. 1994;**2**:1203-1208

Chapter 10

Applications of Artificial Neural Networks in Biofuels

Alex Oliveira Barradas Filho and
Isabelle Moraes Amorim Viegas

Additional information is available at the end of the chapter

http://dx.doi.org/10.5772/intechopen.70691

Abstract

This chapter is focused on the application of artificial neural networks (ANNs) in the development of alternative methods for biofuel quality issues. At first, the advances and the proliferation of models and architectures of artificial neural networks are highlighted in the text by the characteristics of robustness and fault tolerance, learning capacity, uncertain information processing and parallelism, which allow the application in problems of complex nature. In this scenario, biofuels are contextualized and focused on issues of quality control and monitoring. Therefore, this chapter leads to a study of prediction and/or classification of biofuels quality parameters by the description of published works on the topic under discussion. Afterwards, a case study is performed to demonstrate, in a practical way, the steps and procedures to build alternative models for predicting the oxidative stability of biodiesel. The procedure goes from the processing of the data obtained by the near infrared until the evaluation of the alternative method developed by the neural network. In addition, some evaluation parameters are described for the assessment of the alternative method built. As a result, the feasibility and practicality of the application of neural networks to the quality of biofuels are proven.

Keywords: artificial neural network, biofuel, calibration, classification, quality parameters, oxidative stability

1. Introduction

In the last decades, artificial neural networks (ANNs) have undergone several transformations and improvements, which allowed their application in different areas of knowledge. Such an approach appreciated by the academic community, ANNs are distributed parallel systems, also known as connectionist systems, inspired by the biology of the human brain [1].

In this context, ANNs are simplified models of the human brain that consist of a large number of processing units (neurons) connected to each other. These units usually calculate mathematical functions (non-linear and/or linear) and form a large network of communication, which allows solving high complexity problems [2].

The architectures that implement the connectionist approach are usually conditioned by a training and learning process rather than being explicitly programmed. In this way, the choice of the architecture has an extremely important character for the solution of certain problems [3].

Among the different tasks appropriate to the application of ANNs are:

- Classification and pattern recognition: process by which a received signal (input) is assigned to a particular group or category;
- Categorization: discovery of well-defined categories or classes in the input data. Unlike classification, classes are not previously known;
- Prediction: estimation of a numerical response based on input values, also called calibration;
- Optimization: characterized by the minimization or maximization of a cost function;
- Noise filtering: extraction of information about a certain response of interest from a noisy dataset.

The variety of ANN applications provide a stimulating scenario for contributions in the field of biofuels, which are defined as renewable fuels derived from biomass that can be used in internal combustion engines or for other types of energy generation. The aim of using biofuels is to reduce external dependence on oil (partial or total replacement of fossil fuels), minimize environmental impacts and develop agricultural production.

The main liquid biofuels produced in the world are ethanol and biodiesel. Ethanol, also known as ethyl alcohol, is a chemical with the molecular formula C_2H_6O, produced by the fermentation of sugars. Under normal conditions, it is a colorless and volatile liquid with an ethereal odor and pungent taste, miscible in water and in different organic solvents.

According to the U.S. Energy Information Administration (EIA), in 2014, the largest ethanol producers on the worldwide are the United States and Brazil [4]. In the USA, the main raw material used for the production of ethanol is corn, while sugarcane is more prominent in Brazil.

Biodiesel is a fuel composed of alkyl esters of long-chain carboxylic acids, produced by the transesterification and/or esterification of fatty material, fats of vegetable or animal origin, with a short-chain alcohol, such as methanol or ethanol [5]. For the production of biodiesel, a variety of raw materials has been used, including edible and non-edible oils, crude oils, fried oils and animal fats. The main raw materials used are soy, palm, cotton, rapeseed, jatropha and sunflower oils and bovine tallow, although it is possible to use all vegetable oils classified as fixed oils or triglycerides, and animal fats [6–8].

Unlike fuel ethanol, the EIA shows that most of biodiesel production in 2014 is not restricted to America alone but also to the continents of Europe, Asia and Oceania [4].

In general, the two biofuels (ethanol and biodiesel) have attracted international attention and, consequently, have had their production increased in comparison to previous years. Some topics studied and related to both ethanol and biodiesel are:

- Production of raw materials;
- Identification of alternative raw materials and other production routes for biofuels;
- Maximization of the production of biofuels;
- Contribution of biofuels to reduce greenhouse gas emissions and environmental impacts;
- Quality control;
- Forms of storage, transportation and distribution of biofuels.

However, despite the diversity of topics and works published in the scientific literature, the present research is targeted to the study of the application of ANNs in the quality control of biofuels [9–15]. Typically, studies related to the quality control of biofuels have the goal to search efficient methods that monitor the fuels produced and commercialized avoiding damages to the environment and consumer injury [9, 16].

It is important to mention that the quality of biofuels is ensured by technical resolutions or standards established by each country which set limit values for contaminants and other parameters [17].

2. State of art: ANN, quality parameters and biofuels

In this section, some papers published in scientific journals, which discuss applications of ANNs to the quality of fuel ethanol (pure or blends) and biodiesel, were selected and discussed. Articles were extracted from the Web of Science database. **Table 1** groups different articles by type of biofuel (ethanol or biodiesel).

In the first article of **Table 1**, Najafi et al., in the paper named "Performance and exhaust emissions of a gasoline engine with ethanol blended gasoline fuels using artificial neural network", proposed an experimental analysis of the performance and pollutant emissions of a four-stroke SI engine operating with mixtures of ethanol and gasoline (0, 5, 10, 15 and 20%), with the aid of ANNs [18]. Analyzes of the fuel ethanol quality parameters were performed based on the standards of the American Society for Testing and Materials (ASTM). The authors showed that blends with ethanol and gasoline provided an increase in engine power and torque output. It was also found that for ethanol blends, specific brake fuel consumption decreases while thermal brake efficiency and volumetric efficiency increased [18].

Concerning to the use of ANNs, the work of Najafi et al. used the backpropagation algorithm and multilayer perceptron (MLP) architecture for non-linear mapping between the inputs (gasoline-ethanol mixtures and engine speed) and the output parameters (engine performance and exhaust emissions). The evaluation of the results was based on three criteria: correlation

Biofuel	Title of publication	Year
Etanol	Performance and exhaust emissions of a gasoline engine with ethanol blended gasoline fuels using artificial neural network	2009
	Ultrasonic determination of water concentration in ethanol fuel using artificial neural networks	2012
	Prediction of ethanol concentration in biofuel production using artificial neural networks	2013
	Application of GRNN for the prediction of performance and exhaust emissions in HCCI engine using ethanol	2016
	Artificial neural network prediction of diesel engine performance and emission fueled with diesel-kerosene-ethanol blends: a Fuzzy-based optimization	2017
Biodiesel	Application of artificial neural network to predict properties of diesel-biodiesel blends	2010
	Inference of the biodiesel cetane number by multivariate techniques	2013
	Neural network prediction of biodiesel kinematic viscosity at 313 K	2014
	Application of artificial neural networks to predict viscosity, iodine value and induction period of biodiesel focused on the study of oxidative stability	2015
	Attesting compliance of biodiesel quality using composition data and classification methods	2017

Table 1. ANN works applied to biofuel quality.

coefficient (r), root mean squared error (RMSE) and mean relative error (MRE). Thus, the work proves the feasibility of using the ANN approach to predict motor performance (brake power, torque output, brake thermal efficiency, volumetric efficiency, brake specific fuel consumption and equivalence fuel-air ratio) and the emissions (CO, CO_2, HC and NO_x) [18].

In 2012, the work titled "Ultrasonic determination of water concentration in ethanol fuel using artificial neural networks", published by Liu and Koc, it was determined the concentration of water in ethanol by measurements of ultrasonic velocity and liquid temperature [19]. The aim of the research is to propose an alternative method to contribute to the inspection against the adulteration of fuels, which impairs the vehicle performance and can cause damages to the engine [19].

In the development of an alternative method, the authors Liu and Koc used an ANN based on the MLP architecture. A database was elaborated with 651 samples for the training and validation steps of ANNs. The activation functions, varied for each hidden layer, were the functions logistic sigmoid (logsig), tangent sigmoid (tansig) and linear (purelin), and the results were based on the mean square error (MSE) and on the determination coefficient (R^2). Thus, the research concluded that the results obtained by ANNs were far better when compared with other models [19].

In the paper "Prediction of ethanol concentration in biofuel production using artificial neural networks", the authors Ahmadian-Moghadam et al. carried out, in 2013, an economic bioprocess to supply ethanol from sugar cane molasses. That research aims to contribute to the reduction of biofuel production prices and to have it as a more competitive resource in the market [20].

Ahmadian-Moghadam et al. applied ANNs to estimate the concentration of ethanol based on the sugar concentration and live and dead yeast cells. To do so, a database with 61 samples was divided as follows: 60% for training, 15% for validation and 25% for test [20]. The performance of ANN models was evaluated by the mean absolute deviation (MAD), mean absolute percentage error (MAPE) and MSE. Authors concluded that the results showed the viability of the application of the ANN model to determine the final ethanol concentration in the biofuels production process in a large scale [20].

Bendu et al. pointed out, in the paper "Application of GRNN for the prediction of performance and exhaust emissions in HCCI engine using ethanol" published in 2016, the importance of the evaluation of performance and emission parameters of an ethanol-fueled homogeneous charge compression ignition (HCCI) engine. In addition, the authors identified the nature of the parameters as a non-linear problem, which indicated the need for more robust tools [21].

For this purpose, Bendu et al. used a generalized regression neural network (GRNN) consisting of four layers (input layer, radial layer, regression layer and output layer). The input parameters were the charge temperature and the engine load, while the performance and emission values were set as output parameters.

The engine performance parameters were brake thermal efficiency (BTE), exhaust gas temperature (EGT) and the exhaust emission parameters were NO, CO, smoke and unburned hydrocarbon emission (UHC). Summing up, the authors showed the viability of the method and pointed out that the GRNN model can also be used for the control and testing of the HCCI engine [21].

In 2017, Bhowmik et al. performed a study titled "Artificial neural network prediction of diesel engine performance and emission fueled with diesel–kerosene–ethanol blends: a fuzzy-based optimization" to explore the impact on performance and emission characteristics of a single cylinder indirect injection (IDI) engine fueled with blends of diesel and kerosene [22]. In this research, the authors indicated that the addition of ethanol to the mixtures of diesel and kerosene significantly improved the BTE, brake specific energy consumption (BSEC) and the emissions of NO_X, CO and total hydrocarbon (THC) of the engine [22].

Therefore, Bhowmik et al. built an ANN model to map the inputs (load, kerosene volume percentage and ethanol volume percentage) with respect to the outputs (BTE, BSEC, NO_X, THC and CO). The best topology found had a structure with five hidden neurons and presented satisfactory results for the problem addressed. The criteria for evaluation of the developed ANNs were based on MSE, MAPE and r [22].

In 2010, Kumar and Bansal published the paper "Application of artificial neural network to predict properties of diesel – biodiesel blends" whose aim was to evaluate tools for the determination of physical-chemical properties of diesel-biodiesel mixtures. Choosing an appropriate and efficient alternative method could help to avoid some overly time-consuming and costly experiments [23].

Also in the Kumar and Bansal paper, traditional linear regression (principle of least squares) and ANN were applied and compared. The ANNs optimization process was carried out by varying the architectures and training algorithms. The authors concluded that the best results were obtained by the ANN method [23].

In the work of Nadai et al., entitled "Inference of the biodiesel cetane number by multivariate techniques", a method consisting of successive application of principal components analysis (PCA), fuzzy clustering and ANN in a dataset composed by structural information from proton nuclear magnetic resonance (^{1}H NMR) of biodiesel fatty esters was implemented [24]. The aim of that work was to obtain the cetane number of different types of complex mixtures from data of pure substances (esters). The authors pointed out two main characteristics that affect the cetane number values: the number of carbon-carbon double bonds and the structure of the alcohol moiety in each fatty ester [24].

In 2014, with the research "Neural network prediction of biodiesel kinematic viscosity at 313 K" Meng et al. performed the prediction of the kinematic viscosity property of biodiesel by artificial neural networks. The authors used 105 samples of biodiesel collected from the literature and 19 types of fatty acid methyl esters (FAMEs) were set as inputs. The results obtained suggested ANNs as an option in predicting kinematic viscosity with a correlation coefficient of 0.9774 [25].

In the paper "Application of artificial neural networks to predict viscosity, iodine value and induction period of biodiesel focused on the study of oxidative stability", Barradas Filho and collaborators optimized ANN models to predict viscosity, iodine value and induction period (oxidative stability) of 98 biodiesel samples by its fatty esters composition [26].

Also in the work of Barradas Filho et al., the ANNs optimization occurred by varying the activation functions, the number of neurons in the hidden layers and the convergence methods. The evaluation criteria of the models were MSE, RMSE, MAPE and r and R^2 coefficients. After optimization, the ANN results were compared to other models and obtained the best performance [26].

In 2017, the work "Attesting compliance of biodiesel quality using composition data and classification methods" of Lopes et al. compared four classification methods (decision tree classifier, K-nearest neighbors, support vector machine and artificial neural networks) to evaluate the compliance of biodiesel samples concerning some quality parameters. This work aimed to obtain an alternative method with more accuracy when compared to other alternative methods [27].

3. Performance evaluation parameters

After adjustment of classification or calibration models, it is important to have parameters to evaluate the performance through the results obtained. Some of the most widely used parameters and a few explanations on each of them will be provided in this section. These parameters can also be employed, for instance, to aid comparing and deciding among different methods applied to the same problem addressed.

3.1. Evaluation parameters for classification

The first step to organize classification results for better visualization is to build a confusion matrix, like in the example from **Table 2**. The actual classes are represented in the columns, and the predicted classes, in the rows. The number of apple samples classified as apples is registered in cell AA; the number of apples classified as bananas is in cell AB and those

	Actual class			
		Apple (A)	**Banana (B)**	**Coconut (C)**
Predicted class	**Apple (A)**	9 (AA)	2 (BA)	1 (CA)
	Banana (B)	1 (AB)	5 (BB)	1 (CB)
	Coconut (C)	0 (AC)	2 (BC)	11 (CC)
	Sum	10	9	13

Table 2. 3 × 3 confusion matrix of results of fruits classification.

classified as coconuts are in cell AC. The same goes to the other fruit classes. The principal diagonal of the matrix represents the samples correctly classified (cells AA, BB and CC), and the other cells represent the misclassified ones. An ideal classifier would provide a confusion matrix in which all the cells out of the principal diagonal have zero value.

The evaluation parameters for classification methods are based on rates that can be obtained from the confusion matrix. These rates correspond to integer values as they are the numbers of samples classified and split according to some criteria, as will be explained below.

The example given in **Table 2**, and for banana class, the true positive rate (TP) corresponds to the number of bananas correctly classified as bananas (5 samples, cell BB) and the true negatives (TN) are the samples of the other classes (apple and coconut) classified in any class other than banana (21 samples, cells AA, AC, CA and CC). The false positive rate (FP) is the number of samples of other classes misclassified as bananas (2 samples, cells AB and CB) and the false negative rate (FN) corresponds to the banana samples not classified as bananas (4 samples, cells BA and BC).

For apple class, the TP, TN, FP and FN rates are 9, 19, 3 and 1, respectively, and for coconut class, these rates in the same sequence are 11, 17, 2 and 2. Once the TP, TN, FP and FN rates have been obtained for each class, their average values for all classes together can be used to calculate some global evaluation parameters within which the main ones will be briefly explained with the fruits example.

The accuracy (ACC), given by Eq. (1), reflects the global ability of correctly classification by the method. For the fruits example, ACC is 85.42%, which is the percentage of samples that were classified in its actual classes.

$$\mathrm{ACC} = \frac{\mathrm{TP} + \mathrm{TN}}{\mathrm{TP} + \mathrm{TN} + \mathrm{FP} + \mathrm{FN}} \times 100\% \tag{1}$$

The sensitivity (SENS), also called "recall", can be considered as a global TP rate. The SENS of the fruits classification is 78.13%, calculated by Eq. (2).

$$\mathrm{SENS} = \frac{\mathrm{TP}}{\mathrm{TP} + \mathrm{FN}} \times 100\% \tag{2}$$

The specificity (SPEC) can be calculated by Eq. (3) and it is a global TN rate. For the fruits example, SPEC is 89.06%.

$$\text{SPEC} = \frac{\text{TN}}{\text{TN} + \text{FP}} \times 100\% \tag{3}$$

The false positive rate (FPR) can be interpreted as a global rate of FP for all the classes combined and it is the inversely proportional to the SPEC. In the example discussed here, FPR is 10.94%, calculated by Eq. (4).

$$\text{FPR} = \frac{\text{FP}}{\text{TN} + \text{FP}} \times 100\% = 100\% \text{ - SPEC} \tag{4}$$

Analogously, the false negative rate (FNR) is a global rate of FN (Eq. (5)). For the fruits classification, FNR is 21.87% and it is complementary to the SENS.

$$\text{FNR} = \frac{\text{FN}}{\text{TP} + \text{FN}} \times 100\% = 100\% \text{ - SENS} \tag{5}$$

The ACC, SENS, SPEC, FPR and FNR are some of the main evaluation parameters for classification. Here an example of three classes was presented, giving a 3 × 3 confusion matrix and, therefore, the evaluation parameters should be calculated by the average TP, TN, FP and FN rates.

Problems with only two classes are simpler and more widespread in the literature, usually involving samples that "have" or "do not have" a specific characteristic and giving a 2 × 2 confusion matrix. In this case, TP, TN, FP and FN rates are obtained only for the "positive class" and the evaluation parameters are directly calculated by these rates instead of by the averages.

A two class example, already cited in Section 2, is the classification of biodiesel samples according to their compliance to some quality parameters. For each criteria, the samples were split in "compliant" and "non-compliant" [27].

3.2. Evaluation parameters for calibration

The evaluation parameters for calibration are quite different from those for classification. In calibration, these parameters are based on the difference between the actual response, that obtained experimentally by a reference method, and the predicted response, the one estimated by the calibration method.

The oxidative stability (h) of some biodiesel samples from the case study of Section 4 are show in **Table 3** with the actual (y) and predicted (y') responses given in hours. The residuals are the difference between the actual and the predicted responses. The other columns have values calculated to be used in equations of the evaluation parameters that will be explained.

The RMSE is an average deviation between the actual and the predicted values and it has the same unity from the responses. The example from **Table 3**, the RMSE calculated is 0.34 h, which means that the estimated responses differ, on average, in ±0.34 h from the actual values. In papers, the RMSE is often abbreviated as RMSEC, RMSEP, RMSEV and RMSECV when

Actual response (h) (y)	Predicted response (h) (y')	Residual (h) ($y - y'$)	$(y - y')^2$	$\left(\frac{y_i - y'_i}{y_i}\right) \times 100\%$
19.36	19.20	0.16	0.0256	0.8264
8.93	9.01	−0.08	0.0064	0.8956
7.37	7.35	0.02	0.0004	0.2714
12.77	11.95	0.82	0.6724	6.4213
15.64	15.80	−0.16	0.0256	1.0230
6.60	6.45	0.15	0.0225	2.2727
5.53	5.75	−0.22	0.0484	3.9783
8.01	7.68	0.33	0.1089	4.1199

Table 3. Actual and predicted values of oxidative stability (h) of biodiesel samples.

calculated for the samples of calibration (training), prediction (test), validation and cross-validation, respectively, and it can be given by Eq. (6), in which n is the number of samples ($n = 8$, in this example).

$$\mathrm{RMSE} = \sqrt{\frac{1}{n}\sum_{i=1}^{n}(y_i - y'_i)^2} \tag{6}$$

Another important error metric is the MAPE, which is a relative measure of the prediction accuracy, calculated by Eq. (7). From the example of oxidative stabilities of biodiesel, the MAPE is 2.48%, that is, on average, the predicted values deviate in 2.48% from their actual values.

$$\mathrm{MAPE} = \frac{1}{n}\sum_{i=1}^{n}\left|\frac{y_i - y'_i}{y_i}\right| \times 100\% \tag{7}$$

The Pearson correlation coefficient (r, Eq. (8)) is a measure of the linear relationship between two variables and it is expressed in values from 0 to |1|. The closer to |1|, the more linearly correlated the variables are. In cases of calibration methods, r coefficient is used to compare the actual and the predicted values. Since y and y' are expected to be equal, this represents a direct relationship and, then, the ideal r coefficient is +1.

$$r(y, y') = \frac{n\sum_{i=1}^{n} y_i y'_i - \left(\sum_{i=1}^{n} y_i\right)\left(\sum_{i=1}^{n} y'_i\right)}{\sqrt{\left[n\sum_{i=1}^{n} y_i^2 - \left(\sum_{i=1}^{n} y_i\right)^2\right]\left[n\sum_{i=1}^{n} y'^2_i - \left(\sum_{i=1}^{n} y'_i\right)^2\right]}} \tag{8}$$

For the oxidative stabilities, for example, r is 0.9977, which represents a high correlation between the actual and the predicted responses. However, it is important to perform the graphical analysis of the correlation by a scatter plot of the actual (y in x-axis) and the predicted (y' in y-axis) values, because not all samples with a perfect correlation coefficient are well distributed along the line of the expected identity function for $y = y'$.

Step	Parameter	MLP 4-3-1-1
Training	RMSEC (h)	1.31
	MAPE (%)	8.35
	R^2	0.9306
	r	0.9647
Validation	RMSEV (h)	0.43
	MAPE (%)	5.51
	R^2	0.9733
	r	0.9866
Test	RMSEP (h)	0.67
	MAPE (%)	6.89
	R^2	0.9544
	r	0.9769

Table 4. Evaluation parameters calculated from the results obtained by the ANN MLP 4-3-1-1 for the oxidative stability (h) of biodiesel samples.

Although the R^2 coefficient can be obtained by taking the square of the correlation coefficient, they have different meanings. The R^2, calculated by Eq. (9) in which y_m is the average of the actual values, expresses how much the calibration model explains from the total variance and it can range from 0 to +1. For example, from **Table 4**, the R^2 obtained is 0.9954, which means that 99.54% of total data variance is explained by the regression, and the 0.46% remaining are attributed to residuals.

$$R^2 = r^2 = \frac{\sum_{i=1}^{n} (y'_i - y_m)^2}{\sum_{i=1}^{n} (y_i - y_m)^2} \tag{9}$$

Some of the main evaluation parameters for regression have been explained in this section. Besides the numerical parameters, it is also quite important to perform a graphical evaluation of the results by the correlation and residual plots. More details on this will be provided in the case study of the next section.

4. Case study

Biodiesel, like any other fuel, needs to meet some parameters specifications so it can be marketed with quality and safety. These quality parameters are established by standards in each country or region, such as the standards EN 14214 (Europe), ASTM D6751 (USA) and RANP 45/2014 (Brazil) [27].

Among the parameters of biodiesel quality, there are general parameters, which are also applied to petroleum diesel, and there is a special group of parameters related to the chemical composition and purity of the vegetable oils. These parameters can be grouped into four sets: contaminants from the raw material, parameters related to the evaluation of the production process, properties inherent to molecular structures and parameters related to the storage process [7].

One of the main problems assigned to the quality of biodiesel is the possibility of its oxidation caused by the presence of unsaturations in its ester molecules, which is one of the most relevant differences between biodiesel and mineral diesel composition. The main products formed by the oxidation of biodiesel can cause formation of insoluble gums in the engine, filter clogging, injector cocking and corrosion of the metal parts of the engine. Therefore, the evaluation of the oxidative stability of biodiesel is considered by many researchers in the literature to be a very important analysis that should be done because it is directly related to the deterioration capacity (oxidation) and to the time in which the biofuel can be stored (induction period) [26].

The oxidative stability of biodiesel is measured by the method EN 14112, also called Rancimat method, which consists of a system composed of a reaction vessel connected to a cell monitored by an electrode. The sample is placed in the vessel in a heating block at 110°C and a continuous stream of air is bubbled through. The increase in temperature and the presence of oxygen induce the accelerated oxidation of biodiesel. The primary products are formed, followed by secondary products of the oxidation among which are short chain volatile organic acids. These acids are carried to a cell containing deionized water and promote the increase in conductivity, which is measured by an electrode coupled to a device that records the conductivity as a function of time [28].

The induction period used to evaluate the oxidative stability of biodiesel is the time at which the conductivity curve increases rapidly, corresponding to the emergence of the secondary products of the oxidation. The standards EN 14214 and RANP 45/2014 state that the minimum oxidative stability of biodiesel should be 8 h at 110°C [29, 30], while ASTM D6751 specifies 3 h of oxidative stability [31].

Aiming to reduce the time, complexity and costs of analyzing biodiesel quality parameters, some papers in the literature report analytical methodologies alternative to official methods. In this context, the Rancimat method is a relevant case to be studied due to the long analysis time, since a sample of biodiesel that meets EN 14214 requirements will be under analysis for more than 8 h to obtain an oxidative stability result.

A case study of an application of ANN to predict oxidative stability of biodiesel will be presented below to better illustrate the main steps from data preprocessing and selection of sample sets (for training, validation and test) to the optimization of ANN configuration and application. Finally, some performance measures will be evaluated and discussed in the case study. All data handling, preprocessing, subset partitioning and ANN regression were carried out with software MATLAB® 2013a (MathWorks), PLS_Toolbox (Eigenvector) and an algorithm implemented in MATLAB [32].

4.1. Database acquisition and preprocessing

Biodiesels from soybean, corn, palm and babassu (an oleaginous abundant in the Northeast of Brazil) were synthesized via transesterification by methylic route and homogeneous alkaline catalysis and used to prepare 70 binary, ternary and quaternary mixtures (volumetric fractions) designed by simplex-lattice and centroid-simplex designs.

The oxidative stabilities of the samples were determined by the method EN 14112:2003 [33] using a Rancimat equipment Metrohm model 873. The average of two measurements for each sample was taken. The oxidative stabilities of the mixtures ranged from 4.81 to 25.47 h.

The spectra were acquired using a Fourier transform NIR spectrometer PerkinElmer model Frontier™ with a near infrared reflectance accessory (NIRA), equipped with a fast recovery deuterated triglycine sulfate (FR-DTGS) detector. All spectra were recorded with an average of 16 scans and spectral resolution of 2 cm^{-1}. The measured wavenumber range was 4000–12,000 cm^{-1}, but the work range was restricted to 4000–6100 cm^{-1} because of non-informative signal (close to baseline) and increase of noise as wavenumber gets close to 12,000 cm^{-1}.

The raw spectra (**Figure 1a**) showed bands characteristic of first overtone of C—H stretching (5550–6100 cm^{-1}) and of combination of C—H and C=O stretching modes (4640–4700 cm^{-1}) [34]. The bands around 4262 and 4334 cm^{-1} can be associated to the second overtone of C—H bending and to combination of C—H and C=C stretching modes, respectively [35].

For correction of spectra baseline deviations caused by systematic variations, the first derivative was calculated by the Savitzky-Golay filter [36] with a 15-point quadratic smoothing function. The window size of points to fit the polynomial function of Savitzky-Golay filter depends on how noisy the spectra are. In this case, a 15-point window was enough to smooth the spectral noise. The derivative NIR spectra of the full database can be seen in **Figure 1b**.

After applying Savitzky-Golay filter, the spectra were mean-centered and then used as input data (**X**-matrix) consisting of 1051 variables and, as output variable (response, **y**-vector), it was used the raw oxidative stabilities (h). From this point, only the preprocessed data was used.

4.2. Steps for construction of the ANN model and selection of sample sets

The construction and validation of models for multivariate classification or calibration go through three basic steps, and for each of them it is necessary a sample set. The first step, the training or calibration, consists of model adjustment with pairs of inputs and outputs (**X**, **y**) provided in the database. The coefficients or weights of the model are amended so the response calculated based on variations in **X** data is as closest to the real (experimental) response as possible. In the training, it is important to have representative samples concerning all the possible **X** and **y** variations that real samples can have.

The step of validation (or internal validation) helps assess the progress of optimization and indicates when the model adjustment should be ended, so it occurs simultaneously to the training step. In the beginning of the training, the coefficients and weights are underfit and the errors are large. In the course of training, the errors decrease as the coefficients are adjusted

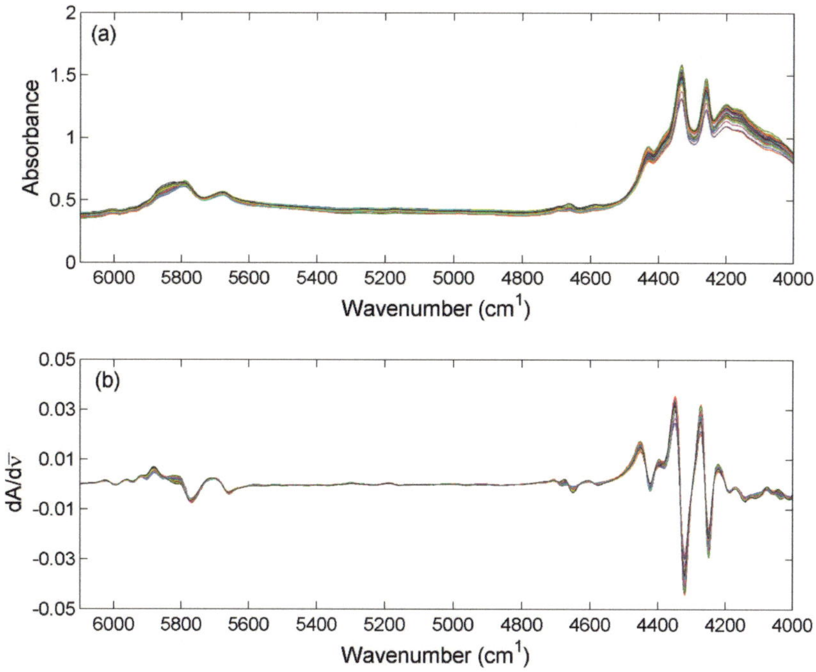

Figure 1. Raw (a) and derivative (b) NIR spectra of the 70 samples of biodiesel mixtures.

and begin to model even the natural noise coming from systematic errors of experimental measurements. At this stage, it occurs the so-called overfitting and the model will not be able to predict or classify external samples with accuracy, although the training and validation errors are small. Therefore, the aim of internal validation is to aid choosing the number of neurons and hidden layers in such a way to balance underfitting and overfitting.

The last step is the test (or external validation), in which samples that were not used during training or internal validation are estimated or classified by the optimized model, simulating a real application. The neural networks learn from the past (training samples) to estimate future cases (test samples).

There are some methods for selection of samples for training, validation and test. In this case study, it will was used the SPXY method (Sample set Partitioning based on joint **x-y** distances), which is based on the variability of both input (NIR spectra) and output (oxidative stability) variables [32]. The test set consisted of 30% of the database (21 samples), while the 49 remaining samples were split for training (39 samples) and validation (10 samples).

4.3. Dimensionality reduction and ANN configuration

As the **X**-matrix is composed of 1051 variables, it is necessary to apply a method for dimensionality reduction before the training of the neural networks. Otherwise, the modeling would consider too much noise and, because of the large number of input neurons, the ANNs would take too long to converge.

The partial least squares regression (PLS) was used for dimensionality reduction. The number of latent variables (LVs) was optimized based on full cross-validation method. Four LVs explained 99.15% of the **X**-variance and 82.85% of **y**-variance.

The feedforward MLP ANNs were trained using backpropagation algorithm with a fixed learning rate (0.125) as convergence method to minimize the RMSEC. The input layer is formed by four neurons receiving the four LVs, and the output layer is constituted of one neuron (oxidative stability). The number of neurons in the first hidden layer ranged from 1 to 20, and in the second hidden layer, from 1 to 10. It was also tested a topology with only one hidden layer. The hyperbolic tangent (tanh, Eq. (10)) and purelin (Eq. (11)) functions were used as activation functions (or transfer functions) of the hidden and output layers, respectively.

$$f(x) = \tanh(x) = \frac{e^x - e^{-x}}{e^x + e^{-x}} \tag{10}$$

$$f(x) = x \tag{11}$$

4.4. Results and discussion

As the validation is the step that aids to assess and choose the best fit under varying conditions during optimization, the RMSEV was the criteria taken to choose the best number of hidden layers and neurons. The RMSEVs of the biodiesel oxidative stabilities (h) predicted by ANNs with different numbers of neurons in the hidden layers are represented in **Figure 2**, showing the dependence of the RMSEV on the ANN topology.

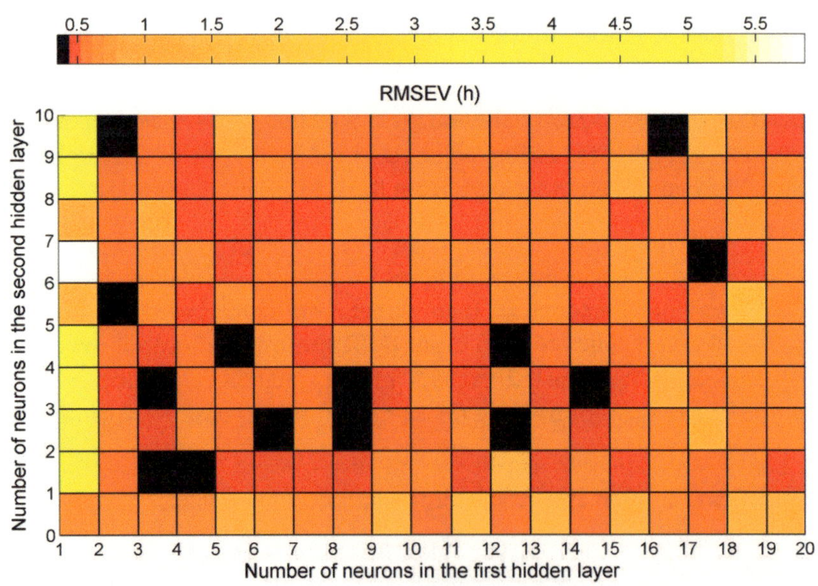

Figure 2. Dependence of the RMSEV of the biodiesel oxidative stability predicted by ANNs with different numbers of neurons in first and second hidden layers.

http://dx.doi.org/10.5772/intechopen.70691

The RMSEVs when number of neurons in the second hidden layer is zero correspond to the topologies having only one hidden layer (the first one, varying from 1 to 20 neurons). These results presented high RMSEVs that did not vary much with the number of the hidden neurons, evidencing the convergence difficulty of the ANNs with only one hidden layer. Hence, the second layer was added to the optimization process.

Few neural network topologies presented RMSEV lower than 0.5 h, but the best ones are those represented by the black squares in **Figure 2**: MLP 4-2-5-1, MLP 4-2-9-1, MLP 4-3-1-1, MLP 4-3-3-1, MLP 4-4-1-1, MLP 4-5-4-1, MLP 4-6-2-1, MLP 4-8-2-1, MLP 4-8-3-1, MLP 4-12-2-1, MLP 4-12-4-1, MLP 4-14-3-1, MLP 4-16-9-1 and MLP 4-17-6-1. In the notation MLP A-B-C-D, A is the number of input neurons (four LVs), B and C are the number of neurons in the first and second hidden layers, respectively, and D is the number of output neurons (one, oxidative stability).

The 14 best topologies above mentioned had had RMSEV less than or equal to 0.43 h. For choosing among them, the smaller number of neurons is preferred (principle of parsimony: the simpler the better). Therefore, the topology MLP 4-3-1-1 was selected to expand results and predict the oxidative stability of the test samples, but the topologies MLP 4-3-3-1 and MLP 4-4-1-1 should provide similar results.

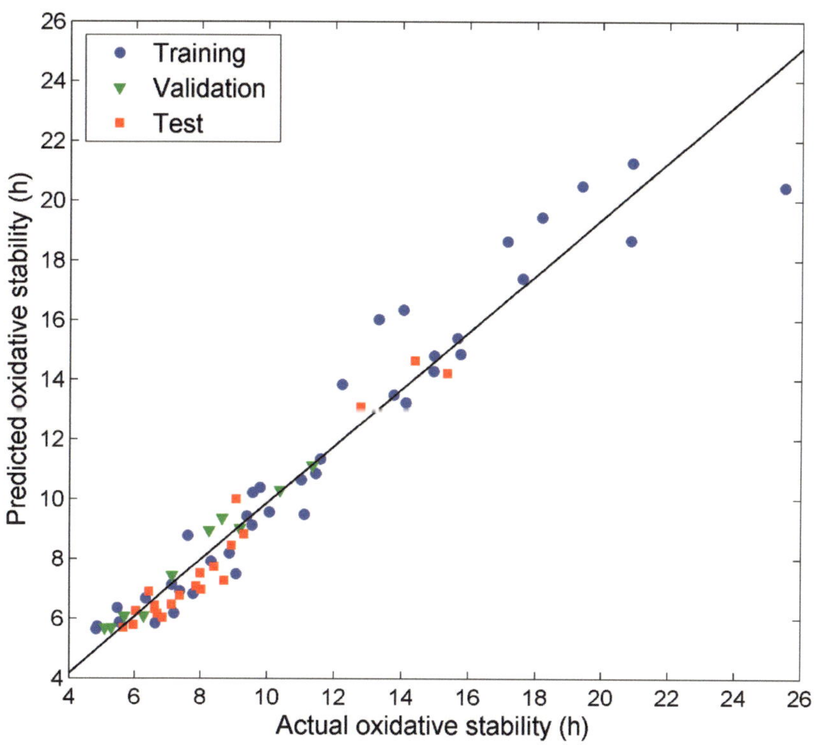

Figure 3. Scatter plot of the biodiesel oxidative stability values predicted by the ANN MLP 4-3-1-1 against the actual values measured by the method EN 14112.

The evaluation parameters calculated for the ANN MLP 4-3-1-1 can be verified in **Table 4**. These parameters can be interpreted as in Section 3.2.

The most important to evaluate the optimized model are the parameters obtained for the test dataset, since these samples simulate a real application with data not used to build nor optimize the model. The RMSEP was 0.67 and the MAPE for test samples was 6.89%, which means that the predicted oxidative stabilities for real samples differed in ±0.67 h from the actual values and deviated about 6.89%, related to their actual values.

Still for the test samples, the correlation coefficient was 0.9769, indicating a high correlation between the actual and the predicted values of oxidative stability. The determination coefficient was also high, meaning that the ANN MLP 4-3-1-1 explained 95.44% of the total data variance, and the prediction errors represents 4.56% of the total variance.

The correlation plot for samples of all the three steps can be seen in **Figure 3**, in which the samples are well distributed along the line, especially the validation and test samples, leading to correlation coefficients higher than 0.96 for the three steps.

In residual plot (**Figure 4**), it is important to have approximately the same quantity of samples with positive and negative residuals, and the closer to the central line ($y = 0$) the smaller the RMSEs. In this case study, the majority of samples had residual lower than ±1.5 h and they are well divided with positive and negative residuals. The higher residuals belong to the training samples, which indeed had the highest RMSE (1.31 h).

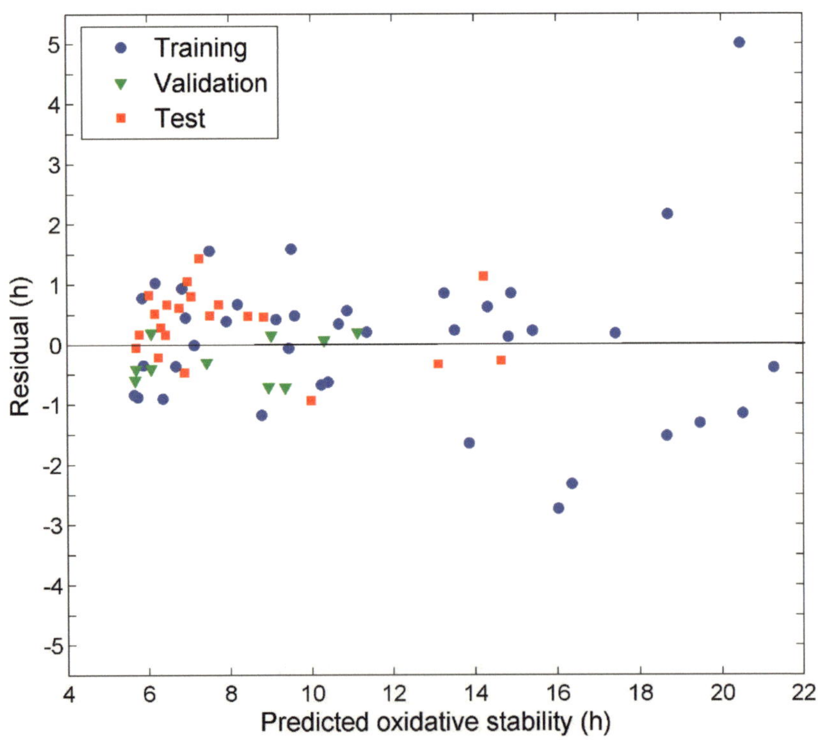

Figure 4. Residual plot the biodiesel oxidative stability values predicted by the ANN MLP 4-3-1-1.

http://dx.doi.org/10.5772/intechopen.70691

5. Conclusion

The literature presents a variety of published works involving the feasibility of the application of artificial neural networks to biofuels. In this way, the increasing importance of the biofuels theme becomes more evident in the global energetic scenario.

The ANNs proved to be a promising tool in the development of more efficient and cost-effective alternative methods to control and monitor the quality of biofuels, when compared to official methods.

In addition, a presented case study allowed to understand, in practice, the procedures to be performed in the process of predicting a physical-chemical property of biodiesel, the oxidative stability, since data preprocessing, ANN setup and training and calculating and interpretation of the evaluation criteria.

Although the practical development was carried out by a regression approach, this work also explained about classifiers and procedures for both the construction and evaluation of models. Therefore, the present work can be helpful to instruct the basic procedures in the application of ANNs to the quality of biofuels.

Acknowledgements

The authors would like to thank the Foundation for Research and Scientific and Technological Development of Maranhão (FAPEMA) and the National Council for Scientific and Technological Development from Brazil (CNPq) for the financial support and fellowships received. We also thank the laboratories LAPQAP/NEPE from the Federal University of Maranhão and LAC from the Federal University of Pernambuco.

Author details

Alex Oliveira Barradas Filho[1]* and Isabelle Moraes Amorim Viegas[2]

*Address all correspondence to: alex.barradas@ecp.ufma.br

1 Federal University of Maranhão, São Luís, MA, Brazil

2 Federal University of Pernambuco, Recife, PE, Brazil

References

[1] Braga AP, Carvalho APLF, Ludermir TB. Redes Neurais Artificiais. Teoria e Aplicações. 2nd ed. Rio de Janeiro: LTC; 2007. 238 p. ISBN: 978-8521615644

[2] Haykin S. Neural Networks: A Comprehensive Foundation. 2nd ed. Upper Saddle River: Prentice Hall, 1998. ISBN: 978-0132733502

[3] Jain AK, Mao J, Mohiuddin KM. Artificial neural networks: A tutorial. Computer. 1996; **29**:31-44. DOI: 10.1109/2.485891

[4] U.S. Energy Information Administration (EIA). International Energy Statistics, 2014. Available from: https://www.eia.gov/tools/ [Accessed: 01-07-2017]

[5] Verma P, Sharma MP. Review of process parameters for biodiesel production from different feedstocks. Renewable & Sustainable Energy Reviews. 2016;**62**:1063-1071. DOI: 10.1016/j.rser.2016.04.054

[6] Moser BR. Influence of extended storage on fuel properties of methyl esters prepared from canola, palm, soybean and sunflower oils. Renewable Energy. 2011;**36**:1221-1226. DOI: 10.1016/j.renene.2010.10.009

[7] Lôbo IP, Ferreira SLC, Da Cruz RS. Biodiesel: parâmetros de qualidade e métodos analíticos. Química Nova. 2009;**32**:1596-1608. DOI: 10.1590/S0100-40422009000600044

[8] Schuchardt U, Sercheli R, Vargas RM. Transesterification of vegetable oils: A review. Journal of the Brazilian Chemical Society. 1998;**9**:199-210. DOI: 10.1590/S0103-50531998000300002

[9] Sajjadi B, Raman AAA, Arandiyan H. A comprehensive review on properties of edible and non-edible vegetable oil-based biodiesel: Composition, specifications and prediction models. Renewable & Sustainable Energy Reviews. 2016;**63**:62-92. DOI: 10.1016/j.rser.2016.05.035

[10] Saldana DA, Starck L, Pascal M, Rousseau B, Ferrando N, Creton B. Prediction of density and viscosity of biofuel compounds using machine learning methods. Energy & Fuels. 2012;**26**:2416-2426. DOI: 10.1021/ef3001339

[11] Balabin RM, Safieva RZ. Near-infrared (NIR) spectroscopy for biodiesel analysis: Fractional composition, iodine value, and cold filter plugging point from one vibrational spectrum. Energy & Fuels. 2011;**25**:2373-2382. DOI: 10.1021/ef200356h

[12] Balabin RM, Lomakina EI, Safieva RZ. Neural network (ANN) approach to biodiesel analysis: Analysis of biodiesel density, kinematic viscosity, methanol and water contents using near infrared (NIR) spectroscopy. Fuel. 2011;**90**:2007-2015. DOI: 10.1016/j.fuel.2010.11.038

[13] Przybylski R, Zambiazi RC. Predicting oxidative stability of vegetable oils using neural network system and endogenous oil components. Journal of American Oil Chemistry Society. 2000;**77**:925-932. DOI: 10.1007/s11746-000-0146-x

[14] Ramadhas AS, Jayaraj S, Muraleedharan C, Padmakumari K. Artificial neural networks used for the prediction of the cetane number of biodiesel. Renewable Energy. 2006;**31**:2524-2533. DOI: 10.1016/j.renene.2006.01.009

[15] Saeid B, Aroua MK, Raman AAA, Sulaiman NMN. Estimation of vegetable oil-based ethyl esters biodiesel densities using artificial neural networks. Journal of Applied Sciences. 2008;**8**:3005-3011. DOI: 10.3923/jas.2008.3005.3011

[16] Marques DB, Barradas Filho AO, Romariz ARS, Viegas IMA, Luz DA, Barros Filho AKD, Labidi S, Ferraudo AS. Recent developments on statistical and neural network tools

focusing on biodiesel quality. International Journal of Computer Science and Applications. 2014;**3**:97-110. DOI: 10.14355/ijcsa.2014.0303.01

[17] Hoekman SK, Broch A, Robbins C, Ceniceros E, Natarajan M. Review of biodiesel composition, properties, and specifications. Renewable and Sustainable Energy Reviews. 2012;**16**:143-169. DOI: 10.1016/j.rser.2011.07.143

[18] Najafi G, Ghobadian B, Tavakoli T, Buttsworth DR, Yusaf TF, Faizollahnejad M. Performance and exhaust emissions of a gasoline engine with ethanol blended gasoline fuels using artificial neural network. Applied Energy. 2009;**86**:630-639. DOI: 10.1016/j.apenergy.2008.09.017

[19] Liu B, Koc AB. Ultrasonic determination of water concentration in ethanol fuel using artificial neural networks. Transactions of the ASABE. 2012;**55**:1865-1872. DOI: 10.13031/2013.42339

[20] Ahmadian-Moghadam H, Elegado FB, Nayve R. Prediction of ethanol concentration in biofuel production using artificial neural networks. American journal of Modeling and. Optimization. 2013;**1**:31-35. DOI: 10.12691/ajmo-1-3-2

[21] Bendu H, Deepak BBV, Murugan S. Application of GRNN for the prediction of performance and exhaust emissions in HCCI engine using ethanol. Energy Conversion and Management. 2016;**122**:165-173. DOI: 10.1016/j.enconman.2016.05.061

[22] Bhowmik S, Panua R, Debroy D, Paul A. Artificial neural network prediction of diesel engine performance and emission Fueled with diesel–kerosene–ethanol blends: A fuzzy-based optimization. Journal of Energy Resources Technology. 2017;**139**. DOI: 10.1115/1.4035886

[23] Kumar J, Bansal A. Application of artificial neural network to predict properties of diesel-biodiesel blends. Journal of Science, Engineering and Technology. 2010;**6**:98-103. DOI: 10.3126/kuset.v6i2.4017

[24] Nadai DV, Simões JB, Gatts CEN, Miranda PCML. Inference of the biodiesel cetane number by multivariate techniques. Fuel. 2013;**105**:325-330. DOI: 10.1016/j.fuel.2012.06.018

[25] Meng X, Jia M, Wang T. Neural network prediction of biodiesel kinematic viscosity at 313 K. Fuel. 2014;**121**:133-140. DOI: 10.1016/j.fuel.2013.12.029

[26] Barradas Filho AO, Barros AKD, Labidi S, Viegas IMA, Marques DB, Romariz ARS, de Souza RM, Marques AL, Marques EP. Application of artificial neural networks to predict viscosity, iodine value and induction period of biodiesel focused on the study of oxidative stability. Fuel 2015;**145**:127-135. DOI: 10.1016/j.fuel.2014.12.016

[27] Lopes MV, Barradas Filho AO, Barros AK, Viegas IMA, Silva LCO, Marques EP, Marques ALB. Attesting compliance of biodiesel quality using composition data and classification methods. Neural Computing and Applications. 2017. DOI: 10.1007/s00521-017-3087-4

[28] Yaakob Z, Narayanan BN, Padikkaparambil S, Unni KS, Akbar PM. A review on the oxidation stability of biodiesel. Renewable and Sustainable Energy Reviews. 2014;**35**:136-153. DOI: 10.1016/j.rser.2014.03.055

[29] EN 14214. Liquid Petroleum Products—Fatty Acid Methyl Esters (FAME) for Use in Diesel Engines and Heating Applications—Requirements and Test Methods. Comité Européen de Normalisation. 2012.

[30] RANP 45/2014. Resolução ANP n° 45, de 25 de agosto de 2014 - DOU 26.08.2014. Agência Nacional do Petróleo, Gás Natural e Biocombustíveis. p. 2014

[31] ASTM D6751. Standard Specification for Biodiesel Fuel Blend Stock (B100) for Middle Distillate Fuels. American Society for Testing and Materials. 2012.

[32] Galvão RKH, Araujo MCU, José GE, Pontes MJC, Silva EC, Saldanha TCB. A method for calibration and validation subset partitioning. Talanta. 2005;**67**:736-740. DOI: 10.1016/j.talanta.2005.03.025

[33] EN 14112. Fat and Oil Derivatives—Fatty Acid Methyl Esters (FAME) - Determination of Oxidation Stability (Accelerated Oxidation Test). Comité Européen de Normalisation. 2003.

[34] Oliveira JS, Montalvão R, Daher L, Suarez PAZ, Rubim JC. Determination of methyl ester contents in biodiesel blends by FTIR-ATR and FTNIR spectroscopies. Talanta. 2006;**69**: 1278-1284. DOI: 10.1016/j.talanta.2006.01.002

[35] De Lira LFB, de Albuquerque MS, Pacheco JGA; Fonseca TM, Cavalcanti EHS, Stragevitch L, Pimentel MF. Infrared spectroscopy and multivariate calibration to monitor stability quality parameters of biodiesel. Microchemical Journal 2010;**96**:126-131. DOI: 10.1016/j.microc.2010.02.014

[36] Savitzky A, Golay MJE. Smoothing and differentiation of data by simplified least squares procedures. Analytical Chemistry. 1964;**36**:1627-1639. DOI: 10.1021/ac60214a047

Chapter 11

ANN Modelling to Optimize Manufacturing Process

Luigi Alberto Ciro De Filippis, Livia Maria Serio,
Francesco Facchini and Giovanni Mummolo

Additional information is available at the end of the chapter

http://dx.doi.org/10.5772/intechopen.71237

Abstract

Neural network (NN) model is an efficient and accurate tool for simulating manufacturing processes. Various authors adopted artificial neural networks (ANNs) to optimize multiresponse parameters in manufacturing processes. In most cases the adoption of ANN allows to predict the mechanical proprieties of processed products on the basis of given technological parameters. Therefore the implementation of ANN is hugely beneficial in industrial applications in order to save cost and material resources. In this chapter, following an introduction on the application of the ANN to the manufacturing process, it will be described an important study that has been published on international journals and that has investigated the use of the ANNs for the monitoring, controlling and optimization of the process. Experimental observations were collected in order to train the network and establish numerical relationships between process-related factors and mechanical features of the welded joints. Finally, an evaluation of time-costs parameters of the process, using the control of the ANN model, is conducted in order to identify the costs and the benefits of the prediction model adopted.

Keywords: modelling, simulation, control and monitoring of manufacturing processes, simulation technologies

1. Introduction

The use of artificial intelligence and specifically artificial neural networks (ANNs) has allowed yielding revolutionary advances in manufacturing. However, most of the applications of artificial intelligence in the production field concerned expert systems and fewer attentions were paid to neural networks (NNs). Most important characteristics of the ANNs are:

- the self-adaptive behaviour that allows to adapt the forecast to changing of the environment, in this way improve the networks' ability to learn and to predict;

- the parallel computing architecture, that has a great impact in multiple disciplines and applications, from speech and natural language processing, to image processing or problems in bioinformatics and biomedical engineering.

Therefore, they could be of great help for today's computer integrated manufacturing and in smart factories, according to Industry 4.0 paradigm. Currently, the nature of the manufacturing process is changing with great speed, becoming more sophisticated and continuous variations are occurring due to changes in customer demand and reduced product life cycle. This requires manufacturing technologies that can easily adapt to such changes. In this context, artificial neural networks are a powerful technology to solve this problem. The use of ANNs is also widely used for process monitoring and control applications. The quality of a process can only be provided by in process monitoring through proper measurements. To ensure a high quality of a process, you must follow the following technological steps [1]:

- Identify the characteristic changes of a process;
- To estimate the changes of the product quality;
- Correct any process operations as a result of any anomalies detected from the comparison between the obtained and the desired quality.

These steps should be followed with minimal supervision and assistance from operators, if possible in unmanned manner. In addition, all processes should be implemented with special features such as: storing information, decision making, learning and integration. It should be noted that most manufacturing processes are regulated by many variable parameters and for this reason, such systems have a random, complex and uncertain nature.

This may be attributable to the fact that they are exposed to external disturbance and noise and often subjected to parameter variations. Furthermore, there is often a great interaction between variables and therefore it is not possible to properly define the final quality of the product and the variables that influence it. Due to these characteristics the quality often varies from product to product, impairing its uniformity and decreasing the yield of the product. So, all changes that may occur in manufacturing environments cannot be easily observed by an operator, so in recent years the use of neural networks applied to process monitoring and control has been of great interest. Indeed, it has been shown that the use of artificial intelligence can overcome the above-mentioned problems [2]. The research efforts in this direction will be accelerated with greater interest in the future and will lead to the development of truly intelligent manufacturing systems that are capable of producing products without the supervision or assistance of human operators [1]. **Figure 1** classifies the functionalities needed to imbed the artificial neural networks on manufacturing processes and summarizes the current developments in manufacturing application areas.

The real world applications here in manufacturing include the modelling, monitoring and control, identification, planning and scheduling associated with the processes. The purpose of this chapter is to present some applications of artificial neural networks in manufacturing process monitoring and control, among which particular attention will be paid to the study that has been published in international journals and that has investigated the use of the

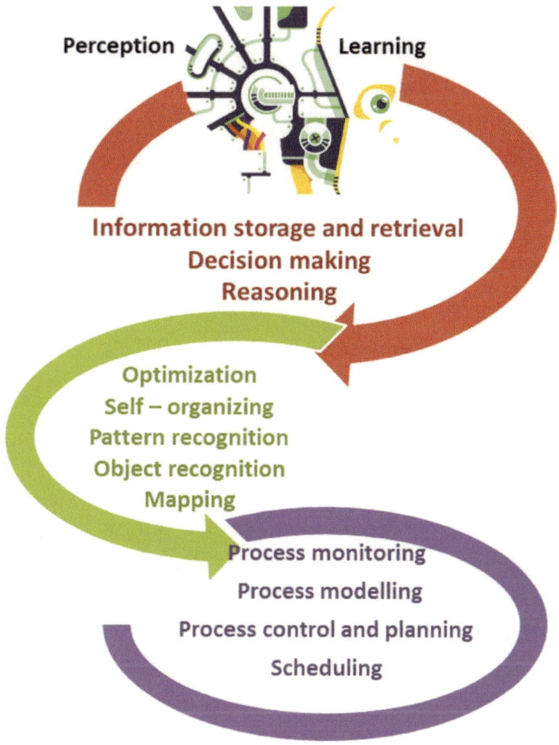

Figure 1. Functionality of the artificial neural networks and their manufacturing applications.

ANNs for the monitoring, control and optimization of a welding processes. Experimental observations were collected in order to train the network and establish numerical relationships between process-related factors and mechanical properties of the welded joints. Finally, an evaluation of the time-cost parameters of the process, using the control of the ANN model, is conducted in order to identify the costs and benefits of the prediction model adopted.

2. Manufacturing applications

Due to many external disturbances and many variations in process parameters, many production processes are complex and time-consuming. For these reasons, it is not always possible to identify the relationship between the product quality and the input variables of the process. Thus, there is interest to integrate the artificial intelligence into the production processes for storing, learning, reasoning and decision making. Such systems are able to adapt to changes in its environment and can truly realize unmanned operations of processes. The adoption of the neural network can be devoted to monitoring and to prediction of different parameters in many industrial areas, in order to solve issue relating to the manufacturing system design, process planning, as well as operational decision making. A summary of main NN applications field is shown in **Table 1**.

Category	Manufacturing		
Application topic	• Manufacturing system design	Author Ref. num.	Moon and Chi [53] Kaparthi and Suresh [54] Lee et al. [55] Moon [56] Wu [57]
	• Manufacturing process control		Cook and Shannon [58] Wu [57]
	• Robot scheduling		Yih et al. [59]
	• Manufacturing operational decision		Chryssolouris et al. [60]

Table 1. Summary of neural network manufacturing applications.

Manufacturing information, such as the sequence of operations, lot size; multiple process plans were given special consideration in their approach to solve the generalized part family formation problem. Many authors also point out that the method of artificial neural networks is flexible and can be efficiently integrated with other manufacturing functions. Below, from the literature, some important artificial intelligence applications to particular production processes are described.

2.1. Injection moulding processes

Injection moulding processes are characterized by dynamic characteristics since process input variables are the melting temperatures, the velocity of the cylinder, the holding, the pressure that produces the polymer flow into the model cavity and they vary in a complex manner. The phenomena occurring in the process are very complex, time-varying, nonlinear and uncertain. This complexity makes it difficult to relate the input operating variables to the product quality such as geometry accuracy and geometry surface smoothness. These processes have been implemented and optimized with the use of artificial intelligence with the use of *multi-layer perceptron* which is found to be the most popular network and tries to model the process dynamics and based on this to predict the part quality [3–9].

2.2. Gas metal arc welding processes

In gas metal arc (GMA) welding processes [10–12], the flow of an electric current is generated by an electric arc that is maintained between the consumable wire electrode and the welding metal as shown in **Figure 2**.

Both the filling metal and the consumable electrode are automatically fed by a wire feeding device. A good quality of the welds is determined by the relatively high depth to width ratio of the molten welding pool. So, the monitoring and control of weld geometry and the surface temperatures that are strongly related with the formation of the weld pool, are very important for the penetration depth or the back bead width. For this purpose, the temperatures by noncontact were measured. Infrared temperature sensing system and recent studies conducted the ANN multi-layer perceptron to detect and control with great success all the surface temperature information.

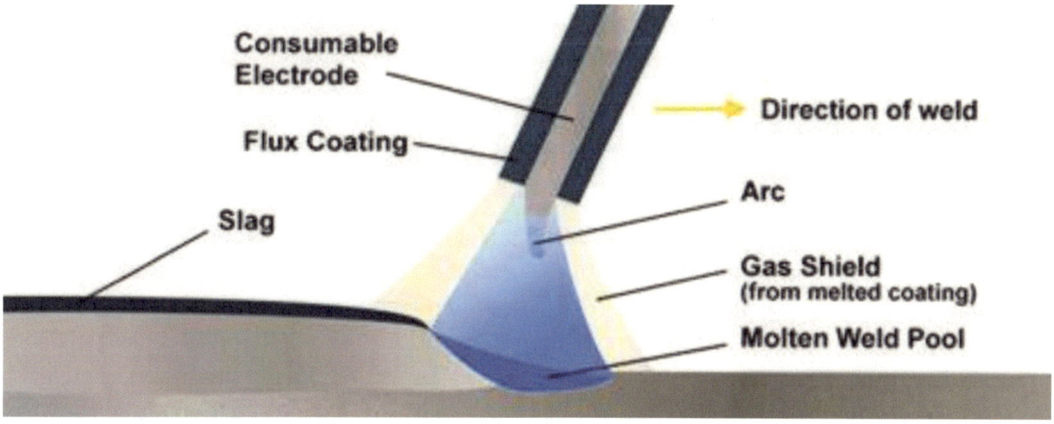

Figure 2. Characteristics of the GMA welding process.

2.3. Arc welding processes

The complexity of the relationship between the process variable and weld quality is the common factor in all manufacturing processes and in particular arc welding processes. For these reasons, the literature documents with some interesting researches, the use of ANNs for quality monitoring and control of the process. In this type of welding process, the ANN input data are generally the surface temperature, the welding voltage and the current and torch speed. The majority type of ANN employed for this case was, again, the multilayer perceptron [10, 13–21]. Their use was found to be very satisfactory to predict the weld defects, the geometry such as bead width, head height and penetration.

2.4. Machining processes

To perform a correct quality control in all machining systems, it is very important to check particular parameters such as the cutting tool state, the vibrations, the forces and the temperature obtained during real-time machining operation. To optimize this particular type of supervision of the cutting tool state, some authors document in literature the use of the ANNs which used the above-mentioned process data to classify the status of tool wear, prediction tool life and detect tool failure in an on-line manner. Examples of typical sensors are tool dynamometers, acoustic emission sensor accelerometers and thermocouples. In this process, the networks in frequent use are the multilayer perceptron and Kohonen [22–46].

2.5. Semiconductor manufacturing processes

The complexity of plasma etching processes in integrated circuits fabrication promoted the use of ANNs for monitoring and control. In this field, the use of artificial intelligence brings advantages that could not be achieved with traditional open loop controls. Where used the multilayer perceptron networks that are the most popular for this process. The ANNs use the fundamental parameters that affecting process dynamics, such as power, gas flow rate, dc bias voltage and throttle positioning. Proper use of networks in this field allows real-time monitoring and estimation of quality variables such as the etching thickness and the etching time [47–52].

3. Development and implementation of ANN

The origin of artificial neural networks is based on learning technique that mimics the biological learning process occurring in the brain. Neural networks present a robust way to predict an actual value after a learning activity from a supplied sample set [61]. The ANNs are based on a concept that combines a set of computational procedures with a theoretical basis in order to predict the unknown output parameter in various processes. Generally, neural networks are adopted to subordinate knowledge to observations or when data or activity is so complex that is not allows to identify an optimal solution in a reasonable time. It is difficult in each field of application and even for each task, to compare the use of neural networks versus other prediction techniques (e.g., statistical methods or a support vector machine) because, on the contrary to the conventional computational techniques, they are able to solve nonlinear and ill-defined problems. Many factors underlie this trend, most of them are related to reliability of the predictions, to the robustness and adaptability of the results as well as the learning ability of the neural process. In many cases the forecasts generated by ANNs, if correctly designed, significantly improve with increasing of dataset used as training subset. Consistently, in last years, the adoption of the ANNs in many business areas is increased exponentially and the number of publications, in high-level journals, was grown [62] (**Figure 3**).

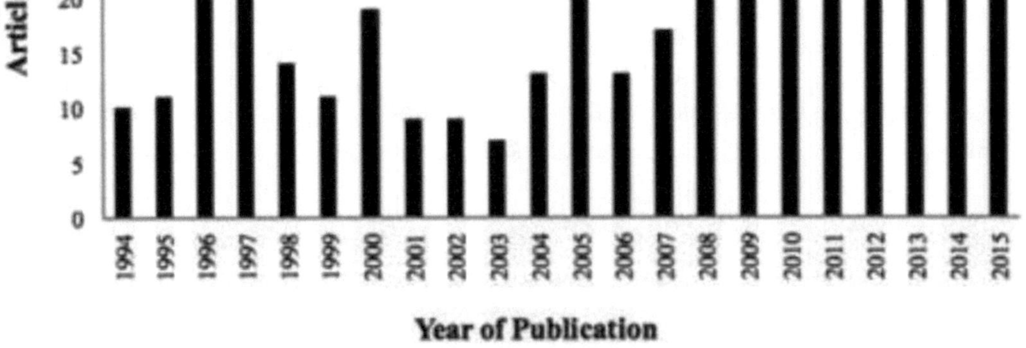

Figure 3. Distribution of ANN-papers by year.

Under engineering perspective, a 'good' ANN is based on models able to imitating the proprieties of natural systems, such as cognitive capabilities, flexibility, robustness, ability to learn and fault tolerance. At this scope the structure and the behaviour of the ANN required a study characterized by different hierarchical levels of organization as neurons, layers, synapses and cognition-behaviour functions. Different areas of application are interested by the ANNs, some of them are astronomy, mathematics, physics chemistry, earth and space sciences, life and medical science and engineering. In recent years USA and EU countries, have approved different initiatives for the study of the human brain in these cases, the ANN, in various forms and at different levels, has been included in thesis research projects. The inter-disciplinary given by system adopted for dataset analysis and by the complexity computational required by the elaboration of the data, allows to design and simulate systems capable to satisfying the needs and the challenges of the real world. Japan in 2014 has been developed a project based named as Brain Mapping by Integrated Neurotechnologies for Disease Studies (Brain/MINDS) [63], that will be integrated with new biomedical technologies and neural network systems. In Australia, a specific programme has also been set up with preliminary funds of around $250 million over 10 years with the goal of developing the world's first bionic brain (AusBrain) [64] based on multilayer perceptron (MLP) system. There is also another ambitious initiative in China (Brainnetome) [65], the goals of this are to simulate the brain networks for perception, memory, emotion and their disorders as well as to develop advanced technologies to achieve these goals.

3.1. Designing the ANN

An ANN is a computational model that establishes a relationship between process factors and output variables. Artificial neurons are combined through weights, which work as adjustable coefficients. There are many programs and frameworks, either of general purpose or that simulates functions or neural structures (e.g., IQR, NeuroSpaces, NNET, etc.) but there is not a specific simulator that is currently being used by the whole community since some different approaches are more suitable than others, on the basis of the research task being addressed. Moreover, most simulators can take full advantage of their computational capabilities on the basis of the features of the computer hardware to which it is installed [66].

This correlation depends by the fundamental features of the network, which define the way input and output are connected to each other [67]. The network includes input layer, output layer and a certain number of hidden layers. The fundamental features of the network are:

- Dataset splitting, which identifies the subset data to be adopted for the training, the testing and the validation of the ANN development;
- Architecture, which determines the connections between layers and neurons;
- Learning algorithm, which determines the weights of the links between neurons.

In the following sections the data splitting strategy, the architecture design approach and the learning algorithm identification, is described.

3.1.1. Dataset splitting

The appropriate data splitting can be handled as a statistical sampling problem. Therefore, various classical sampling techniques can be adopted in order to split the data in three subset for training, validation and testing of ANN, most commons are: Simple random sampling (SRS), Trial-and-error methods, Systematic sampling and Convenience sampling. The splitting strategy tries to overcome the high variance of the SRS by repeating the random sampling several times in order to minimize the mean square error (MSE) of the ANN. This technique is high time-consuming and requires significant computational costs. A subset (generally as big as 60% of the available experimental data composed by inputs/output pairs) is used for the ANN training. In this phase, the synaptic weights, which are the links between neurons, have a synaptic weight attached. They are updated repeatedly in order to reduce the error between the experimental outputs and the associated forecasts. A subset (generally as big as 20% of the available experimental data) is adopted for the ANN validation. In particular the validation sets allows to identifying the underlying trend of the training data subset. A subset (generally as big as 20% of the available experimental data) is adopted for testing the forecast reliability of the ANN in the learning phase. In order to deal with the overfitting problem that occurs when the network has memorized the training examples, but it has not learned to generalize to new situations, different approaches are suggested: reduce the number of hidden layers, improve the 'quality' of the training-subset adopted, introduce some noisy data into training set, etc. In Ref. [67] an efficient method is proposed for model establishment by means the identification of a low-dimension ANN learning matrix through the principal component analysis (PCA).

3.1.2. Network architectures

An ANN is a computational model that establishes a relationship between process factors and output variables. Artificial neurons are combined through weights, which work as adjustable coefficients. This correlation depends by the fundamental features of the network, which define the way input and output are connected to each other [67]. The network includes input layer, output layer and a certain number of hidden layers (**Figure 4**). The fundamental steps for the development of a network are:

- Dataset splitting, which identifies the subset data to be adopted for the training, the testing and the validation steps of the ANN development;
- Architecture, which determines the connections between layers and neurons;
- The learning algorithm, which determines the weights of the links between neurons.

Based on the connection pattern (architecture), ANNs can be grouped into two categories:

- Feed-forward networks (e.g., single-layer perceptron, multilayer perceptron, radial basis function nets) in which there are not network connection as loops (as shown in **Figure 4**);
- Recurrent (or feedback) networks, in which different loops occur in network connections (e.g., competitive networks, Kohonen's SOM, Hopfield network, ART models).

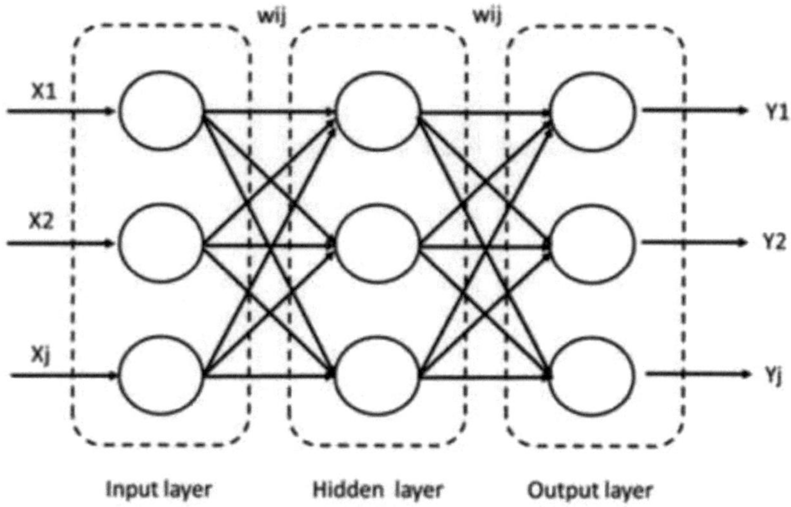

Figure 4. Structure of an ANN.

The first one network are considered "static", in fact they produce only one set of output values rather than a sequence of values from a given input, and they worked in memory-less condition, this means that their response to an input is independent of the previous network state. The 'recurrent networks', on the other hand, are dynamic systems, in which the input pattern leads the network to enter in a new state, when a new input is introduced. Most popular network architecture in use today is the multilayer perceptron neural network (feed-forward network) where the output of a previous layer is the input to the next layer. In this case a biased sum of the weights assigned to different inputs, allows identifying the activation level that, through a transfer function, produces the corresponding output. The network thus has a simple interpretation as a form of input-output model, with the weights and thresholds (biases) the free parameters of the model [68]. The design of the ANN architecture consists of identifying the kind of the structure (between feed-forward and recurrent architectures) and identifies the number of hidden layers and the number of neurons for each layer. On one hand, many neurons can lead to memorize the training sets with lost of the ANN's capability to generalize. On the other hand, a lack of neurons can inhibit the appropriate pattern classification. Many software allows to identify the best number of hidden layer and neurons (for each layer) through a 'trial-and-error' approach. In this case different architectures are iterative tested by software and for each of them, the software provide a "fitness bar" based on the inverse of the mean absolute error (MAE) computed on the testing set. In most cases the higher "fitness bar" identifies the best architecture.

3.1.3. Learning algorithm

The purpose of the learning algorithm is to train the network to predict the output parameter(s) given one or more input parameter(s). There are many types of neural network learning rules. There are three kind of learning algorithm, the first is known as supervised learning, in this case the algorithm allows to predict the output parameter on the basis of a set of known input-output pairs [69, 70]. Second algorithm is unsupervised learning, in this case the output is not given, the aim consisting of inferring a function in order to describe a hidden structure (e.g., clustering, anomaly detection, etc.). Therefore the output parameters are considered 'unlabelled' (the observations are not classified) and is not provided any evaluation about the prediction reliability ensured by the ANN [71]. Third algorithm is named reinforcement learning, in this case a continue interaction between the learning system and the environment allows to identify the input-output mapping minimizing the performance scalar index. The approach is very similar to unsupervised learning (also in this case there are not given input-output pairs), reward or punishment signals are adopted for the prediction of output parameters [72]. In most cases, the unsupervised learning allows to ensuring lower cost function. Three different methods, usually considered to be supervised learning methods, are described in this work: Quick Propagation (QP), Conjugate Gradient (CG) and Levenberg-Marquardt algorithm (LM).

QP is a heuristic modification of the standard back propagation, the output of the *m*th output node for the *p*th input pattern is given by o_{pm} (Eq. (1)).

$$o_{pm} = f\left(\sum_{k=1}^{K} \varpi_{km}\, o_{pk}\right) \tag{1}$$

where *f* is the activation sigmoidal function (Eq. (2)), ϖ_{km} is the weight between the *m*th output neuron and the *k*th hidden neuron. The value of o_{pk} depends by two parameters: the first is given by the weight between *k*th hidden neuron and the *n*th input neuron (ϖ_{nk}). The second parameter is x_{pn} given by *p*th input pattern of *n*th neuron.

$$f(x) = \frac{1}{(1+e^{-x})} \tag{2}$$

All network weights are updated after presenting each pattern from the learning data set.

As far as concern CG method, the learning algorithm starts with a random weight vector that is iteratively updated according the direction of the greatest rate of decrease of the error evaluated as $\omega^{(\tau)}$ in Eq. (3).

$$\Delta\omega^{(\tau)} = -\eta \nabla E_{\omega(\tau)} \tag{3}$$

where E is the error function evaluated at $\omega^{(\tau)}$ and η is the arbitrary learning rate parameter. For each step (τ) the gradient is re-evaluated in order to reduce E. The performance of the gradient descent algorithm is very sensitive to the proper setting of the learning rate, in case η is too high the algorithm can oscillate and become unstable, for η too small the algorithm takes too long to converge. In this case an adaptive learning rate allows to keep the learning step size as large as possible, ensuring, in this way, the learning rate stable. The LM algorithm allows to minimize the squares of the differences (E) between the desirable output, identified as $y_d(t)$, and the predicted output $y_p(t)$ [73]. 'E' is given by the follow equation:

$$E = \frac{1}{2}\sum_{t=1} \left(y_p(t) - y_d(t)\right)^2 \tag{4}$$

LM algorithm is also adopted, which blends the 'Steepest Descent' method and the 'Gauss-Newton', therefore it can converge well even if the error surface is much more complex than the quadratic situation; ensuring, in many cases, speed and stability. LM algorithm can be presented as:

$$w_{k+1} = w_k - (J_k^T J_k + \mu I)^{-1} J_k e_k \tag{5}$$

where J is Jacobian matrix, μ is the 'combination coefficient' (always positive), I is the identity matrix and e represents the error vector. When μ is very small (nearly zero), Gauss-Newton algorithm is used. On the other hand, when μ is very large, steepest descent method is used.

4. Case study: "Prediction of the Vickers microhardness and ultimate tensile strength of AA5754 H111 friction stir welding butt joints using artificial neural network"

Among the artificial neural networks applications to the production processes, this section describes the research of De Filippis et al. [74] in which a simulation model was developed for the monitoring, controlling and optimization of a particular solid-state welding process called friction stir welding (FSW). The approach based on the use of neural networks, using the FSW technique, has allowed identifying the relationships between the process parameters (input variable) and the mechanical properties (output responses) of the AA5754 H111 welded joints. The optimization of the technological parameters has been developed with the aim to produce a stable welding process that can provide welded joints with no defects. The experimental plans that were tested have been constructed by varying the following parameters:

- Tool rotation speed;
- Travel tool speed;
- Position of the samples extracted from the weld bead;
- Thermal data, detected with thermographic techniques for on-line control of the joints.

The quality of welded joints was evaluated through the following destructive and non-destructive tests:

- Visual tests;
- Macro graphic analysis;
- Tensile tests;
- Indentation Vickers hardness tests
- Thermographic controls.

The simulation model was based on the adoption of artificial neural networks (ANNs) using a back-propagation learning algorithm. Different types of architecture were analysed, which were able to predict with good reliability the FSW process parameters for the welding of the AA5754 H111 in Butt-Joint configuration.

4.1. About the friction stir welding process

The process of friction stir welding (FSW) is a solid-state welding method based on frictional and stirring phenomena, which was discovered and patented by the Welding Institute of Cambridge in 1999. In this process, a rotating non-consumable tool that plunges into the work piece and moves forward produces the heat necessary to weld the parts together. Therefore, given the particular geometry of the tool used, as shown in **Figure 5**, the following actions are performed in the process:

- The tool shoulder generates heat with the base material,
- The tool pin generates plastic deformation and mixing of the material.

The much lower temperatures compared with those achieved in traditional welding processes by melting, determine the main advantages of this process. In fact, there is minimal mechanical distortion, with minimal Heat Affected Zone (HAZ), and an excellent surface finish.

No crack formation and porosity right after welding thanks to the low input of total heat.

The main parameters of the friction stir welding process are the tool rotation speed (n) and the tool travel speed (v). The friction stir welding process enjoys major successful applications

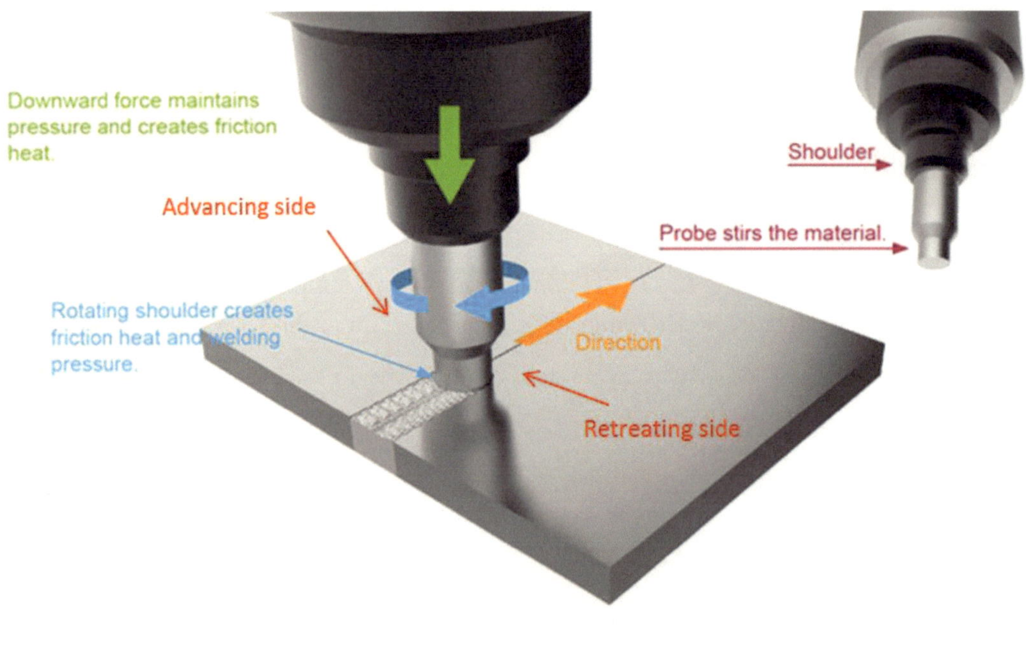

Figure 5. Schematic diagram of the FSW process.

in many fields, such as aeronautics, aerospace, rail, automotive, computer science, marine, chemical and petrochemical industries. Important advantages are also documented in the application of FSW processes on dissimilar materials, Al alloys, Cu alloys, Ti alloys and steel. The main applications are on aluminium alloys because these materials, due to their high strength-to-weight ratio, low density, forming properties, low cost and recyclability, are the main metals used in automotive, marine and aerospace applications. An aluminium alloy of large aeronautical and automotive interest is the AA5754 H111; on this material, there are still few researches about the advantages to apply the FSW. It has been shown that the mechanical properties of the AA5xxx friction stir welded joints depend mainly on the grain size and the dislocation density, due to the phenomena of plastic deformation and recrystallization occurring during the FSW process. To study and optimize properly the friction stir welding process, it is necessary to know the influence of process parameters on the mechanical properties of the joints. In general, the traditional process control techniques cannot provide information about the performance of the process during welding and require lengthy testing times, making them feasible for the industrial field. Therefore, in the production engineering, the control and the optimization of the manufacturing processes is becoming increasingly important. For the FSW process is necessary to carry out a control of the significant variables, in addition to the use of thermographic techniques. This justifies the deepening and use of information technology for enhancing the quality of manufacturing systems. The implementation of numerical and analytical models can reduce time and cost for experiment and analysis through quantitative solutions.

4.2. ANN simulation model for the monitoring of the friction stir welding process

The research interest to developing new technological tools for the control and optimization of manufacturing processes is growing. Such developments are crucial elements for the production engineering. Within the FSW process, many experiments are needed to understand the process-related dynamics and to control all the significant variables and the thermographic techniques are a valuable help but it is necessary to increase and optimize control techniques with new information tools for enhancing the quality of manufacturing systems. The reduction in time and cost of the experiments can be reduced by the implementation of numerical and analytical models. Thus the relationship between the process parameters and the quality of the weld can be easily identified by a model based on the adoption of one or more artificial neural networks (ANNs). Neural networks software packages are very common among scientists and manufacturing researchers. In particular, their applications in the field of welding have showed good success. As far as concern the FSW process, in scientific literature, there are only few papers that discuss the modelling of this welding process by a neural network [75–79]. In particular, a very interesting work is the study of Shojaeefard et al. [80] who studied the adoption of the neural network trained with Particle Swarm Optimization (PSO) for modelling and forecasting of the mechanical properties of the friction stir welding butt joints in AA7075/AA5083. A further contribution is provided by Asadi et al. [81], which with the use of ANN found a relationship between the grain size and the hardness of nanocomposites in FSW process. In this particular case study, an effective simulation model was developed for predicting, monitoring and controlling the mechanical properties of welded AA5754 H111 plates, using the ANNs with the FSW process parameters as input variables. The data set for training, testing and validation of the ANN were the results obtained by experimental cases [82–84], in which all welded joints were performed by non-destructive (visual inspection) and destructive testing (macrographic tests). These tests have been useful for detecting macro defects present on the surface and within the welded area. An accurate quantitative analysis of the FSW process was carried out using the results of the destructive tests of each welded specimen in terms of ultimate tensile strength (UTS) and Vickers micro hardness. Thermographic techniques were used to study the thermal behaviour of FSW process. In the thermal analyses, two thermal parameters were considered: the maximum temperature and the slope of the heating curve measured during the FSW process, along the two sides of the weld ($MSHC_{RS}$ and $MSHC_{AS}$, respectively). The analysis established that there is a correlation between the data derived from the thermographic controls and the quality of the welded joints, in terms of UTS. Thus this work defines the importance and effectiveness of the use of infrared technology for monitoring the FSW process in a quantitative manner, giving important information on the thermal behaviour of joints during the process. Finally, the purpose of this case study was to correlate the mechanical properties of welded joints in terms of UTS and microhardness to the thermal parameters with the use of the ANN. The results obtained have defined a model with the use of the neural networks that can predict quantitatively the mechanical behaviour of the FSW joints, as shown in **Figure 6**.

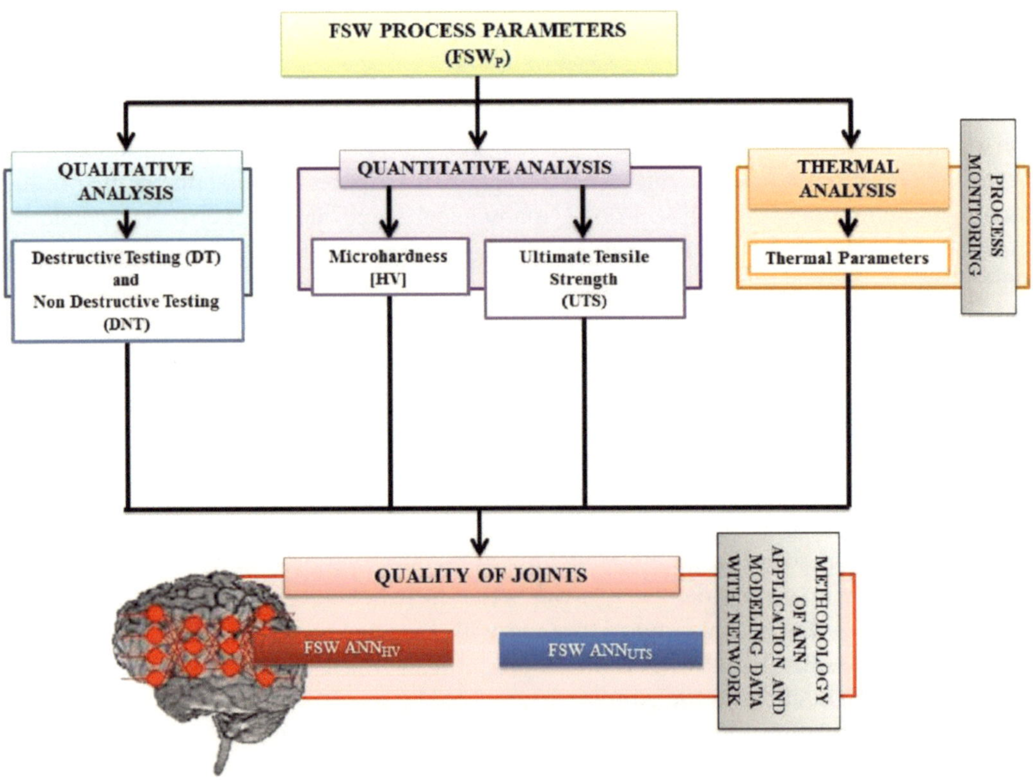

Figure 6. Approaches used for evaluating the quality of FSW process through destructive and non-destructive tests.

http://dx.doi.org/10.5772/intechopen.71237

The results of all tests are summarized in **Table 2** and the same data were used to train the ANN.

In order to establish a relationship between the mechanical properties of the FSW joints and the process parameters, a simulation model was developed. In the development of the model two different ANNs were used, as follows: in the first network, called "ANN_{HV}", was used as output variable, Vickers micro hardness of HAZ; in the second network, called "ANN_{UTS}" was used as the output variable the ultimate tensile strength. Both have used process parameters as inputs. The ANNs were implemented using Alyuda NeuroIntelligence™-Neural networks software (2.2, Alyuda Research Company, LLC., Cupertino, CA, USA). The first network ANN_{HV} was developed with five input nodes (n, v, p, $MSHC_{RS}$, and $MSHC_{AS}$) and only one response node

Input					Output			
n^1[RPM]	v^2[cm/min]	p^3[mm]	$MSHC_{RS}{}^4$ [°]	$MSHC_{AS}{}^5$ [°]	$HV_{haz}{}^6$	$HV_{haz\ norm.}{}^7$	UTS^8[MPa]	$UTS_{norm.}{}^9$[MPa]
20	500	20	86,05	85,83	60,88	0,50	166,69	1,00
30	700	20	87,37	87,37	61,93	0,70	70,25	0,21
20	700	20	87,12	87,92	63,33	0,97	120,75	0,62
30	500	20	86,88	86,85	61,72	0,66	80,05	0,29
20	500	120	87,25	86,80	60,88	0,50	90,66	0,38
30	700	120	88,14	88,15	61,93	0,70	44,29	0,00
20	700	120	87,23	87,91	63,33	0,97	56,06	0,10
30	500	120	87,97	87,91	61,72	0,66	71,99	0,23
20	500	20	86,60	86,16	62,02	0,72	132,43	0,72
30	700	20	87,74	88,23	62,72	0,85	114,87	0,58
20	700	20	86,53	88,00	58,23	0,00	51,86	0,06
30	500	20	89,07	87,23	63,50	1,00	97,43	0,43
20	500	120	87,59	87,43	62,02	0,72	99,06	0,45
30	700	120	88,53	88,32	62,72	0,85	59,95	0,13
20	700	120	87,48	87,74	58,23	0,00	46,55	0,02
30	500	120	87,58	88,45	63,50	1,00	113,98	0,57

[1]Tool rotation speed.

[2]Tool travel speed.

[3]Position of the sample along the welding direction.

[4]Maximum Slope of Heating Curve of thermal profiles evaluated on the surface of joints along the retreating side.

[5]Maximum Slope of Heating Curve of thermal profiles evaluated on the surface of joints along the advancing side.

[6]Vickers microhardness values measured in the HAZ.

[7]Vickers microhardness normalized values measured in the HAZ.

[8]Ultimate tensile strength values.

[9]Ultimate tensile strength normalized values.

Table 2. Measured data used to train the ANN.

(output node), identified as the micro hardness of the Heat Affected Zone of the welds, HVhaz. "Trial-and-error approach" was used to investigate and analyze more than 1000 different network architectures to identify the best architecture for the first network (ANN_{HV}). The network fitness score was calculated for each network with different design (number of hidden layers, number of nodes, etc.), based on the inverse of the mean absolute error (MAE) on the testing set. The best network architecture has been identified with the higher fitness score. The best accuracy and minimum prediction error was obtained by adopting an ANN_{HV} characterized by only one hidden layer with 12 neurons as shown in **Figures 7–9**.

The second network (ANN_{UTS}) was developed with six input nodes (n, v, p, $MSHC_{RS}$, $MSHC_{AS}$ and HV_{haz}) and one response node (output) identified as the ultimate tensile strength of the welds (UTS). Even in this second analysis the methodology chosen for identifying the architecture of the network are the same of the ANN_{HV}. The "best" reliability of the prediction was achieved, adopting an ANN_{UTS} characterized by only one hidden layer with four neurons, as shown in **Figures 10–12**.

The reliability of the estimation of the mechanical properties predicting by the ANN simulation model was evaluated by comparing the data with the experimental results. For this purpose, the mean absolute percentage error (MAPE) was calculated for the two ANNs modelled. **Table 3** summarizes the results of this analysis that demonstrated that the values derived from ANN simulation have a higher level of reliability. Therefore, the neural networks were able to predict, with significant accuracy, the mechanical properties of the friction stir welding joints, under a given set of welding conditions.

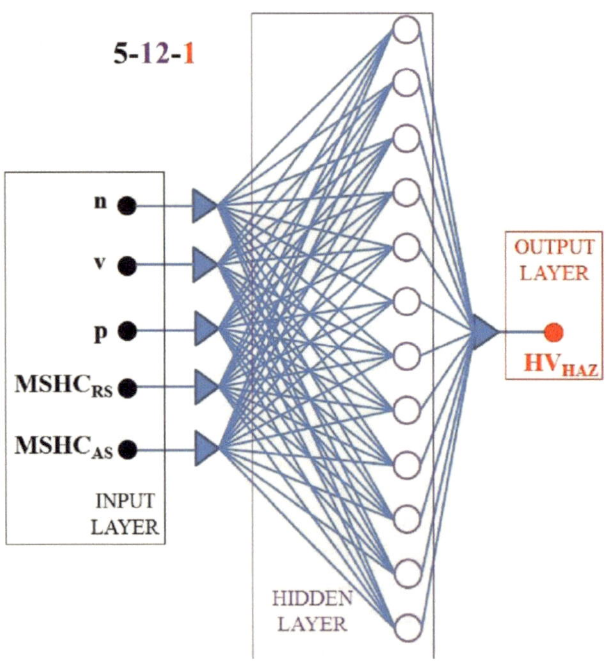

Figure 7. Back-propagation neural network used to foresee the Vickers micro hardness of the Heat Affected Zone (HAZ).

http://dx.doi.org/10.5772/intechopen.71237

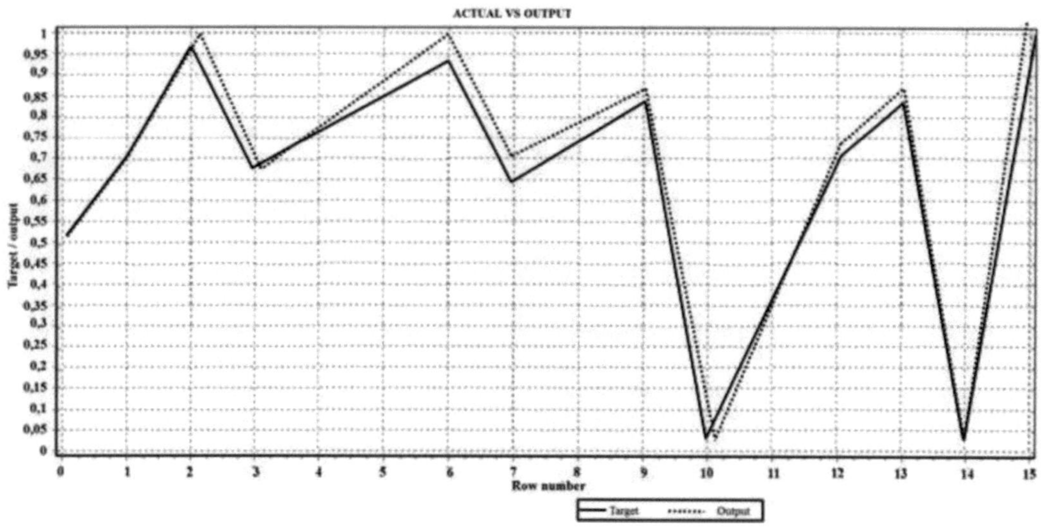

Figure 8. Predicted Vickers HAZ micro hardness by ANN versus the experimental data.

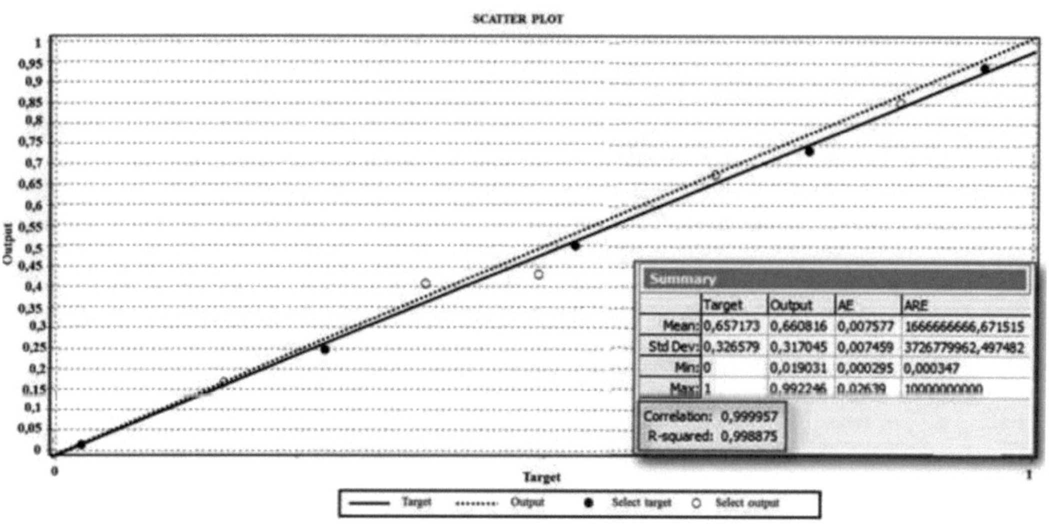

Figure 9. Regression line at the training stage.

Starting from the results obtained in previous researches [84] where the most significant FSW process parameters for AA5754 H111 plates were identified, the development of this ANN model could be used to identify the optimal process parameter setting in order to achieve the desired welding quality.

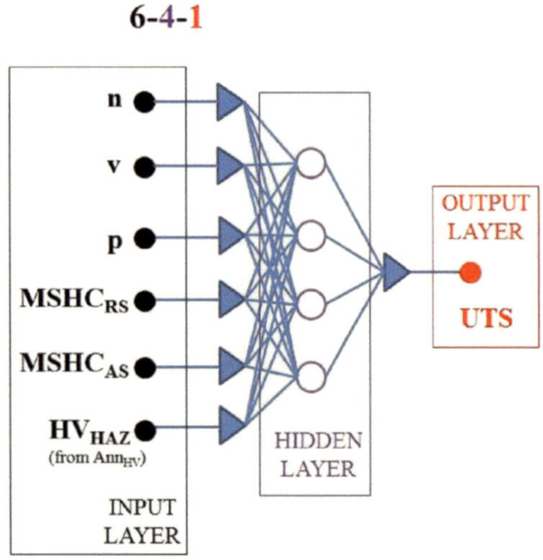

Figure 10. Back-propagation neural network used to foresee the ultimate tensile strength.

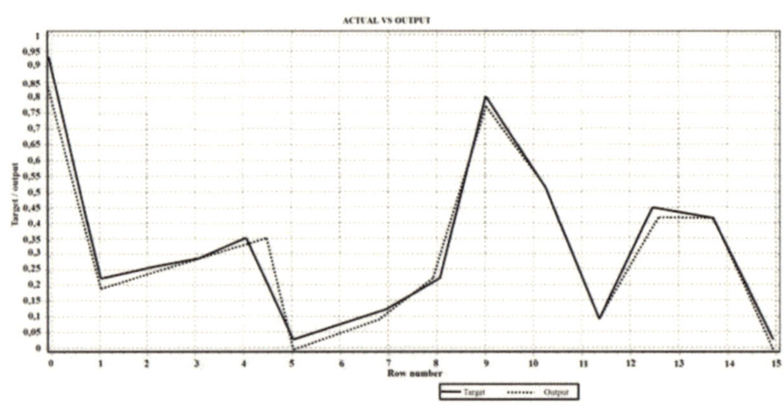

Figure 11. Predicted ultimate tensile strength by ANN versus the experimental data.

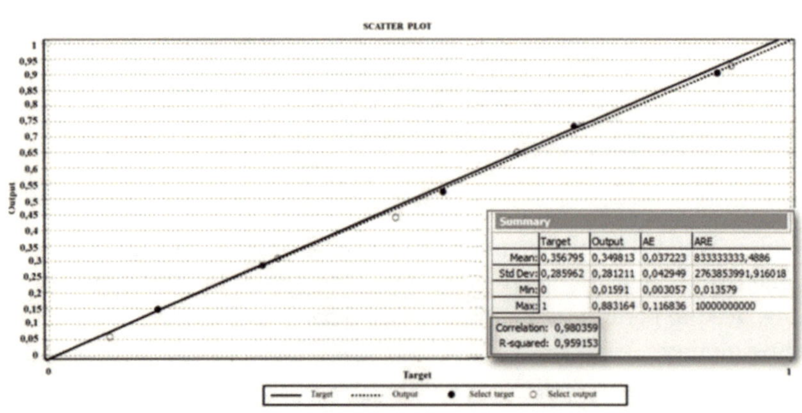

Figure 12. Regression line at the training stage.

ANN model	Input parameters	Output parameters	MAPE (%)
ANN_{HV}	- n - v - p - $MSHC_{AS}$ - $MSHC_{RS}$	HV_{haz} Vickers micro hardness of the Heat Affected Zone	0.29
ANN_{UTS} (in cascade)	- n - v - p - $MSHC_{AS}$ - $MSHC_{RS}$ - HV_{haz} (predicted with the ANN_{HV} model)	UTS ultimate tensile strength	9.57

AA5754 H111 plates welded with the friction stir welding process.

Table 3. Mean absolute percentage error computed for hardness and ultimate tensile strength of AA.

5. Conclusions

The interest in ANN is growing so much that its models and algorithms are becoming standard tools in computer science and information engineering. This highlights the fact that after a long and productive youth, neural networks have formed a robust set of computation procedures with a robust theoretical base and undeniable effectiveness in solving real problems in different fields of information processing. In case study discussed in this work, the analysis performed has shown that the ANN simulation model can be used as a further effective method for predicting the FSW process. The MAPE obtained for the outputs micro hardness (HAZ) and ultimate tensile strength (UTS) were, respectively, 0.29% and 9.57%; R2 values were, in all cases, bigger than 0.90. Although the prediction of UTS was characterized by more high level of MAPE, if it is compared to HAZ estimated value, it was considered acceptable to ensure a model characterized by high reliability. The adoption of the simulation model can be very useful for the friction stir welding process. In fact, the use of tools for predicting the mechanical properties of the welds and for controlling the welding process, allows the production of welds with fewer defects. This reduces the number of repairs and costs, associated with the reiteration of the process. In the context of neural networks, the biggest question is "are we currently capable of building a human brain?" [85]. Undoubtedly, the achievement of these challenges is very ambitious, considering that the human brain has around 90 billion neurons shaping an extremely complex network, but in many cases the ANN can support the human behaviour, simplifying the decision making process, increasing the level cognition, under stress conditions, and increasing the capacity in evaluation and analysis of complex processes.

Author details

Luigi Alberto Ciro De Filippis, Livia Maria Serio, Francesco Facchini* and Giovanni Mummolo

*Address all correspondence to: francesco.facchini@poliba.it

Department of Mechanics Mathematics & Management, Polytechnic University of Bari, Italy

References

[1] Cho HS, Leu MC. Artificial neural networks in manufacturing processes. IFAC Proceedings Volumes. 1998;**31**(15):529-537. DOI: S1474-6670(17)40607-0

[2] Huang SH, Zhang H-C. Artificial neural networks in manufacturing: Concepts, applications, and perspectives. IEEE Transactions on Components Packaging and Manufacturing Technology Part A. 1994;**17**(2):212-228. DOI: 10.1109/95.296402

[3] Lilly KW, Melligeri AS. Dynamic Simualtion and Neural Network Compliance Control of an Intelligent Forging Center. Journal of Intelligent and Robotic Systems. 1996;**17**:8199

[4] Kim DJ, Kim BM, Choi C. Determination of the initial billet geometry for a forged product using neural networks. Journal of Material Processing Technology. 1997;**72**:86-93

[5] Lee WH, Cho HS. Design of a CMAC controller for hydro-forming process. Journal of Institute of Control, Robotics and Systems. 2000;**6**(3):329-337

[6] Hyun BS, Cho HS. Prediction of fonning pressure curve for hydroforming processes using artificial neural network. Proceedings of the Institution of Mechanical Engineers. 1994;**208**(part I):108-121

[7] Park HJ, Cho HS. A CMAC-based learning controller for pressure tracking control of hydroforming processes. In: ASME Winter Annual Meeting, Dollars, Texas, USA. 1990

[8] Hamdi Demirci H, Coulter JP. Neural network based control of molding processes. Journal of Materials Processing & Manufacturing Science. 1994;**2**:335-353

[9] Lim TG, Cho HS, Chang HS. The use of artificial neural networks in the monitoring of spot weld quality. Journal of Korean Welding Society. 1993;**11**(2):39-53

[10] Kim YS, Kim BM, Cho HS. A robust on-line quality monitoring method for butt welding process under gap size change using artificial neural network. Pacific Conference on Manufacturing. 1996;**2**:639-644

[11] Lim TG, Cho HS. Estimation of weld pool sizes in GMA welding process using neural networks. Proceedings of the Institution of Mechanical Engineers. 1993;**207**:15-26

[12] Cho HS. AI applications in welding process monitoring and control. In: Japan-Korea FA Sym, Tokyo, Japan. 1991

[13] Lim TG, Cho HS. Weld pool size control based upon direct estimation of weld pool geometry in GMA welding processes. In: Asian Control Conference, Japan. 1994

[14] Ulrich D, Jens H. Using weld Al-methods for parameter geometry determination in scheduling, quality control GMA-welding. ISIJ International. 1999;**39**:1067-1074

[15] Mirapeix J, García-Allende PB, Cobo A, Conde OM, López-Higuera JM. Real-time arc-welding defect detection and classification with principal component analysis and artificial neural networks. NDT & E International. 2007;**40**(4):315-323

[16] Anderson K, Cook GE, Karsai G, Ramaswamy K. Artfical neural networks applied to arc welding process modeling and control. IEEE Transactions on Industry Applications. 1990;**26**(5):824-830

[17] Ohshim K, Yamane S, Yabe M, Akita K, Kugai K, Kubota T. Controlling of torch attitude and seam tracking using neuro arc sensor. Proceedings of the International Conference on IECON. 1995;**2**:1185-1189

[18] Quero JM, Millan RL, Franquelo LG. Neural network approach to weld quality monitoring. Proceedings of the International Conference on IECON. 1994;**2**:1287-1291

[19] Matteson MA, Morris RA, Raines D. An optimal artificial neural network for GMAW arc acoustic classification. international trends in welding science and technology, In: Proceedings of the 3rd International Conference on Trends in Welding Rearch, Gatlinburg, Tennessee, USA. 1992. pp. 1031-1035

[20] Li P, Fang MTC, Lucas I. Modelling of submerged arc weld beads using self-adaptive offset neutral networks. Journal of Materials Processing Technology. 1997;**71**:288-298

[21] Ko KW, Kim H, Cho HS, Kong WI. A bead shape classification method using neural network in high frequency electric resistance welding. Journal of KSPE. 1995;**12**(9):86-94

[22] Teshima T, Shibasaka T, Takuma M, Yamamoto A. Estimation of cutting tool life by processing tool image data with neural network. Annals of the CIRP. 1993;**42**:59-62

[23] Monostori L. A step towards intelligent manufacturing: modeling and monitoring of manufacturing processes through artifitial neural networks. Annals of the CIRP. 1993;**42**(I):485-488

[24] Malakooti BB, Zhou YQ, Tandler EC. In-process regressions and adaptive multi-criteria neural networks for monitoring and supervising machining operations. Journal of Intelligent Manufacturing. 1995;**1**(6):53-66

[25] Rangwala S, Dornfeld D. Sensor integration using neural networks for intelligent tool condition monitoring. Journal of Engineering for Industry. 1990;**112**:219-228

[26] Sunil Elanayar VT, Shin YC. Design and implementation of tool wear monitoring with radial basis function neural networks. In: Proceeding of American Control Conference. 1995. pp. 1722-1725

[27] Ali Zilouchian and Oren Masory. Neural network controller for turning operation of a metal cutting process. Proceedings of the American Control Conference. 1995;713-717

[28] Huang S-J, Ching Chiou K. The application of neural networks in self-tuning constant force control. International Journal of Machine Tools and Manufacture. 1996;**36**(I):17-31

[29] Chryssolouris G, Domroese M, Beaulieu P. Sensor synthesis for control of manufacturing processes. Journal of Engineering for Industry. 1992;**114**(I):158-174

[30] Leem CS, Dreyfus SE. A Neural network approach to feature extraction in sensor signal processing for manufacturing automation. Journal of Intelligent Material Systems and Structures. 1994;**5**:247-257

[31] Leem CS, Dornald DA, Dreyfus SE. A customized neural network for sensor fusion in on-line monitoring of cutting tool wear. Journal of Engineering for Industry. 1995; **117**:152-159

[32] Chao PY, Hwang YD. An improved neural network model for the prediction of cutting tool life. Journal of Intelligent Manufacturing. 1997;**8**:107-115

[33] Balazinski M, Czogala E, Sadowski T. Control of metal-cutting process using neural fuzzy controller. In: 2nd IEEE International Conference Fuzzy Systems. 1993. pp. 161-166

[34] Venkatesh K, Zhou M, Caudill R. Design of artificial neural networks for tool wear monitoring. Journal of Intelligent Manufacturing. 1997;**8**:215-226

[35] Mou I. A method of using neural networks and inverse kinematics for machine tools error estimation and correction. Journal of Manufacturing Science and Engineering. 1997;**119**:247-254

[36] Grabec I, Kuljanic E. Characterization of manufacturing processes based upon acoustic emission analysis by neural networks. Annals of the CIRP. 1994;**43**:77-80

[37] Govekar E, Grabec I. Self-qrganizing neural network application to drill wear classification. Journal of Engineering for Industry. 1994;**116**:233-238

[38] Tamg YS, Li TC, Chen MC. On-line drilling chatter recognition and avoidance using an ART2-A neural network. International Journal of Machine Tools and Manufacture. 1994;**34**(7):949-957

[39] Lin SC, Ting CI. Drill wear monitoring using neural networks. International Journal of Machine Tools and Manufacture. 1996;**36**(4):465-475

[40] Ko TI, Cho DW. Cutting state monitoring in milling by a neural network. International Journal of Machine Tools and Manufacture. 1994;**34**(5):659-676

[41] Tamg YS, Hseih YW, Hwang ST. Sensing tool breakage in face milling with a neural network. International Journal of Machine Tools and Manufacture. 1994;**34**(3):341-350

[42] Ko TI, Cho DW, Jung MY. On-line monitoring of tool breakage in face milling using a self-organized neural network. Journal of Manufacturing Systems. 1995;**42**(2):80-90

[43] Tansel IN, Mekdeci C, McLaughlin C. Detection of Tool Failure in End Milling with Wavelet Transformations and Neural Networks. International Journal of Machine Tools and Manufacture. 1995;**35**(8):1137-1147

[44] Liu H, Chen T, Qui L. Predicting grinding bum using artificial neural networks. Journal of Intelligent Manufacturing. 1997;**8**:235-237

[45] Kao IY, Tang YS. A neural-network approach for the on-line monitoring of the electrical discharge machining process. Journal of Materials Processing Technology. 1997; **69**:112-119

[46] Himmel CD, Kim TS, Krauss A, Kamen EW, May GS. Real-time predictive control of semiconductor manufacturing processes using neural networks. In: Proceedings of the American Control Conference, 1995. pp. 1240-1244

[47] Bushman S, Edgar TF, Trachtenberg I. Modeling of plasma etch systems using ordinary least squares, recurrent neural network, and projection to latent structure models. Journal of the electrochemical society. 1997;**144**(4):1379-1389

[48] Rietman EA. A neural network model of a contact plasma etch process for VLSI production. IEEE Transactions on Semiconductor Manufacturing. 1996;**9**(1):95-100

[49] Nami Z, Misman O, Erbil A, May GS. Semi-empirical neural network modeling of metal-organic chemical vapor deposition. IEEE Transactions on Semiconductor Manufacturing. 1997;**10**(2):288-294

[50] Rietman EA, Lory ER. Use of neural networks in modeling semiconductor manufacturing processs: An example for plasma etch modeling. IEEE Transactions on Semiconductor Manufacturing. 1993;**6**(4):343-347

[51] Baker MD, Himmel CD, May GS. In-situ prediction of reactive ion etch endpoint using neural networks. IEEE Transactional on Components, Packaging and Manufacturing Technology-Part A. 1995;**18**(3):478-483

[52] Wang Q, Sun X, Golden BL, DeSilets L, Edward AWII, Luco S, Peck A. A neural network model for the wire bonding process. Computers & Operations Research. 1993; **20**(8):879-888

[53] Moon YB, Chi SC. Generalized part family formation using neural network techniques. Journal of Manufacturing Systems. 1992;**1**(3):149-159

[54] Kaparthi S, Suresh NC. Machine-component cell formation in group technology: A neural network approach. International Journal of Production Research. 1992;**30**(6):1353-1367

[55] Lee H, Malave CO, Ramachandran S. A selforganizing neural network approach for the design of cellular manufacturing systems. Journal of Intelligent Manufactuting. 1992;**3**:325-332

[56] Moon YB. Establishment of a neurocomputing model for part family/machine group identification. Joumal of Intelligent Manufacturing. 1992;**3**:173-182

[57] Wu B. An introduction to neural networks and their applications in manufacturing. Journal of Intelligent Manufacturing. 1992;**3**:391-403

[58] Cook DF, Shannon RE. A predictive neural network modelling system for manufacturing process parameters. International Journal of Production Research. 1992;**30**(7):1537-1550

[59] Yih Y, Liang T-P, Moskowitz H. Robot scheduling in a circuit board production line: A hybrid OR/ANN approach. ZZE Transactions. 1993;**25**(2):26-33

[60] Chryssolouris G, Lee M, Domroese M. The use of neural networks in determining operational policies for manufacturing systems. Journal of Manufactuting Systems. 1991;**10**(2):166-175

[61] Facchini F, Mossa G, Mummolo G. A model based on artificial neural network for risk assessment to polycyclic aromatic hydrocarbons in workplace. In: 25th European Modeling and Simulation Symposium. 2013. pp. 282-289

[62] Verner MTR. Artificial neural networks in business: Two decades of research. Applied Soft Computing. 2016;**38**:788-804

[63] Brain Mapping by Integrated Neurotechnologies for Disease Studies [Internet]. Available from: http://brainminds.jp/en/

[64] Available from: https://www.science.org.au/publications/inspiring-smarter-brain research-australia

[65] Brainnetome Project [Internet]. Available from: http://www.brainnetome.org/en/brainnetomeproject.html

[66] Prieto A, Prieto B, Ortigosa EM, Ros E, Pelayo F, Ortega J, Rojas I. Neural networks: An overview of early research, current frameworks and new challenges. Neurocomputing. http://dx.doi.org/10.1016/j.neucom.2016.06.014

[67] Casalino G, Facchini F, Mortello M, Mummolo G. ANN modelling to optimize manufacturing processes: The case of laser welding. IFAC-PapersOnLine. 2016;**49**(12):378-383

[68] Jin L, Kuang X, Huang H, Qin Z, Wang Y. Study on the overfitting of the artificial neural network forecasting model. Acta Meteorologica Sinica. 2004;**19**:216-225

[69] Karthick Anand Babu AB. Design and development of artificial neural network based tamil unicode symbols identification system. International Journal of Computer Science Issues (IJCSI). 2012;**9**(1):388

[70] Jordan MI, Rumelhart DE. Forward models: Supervised learning with a distal teacher. Cognitive Science. 1992;**16**(3):307-354

[71] Bousquet O, Raetsch G, von Luxburg U. Advanced Lectures on Machine Learning. Lecture Notes in Artificial Intelligence. Berlin: Springer Verlag; 2004

[72] Sutton RS, Barto AG. Reinforcement Learning. An Introduction. MIT Press. 2014, 2015, 2016 A Bradford Book The MIT Press Cambridge, Massachusetts London, England

[73] Casalino G, Losacco AM, Arnesano A, Facchini F, Pierangeli M, Bonserio C. Statistical analysis and modelling of an Yb: KGW femtosecond laser micro-drilling process. 10th CIRP Conference on Intelligent Computation in Manufacturing Engineering—CIRP ICME 2016. 2017;**62**:275-280

[74] De Filippis LAC, Serio LM, Facchini F, Mummolo G, Ludovico AD. Prediction of the vickers microhardness and ultimate tensile strength of AA5754 H111 friction stir welding butt joints using artificial neural network. Materials. 2016;**9**(11):915

[75] Ghetiya ND, Patel KM. Prediction of tensile strength in friction stir welded aluminium alloy using artificial neural network. Procedia Technology. 2014;**14**:274-281

[76] Yousif YK, Daws KM, Kazem BI. Prediction of friction stir welding characteristics using neural network. Jordan Journal of Mechanical and Industrial Engineering. 2008;**2**:151-155

[77] Fratini L, Buffa G, Palmeri D. Using a neural network for predicting the average grain size in friction stir welding processes. Computers and Structures. 2009;**87**:1166-1174

[78] Boldsaikhan E, Corwin EM, Logar AM, Arbegast WJ. The use of neural network and discrete Fourier transform for real-time evaluation of friction stir welding. Applied Soft Computing. 2011;**11**:4839-4846

[79] Shojaeefard MH, Akbari M, Tahani M, Farhani F. Sensitivity analysis of the artificial neural network outputs in friction stir lap joining of aluminum to brass. Advances in Materials Science and Engineering. 2013;7

[80] Shojaeefard MH, Behnagh RA, Akbari M, Givi MKB, Farhani F. Modelling and Pareto optimization of mechanical properties of friction stir welded AA7075/AA5083 butt joints using neural network and particle swarm algorithm. Materials and Design. 2013;**44**:190-198

[81] Asadi P, Givi MKB, Rastgoo A, Akbari M, Zakeri V, Rasouli S. Predicting the grain size and hardness of AZ91/SiC nanocomposite by artificial neural networks. International Journal of Advanced Manufacturing Technology. 2012;**63**:1095-1107

[82] Serio LM, Palumbo D, Galietti U, De Filippis LAC, Ludovico AD. Analisi del processo di Friction Stir Welding applicato alla lega AA5754-H111: Comportamento meccanico e termico dei giunti. Riv. Ital. Saldatura. 2014;**66**:509-524

[83] Serio LM. Control, Monitoring and Optimization of the Friction Stir Welding Process [PhD thesis]. Bari, Italy: Polytechnic of Bari; 2015

[84] Serio LM, Palumbo D, De Filippis LAC, Galietti U, Ludovico AD. Effect of friction stir process parameters on the mechanical and thermal behavior of 5754-H111 aluminum plates. Materials. 2016;**9**:122

[85] Costandi M. How to buil a brain July. Sciencefocus.com. 2012:32-38

Chapter 12

Artificial Neural Networks (ANNs) for Spectral Interference Correction Using a Large-Size Spectrometer and ANN-Based Deep Learning for a Miniature One

Z. Li, X. Zhang, G. A. Mohua and Vassili Karanassios

Additional information is available at the end of the chapter

http://dx.doi.org/10.5772/intechopen.71039

Abstract

Artificial neural networks (ANNs) are evaluated for spectral interference correction using simulated and experimentally obtained spectral scans. Using the same data set (where possible), the predictive ability of shallow depth ANNs was validated against partial least squares (PLS, a traditional chemometrics method). Spectral interference (in the form of overlaps between spectral lines) is a key problem in large-size, long focal length inductively coupled plasma-optical emission spectrometry (ICP-OES). Unless corrected, spectral interference can be sufficiently severe to the point of preventing precise and accurate analytical determinations. In miniaturized, microplasma-based optical emission spectrometry with a portable, short focal length spectrometer (having poorer resolution than its large-size counterpart), spectral interference becomes even more severe. To correct it, we are evaluating use of deep learning ANNs. Details are provided in this chapter.

Keywords: artificial neural networks (ANNs), artificial intelligence, machine learning, deep learning, spectral interference, PLS, ICP, microplasma, portable optical emission spectrometry

1. Introduction

According to Webster's dictionary, a neural network is defined as *"a computer architecture in which a number of processors are interconnected in a manner suggestive of the connections between neurons in a human brain and which is able to learn by a process of trial and error"*. The *"processors"* maybe individual computers, but they do not have to be. Typically, such "processors" reside in the same computer and most frequently are referred to as *"neurons"*. Also according to Webster's dictionary, artificial is something *"made or produced by human beings rather than occurring naturally, typically as a copy of something natural"*. In this chapter, spectral interference correction in optical emission spectrometry (OES) will be discussed, using artificial neural networks (ANNs).

Spectral interference (a long standing problem in optical atomic spectrometry [1–4]) arises when a spectral line emitted from an **analyte** (defined as the chemical species of interest) in an **analytical sample** (i.e., one to be used in chemical analysis) is overlapped with (or **interfered** by) a spectral line emitted from another chemical constituent that is also present in the same sample or in the sample's **matrix** (defined as whatever an analyte is in). For example, Zinc (Zn) as an analyte (**A**) in an iron-rich soil matrix. In a widely used, 6000–10,000 K hot, inductively coupled plasma (ICP), iron (Fe) can emit as many as 4000 spectral lines, whereas Zn has less than 10 sensitive (i.e., analytically useful) lines, thus making interference from an Fe line (e.g., from the soil matrix) on a Zn line likely. An additional example will be discussed in conjunction with the simulated spectral windows shown in **Figure 1**.

Assuming that all species involved (per legend of **Figure 1**) are present in a sample and that they all are at equal concentrations, only Copper (Cu, at 213.853 nm) and Nickel (Ni, at 213.856 nm) are shown to overlap with the Zn spectral line (at 213.856 nm). Per legend, and

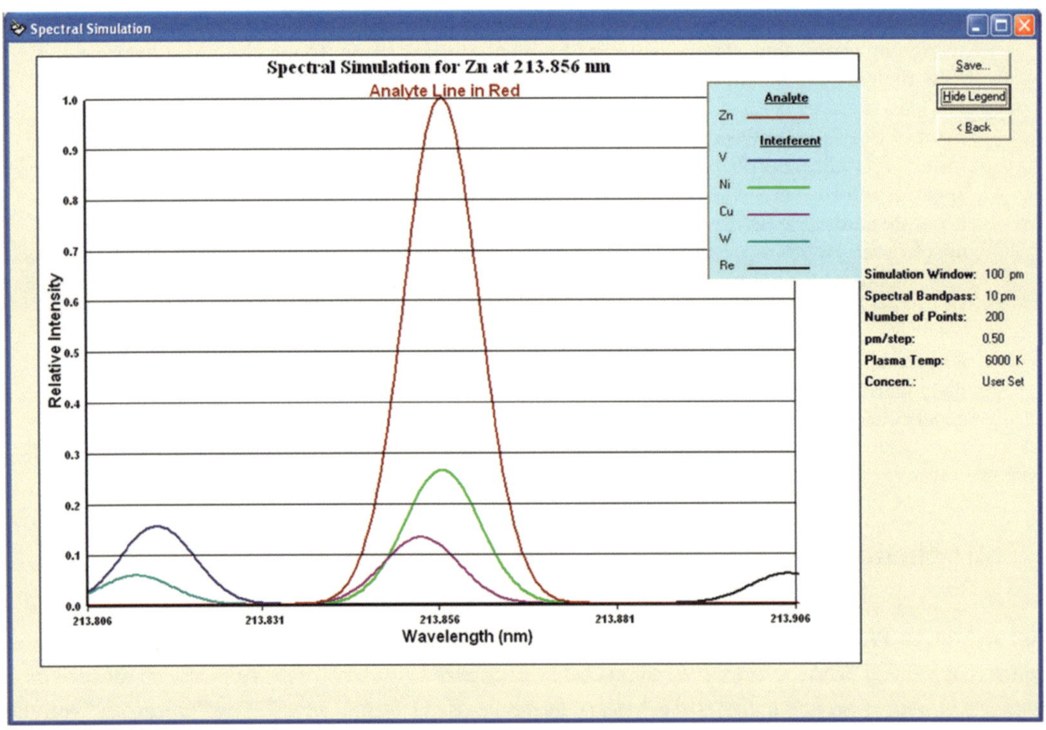

Figure 1. Spectral interferences in a simulated 100 pico-meter (pm)-wide spectral window (between 213.806 and 213.906 nm) centered on the analyte zinc (Zn) 213.856 nm spectral line.

with all participating species at equal concentrations, the spectral lines of V (Vanadium), W (Tungsten) and Re (Rhenium) are not sufficiently intense to be considered (or even to be graphed). However, if the concentrations of these elements is higher (e.g., by 10–100 times) rather than equal to that of the analyte Zn, they will have to be considered. Other elements from the periodic table do not have to be considered even if they are present in the sample or its matrix, because they do not emit spectral lines in the 100 pm-wide spectral window of interest. From this, the significance of spectral interference begins to emerge.

A more dramatic (and yet very realistic example) will be drawn from the practice of elemental analysis by optical emission spectrometry and will be discussed in conjunction with the data shown in **Figure 2**. In this example, Arsenic (As) is the **Analyte** (or simply **A**) and Cadmium (Cd) is the **Interferent** (or simply **I**). It is worth noting that water contaminated by As is a key problem worldwide affecting the health and well-being of more than 100 million inhabitants worldwide because As occurs naturally in the soil surrounding water wells used as drinking water supply in many parts of the world.

In the example shown in **Figure 2**, the intensities of the spectral lines of the As (**Analyte, A**) and of Cd (**Interferent, I**) are about equal (as indicated by the horizontal dashed line positioned on the intensity axis) crossing at 1 (the intensity axis was normalized to the maximum intensity of the As spectral line, the intensity of the Cd line was scaled accordingly). To produce a 1:1 intensity ratio of **A:I**, the concentration ratio of **A:I** was 1:0.3 (due to the different sensitivities of the spectral lines involved). Furthermore, in actual practice, an analyst would

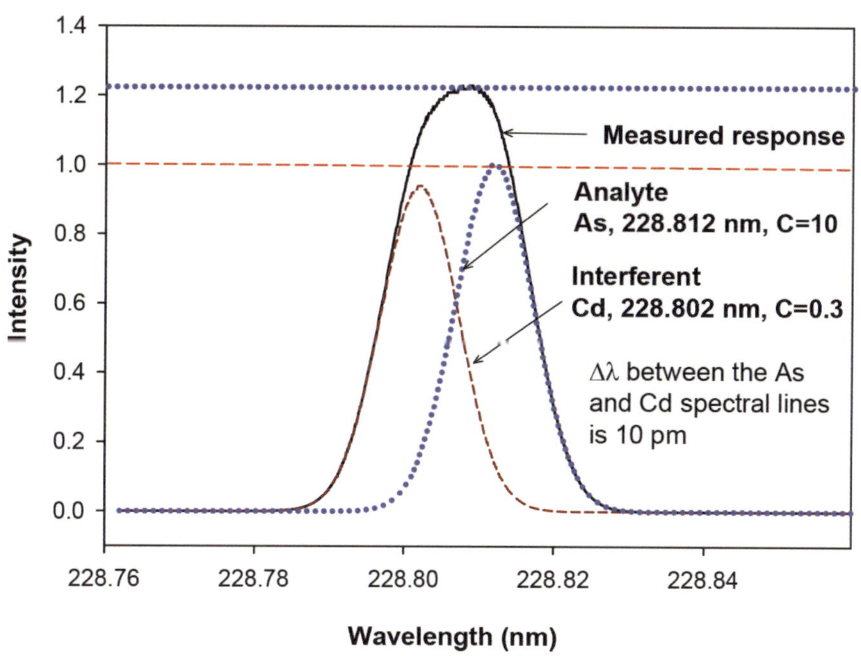

Figure 2. Simulation of the spectral response obtained from a spectral scan (solid line) when using an optical emission spectrometer and a mixture containing arsenic (As) as the analyte **(A)** and cadmium (Cd) as the Interferent **(I)**. C = concentration (regardless of units).

only observe the "added" or measured response shown by the solid line in **Figure 2**. The individual responses obtained by the simulations (shown in using the dashed and the dotted lines in **Figure 2**) will not be observed and they have been added to facilitate discussion.

In this example, the intensity of the combined spectral response for As and Cd (i.e., one obtained by adding the individual responses for As and Cd from a sample containing both As and Cd, and shown by the solid line in **Figure 2** or by experimentally measuring the combined response), is slightly more than 1.2 (indicated by the horizontal dotted line). Clearly, if the Cd interference on As is left uncorrected, the concentration of As will be reported to be higher than it actually is, in this example, by about 20%. Errors as large as the one discussed here are unacceptable in analytical determinations due to potential legal or regulations compliance reasons or health implications (e.g., as used in clinical analysis for medical diagnostics). In analytical practice (e.g., by commercial chemical analysis laboratories), spectral interference is addressed routinely using a number of methods, as will be briefly outlined below.

Several approaches have been used to correct the adverse effects of spectral interference. These traditional methods can be roughly divided into three categories: **Chemistry-based approaches** (i.e., via a chemical separation of an analyte from its matrix), **Physics-based approaches** (e.g., through use of high resolution spectrometry) and **Mathematics-based (or statistics-based) approaches** (e.g., via use of inter element correction factors or through use of Chemometrics). Briefly:

- ***Chemistry-based*** approaches involve removal of either the analyte or the interferent using, for instance, some form of sample processing (e.g., via chemical separation). In general, approaches that require use of additional sample processing and manipulation steps are time-consuming and labor-intensive, thus adding to the overall cost per analysis [1–4].
- ***Physics-based approaches,*** such as use of high resolution spectrometry.
  - Use of high resolution spectrometry [1] to resolve spectral interferences is not feasible in routine analytical laboratories because spectrometers with high resolution (e.g., those with a long focal length) are expensive and they drift.
  - Use of a non-interfered spectral line. This is not always possible, especially if an analyte has few spectral lines useful for analytical determinations and the interferent has many (per Zn and Fe example discussed in the introduction).
- ***Mathematics-based (or statistics-based) approaches,*** include:
  - Use of inter element correction (IEC) factors [5], in which the intensity of a spectral line of an interferent is measured at a different wavelength, and a correction factor is applied. Depending on the type of spectrometer used, this is not always possible.
  - Use of *chemometrics* methods [6–15], defined as those involving the *"application of mathematical or statistical methods for the treatment of chemical data"*. Among others, examples of chemometrics approaches include adaptive filtering, factor analysis, orthogonal polynomials or curve fitting techniques.

Unlike the traditional approaches outlined above, ANNs have been *"designed to find relationships in multi-variate data through learning"* [16–19] that is to *"learn by example'*. As such, they provide an attractive alternative to the traditional methods mentioned above. Due their unique capabilities and their significance in this work, a brief background on ANNs will be provided next.

2. Brief background on ANNs

ANNs fall under the umbrella of artificial intelligence (AI), a general term used to describe *machines displaying human-like intelligence* (presently, only in specific domains). Synonyms used in this field are reflective of the preferences of individual research groups. Examples of synonyms include cognitive computing, computational intelligence, and machine learning in which a machine is trained to use data (e.g., spectra, images, text, or speech) so that it can learn from examples on how to perform a task. These AI methods (no matter what they are called) are contrary to conventional programming paradigms in which explicit program instructions are issued to tell a machine how to perform a task.

ANNs were inspired by biological neurons, and in many respects they mimic them. The ideas behind artificial neurons and their networks date back to the late 1940s and early 1950s followed by the landmark description of the perceptron [20] (a linear classifier, developed in the late 1950s). The influential paper by Hopfield [21] in 1982 addressed the limitations identified by Misnky and Papert and it opened the field of ANNs to their application in a diversity of disciplines [20]. To provide few examples, ANNs have been applied to different areas ranging from finance, to engineering, to physics, to chemistry, to geology, and to medicine and pharmacy. As already been mentioned, a unique advantage of neural networks is their ability to *"learn by example"*.

In chemical analysis, interest in ANNs begun around the mid-1980s. Since then, ANNs have been applied to many chemistry-related areas, limited examples include of IR- and UV-spectra, classification, calibration, nuclear magnetic resonance (NMR), and ion mobility spectrometry (IMS). In my lab, we have been applying ANNs for spectral interference correction in analytical atomic spectrometry [22–27].

A comprehensive description of the theory and practice of ANNs is beyond the scope of this chapter. Briefly [28–32], an ANN is formed by using many individual artificial neurons. An example of an artificial neuron is shown in **Figure 3a**. Neurons are typically organized in layers. The weight (that is the strength of the connection between each neuron) is adjustable. Furthermore, each neuron has its own weighted inputs and its own transfer function (**Figure 3b**). The transfer function is a mapping operation of an input to a neuron or a layer to its output, for example, a linear transfer function (**Figure 3a**); a log-sigmoid function or a hard limit function.

In ANNs, learning can be **supervised or unsupervised**. In supervised learning (used in this work), the network adjusts its internal parameters (e.g., weights) so that a user-specified (i.e., expected) or target-value at the output is reached. At this stage, the error (defined as the difference between the output provided by the network and the target output provided by the user) is computed. Using a **"learning rule"**, the weights are adjusted until the error mentioned above

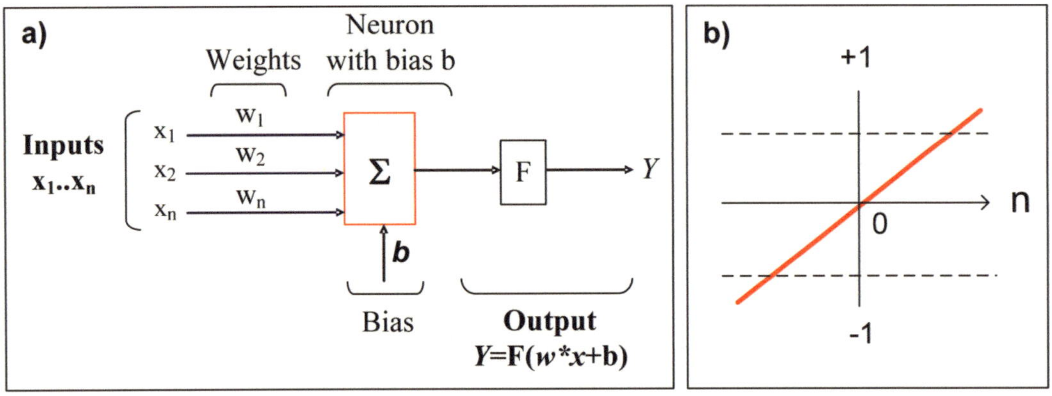

Figure 3. (a) Simplified illustration of a neuron and (b) of a linear transfer function. As shown above, the input to a neuron incorporates an adjustable input bias, ***b***. The input x is multiplied by the strength of the weight (w), and the weight is being adjusted during learning. The product w^*x is passed through a transfer function (F).

is minimized. The learning rate, determining the rate (or speed) at which the weights change is a key parameter. This is because if the learning rate is too fast (and as a consequence the learning step is too large), the network may become unstable. Conversely, if the learning rate is too slow (due to use of a very small learning step), the network may take too long to converge, or it may get trapped at a local minimum. The challenge is to seek a balance between learning rate and convergence to the lowest possible minimum. To find the minimum, a **gradient descent** algorithm (i.e., finding the derivative, typically using the chain rule for derivatives) with **momentum** (m) was used. Specifically, a fraction m is added to the previous weights to update the current weight. This approach ignores small ridges in the error surface, thus reducing the possibility of being trapped at a local minimum. Momentum values ranging anywhere between 0 and 1 can be used. A **backpropagation** of errors algorithm is often used with gradient descent method applied and it was employed here. To generalize, backpropagation strives to find a set of weights that minimize the errors by gradient descent between the output of the network and the target output.

The predictive ability of an ANN depends on the transfer function (**Figure 3b**), on the learning rule applied and on the network's architecture. The **architecture of the network** consists of the number of neurons in each layer, on the number of layers involved, on the transfer function, and on how the layers are connected to each other (and to the network's inputs). Sequential, **feed-forward architecture** is the most the most widely used [28–32]. In this architecture, each neuron is connected to previous neurons and its output becomes an input to the neighboring neurons. An example of spectral scans used for training purposes of a feed-forward network architecture is shown in **Figure 4**.

For validation of network performance (i.e., the ability to predict **A** (analyte) and **I** (Interferent) concentrations) when given an "unknown" scan (i.e., one in which the network is asked to predict the correct or expected value), one spectral scan at a time is fed into the network (bottom frame of **Figure 4**) and the network returns a "predicted" concentration for the Analyte (**A**) and for the Interferent (**I**). For validation (as is typical in this field of research), the performance of ANNs was compared with the performance of a typical chemometric method, such as partial least squares (PLS).

http://dx.doi.org/10.5772/intechopen.71039

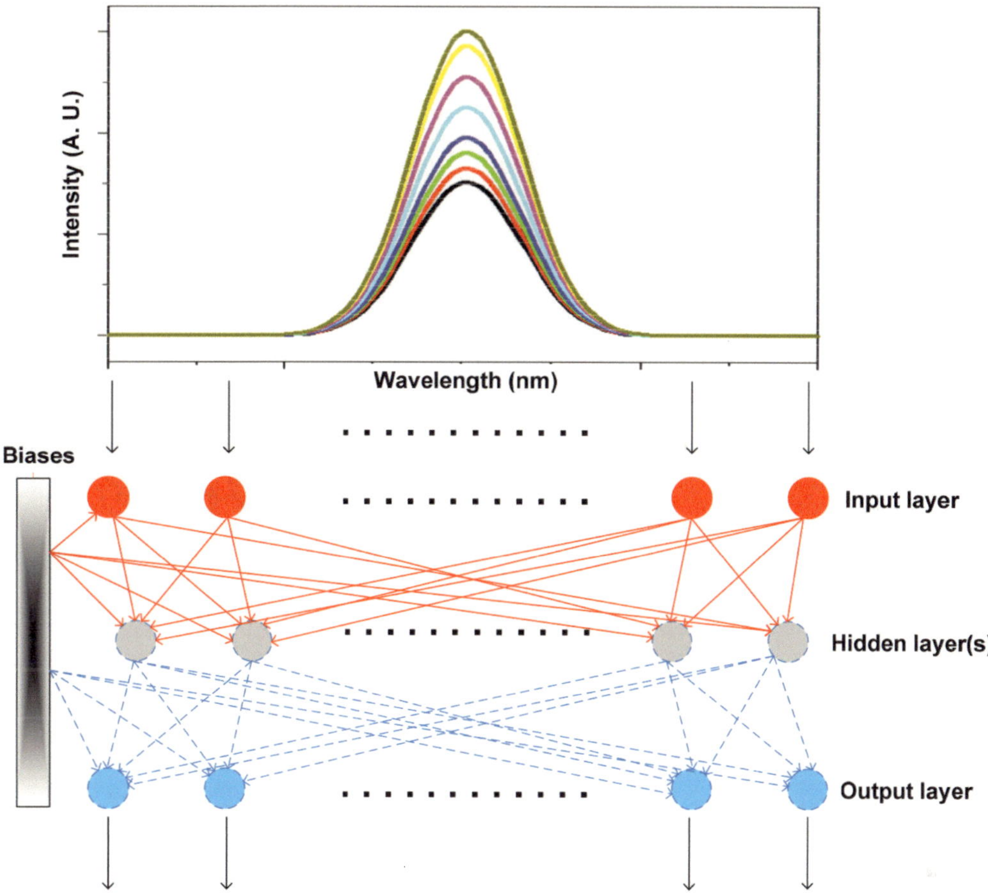

Figure 4. **ANNs**-top frame: Example spectral scans used as a training set. The intensity between scans is different because the concentrations (and hence intensities) of Analyte (**A**) and Interferent (**I**) are different. Multiple scans are shown in the top half, each scan (with data points taken typically every 0.080 nm) was fed individually into the network (bottom half).

3. Brief background on PLS

The key objective in PLS or PLS regression (as it is often called), is to develop a mathematical model relating spectral response (e.g., via spectral scans) in the concentration-range of interest for an interfered analyte. In this case, a calibration model is developed using one of the several PLS algorithms, in this work, a non-linear iterative partial least squares (NIPLS) algorithm was used. For more details on PLS, the review Geladi and Kowalski [33] is recommended. Additional references abound, for brevity only selected few are listed [34–40].

In PLS, an appropriate number of latent variables (or principal components) must be used, otherwise if a small number of variables is employed, the model becomes inadequate; if a large number is utilized both noise and signal are modeled. For comparison purposes, (where possible) the same spectral scans were used to evaluate the predictive ability of PLS and of ANNs. An example of spectral scans used with PLS is shown in **Figure 5**.

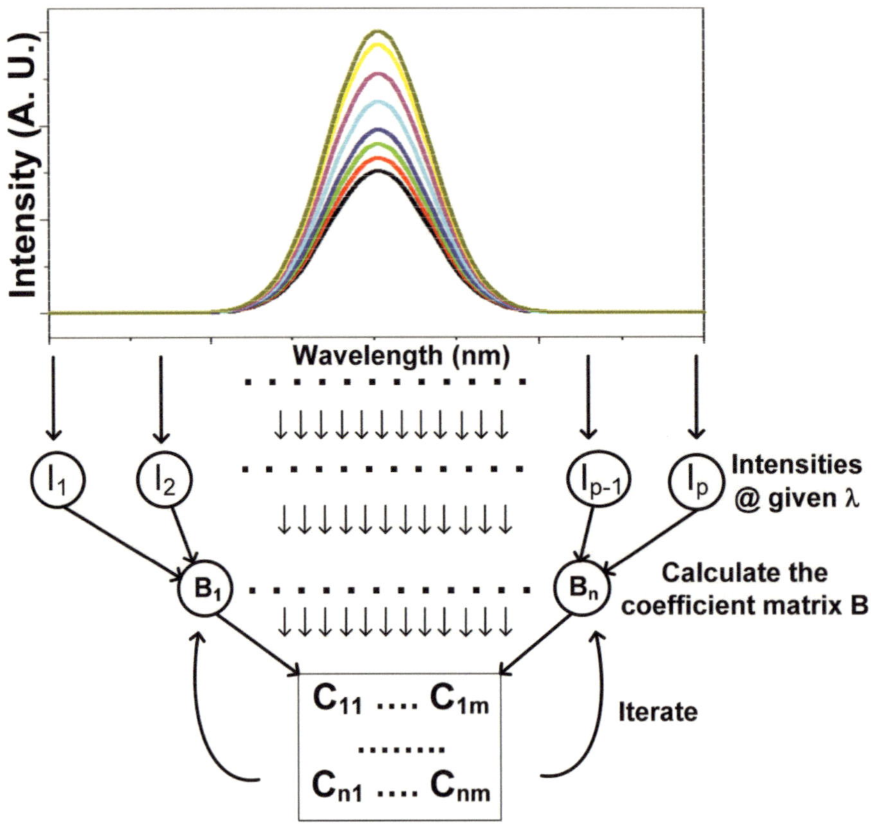

Figure 5. PLS-top frame: Example spectral scans. Bottom frame: Simplified diagram of the PLS algorithm. To facilitate meaningful comparisons, simulations and experimentally obtained spectral scans (where possible) were the same as those used for ANNs.

4. Experimental

For both ANNs and PLS, MatLab (www.mathworks.com) with the neural network and the PLS toolbox were used. To eliminate the effects of instrument-drift (often referred to as 1/f noise) and (potentially) eliminate any other instrument-induced errors, initially both ANNs and PLS were tested using in-house developed spectral simulation software. An example output of this software has been shown in **Figure 1**. The variables tested and the ranges used are listed in **Table 1** and will be briefly discussed next.

Random noise level: Spectral simulations were used to study the effect of random (white) noise, because simulations do not suffer from drift (or 1/f noise) and because a pre-determined amount of noise can be easily added to a simulated spectral scan.

Wavelength separation: What is meant by wavelength separation $\Delta\lambda$ (typically in a few pm) is shown in **Figure 6**. Spectral overlaps can be distinguished as *"direct overlaps"* (**Figure 6a**), intermediate overlaps (**Figure 6b**), and *"wing type"* overlaps (**Figure 6c**). The question

Variables tested	Range of test values	Experimental approach
Random noise level	0, 3, 6, 9 to 18 (%)	Simulations only
Wavelength separation ($\Delta\lambda$)	0, 3, 5, 7, 9, 15 (pm)	Simulations and spectral scans
Intensity ratio	1:0.01 to 1:0.98 (~1:1)	Simulations and spectral scans
Wavelength shift	±0.5 to ±1.8 (pm)	Simulations and aligned spectral scans

Table 1. Variables potentially affecting predictive ability of ANNs and PLS.

addressed was *"how far does an interfering spectral line have to be (in units of $\Delta\lambda$) before its effect on the analyte spectral line is negligible?"* As listed in **Table 1**, the effect of $\Delta\lambda$ on predictive ability was as large as 15 pico-meter (pm).

Intensity ratio A:I affects the measured (or combined) response. For practical reasons, different ratios were used for simulations (**Table 2**) and for spectral scans (**Table 3**). An example is shown in **Figure 7**.

The spectral lines used for the spectral simulations are listed in **Table 2** and those used for the experimentally obtained spectral scans in **Table 3**.

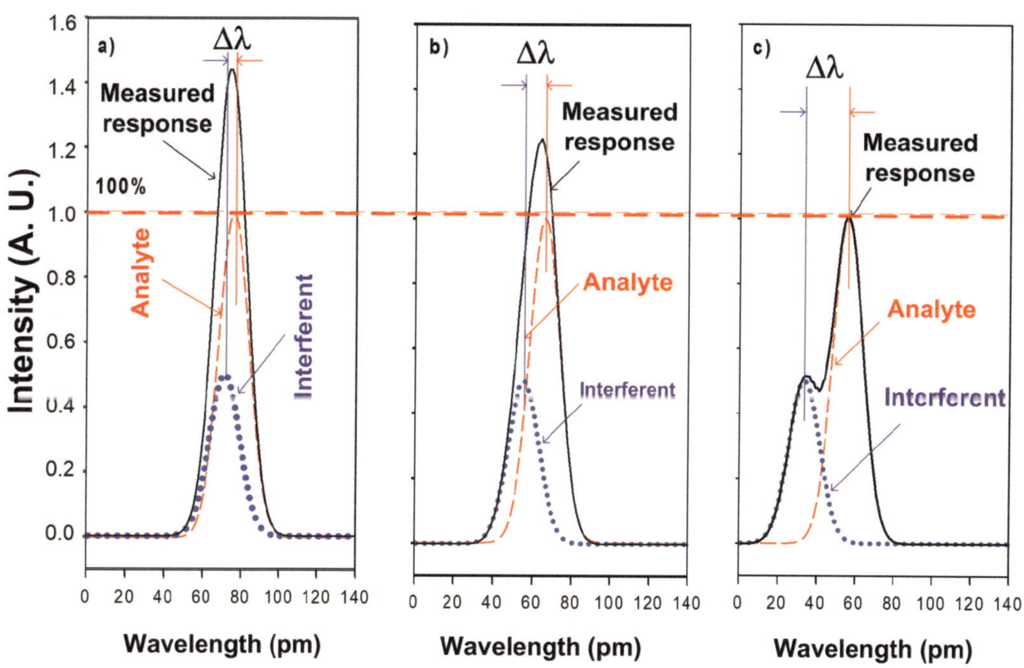

Figure 6. Wavelength separation ($\Delta\lambda$). (a) *"direct spectral overlap"*, small $\Delta\lambda$, (b) intermediate case, (c) *"wing spectral overlap"*, large $\Delta\lambda$. Depending on $\Delta\lambda$, the max measured response in the spectral axis visually "appears" to have shifted (but actually it has not), the visual effect is due to the presence of the interferent. The intensity was scaled to a max of 100% (for **A**) with **I** scaled appropriately. Intensities >100% are due to combined contributions of **A** and **I**.

No.	Elements	Spectral line pairs, wavelength (nm)	Wavelength separation (pm)
1	Zn and Ni	213.856 and 213.856	0
2	Cr and Pt	267.716 and 267.715	1
3	Zn and Cu	213.856 and 213.853	3
4	Ni and Cr	232.003 and 232.008	5
5	B and Mo	208.959 and 208.952	7
6	Ca and Co	315.887 and 315.878	9
7	Be and V	315.042 and 313.027	15

Table 2. Analyte (**A**) and Interferent (**I**) line pairs used in spectral simulations.

No.	Elements	Spectral line pairs, wavelength (nm)	Wavelength separation (pm)
1	Zn and Ni	213.856 and 213.856	0
2	Cr and Pt	267.716 and 267.715	1
3	Zn and Cu	213.856 and 213.853	3
4	Ni and Cr	232.003 and 232.008	5
5	B and Mo	208.959 and 208.952	7
6	Be and V	313.042 and 313.027	15

Table 3. Analyte and Interferent line pairs used for the experimentally obtained spectral scans.

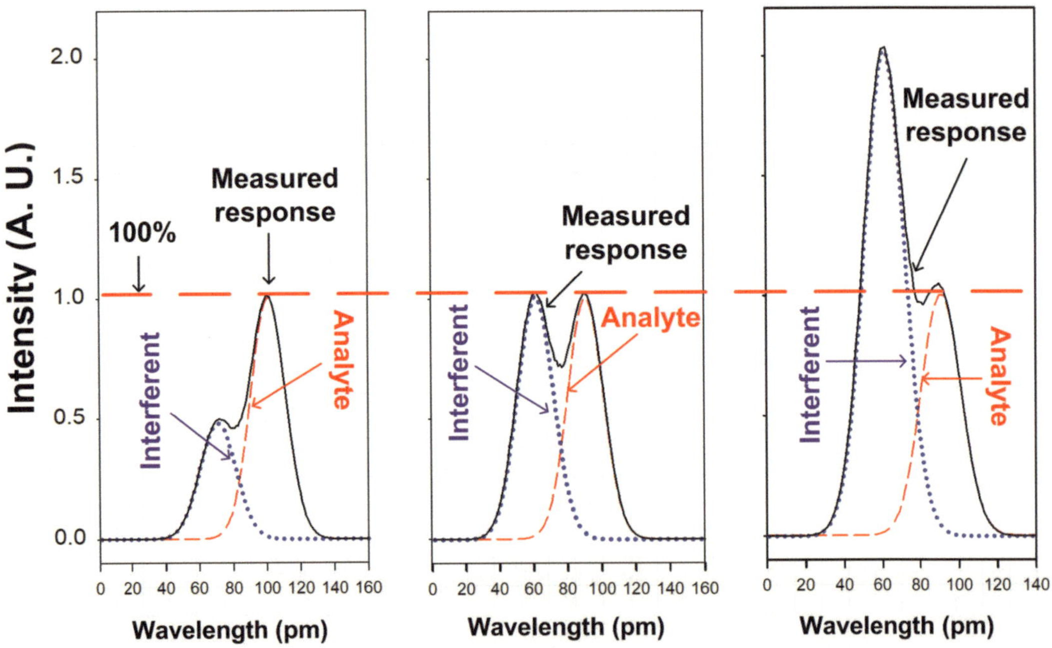

Figure 7. Effect of **A:I** intensity ratio. The intensity axis was scaled to a max of 100% (for **A**) with **I** scaled appropriately. Intensities >100% are due to combined contributions of **A** and **I**.

http://dx.doi.org/10.5772/intechopen.71039

For the experimentally measured scans, a sequential, optical emission spectrometer (OES, a Czerny-Turner scanning monochromator) with a focal length of 0.75 m, an 1800 grooves/mm holographic grating, a photo multiplier tube (PMT) detector, and an ICP were used (Varian Liberty 100). The total weight of this instrument was 300 kg. This ICP-OES system was selected due to its spectral resolution and its ability to scan user-defined spectral windows. A diagram is shown in **Figure 8** and it included here to facilitate explanations of some experimental observations made during the course of this research.

A liquid sample is introduced into a 1–2 kW plasma (**Figure 8**). For simplicity, assume that the plasma generates only two spectral lines (at wavelengths λ_1 for Analyte **A** and λ_2 for Interferent **I**) from a sample introduced into it. Scanning a wavelength-window (dotted line, bottom of **Figure 8**) is accomplished using two mechanisms, one, by initially rotating the computer-controlled grating. Once the beginning of the desired wavelength range has been reached, further scanning is obtained by rotating the computer-controlled scanning plate. To complete a scan,

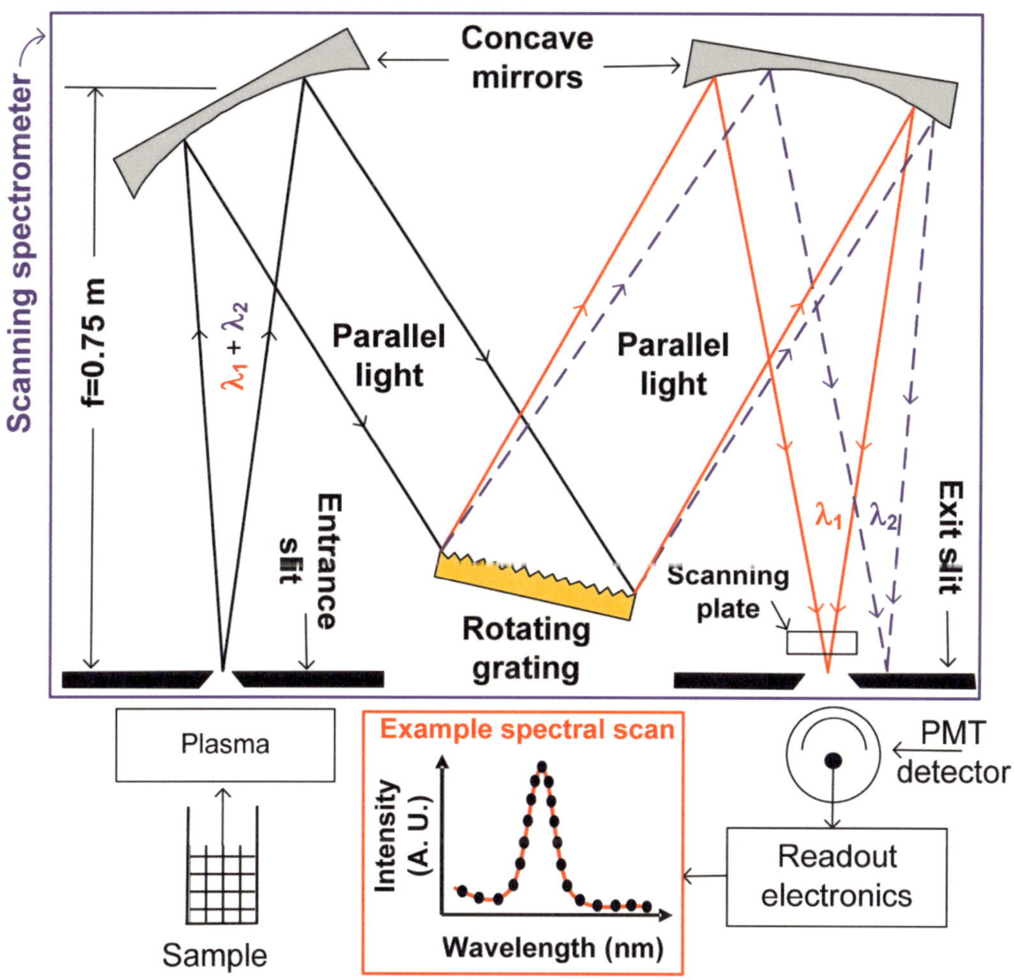

Figure 8. Illustration of the 75 cm focal length (f) scanning spectrometer, scans were 60–160 points.

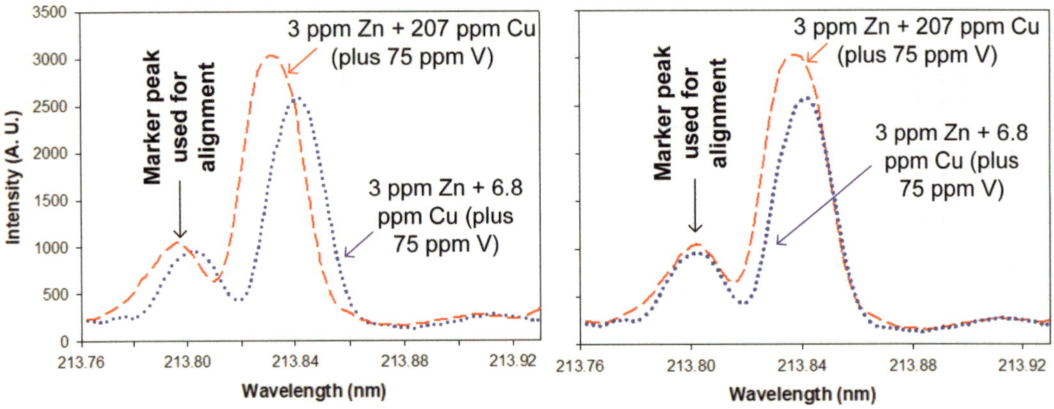

Figure 9. Wavelength shift (misalignment) due to scanning plate (**Figure 8**) reset-errors. (a) Experimentally obtained signal response from Zn (Analyte) + Cu (Interferent) plus V (added to generate a marker peak). And (b) same as (a) but after manual alignment of spectral scans. See text for discussion.

the scanning plate is stopped and a measurement of the intensity is made at the wavelength where the plate was stopped. Then, the wavelength is incremented (typically by about 0.01 nm) by rotating the plate and another measurement of the intensity is made and so on until the desired spectral range has been covered (typically ~0.100 nm). In other words, a scan is accomplished using a step-measure-and-repeat process. The dots in the "example spectral scan" (**Figure 8**) indicate intensity measurements at each step, the presentation software simply *"connects-the-dots"*. Such experimentally obtained spectral scans were used for both ANNs and PLS.

Wavelength shift (misalignment): When repeatedly scanning the same spectral window, it was discovered that scans were offset from each other. An example is shown in **Figure 9a**. To address the effect of this spectrometer limitation, a fixed amount of a reference element was added to the **A** and **I** mixtures. The reference element was selected so that (where possible) its spectral line was separated from the analyte and from the interfering peaks. Subsequently, the spectral scans were corrected by manually aligning them with respect to the marker peak (**Figure 9a**). An example is shown in **Figure 9b**.

The intensity ratio of **A:I** ranged between 1:1, 1:0.01, and 1:0.01, for both simulations and experimental spectral scans. **A:I** ratios higher than 1:1 were not tested because they were deemed too unrealistic for practical analytical applications. If **A:I** is higher than 1:1, an alternative spectral line (if possible) should be used or, the sample may have to undergo some form of chemical separation (per Section 1).

5. Results and discussion

From the large number of experiments that were run (**Tables 2** and **3**), for brevity, only a few results will be included here (and are briefly discussed below).

5.1. Effect of A:I intensity ratio on predictive ability of ANNs and PLS for different $\Delta\lambda$

The predictive performance of ANNs and PLS was found to be inter-dependent on two key variables, specifically **A:I** ratio and $\Delta\lambda$. Experimental results summarizing absolute |Error| are shown in **Figure 10**.

It can be concluded that ANNs (with an average prediction error of the concentration of an Analyte (**A**) of ~4.1%) performed equally as well as PLS (with an average prediction error of ~4.4%).

5.2. Effect of added white (random) noise on prediction of A:I ratios

To avoid the effect of 1/f noise, only simulated spectral scans were used for noise-studies. Noise levels tested were as high as an (unrealistic for practical applicability) 18%. Results are shown in **Figure 11**.

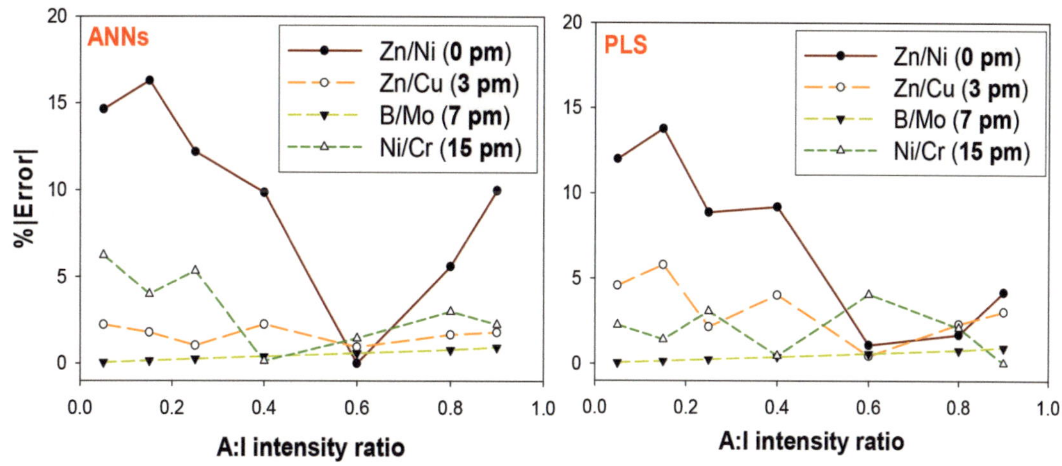

Figure 10. Predictive ability of ANNs and PLS using only four pairs (selected for clarity) of overlapping spectral lines (scans obtained experimentally) with their $\Delta\lambda$ ranging between 0 and 15 pm.

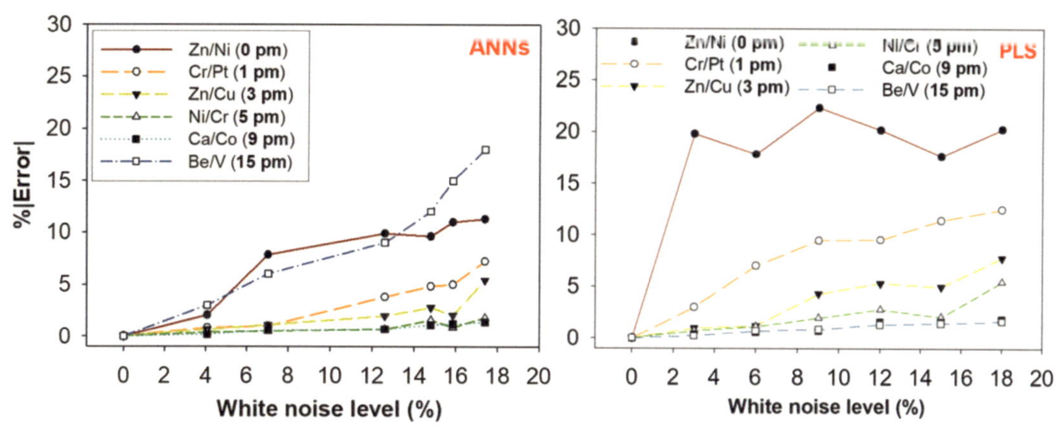

Figure 11. Predictive ability of ANNs and PLS for six pairs of simulated spectral lines with their $\Delta\lambda$ ranging from 0 to 15 pm and with % added random level noise added ranging from 0 to 18% (with two traces overlapping).

The predictive ability of ANNs (on the average) was 5.0%, and of PLS was (on the average) 5.1%. As expected, prediction errors increased as noise levels increased. A key difference between ANNs and PLS is that PLS did poorly when $\Delta\lambda$ was 0 pm (even at very low noise levels). Interestingly, from the simulated spectral scans when 0% noise was added (**Figure 11**) both ANNs and PLS had a prediction errors (on the average) of less than 1%, essentially the predictions were error free. Thus, it can be concluded that (likely) predictive ability was noise-depended (or noise-limited).

6. Conclusions (when using a large-size ICP spectrometer)

Shallow depth ANNs for spectral interference correction were experimentally evaluated using a large-size ICP spectrometer with a scanning monochromator (**Figure 8**) that had resolution typical of commercial systems. The ability of ANNs to predict the concentration of an Analyte (**A**) in a mixture of **A** with an Interferent (**I**) was used a key figure-of-merit and it was studied extensively (**Figures 10** and **11**). To validate predictive ability, predicted **A** concentrations by ANNs were compared with those obtained by PLS. Using experimental spectral scans, the average prediction error for ANNs was 4.1% and for PLS was 4.4%. Simulations were used to understand the origin of prediction errors for both of these methods. The average errors in predictive ability for simulated spectral scans and for Analyte (**A**) by ANNs was 5.0% and for PLS was 5.1%. The higher errors obtained when using simulations over those obtained when using experimentally obtained spectral scans is likely due to use of high (by experimental standards) levels of noise. When low levels of noise were used, the prediction errors were less than 1% (**Figure 11**). In other words the predicted concentrations by both methods were essentially error free. Clearly, methods capable of better discriminating between signals and noise are desirable.

ANNs may also find applicability in portable, miniaturized systems that can be used for *"taking part of the lab to the sample"* types of applications. Due to the short focal length of portable spectrometers employed in miniaturized systems, such spectrometers suffer from significant spectral overlaps (but not from wavelength shift). Interference using miniaturized systems will be discussed next.

7. Spectral interference correction in miniaturization using ANN-based, deep learning approaches

7.1. Why miniaturization?

We have been developing and characterizing miniaturized plasmas in the form of microplasmas [41–48] that we fabricated using a variety of fabrications technologies [49–52] for *taking part of lab to the sample types of applications* [53–60]. Microplasmas are arbitrarily defined as those with one critical dimension in the micrometer regime. To enable use of a non-thermal, non-equilibrium microplasma with an optical emission spectrometer outside of a lab, use of a portable spectrometer is also required.

It is expected that a miniaturized system of the type shown in **Figure 12** will find wide applicability in many analytical situations. For example, in environmental monitoring for testing of water quality *on-site* (e.g., drinking water, lake water, river water, and ground water). Water monitoring is significant to this geographical area because Ontario alone has 250,000 lakes. Outside of Ontario (and Canada), and as already mentioned, Arsenic (As) in water wells affects more than 100 million inhabitants worldwide. Other examples of potential environmental uses include air quality monitoring (e.g., sick building syndrome), safety and security. In clinical analysis, such a portable, ***"shoe-box size"*** instrument could be used to test

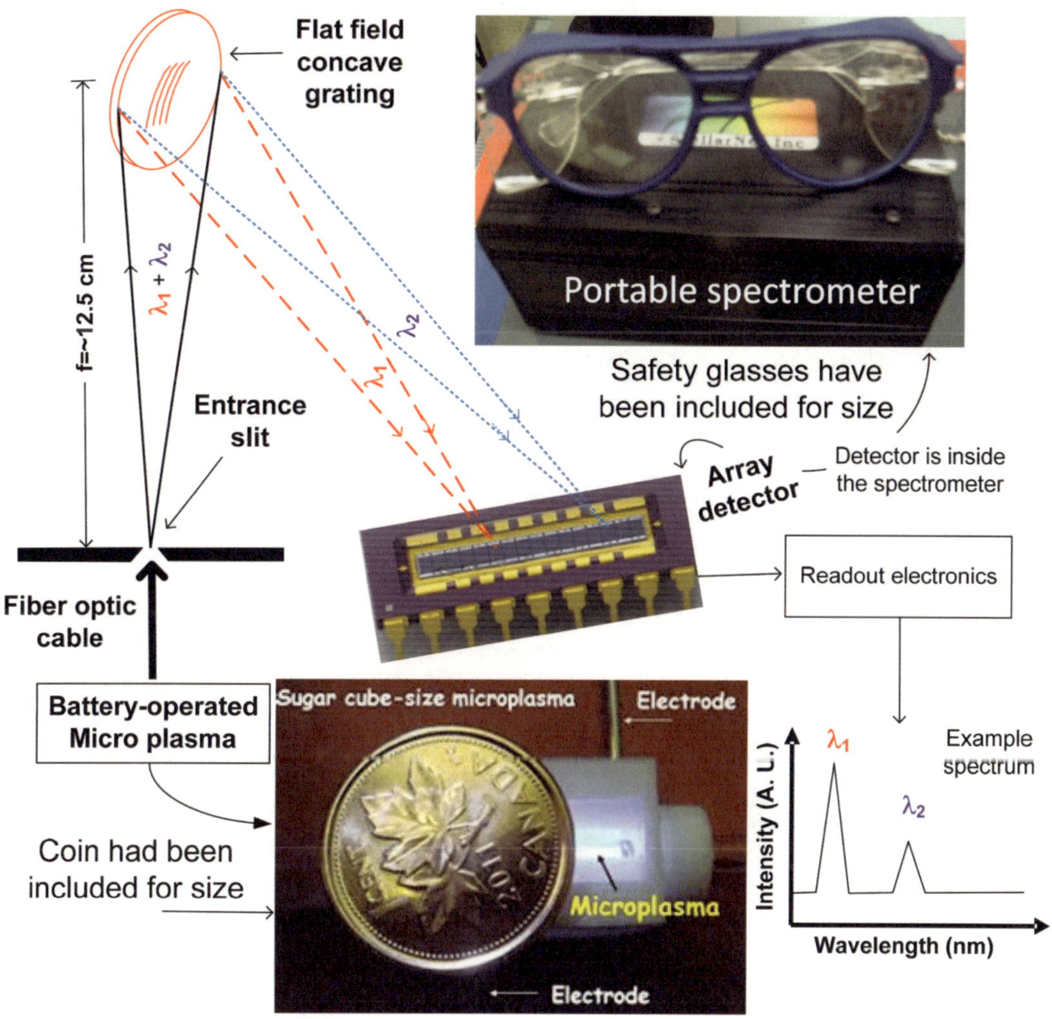

Figure 12. Illustration of a miniaturized microplasma-based optical emission system. Such a system may find use for chemical analysis *on-site*. The ability to obtain analytical results *on-site* and in (near) *real-time* is in stark contrast to the traditional sample collection-in-a-field and chemical analysis-in-a-lab approaches. *On-site* analysis has the potential to alter the traditional chemical analysis paradigm in which samples are collected in a field and are brought to a lab for analysis.

Pb (Lead) concentrations in blood (in the US alone, every child under the age of 7 has to be tested for potential elevated Pb concentrations in their blood); Na and K have to be measured in blood (Na and K concentration-determinations are mandatory in any medical checkup); Li (Lithium) in blood must be measured in certain cases because Li-containing medications are often prescribed as mood stabilizers. In space exploration, a system of the type shown in **Figure 12** may be used in studies involving Ca loss in bones during space flight. This limited set of examples has been included here to highlight potential applicability of miniaturized, microplasma-based optical emission spectrometry systems.

An example of a battery-operated, 3D-printed microplasma coupled to a portable, fiber-optic emission spectrometer is shown in **Figure 12**. All components shown in **Figure 12 can fit inside a shoe box**.

For a system of the type shown in **Figure 12**, in addition to requiring a battery-operated, light-weight, miniaturized plasma source (for use *on-site* rather than in a lab), the spectrometer must also be portable (generally meaning that it must have a short focal length). However, as the focal length of the optical spectrometer is reduced (e.g., from 75 cm as shown in **Figure 8** to about 12.5 cm as shown in **Figure 12**), resolution decreases and spectral overlaps become more prevalent. An example is shown in **Figure 13**.

Some specifics: in optical emission spectrometry, resolution ($R = \lambda/\Delta\lambda$) is defined as the ability to baseline resolve two closely spaced wavelengths (**Figure 13**, left frame). As already mentioned, for use *on-site*, a portable optical spectrometer (with a short focal length) is required. But as focal length decreases, resolution degrades. And as resolution degrades, spectral overlaps become more severe, thus making spectral interference correction essential. To demonstrate the severity of spectral overlaps and the need for spectral interference correction, the superimposed spectra of Europium (Eu), Strontium (Sr), and Lead (Pb) shown in **Figure 14** and will be used as an example.

Shown in **Figure 14** are three spectra obtained by introducing individually (or separately) into a microplasma (**Figure 12**) equal concentrations of Eu, Pb, and Sr. and to facilitate discussion, the spectra have been superimposed and graphed together. In a hypothetical sample

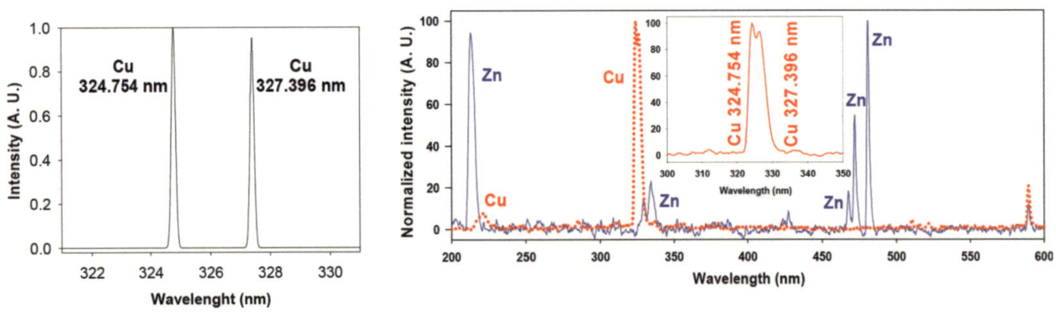

Figure 13. Left frame: Spectral window showing two Cu lines (acquired using a long focal length spectrometer, for example, one shown in **Figure 8**) demonstrating baseline resolution. Right frame, spectra from 200 to 850 nm acquired using a spectrometer with a short focal length (**Figure 12**, StellarNet co, http://www.stellarnet.us/). Right frame (insert): In this case, the same Cu lines cannot be resolved. Each 200–850 nm spectrum (or full spectral scan) is 2048 data points.

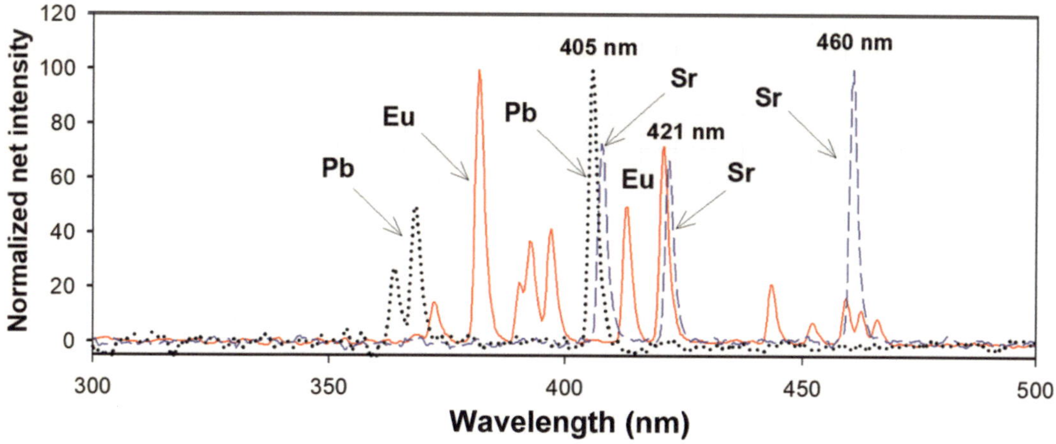

Figure 14. Spectral overlaps observed when using Eu (solid line), Sr (dashed line), and Pb (dotted line).

containing these three elements, Sr. is the analyte and Eu and Pb are the interferents. The most intense Sr. line (at ~460 nm) is directly overlapped by two Eu lines (at ~459 nm). The second most intense Sr. line (at around 407 nm) is overlapped by the most intense Pb line (at 405 nm), and the third most intense Sr. line (~ 421 nm) is also directly overlapped by a Eu spectral line. Clearly in this example interference free determinations of Sr. are not possible, thus making spectral interference correction essential. In this laboratory, an ambitious goal of using ANN-based deep learning approaches is being pursuit. Deep learning approaches can handle larger amounts of data (as opposed to shallow depth ANNs), and they are claimed to have improved abilities to distinguish signals from noise, thus likely having improved predictive abilities.

7.2. ANN-based deep learning

Similar to conventional or shallow depth ANNs (i.e., those with a few network layers, **Figure 4**), deep learning neural nets (or deep neural networks, or DNNs for short), have numerous hidden layers. An example is shown in **Figure 15a**. A key advantage of deep learning [61–65] ANNs versus shallow depth ANNs is that in deep learning the network continues to learn as the amount of data increases, thus increasing its learning and (likely) predictive abilities (thus reducing %|Error| of prediction). In sharp contrast, shallow depth ANNs (e.g., with a few layers) although they may outperform deep learning when using relatively small data sets, their learning and predictive abilities plateau (**Figure 15b**).

At present, deep learning is receiving significant attention. A limited number of examples include **IBM**'s Watson [66], a reportedly $24 billion investment so far); **Google** is offering a time-limited free access to cloud machine learning [67]; **Mobile Eye** is marketing their advanced driver assist system (ADAS) claiming that it has been installed in many self-driving cars [68]; **NVIDIA** is marketing graphics processing units (GPUs) with deep learning abilities [69]; Intel, a semiconductor fabrication house has a sizable investment on deep learning [70]; **OpenText** [71] is using deep learning in the name of Magellan to rival IBM's Watson; **Qualcomm** is a fabrication house of CPUs for smartphones offers a software kit for neural

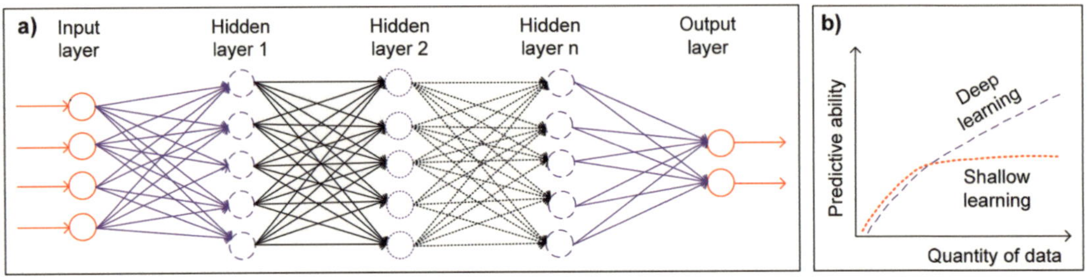

Figure 15. (a) Deep learning neural nets with every neuron connected to all neurons in neighboring layers (where n maybe in the millions of layers). (b) Sketch of predictive (and learning) abilities of shallow depth and deep learning ANNs versus the amount data used in a training set.

networks [72]; **Samsung** is developing deep learning approaches for heath applications [73]; Noah'sArkLab [74] funded by **Huawei** (a telecom company), is heavily investing in deep learning; **Microsoft** is offering a (currently free) "cognitive toolkit" for deployment of deep learning approaches [75]; and **Apple** is offering developers machine learning tools [76] for inclusion into any iOS app. Apple is also publishing their Machine Learning Journal. Overall and one way or another, all of these companies are either using or promoting use of ANN-based deep learning.

We are experimenting with deep learning for spectral interference correction using a miniaturized, portable spectrometer (of the type shown in **Figure 12**) using data of the type shown in **Figures 13** and **14**.

8. Overall conclusions

ANNs proved effective at addressing the key problem of spectral interference encountered in optical emission spectrometry. Due to the relatively small number of data points used (e.g., 60–160), training and validation times did not become bottlenecks. To obtain *method validation* (as is typical in chemical analysis), ANNs were compared to PLS. It was concluded that the predictive ability of both methods was at ~5% and that both methods were noise-limited. Thus, our attention has now been turned to ANN-based deep learning approaches that are reported to have improved abilities to distinguish signals from noise. Deep learning is being evaluated for use in miniaturized systems (with short focal length, portable spectrometers) in which spectral interference is typically more severe than those of long focal length, large-size spectrometers. It is expected that application of deep learning approaches has the potential to lead to portable chemical analysis instruments that are *"smaller, cheaper,* **smarter** *and faster"* at producing precise and accurate analytical results *on-site* [53]. *On-site* analysis capabilities have the potential to cause a paradigm shift in classical chemical analysis (caption of **Figure 12**) by allowing practioners *"to bring part of the lab to the sample"* so that analytical results can be obtained *in-situ* and in (near) *real-time*. Although large-size and miniaturized plasma-based instruments were used as an ANN application example, it is expected that the ideas presented here will have wider applicability to include non-plasma-based chemical analysis instruments regardless of their size.

Acknowledgements

Financial assistance from Natural Sciences and Engineering Research Council (NSERC) of Canada is gratefully acknowledged. A special thank you to Dr. Harold Szu for the numerous discussions we have had (VK) on ANNs during several SPIE conferences.

Author details

Z. Li, X. Zhang, G. A. Mohua and Vassili Karanassios*

*Address all correspondence to: vkaranassios@uwaterloo.ca

Department of Chemistry and Waterloo Institute for Nanotechnology, University of Waterloo, Waterloo, Ontario, Canada

References

[1] Montaser A, Golightly DW, editors. Inductively Coupled Plasmas in Analytical Atomic Spectrometry. 2nd edition. NY: Wiley-VCH; 1992

[2] Boumans PWJM, editor. Inductively Coupled Plasma Emission Spectrometry. Part 2, NY: Wiley; 1987

[3] Tompson M. Handbook of Inductively Coupled Plasma Spectrometry. NY: Chapman Hall; 1989

[4] Nolte J. ICP Emission Spectrometry. NY: Wiley-VCH; 2003

[5] Griffths ML, Svozil D, Worsfold PJ, Denham S, Evans EH. Comparison of traditional and multivariate calibration techniques applied to complex matrices using inductively coupled plasma atomic emission spectroscopy. Journal of Analytical Atomic Spectrometry. 2000;**15**:967-972

[6] Varmuza K, editor. Chemometrics in Practical Applications. InTech, HR; 2012

[7] Lavine BK, Workman Jr. J. Chemometrics. Analytical Chemistry. 2013;**85**(2):705-714

[8] Andrade-Garda JM, editor. Basic Chemometric Techniques in Atomic Spectroscopy, 2nd edition. RSC; 2013

[9] Kumar N, Bansal A, Sarma GS, Rawal RK. Chemometrics tools used in analytical chemistry: An overview. Talanta. 2014;**123**:186-199

[10] Vogt F. Quo vadis, chemometrics? Journal of Chemometrics. 2014;**28**(11):785-788

[11] Jančić-Stojanović B, Rakić T. Chemometrics in data analysis and liquid chromatographic method development. Chapter 13 in Analytical Separation Science. NY: Wiley; 2015

[12] Pawar HA, Kamat SR. Chemometrics and its Application in Pharmaceutical Field. Journal of Physical Chemistry & Biophysics. 2014;**4**(6):169

[13] Mark H, Workman Jr. J. Chemometrics in spectroscopy, a series of tutorial articles in the column entitled Chemometrics in Spectroscopy, appeared from September 2014–June 2017. http://www.spectroscopyonline.com/column-chemometrics-spectroscopy [Accessed July 2017]

[14] Otto M. Chemometrics: Statistics and Computer Application in Analytical Chemistry. 3rd ed. NY: Wiley; 2017

[15] de Harrington PB. Automated support vector regression. Journal of Chemometrics. 2017;**31**(4):1-14

[16] Schalkoff RJ. Artificial Neural Networks. India: McGraw Hill; 2011

[17] Krenker A, Bešter J, Kos A. Introduction to artificial neural networks, Chapter 1. In: Suzuki K, editor. Artificial Neural Networks—Methodological Advances and Biomedical Applications. InTech Open, HR; 2011

[18] Hagan MT, Demuth HB, Beale MH, De Jesús O. Neural Network Design. 2nd ed. Boston: PWS Pub.; 2014

[19] Lin S-B. Limitations of shallow nets approximation. Neural Networks, 2017;**94**:96-102

[20] Marini F, Bucci R, Magri AL, Margi AD. Artificial neural networks in chemometrics: History, examples and perspectives. Microchemical Journal. 2008;**88**:178

[21] Hopfield J. Neural networks and physical systems with emergent collective computational abilities. Proceedings of the National Academy of Sciences. 1982;**79**:2544

[22] Li Z, Karanassios V. Development of artificial neural networks for spectral interference correction in optical emission spectrometry. Proceedings of SPIE. 2011;**8058**:80580J

[23] Li Z, Huang S, Karanassios V. Further development of ANNs for spectral interference correction in optical emission spectrometry. Proceedings of SPIE. 2012;**8041**:8401Y1

[24] Li Z, Zhang X, Karanassios V. Artificial neural networks compared to partial least squares (PLS) for spectral interference correction in optical emission spectrometry. Proceedings of SPIE. 2013;**8750**:87500C1-87500C7

[25] Li Z, Zhang X, Karanassios V. Verification of the performance of artificial neural networks (ANNs) versus partial least squares (PLS) for spectral interference correction in optical emission spectrometry. Proceedings of SPIE. 2014;**87500**:87500C1-87500C7

[26] Li Z, Zhang X, Karanassios V. How do artificial neural networks (ANNs) compare to partial least squares (PLS) for spectral interference correction in optical emission spectrometry? Proceedings of SPIE. 2015;**9496**:94960M1-94960M8

[27] Li Z, Karanassios V. Artificial neural networks (ANNs) versus partial least squares (PLS) for spectral interference correction for taking part of the lab to the sample types of applications: An experimental study. Proceedings of SPIE. 2016;**9871**:97810M1-94960M8

[28] Cirovic DA. Feed-forward artificial neural networks: Applications to spectroscopy. Trends in Analytical Chemistry. 1997;**16**:148

[29] Jansson PA. Neural networks: An overview. Analytical Chemistry. 1991;**63**:357A

[30] Zupan J, Gasteiger J. Neural Networks in Chemistry and Drug Design. 2nd ed. NY: Wiley-VCH; 1999

[31] Harnahan G. Computational neural networks driving complex analytical problem solving. Analytical Chemistry. 2010;**82**:4307

[32] Harnahan G. Artificial Neural Networks in Biological and Environmental Analysis. Boca Raton, FL: CRC Press; 2011

[33] Geladi P, Kowalski BR. Partial least squares regression: A tutorial. Analytica Chimica Acta. 1986;**185**:1-17

[34] Abdi H. Partial least squares regression and projection on latent structure regression (PLS regression). Wiley Interdisciplinary Reviews: Computational Statistics. 2010;**2**(1):970106

[35] Hanrahan G. Environmental Chemometrics (Analytical Chemistry). FL: CRC Press; 2011

[36] Andrade-Garda J. Basic Chemometric Techniques in Atomic Spectroscopy. UK: RSC; 2013

[37] Ballabio D, Consonnia V. Classification tools in chemistry. Part 1: Linear models. PLS-DA. Analytical Methods. 2013;**5**:3790-3798

[38] Xu L, Goodarzi M, Shi W, Cai C-B, Jiang J-H. A MATLAB toolbox for class modeling using one-class partial least squares (OCPLS) classifiers. Chemometrics and Intelligent Laboratory Systems. 2014;**139**:58-63

[39] Shan P, Peng S, Tang L, Yang C, Zhao Y, Xie Q, Li Q. A nonlinear partial least squares with slice transform based piecewise linear inner relation. Chemometrics and Intelligent Laboratory Systems. 2015;**143**:97-110

[40] Hair J, Hult GTM, Ringle CM, Sarstedt M. A Primer on Partial Least Squares Structural Equation Modeling (PLS-SEM). CA: SAGE; 2017

[41] Karanassios V. Microplasmas for chemical analysis: Analytical tools or research toys? Spectrochimica Acta Part B. 2004;**59**:909-928

[42] Karanassios V, Johnson K, Smith AT. Micromachined, planar-geometry, atmospheric-pressure, battery-operated microplasma devices (MPDs) on chips for microsamples of liquids, gases or solids by optical emission spectrometry. Analytical and Bioanalytical Chemistry. 2007;**388**:1595-1604

[43] Weagent S, Karanassios V. Helium-hydrogen microplasma device (MPD) on postage-stamp-size plastic-quartz chips. Analytical and Bioanalytical Chemistry. 2009;**395**:577-589

[44] Weagant S, Chen V, Karanassios V. Battery-operated, argon-hydrogen microplasma on hybrid, postage stamp-size plastic-quartz chips for elemental analysis of liquid

microsamples using a portable optical emission spectrometer. Analytical and Bioanalytical Chemistry. 2011;**401**:2865-2880

[45] Abbaszadeh S, Karim KS, Karanassios V. Measurement of UV from a microplasma by a microfabricated amorphous selenium detector. IEEE Transactions on Electron Devices. 2013;**60**(2):880-883

[46] Nguon O, Gauthier M, Karanassios V. Determination of the loading and stability of Pd in an arborescent copolymer in ethanol by microplasma-optical emission spectrometry. RSC Advances. 2014;**4**:8978-8984

[47] Nguon O, Huang S, Gauthier M, Karanassios V. Microplasmas: From applications to fundamentals. Proceedings of SPIE. 2014;**9105**:9101061-9101067

[48] Weagent S, Dulai G, Li L, Karanassios V. Characterization of rapidly-prototyped, battery-operated, argon-hydrogen microplasma on a chip for elemental analysis of microsamples by portable optical emission spectrometry. Spectrochimica Acta Part B. 2015;**106**:75-80

[49] Weagant S, Li L, Karanassios V. Rapid Prototyping of Hybrid, Plastic-Quartz 3D-Chips for Battery-Operated Microplasmas. InTech Publishing, HR; 2011. Chapter 10, pp. 1-18

[50] Weagant S, Karanassios V. Battery-operated, planar-geometry microplasma on a postage-stamp size chips: Some fundamentals. Proceedings of SPIE. 2011;**8024**:80240L

[51] Zhang X, Karanassios V. Rapid prototyping of solar-powered, battery-operated, atmospheric-pressure, sugar-cube size microplasma on hybrid, 3D chips using a portable optical emission spectrometer. Proceedings of SPIE. 2012;**8366**:83660D

[52] Shatford R, Karanassios V. Microplasma fabrication: From semiconductor technology for 2D-chips and microfluidic channels to rapid prototyping and 3D-printing of microplasma devices. Proceedings of SPIE. 2014;**9106**:9106H1-9106H7

[53] Weagant S, Smith AT, Karanassios V. Mobile micro- and nano-instruments: Small, cheap and under wireless control. ECS Transactions. 2010;**28**(14):1-6

[54] Trzcinski P, Weagent S, Karanassios V. Wireless data acquisition of transient signals for mobile spectrometry applications. Applied Spectroscopy. 2016;**70**:905-915

[55] Abbaszadeh S, Karim KS, Karanassios V. A microfabricated, low dark current a-Se detector for measurement of microplasma optical emission in the UV for possible use on-site. Proceedings of SPIE. 2013;**8726**:87260S

[56] Lee D, Dulai G, Karanassios V. Survey of energy harvesting and energy scavenging approaches for on-site powering of wireless sensor- and microinstrument-networks. Proceedings of SPIE. 2013;**8028**:8720S1

[57] Badiei HR, McEnaney J, Karanassios V. Bringing part of the lab to the field: On-site chromium speciation in seawater by electrodeposition of Cr(III)/Cr(VI) on portable coiled-filament assemblies and measurement in the lab by electrothermal, NTV

sample introduction and inductively coupled plasma-atomic emission spectrometry. Spectrochimica Acta Part B. 2012;**78**:42-49

[58] Badiei HR, Lai B, Karanassios V. Micro- and nano-volume samples by electrothermal, near-torch vaporization sample introduction using removable, interchangeable and portable rhenium coiled-filament assemblies and axially-viewed inductively coupled plasma-atomic emission spectrometry. Spectrochimica Acta Part B. 2012;**77**:19-30

[59] Badiei HR, Liu C, Karanassios V. Taking part of the lab to the sample: On-site electrodeposition of Pb followed by measurement in the lab using electrothermal, NTV sample introduction and ICP-AES. Microchemical Journal. 2013;**108**:131-136

[60] Trizcinski P, Nathan A, Karanassios V. Approaches to energy harvesting and energy scavenging for energy autonomous sensors and microinstruments. Proceedings of SPIE. 2017;**10194**:10194A1-10194A9

[61] Deng L, Yu D. Deep learning: Methods and applications. Foundations and Trends in Signal Processing. 2014;**7**(3-4):197-387

[62] Schmidhuber J. Deep learning in neural networks: An overview. Neural Networks. 2015;**61**:85-117

[63] Le Cun Y, Bengio Y, Hinton G. Deep learning. Nature. 28-05-2015;**521**:436-444

[64] Bengio Y. Machines who learn. Scientific American. 2016;**314**(6):46-51

[65] Gopnik A. Making AI more human. Scientific American. 2017;**316**(6):60-65

[66] www.ibm.com/watson/ [Accessed: July 2017]

[67] cloud.google.com/products/machine-learning/ [Accessed: July 2017]

[68] http://www.mobileye.com/future-of-mobility/mobileye-advanced-technologies/ [July 2017]

[69] www.nvidia.com/en-us/deep-learning-ai/ [Accessed: July 2017]

[70] https://software.intel.com/en-us/ai-academy/training [Accessed: July 2017]

[71] https://blogs.opentext.com/introducing-opentext-magellan-power-ai-pre-integrated-platform-machine-assisted-decision-making/ [Accessed: July 2017]

[72] https://www.qualcomm.com/news/onq/2017/07/25/device-ai-qualcomm-snapdragon-neural-processing-engine-sdk [Accessed: July 2017]

[73] http://www.samsung.com/global/business/healthcare/insights/news/samsung-applies-deep-learning-technology-to-diagnostic-ultrasound-imaging [Accessed: July 2017]

[74] http://www.noahlab.com.hk/ [Accessed: July 2017]

[75] https://www.microsoft.com/en-us/cognitive-toolkit/toolkit [Accessed: July 2017]

[76] https://developer.apple.com/machine-learning/ [Accessed: July 2017]

Chapter 13

Solar Radiation Prediction Using NARX Model

Ines Sansa and Najiba Mrabet Bellaaj

Additional information is available at the end of the chapter

http://dx.doi.org/10.5772/intechopen.70570

Abstract

The human brain, like every vital organ, is constituted of neurons. It is through this organ that we can learn and reason, reflect and memorize. The geniality of human brain and more particularly of its neurons motivates several researchers to interest to this research and to benefit from its biological aspect. The idea was to reproduce, in an artificial way, the behaviors observed in man. It was in 1943 that the first artificial neural network (ANN) was created by Warren McCulloch and Walter Pitts. It is a simple elementary processor imitating the structure and the functioning from the biological neuron. Artificial neural network is characterized by its capacity to learning and generalizing. It represents a very powerful tool. It provided multiple solutions to different complex problems. In these recent years, its effectiveness is proved in various researches fields. ANN is subdivided on two main groups, the static and dynamic neural network. The choice of the one or the other neural network type depends to the application to be processed and the complexity of model. For static neural network, information propagates in a single direction, layer by layer, and from the inlet to the outlet. They are generally used in various applications such as classifications, pattern recognition, and functions approximation. For the dynamic neural network dynamic neural network is not limited. Each neuron can send and receive information from all other neurons. The dynamic neural network architecture includes frequently one or more cycles which necessarily contain at least one delay connection. This gives rise to the dynamism notion. This neural network type is more complex than the static one, but it is more efficient for some particular applications such as dynamic modeling, monitoring, and process control. In this chapter, nonlinear autoregressive models with exogenous input (NARX) model, as type of dynamic neural network, will be used to the solar radiation prediction. Simulation results will be presented to prove the effectiveness of this model compared to those obtained using the static one.

Keywords: static neural network, NARX model, solar radiation prediction

1. Introduction

The human brain, like every vital organ, is constituted of a set of cells which are called neurons. It is through this organ that we can learn and reason, reflect and memorize. The geniality of human brain and more particularly of its neurons motivates several researchers to interest to this research and to benefit from its biological aspect. The idea was to reproduce, in an artificial way, the behaviors observed in man. It was in 1943 that the first artificial neural network was created by Warren McCulloch and Walter Pitts. It is a simple elementary processor imitating the structure and the functioning from the biological neuron. Artificial neural network is characterized by its capacity of learning and generalizing. It represents a very powerful tool; it provided multiple solutions to different complex problems. In these recent years, its effectiveness is proved in various researches fields. Artificial neural network are subdivided on two main groups, the static and dynamic neural network. The choice of the one or the other neural network type depends on the application to be processed and the complexity of model. For static neural network, information propagates in a single direction, layer by layer, and from the inlet to the outlet. They are generally used in various applications such as classifications, pattern recognition, and functions approximation. The connectivity between neurons in dynamic neural network is not limited. Each neuron can send and receive information from all other neurons. The dynamic neural network architecture includes frequently one or more cycles which necessarily contain at least one delay connection. This gives rise to the dynamism notion. This neural network type is more complex than the static one, but it is more efficient for some particular applications such as dynamic modeling, monitoring, and process control. In this chapter, nonlinear autoregressive models with exogenous input (NARX) model, as type of dynamic neural network, will be used to the solar radiation prediction. Simulation results will be presented to prove the effectiveness of this model compared to the static one.

2. Static neural network

Static neural network was the first and simplest type. It is a nonlooped network since it does not contain a feedback or delay connection [1]. It is a statistical regression tool which allows the approximation of any nonlinear function sufficiently regular. The neural architecture of this network is presented as shown in **Figure 1**. It imitates the structure of the biological neuron. It is composed of a set of layers. The hidden one allows to receive a variable number of inputs, and information is moved only from inputs directly through hidden layer to the output layer without cycles or loops. Each connection is associated with a synaptic weight w, which represents the strength of each connection. The negative weight inhibits its input, while the positive weight accentuates it.

http://dx.doi.org/10.5772/intechopen.70570

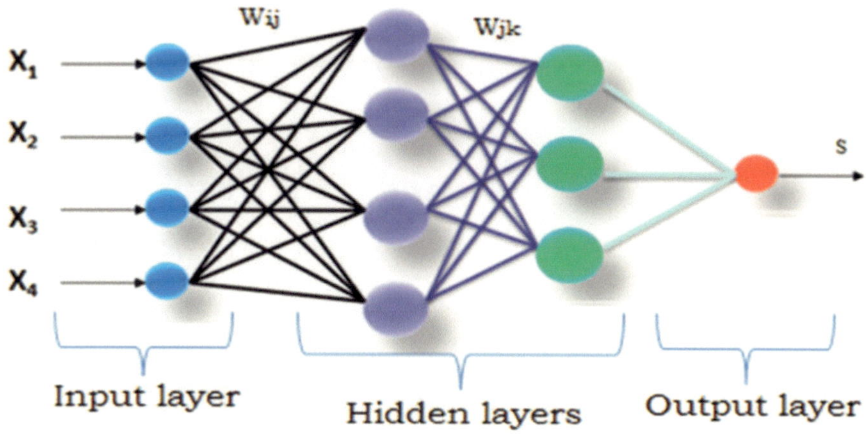

Figure 1. Static neural architecture.

3. NARX model

NARX model is the abbreviation of "nonlinear autoregressive models with exogenous input". It is registered under recurrent dynamic neural networks. It is a nonlinear autoregressive model with exogenous inputs. NARX consists of a linear ARX model with two delays, one for input and the other for output. It is based on the multilayer perceptron and the recurring connections. Its effectiveness has been proven in the research work presented in [2] to predict the PV power. It is also used in other applications such as the electricity prices prediction and the air pollution prediction [3–5]. This model is commonly used for the time series, estimation, and prediction as well as for nonlinear dynamic systems modeling. Compared to other neural network types, NARX model is characterized by a good learning, fast convergence, and better generalization [6]. The PV power prediction results presented in [2] have proven an improvement performance when using NARX model compared to those obtained using the static neural network. NARX model performances are also compared to those of static neural network and radial neural network in the research works presented in [7]. NARX gave also the best prediction results in these studies.

4. NARX model architecture

NARX model defines the output as a function of its inputs and its past outputs as described in the following equation [8],

$$y(t) = f\left[y(t-1), y(t-2), \ldots, y\left(t-d_y\right); u(t-1), u(t-2), \ldots, u\left(t-d_u\right)\right] \tag{1}$$

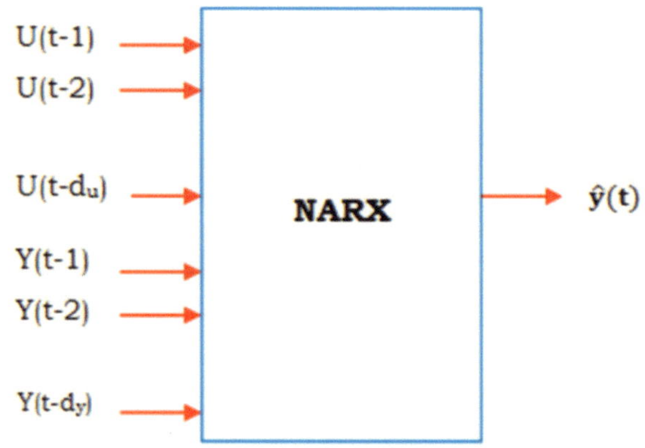

Figure 2. NARX model standard architecture.

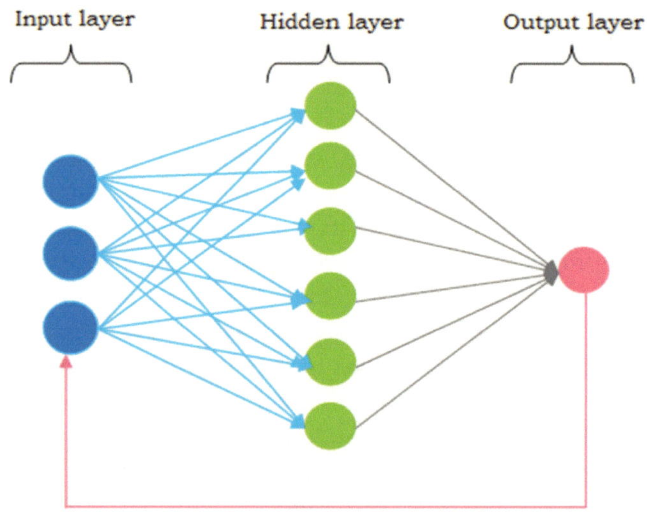

Figure 3. Example NARX model standard architecture *(3 inputs, 1 hidden layer, and 1 output).*

Where u represents the exogenous data and y are the NARX model outputs. d_u and d_y present respectively delays order of inputs u and outputs y. **Figure 2** presents the NARX model standard architecture.

For example, the NARX architecture of a neural network composed of three inputs, one output and six neurons in its hidden layer is presented as shown in the **Figure 3**.

5. Learning and generalization

Learning and generalization are two specifics properties that characterize any neural network. Unlike traditional methods that build programs to solve a problem, neural network operates mainly on a learning basis. We do not program a neural network, but we learn it. This is why the learning phase is among the most important properties of neural network.

The learning phase consists to estimate the parameter of the network in such a way that it can best fulfill the task assigned to it. This phase cannot be effective only after having accumulated a set of inputs/outputs. When creating a neural network, the inputs and outputs are fixed relative to the application to be accomplished, it is the network weights that are modified and adjusted during the learning phase. The weight adjustment cannot be done in a random way but according to a "learning algorithm." The generalization phase, known also the test phase, is one of the characteristics that determines the neural network performance. It consists to treat the output network with respect to the nonlearned inputs. The network generalization capacity degrades in the case of under/on learning.

6. Solar radiation prediction

In the present work, solar radiation will be predicted firstly with static neural network and then with NARX model. This study begins firstly with the observation of the solar radiation data base. In fact, the data base used in this work is composed of a set of solar radiation and temperature measurements correspond to an industrial company located on north of Barcelona [9]. These measurements are taken every day and every 5 minutes throughout 2010. In **Figure 4**, the daily evolution of solar radiation during 2010 is presented.

As shown in the above figure, the presented database is so large. So in order to reduce this annual solar radiation descriptive curve, just the solar radiation weekly averages will be taken into consideration in the solar radiation prediction. The curve presented in **Figure 4** is thus reduced as presented in **Figure 5**.

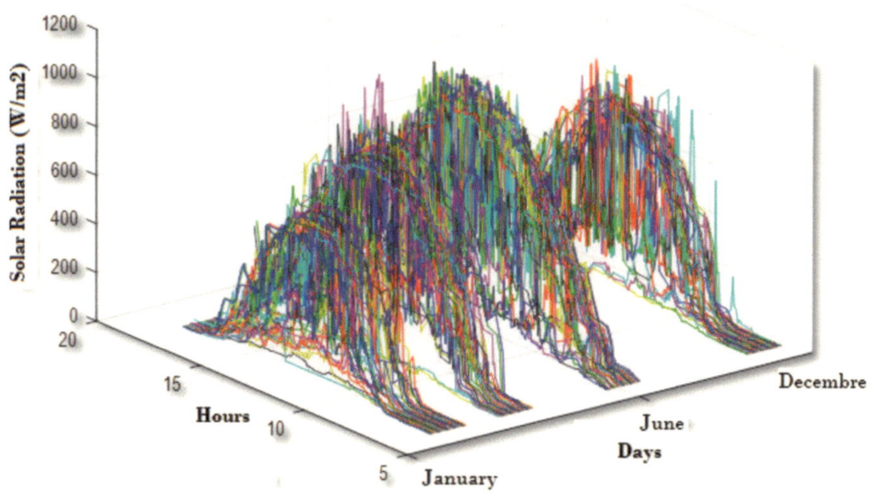

Figure 4. Solar radiation daily evolution during 2010.

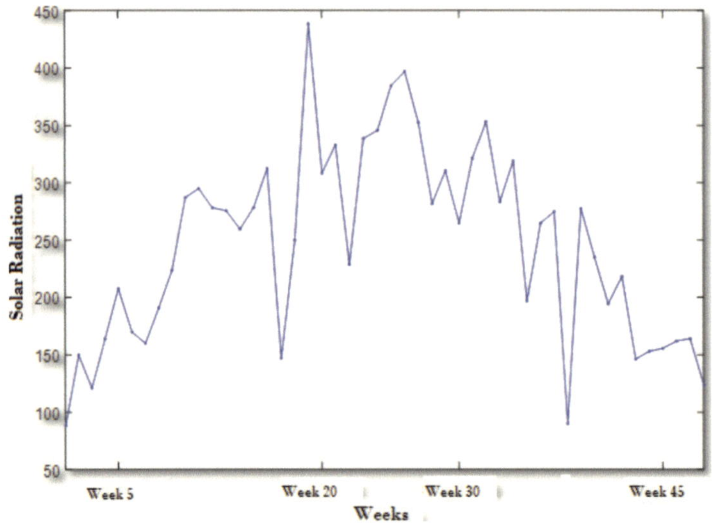

Figure 5. Weekly evolution of solar radiation during 2010.

7. Solar radiation prediction using static neural network

In this paragraph, solar radiation will be predicted using the static neural network. Inputs chosen for this neural network are the temperature and the output will be the radiation as presented in **Figure 6**.

To determine the optimal neural structure for this network, the learning and test performances are treated for different neurons in the hidden layer. The transfer functions chosen for the hidden layer and for the output layer are respectively "tansig" and "purelin." As presented in **Table 1**, the optimal neurons number obtained for this static neural network is equal to 2. The simulation results of learning, test, and validation obtained with this structure are presented in **Figure 7**.

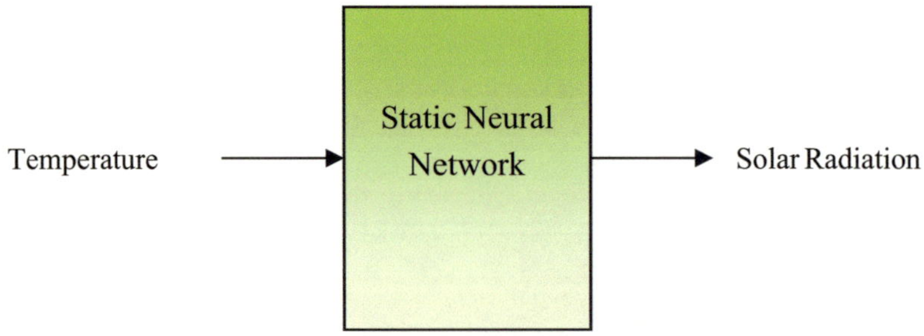

Figure 6. Inputs and the output for the static neural network.

Number of neurons	MSE
1	0.0288
2	**0.0016**
3	0.0140
4	0.0041
5	0.0071
6	0.0298
7	0.0043
8	0.0058
9	0.0106
10	0.0097

Table 1. MSE versus neurons in the hidden layer for static neural network.

The optimal neural structure for the static neural network is thus composed of temperature (T) as input, radiation (R) as output, and one hidden layer which contains two neurons as shown in **Figure 8**.

The results of solar radiations prediction with static neural network are presented in **Figure 9.** All inputs are normalized, so the maximum solar radiation value is equal to 1. The blue curve corresponds to the real solar radiation, and the red one corresponds to the predicted one. As shown in the figure, the predicted solar radiation follows the evolution of the real one, but there is not an

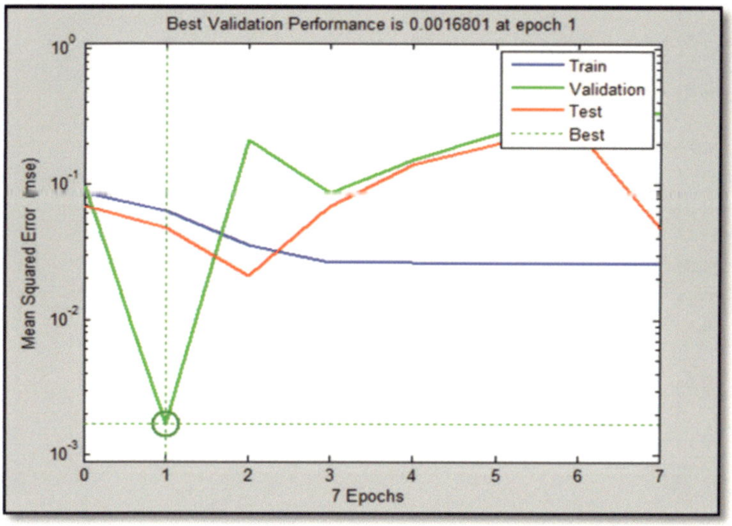

Figure 7. Learning, test, and validation of static neural network.

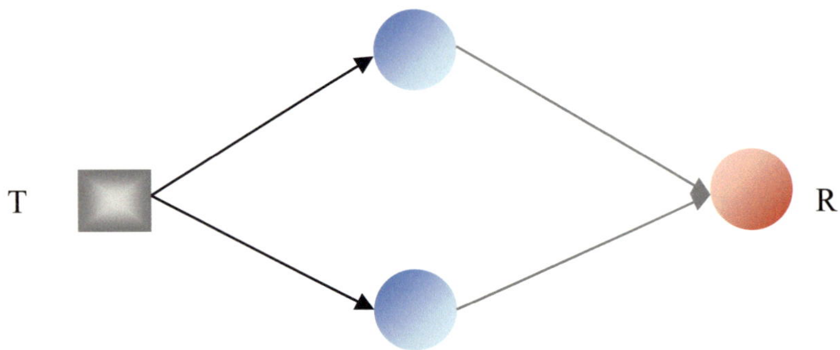

Figure 8. Optimal neural architecture for the static neural network.

approximation between the two curves. This is remarked especially when the solar radiation fluctuations are so important. To better treat these results, prediction error is presented in **Figure 10**, and the different error mean square error (MSE), mean absolute error (MAE), and root mean square error (RMSE) are computed and presented in **Table 2**.

Figure 11 shows that the prediction error is variable. It reaches a maximum value of 0.5 and a minimum value of 0.02. This is shows the performances of static neural network to predict the solar radiation for certain period of time and its weakness to predict it in other periods. The MSE value is equal to 0.0516; it is lower than MAE and RMSE. It is not considered too small, thus shows the inefficiency of the static neural network to best predict the solar radiation.

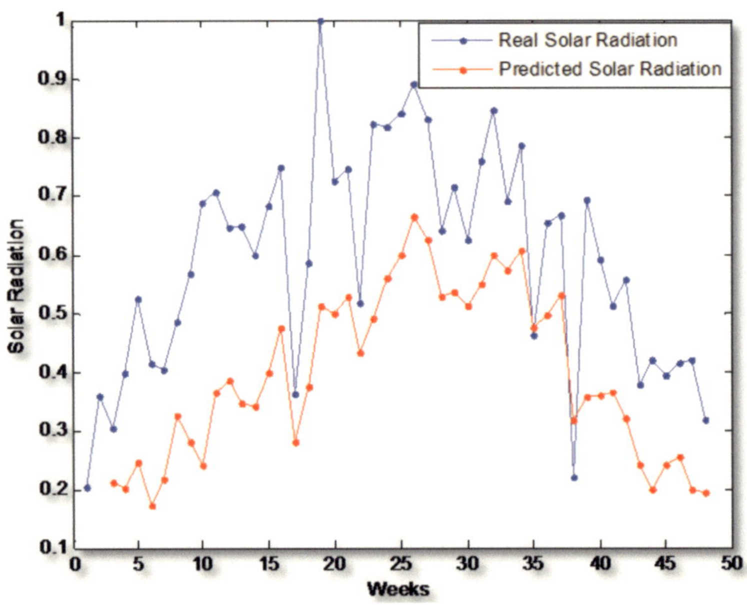

Figure 9. Solar radiation prediction using the static neural network.

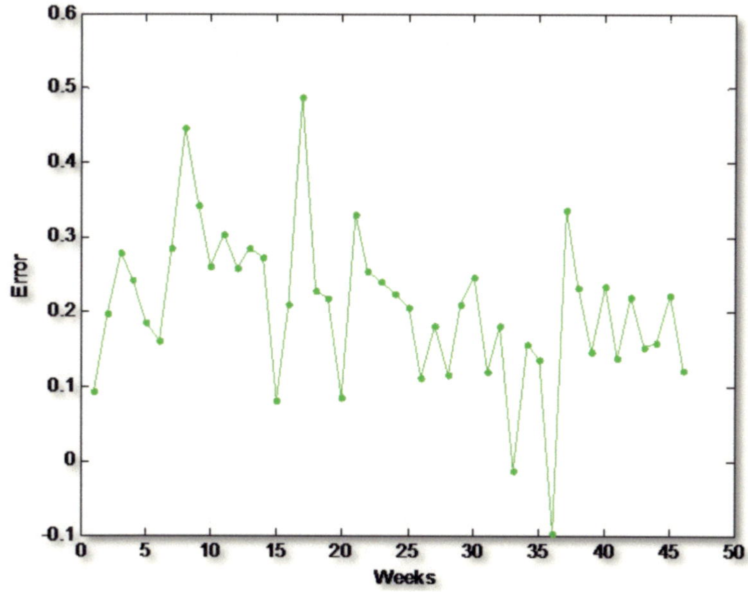

Figure 10. Solar radiation prediction error with the static neural network.

Error	Performances
MSE	0.0516
MAE	0.2076
RMSE	0.2272

Table 2. MSE, MAE, and RMSE for solar radiation prediction with static neural network.

8. Solar radiation prediction using NARX model

In this part, solar radiation will be predicted using the NARX model. As presented in the previous paragraph, to predict a future value, NARX model is based on the historical data related to this value and involves some exogenous data. As temperature influences the solar radiation variation, it is chosen as an exogenous data. So the NARX model inputs will be the historical solar radiation data and temperature data as presented in **Figure 11**.

The hidden layers number and their neurons must be chosen in such a way that they offer the best network performances in learning and in generalization. So in this paragraph, the network performances will be treated for different neural network architecture. Inputs for NARX model correspond to the historical solar radiations (R(t−1) and R(t−2)) and the ambient temperatures (T(t−1) and T(t−2)). The output will be the predicted solar radiation at time t (R(t)) as presented in **Figure 12**. The transfer functions used for the hidden layer and for the output layer are respectively “tansig” and “purelin.”

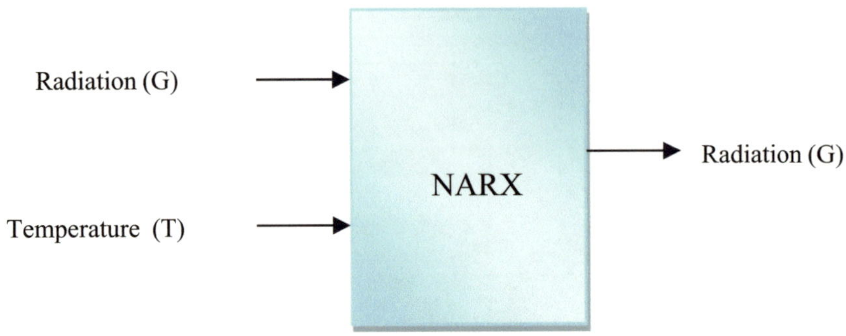

Figure 11. Inputs and output for the NARX model.

First, the network performances will be studied with just one neuron in the hidden layer; then, number of neurons will be incremented and the network performances will be restudied. Network performances are treated by the compute of the mean square error of learning and test (MSE). The optimal neural structure corresponds to the one which presented the minimal MSE. Simulations results for this study are presented in **Table 3** and in **Figure 13**. The optimal neural architecture obtained is the one which its hidden layer contains five neurons as presented in **Figure 14**.

Based on this neural network, solar radiation is predicted by NARX model. Simulation results are presented in **Figure 15**. The blue curve corresponds to the real solar radiation, and the red curve corresponds to the predicted one. As obtained with the static neural network, the predicted solar radiation follows the evolution of the real one. Furthermore, an approximation between the real and predicted curves is remarked, the two curves are overlapped for certain period of time especially when the solar radiation fluctuations are low. So an improvement in the quality of solar radiation prediction with NARX model is remarked compared to that obtained with the static neural network.

To the best evaluation of the NARX model performances, the solar radiation prediction error is presented in **Figure 16**. The different error MSE, MAE, and RMSE are computed and presented in **Table 4**. As presented in **Figure 16**, the maximum error reaches the value of 0.42, and the

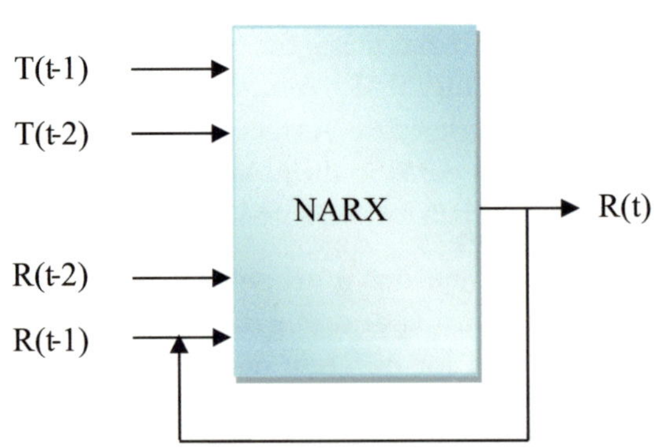

Figure 12. Neural architecture for the NARX model.

minimum one is equal to 0. MSE is always the lowest one. It indicates a value of 0.0348. It is low compared to this one obtained with static neural network. Therefore, the performance of NARX model is proven in this work to predict the solar radiation.

Number of neurons	MSE
1	0.0047
2	0.0217
3	0.0122
4	0.0072
5	**0.00089**
6	0.0016
7	0.0076
8	0.0258
9	0.0784
10	0.0460

Table 3. MSE versus neurons in hidden layer for NARX model.

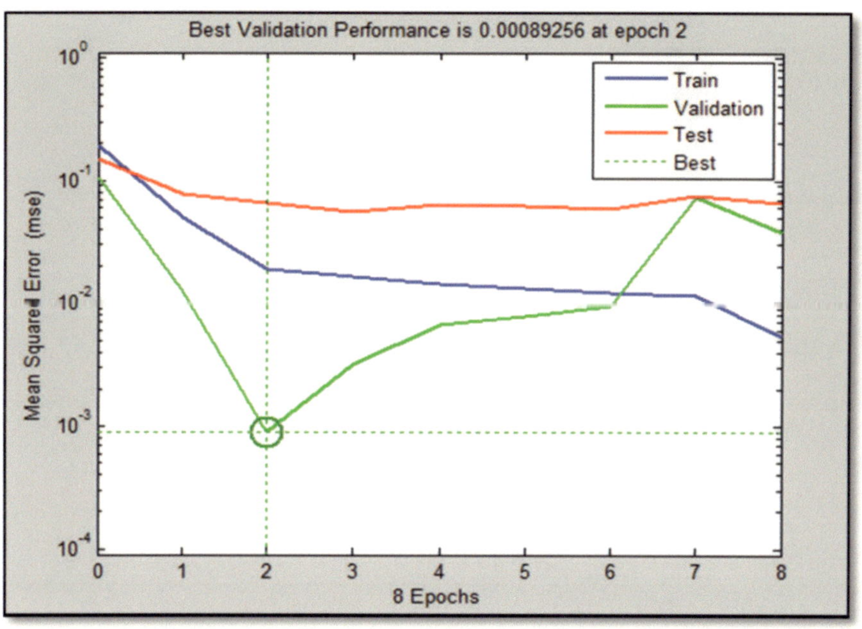

Figure 13. Learning, test and validation of NARX model.

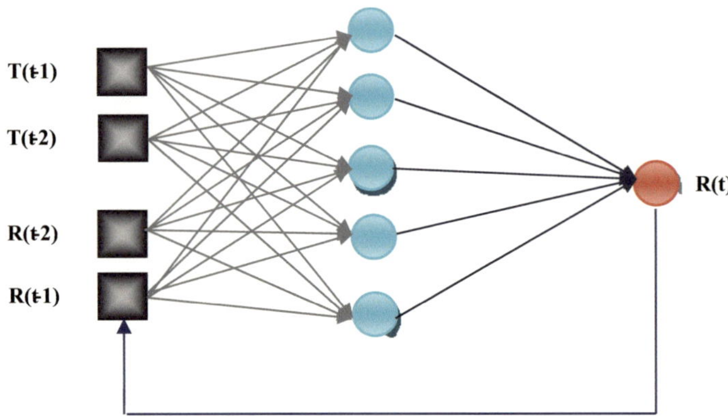

Figure 14. Optimal neural architecture for the NARX model.

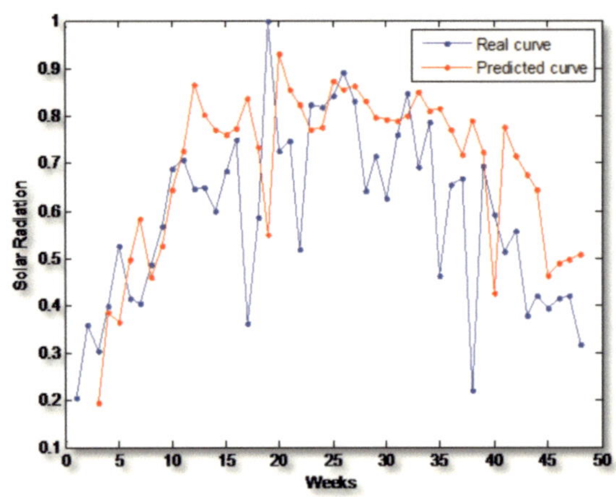

Figure 15. Solar radiation predicted by NARX.

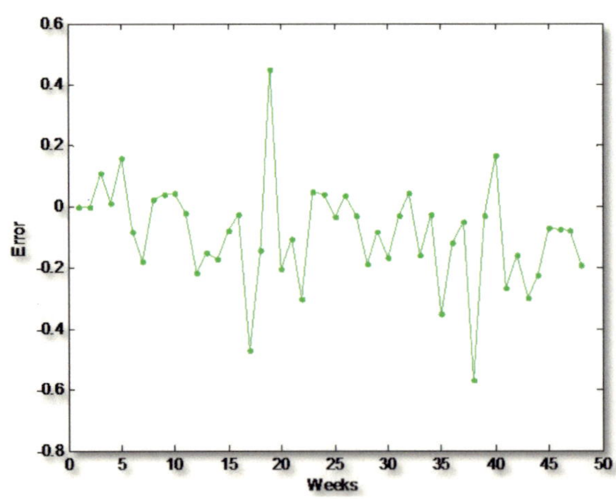

Figure 16. Solar radiation prediction error with NARX model.

http://dx.doi.org/10.5772/intechopen.70570

Error	Performances
MSE	0.0348
MAE	0.1360
RMSE	0.1864

Table 4. MSE, MAE, and RMSE for solar radiation prediction with NARX model.

9. Conclusion

In this chapter, the solar radiation is predicted using two different neural networks, the static one and the NARX model. Simulations results are presented and are proven the effectiveness of NARX model to predict the solar radiation compared to the static neural network. The efficiency of NARX model is proven especially for the low solar radiation fluctuations. The NARX model is characterized by the presence of a direct feedback of the output which has given it an additional predictive power.

Author details

Ines Sansa* and Najiba Mrabet Bellaaj

*Address all correspondence to: sansa.ines@yahoo.com

Institut supérieur d'informatique, Université de Tunis El Manar, Ecole Nationale d'Ingénieurs de Tunis, Tunis, Tunisia

References

[1] Dreyfus G, Martinez J-M, Samuelides M, Gordon MB, Badran F, Theria S, Herault L. Réseaux de neurones – méthodologie et applications. Edition EYROLLES; janvier 2002

[2] Missaoui S. Prédiction de la production de la puissance PV à l'aide des réseaux de. neurones dynamiques. Mastère en systèmes électriques, Laboratoire de système électrique, Ecole nationale d'ingénieurs de Tunis; juillet 2012

[3] Pisoni E, Farina M, Carnevale C, Piroddi L. Forecasting peak air pollution levels using NARX models. Engineering Applications of Artificial Intelligence. 2009;**22**:593-602

[4] José Maria P. Junior and Guilherme A. Barreto. Long-term time series prediction with the NARX network: An empirical evaluation. Neurocomputing. October 2008;**71**(16-18): 3335-3343

[5] Arash A, Atry F. Multi-step ahead forecasts for electricity prices using NARX: A new approach, a critical analysis of one-step ahead forecasts. Energy Conversion and Management. 2009;**50**(3):739-747

[6] Diaconescu E. The use of NARX neural networks to predict chaotic time series. Wseas Transactions on computer research. March 2008;**3**(3)

[7] Zemouri R, Gouriveau R, Zerhouni N. Defining and applying prediction performance metrics on a recurrent NARX time series model. Neurocomputing. 2010;**73**:2506-2521

[8] Khamis A, Nabilah SSBA. Forecasting wheat price using backpropagation and NARX neural network. The International Journal Of Engineering And Science (IJES). 2014;**3**(11): 19-26

[9] Sant Joan les Fonts, Garrotxa. Available from: http://www.noel.es/

Chapter 14

Data Assimilation by Artificial Neural Networks for an Atmospheric General Circulation Model

Rosangela Saher Cintra and
Haroldo F. de Campos Velho

Additional information is available at the end of the chapter

http://dx.doi.org/10.5772/intechopen.70791

Abstract

Numerical weather prediction (NWP) uses atmospheric general circulation models (AGCMs) to predict weather based on current weather conditions. The process of entering observation data into mathematical model to generate the accurate initial conditions is called data assimilation (DA). It combines observations, forecasting, and filtering step. This paper presents an approach for employing artificial neural networks (NNs) to emulate the local ensemble transform Kalman filter (LETKF) as a method of data assimilation. This assimilation experiment tests the Simplified Parameterizations PrimitivE-Equation Dynamics (SPEEDY) model, an atmospheric general circulation model (AGCM), using synthetic observational data simulating localizations of meteorological balloons. For the data assimilation scheme, the supervised NN, the multilayer perceptrons (MLPs) networks are applied. After the training process, the method, forehead-calling MLP-DA, is seen as a function of data assimilation. The NNs were trained with data from first 3 months of 1982, 1983, and 1984. The experiment is performed for January 1985, one data assimilation cycle using MLP-DA with synthetic observations. The numerical results demonstrate the effectiveness of the NN technique for atmospheric data assimilation. The results of the NN analyses are very close to the results from the LETKF analyses, the differences of the monthly average of absolute temperature analyses are of order 10–2. The simulations show that the major advantage of using the MLP-DA is better computational performance, since the analyses have similar quality. The CPU-time cycle assimilation with MLP-DA analyses is 90 times faster than LETKF cycle assimilation with the mean analyses used to run the forecast experiment.

Keywords: artificial neural networks, data assimilation, numerical weather prediction, computer performance, ensemble Kalman filter

1. Introduction

For operating systems in weather forecasting, one of the challenges is to obtain the most appropriate initial conditions to ensure the best prediction from a physical mathematical model that represents the evolution of the atmospheric dynamics. Performing a smooth melding of data from observations and model predictions, the assimilation process carries out a set of procedures to determine the best initial condition. Atmospheric observed data are used to create meteorological fields over some spatial and/or temporal domain.

The analysis, i.e., initial condition, for NWP is combination of measurements and model predictions to obtain a representation of the state of the modeled system as accurate as possible. The analysis is useful in itself as a description of the physical system, but it can be used as an initial state for the further time evolution of the system [22]. The research of data assimilation methods has been studied for atmospheric and oceanic prediction, besides other dynamics researches like ionosphere and hydrological. The different algorithms of data assimilation were applied varying in complexity, optimality, and formulation. The approach of Bayesian scheme [31] uses ensembles of integrations of prediction models, where added perturbations to initial conditions and model formulation; the mean of ensemble forecasts can be interpreted as a probabilistic prediction. The ensemble Kalman filter (EnKF) [11, 23] uses a probability density function associated with the initial condition, characterizing the Bayesian approaches [9], and represents the model errors by an ensemble of estimates in state space. The Kalman filter (KF) [27] is one good technique to estimate an initial condition to a linear dynamic system. A useful overview of most common data assimilation methods used in meteorology and oceanography and detailed mathematical formulations can be found in texts such as Daley [9] and Kalnay [29].

The modern DA techniques represent a computational challenge, even with the use of parallel computing with thousands of processors. Nowadays, the operational NWP is using a higher resolution model, and the amount of observations has an exponential growth because of launch of new satellite. There is a computational challenge to get the analysis (initial condition) to run models, and so we need to make a prediction on time. The computational challenge to the data assimilation techniques lies in millions of equations involved in NWP models.

The DA algorithms are constantly updated to improve their performance. The example is the version of the EnKF [11] restricted to small areas (local); the local ensemble Kalman filter (LEKF) [38] is a version of the EnKF. We propose the application of artificial neural networks (NNs) like a DA technique to get a quality analysis and to solve the computational challenge.

First, the application of NN was suggested as a possible technique for data assimilation by [24, 30, 43]. The researches with NN (for data assimilation method) were initiated at INPE (National institute for Space Researcher) with Nowosad [37], see also [44, 5]; they used an NN over all spatial domains. Later, this method was improved by [16, 17], where they introduced a modification on the NN application, in which the analysis was obtained at each grid point, instead of at all points of the domain. They also evaluated the performance of two feed-forward NN (multilayer perceptron and radial basis function) and two recurrent NN (Elman and Jordan, see description in [19, 20]) [17]. Ref. [13] applied NN to emulate the particle filter and the variational data assimilation (4D var) for the Lorenz chaotic system. In 2012, Furtado [40] used an ocean model to emulate a variational method called representer. The NN technique was successful for all experiments, but they use theoretical or low-dimensional models. In 2010, Refs. [6, 7] applied this approach of supervised NN to an atmospheric general circulation model (AGCM) to emulate a LETKF method. This is the experiment described in this paper, this experiment is the first one to use the 3D global atmospheric model; but the NN methodology research continues, see [41, 42], where this method is applied to FSU (Florida State Model) AGCM to emulate the LETKF data assimilation method too.

In every experiment, NNs were applied to mimic other data assimilation methods to obtain the analyses to initiate the forecast models. They do not use an error model estimation or error observation estimation. The main advantage to using NN is the speed-up of the data assimilation process.

This paper presents the approach based on a set of NN *multilayer perceptron* (MLP) [Section 3] employed to emulate the LETKF. The LETKF technique was used as the reference analysis, see [29, 32], Section 2.3. More information about LETKF can be obtained from [2, 26, 35]. The initial conditions generated by NNs are applied to a nonlinear dynamical system; the AGCM is the Simplified Parameterizations PrimitivE-Equation Dynamics (SPEEDY). The DA method is tested with synthetic conventional data, simulating measurements from surface stations (data at each 6 hours on a day) and upper-air soundings (data at each 12 hours on a day). The application of NN produces a significant reduction for the computational effort compared to LETKF. The goal of using NN approach is to obtain a similar quality for analyses with better computational performance for prediction process.

Summarizing, the NN technique uses the function:

$$x^a = F_{NN}\left(y^o, x^f\right) \tag{1}$$

where F_{NN} is the data assimilation process, y^o represents the observations, x^f is a model forecast (simulated), and x^a is the analysis field.

The observations used in operational data assimilation are conventional and satellite data. The observations include surface and upper-air observations; here, we simulate observations of one type of measurement, meteorological balloons. The grid of synthetic observations seeks to reproduce the stations of World Meteorological Organization (WMO) of radiosonde observations.

The experiment was conducted using the SPEEDY model [3, 21], which is a 3D global atmospheric model, with simplified physics parameterization by [36]. The spatial resolution considered is T30 L7 for the spectral method explained in Section 2.2. This paper shows that the analysis computed by the NN has the similar quality as the analysis produced by LETKF with minor computational effort.

2. Methodology

2.1. Artificial neural network (NN)

An NN is composed of simple processing units that compute certain mathematical functions (usually nonlinear). An NN consists of interconnected artificial neurons or nodes, which are inspired by biological neurons and their behavior. The neurons are connected to others to form a network, which is used to model relationships between artificial neurons. NN has the ability to learn and store experimental knowledge. It is a computational system with nodes that can be parallel processing.

Each artificial neuron is constituted by one or more inputs and one output. The neuron processing is nonlinear and adaptable. Each neuron has a function to define the output, associated with a learning rule. The neuron connection stores a nonlinear weighted sum called a weight. The inputs are multiplied by weights, and the results go through the activation function. This function activates or inhibits the next neuron.

Mathematically, we can describe the *i*th input with the following form:

$$\text{input summation: } u_i = \sum_{i=1} \rho_{W_{i \times j \times j}} \tag{2a}$$

$$\text{neuron output: } y_i = \phi(u_i) \tag{2b}$$

where $x_1, x_1, \ldots \cdots, x_p$ are the inputs; $w_{i1}, \cdots, w_{ip}$ are the synaptic weights; u_i is the output of linear combination; $\varphi(\cdot)$ is the activation function, y_i is the *i*th neuron output, and p is number of neurons (**Figure 1(a)**).

A feed-forward network, which processes in one direction from input to output, has a layered structure. The input layer is the first layer of an NN, where the patterns are presented, the hidden layers are the intermediary layers, and the last layer is called the output layer, where the results are presented. The number of layers and the quantity of neurons in each are determined by the nature of the problem. In most applications, a feed-forward NN with a single layer of hidden units is used with a sigmoid activation function, such as the hyperbolic tangent function (Eq. 3)

$$\varphi(v) = \frac{1 - \exp(-av)}{1 + \exp(-av)} \tag{3}$$

The NN has two distinct phases: the training phase (learning process) and the run phase (activation or generalization). An iterative process for adjusting the weights is made for the training phase, where the NN establishes the mapping of input and target vector pairs for the best performance. This phase uses the learning algorithm, i.e., a set of procedures for adjusting the weights. "Epoch" is the name of a training set pass through the iterative network process, testing of the verification set each epoch; the iterative process continues or stops after defined criteria that can be the minimum error of mapping or a determined number of epochs. Once the processing is stopped, the weights are fixed, and the NN is ready to receive new inputs (different from training inputs) for which it calculates the corresponding outputs. The latter phase is called the generalization: each connection (after training) has an associated weight value that stores the knowledge represented in the experimental problem and considers the input received by each neuron of that NN.

Neural network designs or NN architectures are dependent on the learning strategy adopted, see Haykin [19]. The multilayer perceptron (MLP) (**Figure 1(b)**) is the NN architecture used in

http://dx.doi.org/10.5772/intechopen.70791

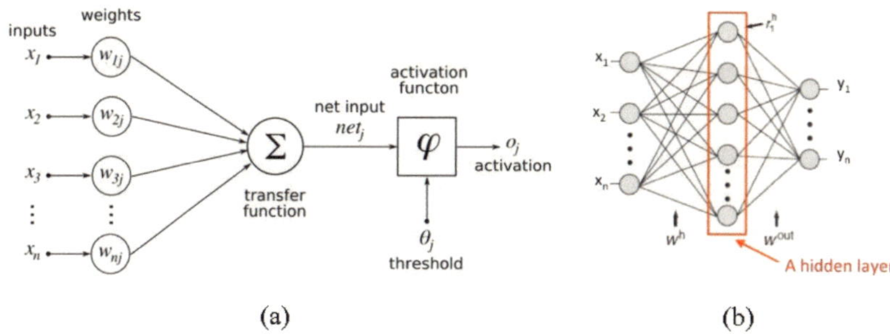

Figure 1. (a) Artificial neural network components and (b) multilayer perceptron.

this study, in which the interconnections between the inputs and the output layer have one intermediate layer of neurons, a hidden layer [14, 20]. NNs can solve nonlinear problems if nonlinear activation functions are used for the hidden and/or the output layers. In this work, during the training phase, the nonlinear activation functions employ the delta rule. Developed by [45], the delta rule is a version of the least mean square (LMS) method. The delta rule algorithm is summarized as follows:

1. Compute the error function $E(w_{ij})$, defining the distance between the target and the NN calculated output: $E(w_{ij}) \equiv \left[x^a_{ref} - x^a_{NN}\right]^2$

2. Compute the gradient of the error function $\partial E(w_{ij})/\partial w_{ij} = \delta_j y_i$, defining which direction should move in weight space to reduce the error, with $\delta_j \equiv \left(x^a_{ref} - x^a_{NN}\right)\varphi'(v)$.

3. Select the learning rate η which specifies the step size taken in the weight space of updating equation;

4. Update the weight, k: $w^k_{ij} = w^{k-1}_{ij} + \Delta w_{ij}$, where $\Delta w_{ij} = -\eta E(w_{ij})/\partial w_{ij}$. One epoch or training step is a set of update weights for all training patterns, η is the learning rating.

5. Repeat Step 4 until the NN error function reaches the required precision. This precision is a defined parameter to stop the iterative process.

The supervised learning process, the functional to be minimized is treading as a function of the weights w_{ij} (Eq. 2) instead of the NN inputs. For a given input vector x, x^a_{NN} is compared to the target answer x^a_{ref}. If the difference is smaller than a required precision, no learning takes place; on the other hand, the weights are adjusted to reduce this difference. The goal is to minimize the error between the actual output y_i (or x^a_{NN}) and the target output (d_i) (or x^a_{ref}) of the training data. The set of procedures to adjust the weights is the learning algorithm *back propagation,* which is generally used for the MLP training. It performs the delta rule, considering a set of (input and target) pairs of vectors $\{(x_0, d_0),\ (x_1, d_2), \cdots, (x_N, d_N)\}^T$, where N is the number of patterns (input elements) and one output vector $y = [y_0, y_1, y_2, \cdots, y_N]^T$. The MLP performs a complex mapping $y = \varphi(w, x)$ parameterized by the synaptic weights w, and the functions $\varphi(\cdot)$ that provide the activation for the neuron. That is, for each (input/output) training pair, the delta rule determines the direction you need to be adjusted to reduce the error. In the back-propagation supervised algorithm, the adjustments to the weights are conducted by back propagating of the error and the target output is considered the supervisor. Ref. [14] included brief introductions of MLP and the back-propagation algorithm.

The NN applications, generally, are on function approximation of modeling of nonlinear transfer functions and pattern classifications. Refs. [18, 25] reviewed applications of NN in environmental science including atmospheric sciences. They reviewed some NN concepts and some NN applications; these reviews were also for other estimation methods and its applications. Other reviews for NN applications in the atmospheric sciences, looking at prediction of air-quality, surface ozone concentration, dioxide concentrations, severe weather, etc., and pattern classifications applications in remote sensing data to obtain distinction between clouds and ice or snow were presented by [14]. Refs. [18, 25] also presented applications on classification of atmospheric circulation patterns, land cover and convergence lines from radar imagery, and classification of remote sensing data using NN. Data assimilation was not mentioned in such reviews.

2.2. SPEEDY model

The SPEEDY computer code is an AGCM developed to study global-scale dynamics and to test new approaches for numerical weather prediction (NWP). The dynamic variables for the primitive meteorological equations are integrated by the spectral method in the horizontal grid at each vertical level, more details in [3, 21]. The model has a simplified set of physical parameterization schemes that are similar to realistic weather forecasting numerical models. The goal of this model is to obtain computational efficiency while maintaining characteristics similar to the state-of-the-art AGCM with complex physics parameterization [32].

According to Ref. [36], the SPEEDY model simulates the general structure of global atmospheric circulation (**Figure 2**), and some aspects of the systematic errors are similar to many errors in the operational AGCMs. The package is based on the physical parameterizations adopted in more complex schemes of the AGCM, such as convection (simplified diagram of mass flow), large-scale condensation, clouds, short-wave radiation (two spectral bands), long-wave radiation (four spectral bands), surface fluxes of momentum, energy (aerodynamic formula), and vertical diffusion. Details of the simplified physical parameterization scheme can be found in Ref. [36].

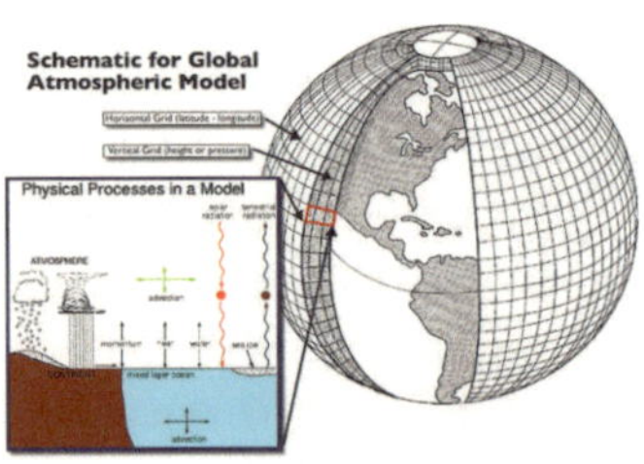

Figure 2. Schematic for global atmospheric model. **Source:** Center for Multiscale Modeling of Atmospheric Processes.

The boundary conditions of the SPEEDY model include topographic height and land-sea mask, which are constant. Sea surface temperature (SST), sea ice fraction, surface temperature in the top soil layer, moisture in the top soil layer, the root-zone layer, snow depth, all of which are specified by monthly means. Annual-mean fields specify bare-surface albedos, and fraction of land-surface covered by vegetation. The lower boundary conditions such as SST are obtained from the ECMWF's reanalysis in the period 1981–1990. The incoming solar radiation flux and the boundary conditions are updated daily. The SPEEDY model is a hydrostatic model in sigma coordinates. Ref. [3] also describes the vorticity-divergence transformation scheme.

The SPEEDY model is global with spectral resolution T30L7 (horizontal truncation of 30 numbers of waves and 7 levels). The vertical coordinates are defined on sigma ($\sigma = p/p_0$, where p_0 is the surface pressure) surfaces, corresponding to 7 vertical pressures levels (100, 200, 300, 500, 700, 850, and 925 hPa). The horizontal coordinates are latitude and longitude on regular grid, corresponding to a regular grid with 96 zonal points (longitude) and 48 meridian points (latitude). The schematic for global model and its physical packages can be seen at **Figure 2**. The prognostic variables for the model input and output are the absolute temperature (T), surface pressure (p_s), zonal wind component (u), meridional wind component (v), and an additional variable and specific humidity (q).

2.3. Brief description on local ensemble transform Kalman filter

The analysis is the best estimate of the state of the system based on the optimizing criteria. The probabilistic state-space formulation and the requirement for updating information when new observations are encountered are ideally suited to the Bayesian approach. The Bayesian approach is a set of efficient and flexible Monte Carlo methods for solving the optimal filtering problem. Here, one attempts to construct the posterior probability density function (pdf) of the state using all available information, including the set of received observations. Since this pdf embodies all available statistical information, it may be considered as a complete solution to the estimation problem.

In the field of data assimilation, there are only few contributions in sequential estimation (EnKF or PF filters). The EnKF was first proposed by [11] and was developed by [4, 12]. It is related to particle filters [1, 10] in the context that a particle is identified as an ensemble member. EnKF is a sequential method, which means that the model is integrated forward in time and whenever observations are available; these EnKF results are used to reinitialize the model before the integration continues. The EnKF originated as a version of the Extended Kalman Filter (EKF) [28]. The classical KF method, see [27], is optimal in the sense of minimizing the variance only for linear systems and Gaussian statistics. Analysis perturbations are added to run the ensemble forecasts, the mean of ensemble forecasts is the estimation error for analysis. Ref. [35] added Gaussian white noise to run the same forecast for each member of the ensemble in LETKF. The EnKF is a Monte Carlo integration that governs the evolution of the pdf, which describes the *a priori* state, the forecast and error statistics. In the analysis step, each ensemble member is updated according to the KF scheme and replaces the covariance matrix by the sampled covariance computed from the ensemble forecasts. Ref. [23] applied the EnKF to an atmospheric system. They applied a state model ensemble to represent the statistical model error. The scheme of analysis acts directly on the ensemble of state models, when observations are assimilated. The ensemble of analysis is obtained by assimilation for each member of the reference model. Several methods have been developed to represent the modeling error covariance matrix for the analysis applying the EnKF approach; the local ensemble transform Kalman filter (LETKF) is one of them. Ref. [26] proposed the LETKF scheme as an efficient upgrade of the local ensemble Kalman filter (LEKF). The LEKF algorithm creates a close relationship between local dimensionality, error growth, and skill of the ensemble to capture the space of forecast uncertainties formulated with the EnKF scheme (e.g., [45]). In addition, Ref. [29] describes the theoretical foundation of the operational practice of using small ensembles, for predicting the evolution of uncertainties in high-dimension operational NWP models.

The LETKF scheme is a model-independent algorithm to estimate the state of a large spatial temporal chaotic system [38]. The term "local" refers to an important feature of the scheme: it solves the Kalman filter equations locally in model grid space. A kind of ensemble square root filtering [32, 45], in which the analysis ensemble members are constructed by a linear combination of the forecast ensemble members. The ensemble transform matrix, composed of the weights of the linear combination, is computed for each local subset of the state vector independently, which allows essentially parallel computations. The local subset depends on the error covariance localization [33]. Typically, a local subset of the state vector contains all variables at a grid point. The LETKF scheme first separates a global grid vector into local patch vectors with observations. The basic idea of LETKF is to perform analysis at each grid point simultaneously using the state variables and all observations in the region centered at given grid point. The local strategy separates groups of neighboring observations around a central point for a given region of the grid model. Each grid point has a local patch; the number of local vectors is the same as the number of global grid points [35].

The algorithm of EnKF follows the sequential assimilation steps of classical Kalman filter, but it calculates the error covariance matrices as described below:

Each member of the ensemble gets its forecast $\left\{x_{n-1}^{f}\right\}^{(\mathrm{i})}$: $i = 1,2,3,\cdots,k$, where k is the total members at time tn, to estimate the state vector $\overline{x}^f$ of the reference model. The ensemble is used to calculate the mean of forecasting $\left(\overline{x}^f\right)$:

$$\overline{x}^f \equiv k^{-1} \sum_{i=1}^{k} \{x^f\}^{(i)}. \tag{4}$$

Therefore, the model error covariance matrix:

$$P^f = (k-1)^{-1} \sum_{i=1}^{k} \left(\{x^f\}^{(i)} - \overline{x}^f\right)\left(\{x^f\}^{(i)} - \overline{x}^f\right)^T. \tag{5}$$

The analysis step determines a state estimate to each ensemble member:

http://dx.doi.org/10.5772/intechopen.70791

$$\{x^a\}^{(i)} = \{x^f\}^{(i)} + W_K\left[x^{obs} - H\left(\{x^f\}^{(i)}\right)\right] \tag{6}$$

$$W_K = P^f H^T\left[HP^f H^T + R\right]^{-1}. \tag{7}$$

The analysis $\{x^a\}^{(i)}$ $i = 1,2,3,\cdots,k$, (Eq. 6) by solving (Eq. 7) for W_k to get the optimal weight (e.g., Kalman gain). The matrix H represents the observation operator. The covariance matrix R identifies the observation error. The analysis step also updates the covariance error matrix P^a (Eq. 8)

$$P^a = (k-1)^{-1}\sum_{i=1}^{k}\left(\{x^a\}^{(i)} - \overline{x}^a\right)\left(\{x^a\}^{(i)} - \overline{x}^a\right)^T \tag{8}$$

with the appropriate ensemble analyses mean:

$$\overline{x}^a \equiv k^{-1}\sum_{i=1}^{k}\{x^a\}^{(i)}. \tag{9}$$

The LETKF scheme has been applied to a low-dimensional AGCM SPEEDY model [32], a realistic model according to [42]. The LETKF scheme was also employed in the following: the AGCM for the Earth Simulator by [35] and the Japan Meteorological Agency operational global and mesoscale models by [34]; the Regional Ocean Modeling System by [41]; the global ocean model known as the Geophysical Fluid Dynamics Laboratory (GFDL) by [39]; and GFDL Mars AGCM by [15].

3. MLP-DA in assimilation for SPEEDY model

The NN configuration for this experiment is a set of multilayer perceptron, hereafter, referred to as MLP-DA. On the present paper, the NN configuration (number of layers, nodes per layer, activation function, and learning rate parameter) was defined by empirical tests, and we found the following characteristics:

1. two input nodes, one node for the meteorological observation vector and the other for the 6-hour forecast model vector;
2. one output node for the analysis vector results;
3. one hidden layer with 11 neurons;
4. the hyperbolic tangent (Eq. 3) as the activation function (to guarantee the nonlinearity for results);
5. learning rate η is defined do each MLP; and
6. training stops when the error reaches 10–5 or after 5000 epochs, which criterion first occurs.

The vectors values represent individual grid points for a single variable with a correspondent observation value on model point localization. The grid points is considered where observation value exists, see **Figure 3**. In the training algorithm, the MLP-DA computes the output and compared it with the "input" analysis vector of LETKF results (the target data), but it is not a node for the MLP generalization. The output vectors represent the analysis values for one grid point too. Care must be taken in specifying the number of neurons. Too many neurons can lead the NN to memorize the training data (over fitting), instead of extracting the general features that allow the generalization. Too few neurons may force the NN to spend too much time trying to find an optimal representation and thus wasting valuable computation time.

One strategy used to collect data and to accelerate the processing of the MLP-DA training was to divide the entire globe into six regions: for the Northern Hemisphere, 90° N and three longitudinal regions of 120° each; for the Southern Hemisphere, 90° S and three longitudinal regions of 120° each. This division provides the same size for each region, but the number of observations is distinct, as illustrated by **Figure 3**. This regional division is applied only for the MLP-DA; the LETKF procedures are not modified.

The MLP-DA scheme was developed with a set of 30 NN (six regions with five prognostic variables (p_s, u, v, T, and q)). Each grid point has all vertical layers values for the model. One MLP with characteristics described above was designed for each meteorological variable of the SPEEDY model and each region. Each MLP has two *inputs* (model and observation vectors), one output neuron which is the *analysis* vector, and the training scheme is the back-propagation algorithm.

The MLP-DA is designed to emulate the global LETKF analysis for SPEEDY initial condition. The LETKF analysis is the mean field of an ensemble of analyses. Fortran codes for SPEEDY and LETKF [32] were adapted to create the training data set for that period. The upper levels and the surface covariance error matrices to run the LETKF system, as well as the SPEEDY model boundary conditions data and physical parameterizations, are the same as those used for Miyoshi's experiments.

The initial process is the implementation of the model, it assumes that it is perfect (initialization = 0); and the SPEEDY model T30 L7 was integrated for 1 year of spin-up, i.e., the period required for a model to reach steady state and obtain the simulated atmosphere. The model

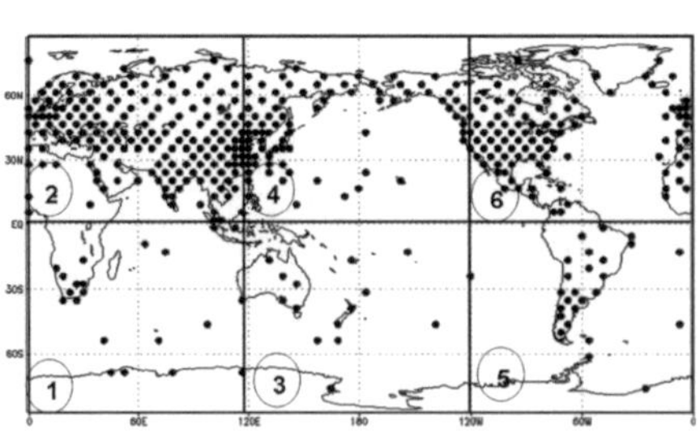

Figure 3. Observations localizations in global area. The dot points represent radiosonde stations (about 415) divided in six regions.

ran (without interruption) four times per day, from 01 January 1981 until 31 December 1981 and the last result is the initial condition for SPEEDY to 01 January 1982 0000 UTC. The model fields, so-called "true" (or control) model, are generated without data assimilation (each 6 hours forecast, is the initial condition for the next execution). The "true" model forecasts collected for executions without DA, considered four times per day (0000, 0600, 1200, 1800 UTC), the model run from 01 January 1982 through 31 December 1984 and collected analysis for each run.

The synthetic observations are generated, reading the "true" SPEEDY model fields, adding a random noise of meteorological variables: surface pressure (*ps*), zonal wind component (u), vertical wind component (v), absolute temperature (T), and specific humidity (q). The observation localization is on grid model point. An observation *mask* is designed, adding a positive flag to grid point, where the observation should be considered; the locations simulate the WMO data stations observations from radiosonde (**Figure 3**). Except for *ps* observations, the other observations are upper level with seven levels. Both assimilation schemes, LETKF and MLP-DA, use the same number of observations at the same grid point, i.e., the observation localization mask.

3.1. Training process

The training process for the experiment is conducted with data obtained from the SPEEDY model and the LETKF analyses. The LETKF analyses are executed with synthetic observations: upper levels wind, temperature and humidity, and surface pressure to 0000 and 1200 UTC and 0600 and 1800 UTC with surface observations only. The LETKF runs generate the analyses target vectors, the input observations vectors, and analyses field to run the SPEEDY model, which generates the input forecasts vectors for training the MLP-DA. The training is made with back-propagation algorithm.

Executions of the model with the LETKF data assimilation are made for the same period mentioned for the true model: from 01 January 1982 through 31 December 1984. The ensemble forecasts/analyses of LETKF have 30 members. The ensemble average of the forecasts and analyses fields, to this training process, is obtained by running SPEEDY model with the LETKF scheme.

These data are collected, initially, by dividing the globe into two regions (northern and southern hemispheres), but the computational cost was high because the training process took 1 day for the performance to converge. Next, the two regions were divided each into three regions, for a total of six regions. Then, we use this division strategy to collect the 30 input vectors (observations, mean forecasts, and mean analyses) at chosen grid points by the observation mask during LETKF process. The NN training process begin after collecting the input vectors for whole period (3 years), the training took about 15 min, for a set of 30 NN.

The MLP-DA data assimilation scheme has no error covariance matrices to spread the observation influence. Therefore, it is necessary to capture the influence of observations from the neighboring region around a grid point considered as a "new" observation. This calculation is based on the distance from the grid point related to observations inside a determined neighborhood (initially: $\gamma = 0$)

$$\widehat{y}^{o}_{i\pm m,j\pm m,k\pm m} = \frac{y^{o}_{ijk}}{(6-\gamma)r^{2}_{ijk}} + \sum_{l=1}^{6}\alpha_l \frac{y^{o}_{i\pm m,j\pm m,k\pm m}}{r^{2}_{ijk}}$$

$$(m = 1, 2, \ldots, M) \tag{10}$$

$$\alpha_l = \begin{cases} 0 & (if\ \ there\ \ is\ \ no\ \ observation) \\ 1 & (if\ \ there\ \ is\ \ observation,\ \ and: \gamma_{new} = \gamma_{old} + 1) \end{cases}$$

where $\widehat{y}^{o}$ is the weighted observation, M is the number of discrete layers considered around observation,

$r^{2}_{ijk} = (x_p - y^{o}_{i})^2 + (y_p - y^{o}_{j})^2 + (z_p - y^{o}_{k})^2$, where (x_p, y_p, z_p) is coordinate of the grid point, and the $(y^{o}_{i}, y^{o}_{j}, y^{o}_{k})$ is the coordinate of the observation, and γ is a counter of grid points with observations around that grid point $(y^{o}_{i}, y^{o}_{j}, y^{o}_{k})$. If $\gamma = 6$, there is no influence to be considered. Each observation's influence computed on a certain grid point is a new location, hereafter referred to as pseudo-observation, which adds values to the three input vectors to NN training process and also adds positive flags in the observation mask.

Then, the grid points to be considered in MLP-DA analysis are greater than grid points considered to LETKF analysis, although these calculations are made without interference on LETKF system. The back-propagation algorithm stops the training process using the criteria cited at item 6 above (Section 3), after obtaining the best set of weights; it is a function of *smallest error* between the MPL-NN analysis and the target analysis (e.g., when the root mean square error between the calculated output and the input target vector is less than 10^{-5}). The learning process is the same for each MLP of the set of 30 NN and takes about 15 min to get the fixed weights before the MLP-DA data assimilation cycle or generalization process of MLP-DA.

3.2. Generalization process

The training is performed with combined data from January, February, and March of 1982, 1983, and 1984, and in generalization process, MLP-DA is able to perform analyses similar to the LETKF analyses.

The generalization process is indeed the data assimilation process. The MLP-DA results a global analysis field. The MLP-DA activation is entering by input values (only 6 hours forecast and observations) at each grid point once, with no data used in the training process. The input vectors are done at grid model point, where it is marked (by positive flag mask) with observation or pseudo-observation (Eq. 10). The procedure is the same for all NN but one NN for each region, and each prognostic variable has own connection weights. All NNs have one hidden layer, with the same number of neurons for all regions. The regional grid points are put in the global domain to make the analysis field after generalization process of the MLP-DA, e.g., the activation of 30 NN results a global analysis. The regional division is only for inputting each NN activation.

The MLP-DA data assimilation is performed for 1-month cycle. It starts at 0000 UTC 01 January 1985, generating the initial condition to SPEEDY model. Running the SPEEDY model starting at 31 December 1984 1800 UTC carried out the previous model prediction. There were observations available at 0000 UTC 01 January 1985. Therefore, an analysis was computed for the SPEEDY model at 0000 UTC 01 January 1985. The SPEEDY model is re-executed with the former analysis, producing a new 6 hours forecast. The process is repeated at each 6 hours.

In this experiment, the MLP-DA begins the activation at 01 January 1985 0000 UTC and generates analyses and 6 hours forecasts up through 31 January 1985 1800 UTC.

4. Results

The input and output values of prognostic variables (p_s, u, v, T, and q) are processed on grid model points for time integrations to an intermittent forecasting and analysis cycle. Taking into account the pseudo-observation (Eq. 10), two grid layers ($M = 2$) around a given observation are considered.

The results show the comparison of analysis fields, generated by the MLP-DA, the LETKF, and the true model fields. The global surface pressure fields (at 11 January 1985 1800 UTC) and differences between the analyses are shown in **Figure 4**. The analysis fields and the differences between both assimilation, for 11 January 1985 at 1800 UTC at 950 and 500 hPa are also shown, for at 18 UTC at levels 950 hPa (near surface) and 500 hPa are also shown, for T, u, v, and q meteorological global fields, in **Figures 5–10**. These results show that the application of MLP-DA, as an assimilation system, generates analyses similar to those calculated by the LETKF system. Sub-figure (d) from **Figures 5–10** shows very small differences between the MLP-DA and LETKF analyses. The difference field of absolute temperature (K) at 500 hPa is about 3 degrees; and the difference field of humidity at 950 hPa is about 0.002 kg/kg.

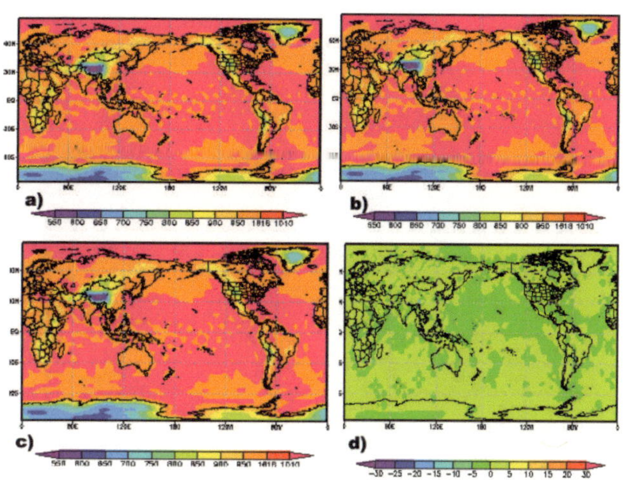

Figure 4. Surface pressure (PS) [Pa]—Jan/11/1985 at 18 UTC (a) LETKF analysis, (b) ANN analysis, (c) true model, and (d) differences analysis.

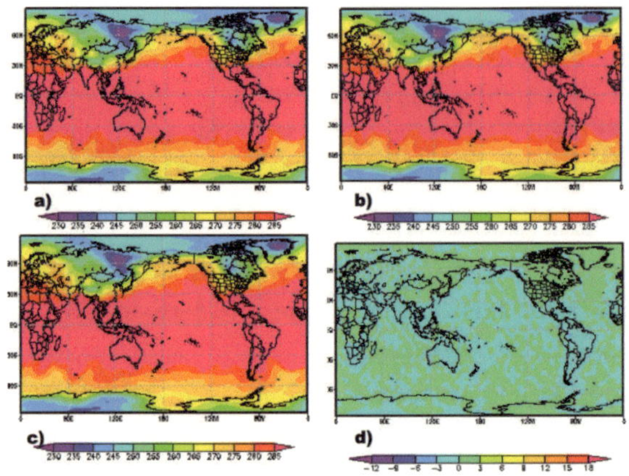

Figure 5. Absolute temperature (T) [K] Fi-950 hPa, Jan/11/1985 at 18 UTC. (a) LETKF analysis, (b) ANN analysis, (c) true model, and (d) differences analysis.

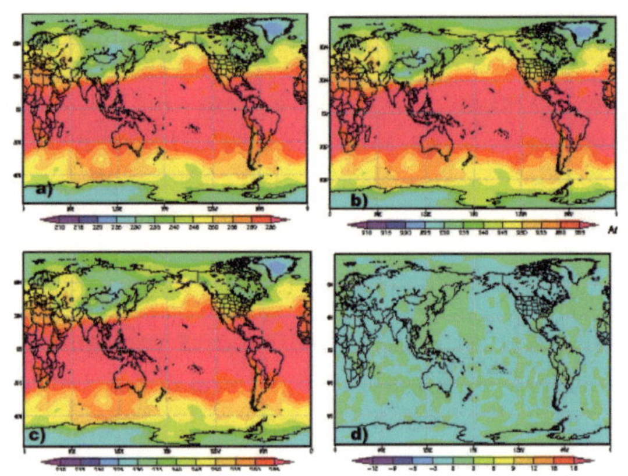

Figure 6. Absolute temperature (T) [K] at 500 hPa—Jan/11/1985 at 18 UTC (a) LETKF analysis, (b) ANN analysis, (c) true model, and (d) differences analysis.

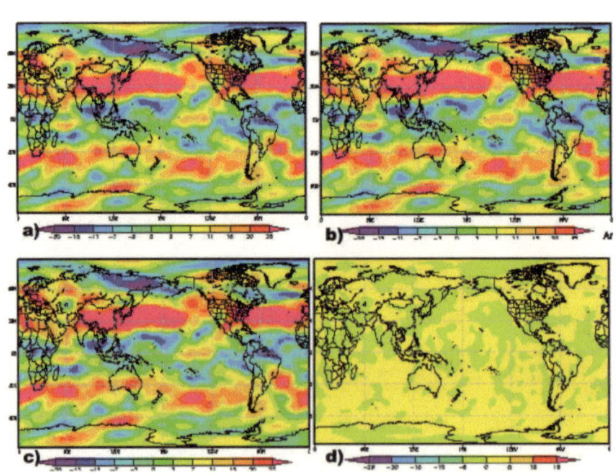

Figure 7. Zonal wind component (u) [m/s] at 500 hPa—Jan/11/1985 at 18 UTC. (a) LETKF analysis, (b) ANN analysis, (c) true model, and (d) differences analysis.

http://dx.doi.org/10.5772/intechopen.70791

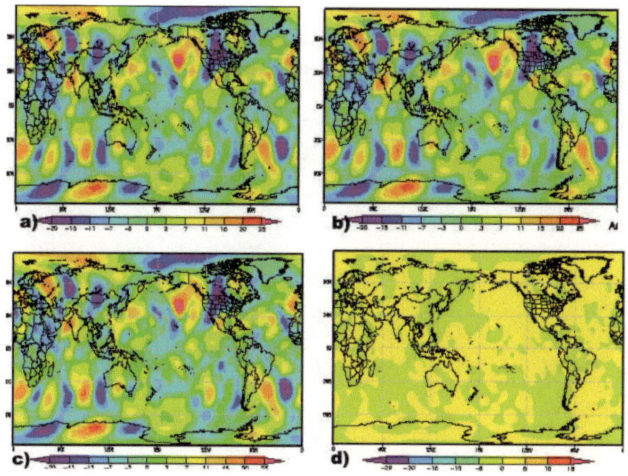

Figure 8. Meridional wind component (v) [m/s] fields at 500 hPa—Jan/11/1985 at 18 UTC (a) LETKF analysis, (b) ANN analysis, (c) true model, and (d) differences analysis.

Monthly average of absolute temperature analyses fields was obtained. The field of differences between the analyses (LETKF and MLP-DA) for data assimilation cycles is shown in **Figure 11**. The differences are slightly larger in some regions, such as the northeast regions of North America and South America.

The root mean square error (RMSE) of the absolute temperature analyses related to true model is calculated by fixing a point at longitude (87 W) for all latitude points. **Figure 12** shows the temperature RMSEs for the entire period of the assimilation cycle (January 1985). Subfigure (a) for **Figure 12** shows the RMSE of the LETKF analysis by line and the RMSE of the MLP-DA analysis by circles; and subfigure (b) for **Figure 12** shows the differences between LETKF and MLP-DA analyses RMSE. The differences are less than 10^{-3}.

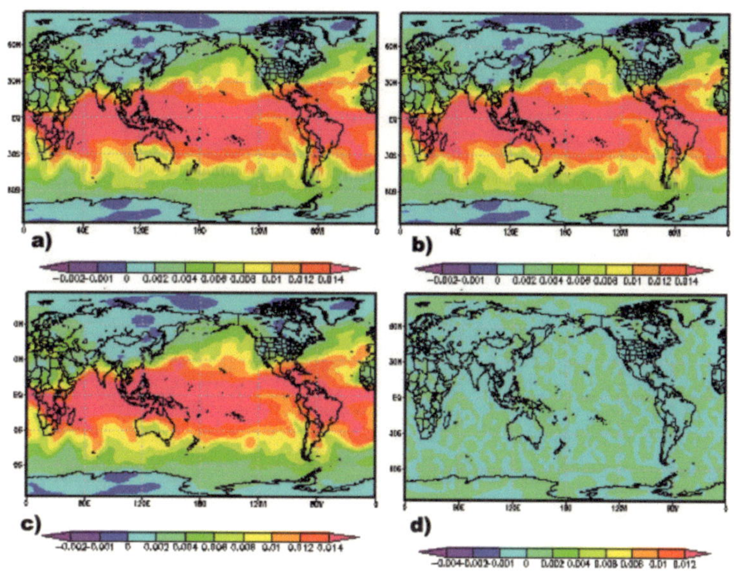

Figure 9. Specific humidity (q) at 950 hPa—Jan/11/1985 at 18 UTC (a) LETKF analysis, (b) ANN analysis, (c) true model, and (d) differences analysis.

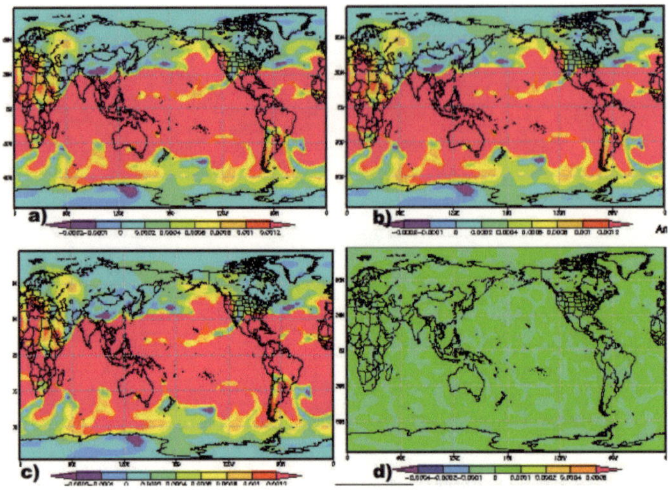

Figure 10. Specific humidity (q) at 950 hPa—Jan/11/1985 at 18 UTC (a) LETKF analysis, (b) ANN analysis, (c) true model, and (d) differences analysis.

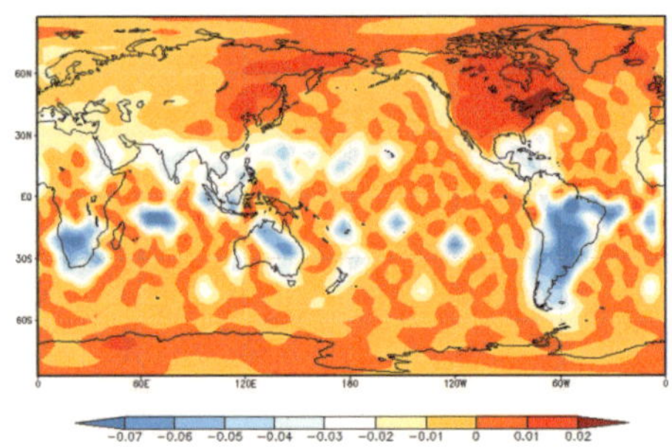

Figure 11. Differences field of the average of absolute temperature MLP-DA analysis and LETKF analysis for the assimilation cycle.

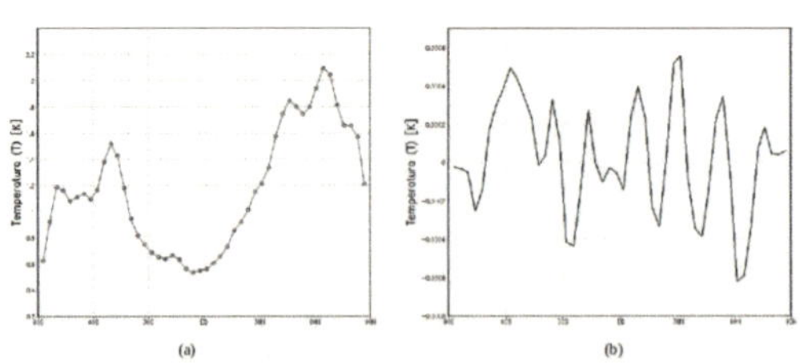

Figure 12. Meridional root mean square error for entire period of the assimilation cycles. RMSE analyses to the "true" state to (a) the errors of the LETKF analysis (line) and the errors of MLP-DA analysis (circles) to the absolute temperature at 500 hPa. (b) Differences of RMSE analyses.

4.1. Computer performance

Several aspects of modeling stress computational systems and push the capability requirements. These aspects include increased grid resolution, the inclusion of improved physics processes and concurrent execution of earth-system components, and coupled models (ocean circulation and environmental prediction, for example).

Often, real-time necessities define capability requirements. In data assimilation, the computational requirements become much more challenging. Observations from Earth-orbiting satellites in operational numerical prediction models are used to improve weather forecasts. However, using the amount of satellite data increases the computational effort. As a result, there is a need for an assimilation method able to compute the initial field for the numerical model in the operational window time to make a prediction. At present, most of the NWP centers find it difficult to assimilate all the available data because of computational costs and the cost of transferring huge amounts of data from the storage system to the main computer memory.

The data assimilation cycle has a recent forecast and the observations as the inputs for assimilation system. The described MLP-DA system produced an analysis to initiate the actual cycle. This time simulation experiment is for January 1985 (28 days). There were 2075 observations inserted at runs of 0600 and 1800 UTC for surface variables, and 12,035 observations inserted at runs of 0000 and 1200 UTC for all upper layer variables.

The LETKF data assimilation cycle initiates running the ensemble forecasts with the SPEEDY model, and each analysis produced to each member at the latter LETKF cycle to result 30 (members) 6-hour forecasts; the second step is to compute the average of those forecasts. After, with a set of observations and the mean forecast, the LETKF system is performed. The LETKF cycle results one analysis to each member for the ensemble and one average field of the ensemble analyses. The MLP-DA data assimilation cycle is composed by the reading of 6-hour forecast of SPEEDY model from latter cycle and reading the set of observations to the cycle time, the division of input vectors, the activation of MLP-DA, and the assembly of output vectors to a global analysis field.

The MLP-DA runtime measurement initiates after reading the 6-hour forecast of SPEEDY model from latter cycle and the set of observations. The time of generalization includes the division of observation and prediction fields into regions, and the execution of the various trained networks by gathering all regions in a global analysis. It initiates after reading the mean 6-hours forecast of SPEEDY model and the set of observations. The LETKF time includes the results of 30 analyses and one mean ensemble analysis. The comparison in **Table 1** is the data assimilation cycles for the same observations points and the same model resolution to the same time simulations. LETKF and MLP-DA executions are performed independently. Considering the total execution time of those 112 cycles simulated, the computational performance of the MLP-DA data assimilation is better than that obtained with the LETKF approach. These results show that the computational efficiency of the NN for data assimilation to the SPEEDY model, for the adopted resolution, is 90 times faster and produces analyses of the same quality (**Table 1**). Considering only the analyses execution time of those 112 data assimilation processes simulated, the computational efficiency of MLP-DA is 421 times faster than LETKF process. **Table 2** shows the mean execution time of each element to one cycle of the LETKF data assimilation method (ensemble forecast and analysis) and the MLP-DA method (model forecast and analysis). The computational efficiency of one MLP-DA execution keeps the relationship about speed-up, comparing with one LETKF execution (421 times faster). Details for this experiment can be found in Ref. [6].

Execution of 112 cycles	MLP-DA (hour:min:sec)	LETKF (hour:min:sec)
Analysis time	00:00:25	03:14:55
Ensemble model time	00:00:00	01:05:44
Single model time	00:02:28	00:00:00
Total time	00:02:53	04:20:39

Table 1. Total running time of 112 cycles of complete data assimilation (analysis and forecasting).

Cycle element	hour:min:sec:lll
Ensemble (model)	00:00:35:214
Single model	00:00:01:174
LETKF analysis	00:01:37:463
NN analysis	00:00:00:231

Table 2. Mean time of one execution (hour:min:sec:lll).

5. Conclusions

In this study, we evaluated the efficiency of the MLP-DA in an atmospheric data assimilation context with a 3D global model. The MLP-DA is able to emulate systems for known data assimilation scheme. For the present investigation, the MLP-DA approach is used to emulate the LETKF method, which is designed to improve the computational performance. The another experiments with the same methodology can be found in [7, 8].

The NN learned the whole process of the LETKF scheme of data assimilation through training process. The results for the MLP-DA analyses are very close to the results obtained from the LETKF data assimilation for initializing the SPEEDY model forecast, i.e., the analyses obtained with MLP-DA are similar to analyses computed by the LETKF. The difference between MLP-DA and LETKF analyses to surface pressure fields belongs to interval $[-5, 5]$ hPa. However, the computational performance of the set of 30 NN is better than LETKF scheme. The MLP-DA accelerates the LETKF data assimilation computation.

The application of the present NN data assimilation methodology is under investigation at the Center for Weather Prediction and Climate Studies (Centro de Previsão de Tempo e Estudos Climáticos-CPTEC/INPE) with operational numerical global model and real observations. After investigation with Florida State University model made in 2014, the results are found in [41, 42].

Acknowledgements

The authors thank Dr. Takemasa Miyoshi and Prof. Dr. Eugenia Kalnay for providing computer routines for the SPEEDY model and the LETKF system. This paper is a contribution of the Brazilian National Institute of Science and Technology (INCT) for Climate Change funded by CNPq Grant Number 573797/2008-0 e FAPESP Grant Number 2008/57719-9. Author HFCV also thanks to the CNPq (Grant number 311147/2010–0).

Author details

Rosangela Saher Cintra* and Haroldo F. de Campos Velho

*Address all correspondence to: rosangela.cintra@inpe.br

National Institute for Space Research, São José dos Campos, SP, Brazil

References

[1] Andrieu C, Doucet A. Particle filtering for partially observed Gaussian state space models. Journal of the Royal Statistical Society. 2002;**64**(4):827-836

[2] Bishop HC, Etherton BJ, Majumdar SJ. Adaptive sampling with the ensemble transform Kalman filter. Part I: Theoretical aspects. Monthly Weather Review. 2001;**129**:420-436

[3] Bourke W. A multilevel spectral model: I. Formulation and hemispheric integrations. Monthly Weather Review. 1974;**102**:687-701

[4] Burgers G, van Leeuwen P, Evensen G. Analysis scheme in the ensemble Kalman filter. Monthly Weather Review. 1998;**126**:1719-1724

[5] Campos Velho HF, Vijaykumar NL, Stephany S, Preto AJ, Nowosad AG. A neural network implementation for data assimilation using MPI. In: Brebia CA, Melli P, Zanasi A, editors. Application of High Performance Computing in Engineering. Vol. Section 5. Southampton: WIT Press; 2002. p. 211-220

[6] Cintra RS. Assimilação de dados por redes neurais artificiais em um modelo global de circulação atmosférica. D.Sc. dissertation on Applied Computing. São José dos Campos, Brazil: National Institute for Space Research; 2010

[7] Cintra RS, Campos Velho HF. Data assimilation for satellite temperature by artificial neural network in an atmospheric general circulation model. XVII Congresso Brasileiro de Meteorologia, Gramado, RGS, Brasil, September 23rd–28th, 2012.

[8] Cintra RS, Campos Velho HF, Furtado HC. Neural network for performance improvement in atmospheric prediction systems: Data assimilation. 1st BRICS Countries & 11th CBIC Brazilian Congress on Computational Intelligence. Recife, Brasil, "Porto de Galinhas" Beach, September 8th–11th, 2013.

[9] Daley R. Atmospheric Data Analysis. New York, USA: Cambridge University Press; 1991. 471 pp

[10] Doucet A, Godsill S, Andrieu C. On sequential Monte Carlo sampling methods for Bayesian filtering. Statistics and Computing. 2002;**10**(3):197-208

[11] Evensen G. Sequential data assimilation with a nonlinear quasigeostrophic model using Monte Carlo methods to forecast error statistics. Journal of Geophysics Research. 1994;**99**:10143-10162

[12] Evensen G. The ensemble Kalman filter: Theoretical formulation and practical implementation. Ocean Dynamics. 2003;**53**:343-367

[13] Furtado HC. Redes neurais e diferentes metodos de assimilação de dados em dinâmica não linear. São José dos Campos, Brazil: Brazilian National Institute for Space Research master thesis in Applied Computation program; 2008

[14] Gardner M, Dorling S. Artificial neural networks, the multilayer perceptron. Atmospheric Environment. 1998;**32**(114/15):2627-2636

[15] Greybush S. Mars Weather and Predictability: Modeling and Ensemble Data Assimilation of Space Craft Observations [Ph.D. thesis]. College Park, Maryland, USA: University of Maryland; 2005

[16] Harter F, Campos Velho HF. Recurrent and feedforward neural networks trained with cross correlation applied to the data assimilation in chaotic dynamic. Revista Brasileira de Meteorologia. 2005;**20**:411-420

[17] Harter FP, Campos Velho HF. New approach to applying neural network in nonlinear dynamic model. Applied Mathematical Modeling. 2008;**32**(12):2621-2633. DOI: 10.1016/j.apm.2007.09.006

[18] Haupt SE, Pasini A, Marzban C. Artificial Intelligence Methods in the Environmental Sciences. 1st ed. Springer: Berlin, Heidelberg; 2009. 424 pp

[19] Haykin S. Redes neurais princípios prática. Vol. 2. Porto Alegre: Editora Bookman; 2001

[20] Haykin S. Adaptive Filter Theory. New Delhi, India: Dorling Kinderley; 2007

[21] Held I, Suarez M. A proposal for the intercomparison of dynamical cores of atmospheric general circulation models. Bulletin of American Meteorological Society. 1994;**75**:1825-1830

[22] Ho'lm EV. Lecture Notes on Assimilation Algorithms. Reading, UK: European Centre for Medium-Range Weather Forecasts; 2008. 30 pp

[23] Houtekamer PL, Mitchell HL. Data assimilation using an ensemble Kalman filter technique. Monthly Weather Review. 1998;**126**:796-811

[24] Hsieh W, Tang B. Applying neural network models top prediction and data analysis in meteorology and oceanography. Bulletin of the American Meteorological Society. 1998;**79**(9):1855-1870

[25] Hsieh WW. Machine Learning Methods in the Environmental Sciences: Neural Networks and Kernels. Cambridge University Press: New York, NY, USA; 2009. 349 pp

[26] Hunt B, Kostelich EJ, Szunyogh I. Efficient data assimilation for spatiotemporal chaos: A local ensemble transform Kalman filter. Physica D. 2007;**230**:112-126

[27] Kalman RE. A new approach to linear filtering and prediction problems. Transactions of the ASME Journal of Basic Engineering. 1960;**82**(Series D):35-45

[28] Kalman RE, Bucy RS. New results in linear filtering and prediction theory. Transactions of the ASME Journal of Basic Engineering. 1961;**83**(Series D):95-108

[29] Kalnay E. Atmospheric Modeling, Data Assimilation and Predictability. 2nd ed. New York: Cambridge University Press; 2003

[30] Liaqat A, Fukuhara M, Takeda T. Applying a neural collocation method to an incompletely known dynamical system via weak constraint data assimilation. Monthly Weather Review. 2003;**131**(8):1697-1714

[31] Lorenc AC. Analysis methods for numerical weather prediction. Quarterly Journal of Royal Meteorological Society. 1986;**112**:1177-1194

[32] Miyoshi T. Ensemble Kalman Filter Experiments with a Primitive Equation Global Model [PhD thesis]. College Park, Maryland, USA: University of Maryland; 2005. 197 p

[33] Miyoshi T, Kunii M. The local ensemble transform Kalman filter with the weather research and forecasting model: Experiments with real observations. Pure and Applied Geophysics. 2012;**169**:321-333

[34] Miyoshi T, Sato Y, Kadowaki T. Ensemble Kalman filter and 4D-var intercomparison with the Japanese operational global analysis and prediction system. Monthly Weather Review. 2010;**138**:2846-2866

[35] Miyoshi T, Yamane S. Local ensemble transform Kalman filtering with an AGCM at a T159/L48 resolution. Monthly Weather Review. 2007;**135**:3841-3861

[36] Molteni F. Atmospheric simulations using a GCM with simplified physical parametrizations. I: Model climatology and variability in multi-decadal experiments. Climate Dynamics. 2003;**20**:175-191

[37] Nowosad A, Neto AR, Campos Velho H. Data assimilation in chaotic dynamics using neural networks. International Conference on Nonlinear Dynamics, Chaos, Control and Their Applications in Engineering Sciences. 2000:212-221

[38] Ott E, Hunt BR, Szyniogh I, Zimin AV, Kostelich EJ, Corazza M, Kalnay E, Patil DJ, York J. A local ensemble Kalman filter for atmospheric data assimilation. Tellus A. 2004;**56**:415-428

[39] Penny S. Data Assimilation of the Global Ocean using the 4D Local Ensemble Transform Kalman Filter (4D–LETKF) and the Modular Ocean Model (MOM2) [PhD].

[40] Furtado HCM, Cintra RSC, Campos Velho HF. Artificial neural networks emulating representer method at shallow water model 2D. In: DINCON Conferência Brasileira de Dinâmica. 2015

[41] Cintra RS, Campos Velho HF, Furtado HC. Neural network for performance improvement in atmospheric prediction systems: Data assimilation. 1st BRICS Countries & 11th CBIC Brazilian Congress on Computational Intelligence. Recife, Brasil, Porto de Galinhas Beach, September 8th–11th, 2013.

[42] Cintra RSC, Campos Velho HF, Anochi J, Cocke S. Data assimilation by artificial neural networks for the global FSU atmospheric model: Surface pressure. In: 2nd Latin-American Congress on Computational Intelligence (LA-CCI). 2015. Curitiba. CBIC and LA-CCI 2015.

[43] Cintra RSC, Cocke S. A local ensemble transform Kalman filter data assimilation system for the global FSU atmospheric model. Journal of Mechanics Engineering and Automation. 2015;**5**:185-196

[44] Vijaykumar NL, Campos Velho HF, Stephany S, Preto AJ, Nowosad AG. Optimized neural network code for data assimilation. Brazilian Congress on Meteorology, 12, 38413849. 2002

[45] Widrow B, Hoff M. Adaptive switching circuits. IRE WESCON Conv. Record, Pt.4.94, 95, 96-104. 1960